KEEPING OREGON GREEN

Keeping Oregon Green

LIVABILITY, STEWARDSHIP, AND THE CHALLENGES OF GROWTH 1960–1980

Derek R. Larson

Oregon State University Press   Corvallis

For Theresa

Library of Congress Cataloging-in-Publication Data

Names: Larson, Derek R., author.
Title: Keeping Oregon green : livability, stewardship, and the challenges of growth, 1960–1980 / Derek R. Larson.
Description: Corvallis : Oregon State University Press, 2016. | Includes bibliographical references and index.
Identifiers: LCCN 2016030887 | ISBN 9780870718717 (original trade paperback : alkaline paper)
Subjects: LCSH: Oregon—Environmental conditions—History—20th century. | Environmental policy—Oregon—History—20th century. | Environmentalism—Oregon—History—20th century. | Green movement—Oregon—History—20th century. | Sustainable living—Oregon—History—20th century. | Environmental management—Oregon—History—20th century. | Economic development—Environmental aspects—Oregon—History—20th century. | Social conflict—Oregon—History—20th century. | BISAC: HISTORY / United States / State & Local / Pacific Northwest (OR, WA).
Classification: LCC GE155.O7 L37 2016 | DDC 333.7209795/09046—dc23
LC record available at https://lccn.loc.gov/2016030887

♾ This paper meets the requirements of ANSI/NISO Z39.48-1992 (Permanence of Paper).

First published in 2016 by Oregon State University Press
Printed in the United States of America

Oregon State University Press
121 The Valley Library
Corvallis OR 97331-4501
541-737-3166 • fax 541-737-3170
www.osupress.oregonstate.edu

Contents

Illustrations

Acknowledgments

My love for Pacific Northwest history was undoubtedly kindled by my parents, who invested countless weekends and vacations exploring the region and planted the seeds of historical curiosity in me at an early age. Though I did not recognize it at the time, that curiosity proved invaluable when I began taking courses on regional history and politics from legendary professors Stephen Dow Beckham and Donald Balmer at Lewis and Clark College in Portland. It was under their guidance that I first began to consider academia in general and history in particular as potential career paths. My progress along the way was guided in particular by Dave Thelen, Wendy Gamber, John Bodnar, and Rob Fischman at Indiana University, who oversaw the dissertation that served as the foundation of this project. Their advice, encouragement, and feedback were invaluable in shaping not only my research and writing but my identity as an environmental historian.

My colleagues at the College of St. Benedict and St. John's University supported my work on the book over the long haul, including sabbatical and travel funding that made spending significant periods of time immersed in archival collections in Oregon and Washington, DC, possible. Special thanks are due to Annette Atkins, for both her constant encouragement and her sage advice on the historian's craft. The many students who have passed through my Environmental History and History of the American West classes also deserve recognition, as they have, often unknowingly, helped me sort out the forest from the trees by prompting reflection on the national context of the study.

My research was aided by a phalanx of friendly librarians and archivists. Helpful staff at the Oregon State Library, Oregon State Archives, Oregon Historical Society Research Library, the University of Oregon's Knight Library, and Western Oregon University's Hamersly Library made my numerous research trips more productive by offering advice and quick retrieval of what seemed like endless boxes of records. Their collective interest in the project gave me confidence it would find an audience among general readers as well as academics. Thanks are due to the interlibrary-loan staff of Clemens and Alcuin Libraries at my home institutions as well; they gamely logged countless requests for books and documents during my work on this book, effectively making it possible to conduct research half a continent away from my subject.

Perhaps the greatest pleasure of my research was meeting the many Oregonians who shared their memories of the events and personalities central to the narrative, a fair number of whom did so without any prodding from me. The late Hector Macpherson, the father of Oregon's landmark land use legislation, and Maradel Gale, past president of the Oregon Environmental Council, deserve special recognition for submitting to formal oral history interviews. My understanding of the land use regulation struggle was deeply enriched by the contributions of Ron Eber, formerly of the Oregon Department of Land Conservation and Development (DLCD). Ron provided a large cache of documents from the historical files he amassed as the unofficial agency historian at the DLCD as well as helpful critiques of conference papers and early drafts of the dissertation chapters on which this book is based. Dozens of other individuals, many of them strangers, shared their thoughts and memories at conferences, through informal interviews, and across worktables in archives around the region.

Travel for research was made more pleasant by an extended group of friends and family who hosted me in Portland, Salem, Corvallis, Eugene, and other locations over the years. Rather than huddling in hotel rooms and eating alone at night, research trips became minivacations marked by long days in the archives and delightful evenings and weekends spent in conversation and laughter. Thanks are due in particular to Laura Mundt and Tony Paolucci, whose Portland home became my frequent "field office" for weeks at a time. Judy Spence, Sophia Polasky, Peter Edwards, Ken Dankenbring, Kari Frey, and many others shared their dinner tables and guest rooms with me over the years. While the work was solitary, evening and weekend debriefings with friends made it much more enjoyable.

The staff at Oregon State University Press were a delight to work with from the outset. Mary Braun expressed interest in the project upon our first meeting years ago and encouraged me at every subsequent encounter; her patience and guidance are greatly appreciated. Marty Brown made discussions about design and marketing a breeze, and Joy Margheim's skilled hand in copyediting made the potentially exhausting final stages of work a pleasure. The anonymous reviewers of the manuscript provided invaluable feedback and criticism when it was needed most; when I was immersed in minutia and details they helped me regain a vision of the whole. Though they and many others contributed greatly to the book as a whole, any errors in fact or interpretation of course remain my own.

Finally, my deepest debts are to my family: throughout the years of work on the project they always made me look forward to going home, be it after a day in the campus library or a two-month research trip halfway across the country. My children, Hazel and Piper, accepted these frequent absences without complaint and listened to more stories of archival finds and distant historical events than I had a right to ask of anyone. Their patience and understanding when work drew me away meant very much to me. Ultimately, though, the book would never have been completed without the support of my wife, Theresa Anderson. Her love, encouragement, and assistance with everything from slogging through microfilm rolls to editing drafts not only made completing it possible, but made it much better than I could have on my own. I dedicate the book to her, with my love and gratitude.

Derek R. Larson
Collegeville, MN

Introduction

> We are threatened today by two kinds of environmental degradation:
> one is pollution . . . the other is loss of meaning.
> —Eugene Walter, *Placeways: A Theory of the Human Environment*

The environmental awakening of the 1960s reflected a stark reality of post-war America: the economic expansion that carried consumers to a standard of living once unimaginable to the average citizen came with significant environmental costs. Rising incomes, increasing rates of home ownership, a flood of new consumer goods ranging from televisions to V-8 sedans, and more leisure time buoyed many Americans to levels of affluence their parents could never have imagined. Yet beneath that rising tide lurked the unforeseen consequences of growth, including air and water pollution, fallout from nuclear testing, loss of agricultural land, urban crowding and sprawl, unsustainable resource extraction, and alienation from nature. The alarm bell Rachel Carson sounded with her 1962 book *Silent Spring* was heard by people primed for such a message by witnessing environmental decline in their own communities. When viewed on the national scale these threats seemed daunting, even unmanageable; unsurprisingly, some of the most effective early responses to the environmental crisis were driven by citizen engagement at the local and state levels.

The nascent environmental movement of the 1960s differed from the conservation movement that preceded it in many ways, and dramatically so in its local and regional focus. Rather than emphasizing distant wilderness or natural resource policies impacting most Americans only tangentially, its core concerns revolved around quality of life issues affecting everyone. Clean water, clean air, safe food, access to parks and outdoor recreation opportunities, and managing the impacts of population growth were *community* issues that at least sometimes lent themselves to local solutions. In some cases state-level approaches made more sense, as with industrial regulation or development policies, but those solutions too invited participation on the local level and reflected the experiences of individuals living with the impacts of environmental decline on a daily basis. As citizens called on political leaders, formed new advocacy groups, and took action to preserve or improve quality of life for themselves and their neighbors, they were often responding to a local crisis or a widely perceived sense of loss that was close to home and part of their lived experience. Quality of life concerns were immediate and personal, rather than distant in time or space, and drew the attention of many who had not been mobilized by the traditional conservation agenda of the first half of the twentieth century.

While the direct impacts of industrial air and water pollution were abundantly evident in some parts of the country by the 1950s, declining environmental quality was not so immediately apparent everywhere. In the Pacific Northwest rapid population growth and industrial development were relatively new forces to contend with, legacies of the wartime boom economy and postwar migration of those drawn to the region at least in part by its natural amenities– the forests, rivers, beaches, and mountains that offered a wealth of recreational opportunities and aesthetic value within a short drive of population centers. The region boasted a tradition of environmental exceptionalism that went beyond the economic opportunities afforded by its abundant natural resources to incorporate natural amenities into its inhabitants' collective sense of place. As nineteenth-century pioneers celebrated the temperate climate, fertile soils, lush forests, and productive fisheries in letters home they laid the foundation for imagining the Northwest as "the Eden at the end of the Oregon Trail" or "God's Country." The communities they formed developed amid a culture of abundance that reinforced their belief in an inexhaustible base of natural resources and unlimited room for expansion. In their hands nature was quickly systematized and actively managed, which had clear impacts on the environment as well as the surviving Native American population. Nevertheless, a vision of the region as a natural paradise persisted as commodity production and order replaced the wilderness without erasing it completely from memory.[1]

The events central to this study—a fifteen-year period of environmental conflict in Oregon between 1959 and 1974—took place in a cultural and political milieu in which the nineteenth-century culture of abundance ran headlong into postwar realities of industrialization, pollution, and population growth. Longstanding beliefs and tradition regarding nature were challenged, new ideals and identities developed, and innovative political solutions were proposed as Oregonians realized their quiet corner of the country was no more immune from environmental decay than were Ohio or New Jersey. The clean-flowing rivers, endless forests, abundant farmland, and even the sandy beaches that helped define the state just a generation prior, they feared, might not remain for their children or grandchildren to enjoy in similar fashion. They experienced, as a result, an environmental awakening concurrent with the national conversation on the environment spurred by *Silent Spring* and culminating with the first Earth Day in the spring of 1970. Oregon, however, responded more quickly and forcibly to perceived threats to quality of life than many other states; by 1970 the *New York Times* could report that officials around the country were watching Oregon to learn how to deal with pollution, noting that "strong public outcries" drove political commitment to "forceful leadership, tough standards and the cooperation of industry" to address environmental decay.[2] Soon much of the country would look to Oregon as a model of progressive environmental policies, as its record of innovation and reputation for uncompromising leadership became part of the state's national identity.

Evidence of Oregon's self-conscious role as the nation's environmental bellwether in the 1970s is substantial. This study traces the rise and fall of the state's "environmental era" primarily through public debates over environmental quality, policy, and politics. Central to these debates are claims about the meaning of place, citizens' obligations to the past and future, and the qualities that make Oregon exceptional. Media coverage of environmental issues on the local, state, and national levels provides an ongoing narrative and commentary throughout the period of greatest engagement as solutions to specific environmental problems were proposed within the state. The personal papers of participants in these exchanges, including the central elected officials, are available in regional archives. Public records in the form of published speeches, transcripts of legislative hearings and debates, internal agency documents, and commissioned studies offer another set of views. Oral history interviews offer competing personal perspectives, speak to the individual motivations of participants, and provide details not evident in the public record. The collection and analysis of what ultimately became thousands of such sources forms the foundation of an argument for the importance of the "Oregon story," as it was called in the 1970s, in understanding how the state earned its reputation for environmental leadership and why, ultimately, its example was not so easily replicated elsewhere.

The widespread association of the state of Oregon with popular environmentalism in the public imagination arose out of a series of discrete and identifiable events. By focusing on the public voices of participants in these events, particularly the words and actions of politicians, reporters, and citizens involved, it is possible to trace the emergence of a regional identity based on environmental leadership that not only resulted from these political struggles but helped drive them as well. Rooted in history, sense of place, personal experience, and myth, regional identity is complex and mutable. Developed and passed on primarily in story, it can be mobilized to serve political, commercial, and social ends. Affinity for place, according to the historian William Robbins, is based "in the intimate association between humans and geography," forms a core element of regional identity, and may serve as "a moral force to guide and shape social and environmental policies."[3] Oregonians' sense of common purpose was ill-formed prior to the 1960s, if it existed in widespread fashion at all. By late 1970s, however, it was a central part of the state's internal identity and a dominant factor in external perceptions as well. The content, formation, and application of this emerging regional identity are examined in depth in chapter 1, which explores the historical perception of Oregon as a place characterized by sublime environmental qualities and its residents' ongoing belief that the economic and aesthetic values provided by nature defined their quality of life. Inhabitants of Eden, they came to believe, carried some obligation to care for the gifts they enjoyed.

Chapter 2, which examines the fight to create a national park in the Oregon Dunes, argues that in the late 1950s conservation remained largely the province of urban elites, who failed to mobilize the broad political support necessary to overcome localized opposition to the type of traditional wilderness preservation advocated by park proponents. Fought largely in Washington, DC, between politicians and bureaucrats and in missives exchanged in the Oregon press, the dunes park battle was not unlike simultaneous attempts to create similar coastal parks in Massachusetts and Texas. The key differences are that the Oregon case provides evidence of early attempts to appeal to an Oregon sense of place rooted in environmental quality and that it ultimately failed to win approval, while other efforts succeeded. From these events a baseline can be established to demonstrate the scope of change that occurred over the following decade as environmental issues made a rapid transition from the province of a distant Congress to the front pages of Oregon's newspapers. Tellingly, the battle over the Oregon Dunes is largely forgotten today by Oregon residents, and no mention of the plan exists at the federal recreation area ultimately established there in lieu of a national park.

A scant few years after the dunes controversy peaked, the concerns that previously had failed to find a widespread audience (factors such as population growth, preservation of wild areas, resource use, and environmental degradation) met with a much different reception upon their reintroduction. In the intervening time Carson's *Silent Spring*, Stewart Udall's *The Quiet Crisis* (1963), and similar works had alerted the citizenry to threats evident in their immediate communities. Concern over environmental decline began to drive political energy away from the parks and wilderness, the traditional mainstays of the conservation movement, to the quality of life issues that would carry popular environmentalism into the 1970s. This transition was amplified in Oregon by an event no less significant than Carson's book: the 1962 broadcast of a locally produced television documentary called *Pollution in Paradise* and the subsequent campaign to clean up the Willamette River. Chapter 3 treats this campaign and the rise of environmental concern among the public as critical to the development of a regional culture of stewardship and of Oregon's national environmental reputation. In providing the state's most visible victory over pollution and in transforming reporter Tom McCall's political career, the Willamette cleanup both mobilized public opinion in support of environmental restoration and provided the first avenue by which concerns about quality of life came to trump traditional conservation as the central issue in environmental politics in the state.

The rhetorical creation of a shadowy cadre of "Californian developers" played an important role in the crusade to save Oregon's public beaches in 1967, the subject of chapter 4. Then-governor McCall encouraged Oregonians' belief that growth and development were the fundamental causes of environmental degradation and that external forces, often conveniently labeled "Californian," were to blame for the decline. Preserving the tradition of public beach access is the cause most clearly linked with the mythology of stewardship, as proponents frequently made historical claims about Governor Oswald West, who proclaimed the beaches to be highways in 1914, and interpreted his actions as part of an ongoing environmental tradition they wished to continue. While elements of class conflict did appear in this case, as between wealthy beachfront developers and the working-class residents who used the beaches for free recreation, supporters of public beaches joined across political and economic divides, particularly in response to McCall's appeals to the legacy of Governor West, inundating elected officials with demands to preserve the public beaches for themselves and their descendants. Thus appeals based on history and tradition were made in support of environmental causes that would benefit posterity, a tactic that proved a powerful weapon in mobilizing public support and in deflecting criticism from opponents. In the views of those defending traditional beach access, the forces driving environmental decay and loss of open space were external ones, actions promulgated by and benefiting people seen to be "not like us" and not understanding what was often referred to as "the Oregon way." In avoiding the temptation to frame the public beach issue as a class conflict, proponents made it possible for wealthy *individual* beachfront property owners to join their cause out of sympathy for tradition or antipathy toward the small group of developers seeking to profit from coastal tourism or otherwise restrict access for their private benefit.

Efforts to improve the aesthetic appearance of the state, and especially its roadside areas, are at the center of chapter 5. Not long after national beautification campaigns helped make litter and visual blight significant political issues in the 1960s, efforts arose to remove both billboards and trash along Oregon's highways. Although attempts to regulate roadside advertising were made as early as 1923, it was not until the late 1950s that concern over billboard proliferation became sufficiently widespread to prompt serious efforts at a ban. Coinciding with federal bills for billboard regulation, the Oregon case demonstrates significant parallels between attitudes in the Pacific Northwest and the rest of the nation in that period. By the end of the 1960s, however, the lead villain in roadside blight became litter rather than advertising, and Oregon led the nation by proposing a novel solution to the problem. When it was determined that the bulk of roadside trash was discarded beverage containers—primarily glass bottles and metal cans—one Oregon resident made a personal crusade of placing a price on their heads. While his proposal for a bottle deposit and a corresponding ban on single-use containers did not attract immediate support, it would ultimately become one of the signature policies by which the state's environmental reputation was earned. In this case proponents of the "Bottle Bill" employed appeals to the culture of stewardship and aesthetic arguments not only to sway their fellow citizens but in opposition to a well-funded and organized industry lobby supporting the status quo of disposable containers. By 1970 many Oregonians were conscious of their position as the nation's environmental leader and perceived a victory on the Bottle Bill as important to maintaining that position. Setting a precedent for the rest of the nation to follow thus became a key point in the debate, with both sides certain that whatever happened in Oregon, the rest of the nation would follow.

By the early 1970s many of the most pressing environmental issues facing the state had been addressed: polluted air and rivers had been cleaned up, the state's beaches had been reserved for public use, and the highways were substantially cleared of litter. Despite these victories a sense of impending crisis was prevalent in newspaper stories and politicians' speeches; most often the source of this unease was population growth and the urban sprawl that accompanied it. Though tourism had played a key role in Oregon's economy for at least a half century, citizens and politicians alike became suspicious of boosterism in the 1960s, seeing it as a driving force for in-migration. This fed upon a tradition of distrust of outsiders, and Californians in particular, to erupt into full-blown xenophobia by the 1970s. Conditions outside of Oregon were bad, and anyone who came from outside would bring those things with them, decried the xenophobes. When report after report began to project population growth as the next big environmental threat facing the state, people spoke out against growth directly, targeting both raw increases in population (Oregon grew faster than the national average in this period) and what was labeled "California-style growth" in reference to urban sprawl and loss of open space seen in places such as Orange County. Chapter 6 explores the political manifestation of these concerns, which took the form of a statewide land use zoning program to restrict the ability of private property owners to convert farmland to subdivisions, force a set of mandatory environmental goals upon local planners, and provide a system of structured growth meant to preserve open space into the next century. As might be expected, the sweeping goals of the proposal, its limited-growth perspective, and its impact on private property rights were extremely controversial, but once again proponents drew on the growing culture of stewardship to convince Oregonians that such planning was in keeping with their tradition of respect for the environment and would ensure future generations' enjoyment of all the natural resources and amenities that contributed to their own quality of life.

During the period of this study the phrase "quality of life" was used by advocates of environmental regulation and restoration, but they increasingly turned to the more nuanced word "livability" in the 1970s. Quality of life, of course, suggested something of a spectrum, and one could imagine that a range of points on that spectrum would be acceptable depending on an individual's personal preferences, means, and values. But livability was binary: a place was either livable or not. Historically associated with indoor habitats or the basic capacity to support life, the term's widespread adoption in Oregon's environmental era signaled simultaneously a growing concern that certain places might become unlivable due to pollution and the belief that natural amenities like green space were critical to quality of life, not just adjuncts. The concept of livability offered environmental advocates the means to counter economic arguments against regulation, as it could be argued that while growth might produce jobs or even wealth, they were of little utility if the resulting place was "unlivable" due to their environmental impacts. The limits to growth were central to the national environmental debate of the 1970s, and in Oregon the dividing line was drawn rhetorically at livability. The hard task, of course, was defining exactly what that meant.

During the short span covered in these case studies the state of Oregon garnered a widespread reputation as a national leader in environmental policy. Many of its high-profile environmental actions, such as the ban on nonreturnable beverage containers, were duplicated by other state legislatures and even debated in the U.S. Congress, though few of these attempts met with the same success they found in Oregon. Key to Oregon's environmental achievements was the degree to which claims about what needed to be done for the environment resonated with individual and collective understandings of an "Oregon way" and the connections between politics and sense of place that helped environmental advocates form coalitions across traditional divisions of class, party, ideology, and geography to mobilize citizens who felt a sense of responsibility both to a mythologized past and to posterity. While the environmental issues that galvanized Oregon politics from the mid-1960s through the mid-1970s had their counterparts in other regions, the way these particular battles played out reflects the unique history of the Pacific Northwest and the degree to which nature and culture informed people's understanding of who they were. This was a process clearly rooted in a place that, as was once noted in a study of regional identity, "has been almost universally praised and idealized in popular discourse" and has yielded an understanding of history for generations of residents to incorporate into their own sense of place, while simultaneously offering an image of the region to outside observers that invites connections between the environment and the cultural and political trends evident therein. This idealization ultimately evolved, in the words of one observer, into a "harmonious viewpoint" that "depicts a beneficent juxtaposition between nature and human activity . . . [in a] landscape in which city and civilization intertwine benignly with field, forest, and wilderness."[4]

In the events explored in the following chapters, one can see not only the emergence of Oregon's mythology of stewardship but its application as well. The appeals to tradition and posterity on behalf of the environment made by Richard Neuberger in 1959–60 fell largely on deaf ears; the people of Oregon were not yet ready to accept his warning of environmental decline or respond to the construction of a stewardship mythology around the value of wilderness preservation by environmental advocates. But by the close of the 1960s a sense of crisis was becoming widespread, and the same sort of appeals made by Neuberger were soon found at the center of political debates over environmental issues, in particular within what are now recognized as the key events of the "Oregon story": the restoration of the Willamette River, the passage of the Beach Bill and the Bottle Bill, and enactment of the state-wide land use zoning program upon which the state's reputation as a national environmental leader was established. In a period in which communities around the United States faced growing concerns about environmental quality, the people of Oregon were seen as uniquely successful in maintaining a quality of life heralded for generations. Their success was based on a long-standing tradition of conservation for use and a growing concern that the changes of the postwar era threatened an idealized way of life based on both the use of the region's abundant natural resources and the celebration of their aesthetic beauty, combined under the umbrella of livability. The culture of stewardship that developed during this time served to support progressive political action on environmental issues and contributed to a sense of regional identity as well. By the end of the twentieth century, these events themselves came to play a part in the culture of stewardship in an almost reflexive fashion. References to the groundbreaking actions of Oregon's environmental era continue to be used today in support of new policies that embody "the Oregon way," a reference to the character and spirit surrounding the political and cultural milieu that gave rise to innovation in the 1960s and 1970s.

The epigraph from Eugene Walter that opens this introduction suggests that loss of meaning may contribute to environmental degradation as inexorably as pollution. The people of Oregon, in finding a way to combat environmental decay by defending the meaning of the places they inhabited, offered the nation a model for addressing the ecological concerns that alarmed many Americans in the 1970s. As the following chapters will illustrate, it was not an easy nor a particularly coordinated response to the environmental crisis but was, in a sense, an organic product of one state's sense of place and the importance its people saw in preserving elements of the past for the sake of the future.

Chapter 1
Preserving Eden

> This state is singularly blessed in soil, climate and natural resources
> of all kinds, and while in the past their very abundance has made us
> profligate of our patrimony, it is fortunate that we are yet in a position
> to conserve them.
>
> —Joseph N. Teal, Oregon State Conservation
> Commission Chairman, 1909

In December 1999, as the rush to catalog and evaluate the events of the closing twentieth century came to its peak, the Associated Press issued a wire report under the headline "Oregon's 20th Century Legacy: Protecting the Environment" that reinforced the popular image of the state as the nation's environmental leader. "The 20th century," the AP proclaimed, "will be remembered for the environmental awareness it instilled in people. And Oregon . . . helped show the way."[1] That perceptions of Oregon should be associated with its natural environment comes as no surprise; from the time of the Lewis and Clark expedition's arrival in the Pacific Northwest the region's natural features attracted and inspired explorers, immigrants, and potential exploiters, drawn by the diversity of natural and scenic resources that marked the landscape as special. Oregon's widespread modern reputation as a bastion of progressive environmental policy, however, raises the basic question of how this reputation for environmental stewardship arose and if it is indeed somehow unique.

Oregon's standing as a source of innovative environmental policy and practice is clearly part of its modern identity, evident both in external assessments like that of the Associated Press and in the collective culture of its inhabitants. The state's residents have in fact cultivated a shared mythology aligning the nineteenth-century encounter with the sublime landscapes of the fertile coast and inland valleys of the region with twentieth-century efforts to maintain those resources as important elements of their quality of life. Subscribers to this mythology view the state's natural environment as the embodiment of the region, an act of cultural "topophilia," what

11

geographer Yi-Fu Tuan called "the affective bond between people and place."[2] The generalized topophilia of Oregonians blends individual perceptions of place with a culturally constructed understanding of how the landscape came to be as it is, providing both an appreciation of natural amenities and a rationale for preserving them that are mutually sustaining.[3] Their sense of what Oregon *means* unites the landscape and most of its prominent features (rivers, mountains, beaches, forests) with their own cultural and personal histories, a process that is at once both shaped and interpreted through tales of past acts of stewardship that are commonly understood as both distinctive and somehow binding on the actions of contemporary residents.

Through this process of integrating landscape and culture Oregonians have cultivated a collective identity as environmental stewards, sometimes quite consciously, as in the formation of environmental policies, and other times indirectly, as through the use of storytelling that propagates this sense of place among children and in-migrants. By perpetuating stories of how certain places or natural features came to be preserved, they take ownership of the landscape in a fashion that reinforces ideas of Oregon's exceptionalism. All mountains, rivers, fields, and forests are not created equal—through these stories other, alien places become object lessons in how *not* to relate to the land, thus reinforcing the uniqueness of the Oregon story. The state's official tourism slogan of the 1980s, "Things Look Different Here," reflected the conscious cultivation of that perceived difference as part of the process of defining what Oregon was, creating meaning from the landscape and an explanation of how it came to be preserved from spoliation as a means of differentiating Oregon from other parts of the country.

Of course, similar processes have played out in other places. It is part of human nature to perceive place as a combination of landscape and history, the canvas on which events are played out, lives are lived, and memories are made. Geographical features or even the built environment can provide a perceptual anchor for any location; think of the Swiss Alps, the pyramids of Giza, New York's Central Park, or the beaches of Normandy. Some may signal the human conquest of nature, such as Mount Rushmore's capitulation to the sculptor's gaze, while others may drive home the insignificance of human endeavors, as has been said of the Grand Canyon. In the United States regional variations in geography and culture are widely recognized, if not always by academics then at least within the vernacular, and they account for much of the popular perception of what these "other" places are like.

The Pacific Northwest, from the time the first reports of Lewis and Clark's journey reached the urban East, has been identified with its environment. It is often said that the land there—specifically, the part lying between the Pacific coast and the western slopes of the Cascade Mountains—is the richest in the world, the most abundant in providing food and useful materials for human consumption. It is not surprising that the Euro-Americans who settled the region and their descendants took to telling stories about the land and their relationships with it as part of the process of defining who they were. Understanding how that process worked, the substance of stories they told, and how the resulting mythology was used can inform broad notions about the uses of history, the formation of regional and state identity, and the ways in which culture impacts political decisions about natural resources and environmental quality. This process took place within a multitude of contexts—national, regional, local, and personal—that merit attention, but it was in debates over environmental issues that these ideals were most often expressed in the critical period when Oregon rose to become the nation's environmental bellwether.

Nature was long celebrated by Oregon residents. By the late nineteenth century the state had developed a regional identity based on common values and emphasizing the rich natural resources and amenities offered by the temperate climate that sheltered the population centers of the western half of the state. Between roughly 1850 and 1890, settlers in Oregon's Willamette Valley (the principal destination for agriculturally inclined immigrants) transformed their environment into a pastoral garden. Forests were cut back from the edge of the valley floor, houses, farms, and villages established, and the "primitive" landscape converted into an ordered vision of civilization. Native Americans were dispossessed of their land, their lifeways and cultures disrupted and their traditional ecological knowledge discounted in the settlement process as well. According to David Lewis, historian for the Confederated Tribes of the Grand Ronde Community, death came to many "through epidemic disease . . . attempted genocide, forced marches onto reservations, reduction of land holdings, broken treaty promises, attempts to destroy tribal culture . . . and termination of federal recognition of sovereign, tribal status."[4] Indigenous people were predominantly relocated to reservations, where federal policy sought their assimilation by compulsion; by the 1880s just six reservations were home to the majority of Oregon's surviving Native population.[5]

Indian removal left what members of the settler society viewed as a blank canvas, a place to build a "civilization" that blended with surrounding natural features like the snow-capped Cascade Mountains to create a thing of beauty unsurpassed by any landscape of the East. As a local newspaper commented in 1873, there could not be "a more charming spot of earth than this blessed valley which offers us a home, with its delightful climate, rich and certain harvests and with its undeveloped resources."[6] Little mention of the prior residents, or to the pioneers' role in their removal, appears in any of the nineteenth-century odes to Oregon's natural bounty. The land use regimes established by generations of Native inhabitants were forgotten even while their impacts on the land remained evident, their hand in shaping the Eden into which Anglo-European migrants poured ignored or at best misunderstood.

The 1890s were marked by the ascendancy of the commercial timber industry in the region, reflecting a utilitarian view of nature that marked the dominant regional mind-set for generations to follow but one still firmly rooted in a culture of abundance. Indeed, by 1894 a regional guidebook was able to predict that "many generations will yet come and pass before the mighty forests here are felled to the ground. It is not unreasonable to hope that the forests of the Pacific Northwest will in the near future be the chief source of supply of the world for lumber."[7] Boosterism notwithstanding, the Northwest did become the chief source of lumber for North America not long after that guidebook was published. In the process, the timber industry became the dominant force in the region's economy and culture, for example, employing 63 percent of Washington State's wage earners at its peak in 1910. In 1938 a high school textbook could announce that the Pacific Northwest contained 55 percent of the nation's virgin timber, while the forest products industry employed 59 percent of all industrial workers and directly supported 25 percent of the region's population.[8] Though the increasing mechanization of logging and lumber production reduced the need for labor in the forests and mills in the following years, the forest products sector remained the primary employer in Washington and Oregon for another half century.

Challenges to the timber industry's economic dominance were few in the early twentieth century, usually taking the form of citizen-led parks groups or the occasional paean to the falling forests. One visitor's reflection on her journey to a logging site, published in 1914, was notable, if not entirely accurate, in its foresight:

> The men are going to fall a tree and you linger a little longer. A strange feeling of impending disaster enfolds you. Timber! Loud and long the call, like the warrior's cry of old; the great tree shudders from root to crest; the crashing of his great body, against his brothers as he sways, fills the air with wild screamings. Now you trudge slowly tentward for you have seen a sight and heard sounds that your children and their children's children will never see or hear. For like the Indian and the buffalo, the firs are passing.[9]

Poetic accounts aside, in a region where "lumber is king" it made little sense economically to criticize the source of so much wealth; falling trees were as much a sign of economic progress in Oregon as were smokestacks in Pittsburgh. In the early 1920s a public crusade to preserve some of Oregon's forests as parks was met with opposition from those who felt the great forests would never be exhausted. In the end the park proponents' plans were reduced to the creation of visual "buffer zones" of uncut trees along major roadways, at once bowing to the utilitarian agenda and perpetuating the culture of abundance among those who saw the forests only from their cars.[10]

While the timber industry propelled the economy, the popular image of the region was also characterized by resource extraction. Though silent films of the 1920s, such as *The Covered Wagon* (1923), emphasized the drama of the overland journey and said little about what waited at the end of the Oregon Trail, the sound era ushered in new visions of Oregon and the Northwest that depended heavily on the environment and the men who toiled in their forests. The drama *God's Country and the Woman* (1937) set a typical romance in the logging camps of Oregon and featured the forests as much as the actors. By the 1950s popular productions like *Big Timber* (1950) and John Wayne's *North to Alaska* (1960) were able to make shorthand references to the logging culture, while film buffs waited until Ken Kesey's *Sometimes a Great Notion* hit the screen in 1971 for a more critical (and grittily realistic) portrayal of the industry.

The importance of timber to the region was obvious even to the casual observer; when Woody Guthrie was hired by the federal government in 1941 to write songs about the federal dams going up along the Columbia River, one of his first compositions was called "Lumber Is King."[11] What Guthrie could not foresee was that the very project he was hired to promote, the harnessing of the Columbia River system for the generation of hydroelectric power and irrigation, would change the environment of the Pacific Northwest on a grander scale than any human enterprise before or since. Beginning at Bonneville in 1933, a series of dams converted the once-feared "River of the West" into what contemporary detractors called "the longest lake in North America." In the process, they provided cheap electricity that reached 97 percent of the region's farms by the early 1950s and provided the energy for the emergent aluminum industry.[12] That the dams were also a death sentence to the runs of wild salmon that pioneers once claimed were "so thick you could cross the river on their backs" was not apparent until years later. In the 1930s the federal dam projects were sold largely as an extension of the existing quality of life in the region; rural farmers who lived off the fertile soils could also now enjoy the benefits of "modern" life in the form of electrically powered labor-saving devices and—likely a stronger selling point—increased production through irrigation made possible by the new impoundments and the electric pumps they would feed.[13] The river once called "the soul of the land to which it belongs" still played a central role in the regional body, but it was now one shaped by human hands.[14]

While one might consider the harnessing of the Columbia and the subsequent rise of industry a departure from the historic vision of the "Eden at the End of the Oregon Trail," both embody the utilitarian values characterizing the nineteenth-century vision of the promised land. Just as the adaptation of the Willamette Valley to pastoral agriculture combined the domination and appreciation of nature in the period from 1850 to 1890, the damming of the Columbia adapted that river and its adjacent lands to power production and irrigated agriculture in the 1930s and 1940s, a feat accompanied by the rhetorical juxtaposition of the beauty of nature and the progress of human achievement. Another of Guthrie's WPA tunes, "Grand Coulee Dam," provides an example:

> She winds down the granite canyon and she bends across the lee
> Like a dancing, prancing stallion down her seaway to the sea,

Cast your eyes upon the biggest thing yet built by human hands
On the King Columbia River, it's the grand Grand Coulee Dam.

Guthrie was certainly not alone in reading the reining in of that "dancing,
prancing stallion" by a dozen concrete dams as a sign of progress.

The dams, of course, were only another part of the shared Northwest
image enjoyed by Oregon and Washington alike. Differentiation occurred
as well; at the height of the Great Depression boosters circulated pamphlets
proclaiming Oregon specifically to be a worker's paradise, often utilizing
language similar to that of their nineteenth-century counterparts: "Oregon
is one of the immensely resourceful states. In productive possibilities it
ranks with the greatest. In variety of actual resources that are convertible
into wealth by the hand of man, it is unquestionably the greatest. The man
who comes to OREGON with the purpose of working with his hands or
investing his money, or both, will come to the right place. . . . All wealth
comes from the soil. . . . OREGON is able to endow millions of men in addition to them that already have come to her."[15] Simultaneously, claims about
the quality of life in the region echoed the "promised land" rhetoric of the
earlier era as well. Local boosters claimed that Coos Bay, a lumber port on
the southern Oregon coast, offered

life and infinite variety. Within a few miles is the turbulent Pacific
Ocean, with its calling magnitude, its eternal change and interest,
its beaches and cliffs and light-houses, its bathing and fishing. [In
the hills] are the tumbling brooks with their trout . . . and their
big game. Deer, bear, grouse, pheasant, and other big game and
wild birds of the woods may be found . . . while Coos Bay has
exceptional climactic advantages—no blizzards, no cyclones, no
snow storms, no freeze-ups, no sweltering summer days or nights.
. . . . There is no malaria and fevers are almost unknown.[16]

No celebration of the Northwest environment would be complete
without a word on the forests, and even the Depression brought out the
best in the timber industry, which reminded people that the "marvelous,
gripping story of lumbering in America" was continuing in the Northwest
even in a time of crisis. "Listening ears are now turned to the Far West,
where great forests of fir so tall 'their tops tickle the soles of the angel's feet,'

of spruce and hemlock, of pine and cedar, of larch and redwood—'The Last Great Stand'—await the pleasure of the nation, ready to provide, for all time, for the needs of a wood-loving people."[17] The "wood-loving people" of the region were themselves believed to embody the influence of an abundant nature. The regional guides produced by the Works Progress Administration in the late 1930s, for example, are marked by references to the healthy bodies and pleasant dispositions produced by the Pacific Northwest's temperate climate. "The sons of Oregon are tall and sturdy, and the complexion of the daughters is faintly like that of the native rose—a hue gained from living and playing in a pleasant outdoors."[18] While this sort of simplistic environmental determinism might quickly collapse under scrutiny, its publication in the WPA guide does suggest the relatively wide acceptance of the notion. It even hinted to potential visitors that a brief stay in the Northwest might beneficially affect them as well. Inhabitants' tastes for outdoor recreation, such as their pioneering use of skis on the slopes of Mt. Hood and their proclivity for hiking within the "awe-inspiring solitude" of the "superb landscape [and] rough, rugged, mountainous country" just miles outside of the city of Portland, were highlighted as experiences accessible to even the greenest tourist.[19] A 1934 feature on Oregon in *National Geographic* spanned sixty pages, including two dozen color illustrations that presented a similar image: Oregon and the Northwest were the pioneers' Eden, where now "cattle graze in the sun-flecked aisles of [the] national forests."[20]

By the mid-twentieth century Oregon lumber, Washington apples, and Idaho potatoes were established symbols of a region that was rapidly modernizing.[21] The nation's cheapest electricity and a growing, affordable housing stock, functions of the hydroelectric and timber industries, combined with abundant opportunities for outdoor recreation and other natural amenities, offered residents of the Pacific Northwest a relatively high quality of life compared to much of the country, despite per capita incomes only slightly higher than the national average in 1950.[22] The natural environment, though, provided the characteristics most associated with the region in national discourse. A 1945 propaganda film produced by the federal Office of War Information captured this well in a narration that described Oregon, Washington, and Idaho as a place apart from the rest of the nation:

Here the west wind moves, and the heavy Pacific moves and lifts against the granite of the Northwest. . . . The air is still bright and

clear. . . . It's a young country, and the people who live here feel it.
They enjoy the snow, and the swiftness of the mountain. They enjoy
the summer of the inland lakes. The run of water sounds in their
memory, and the great sound of the Columbia River. . . . Salmon
are a treasure of the Northwest, as the river itself is a treasure. It is
bridged now. It serves man, and it runs through his cities. There are
mountains behind the cities; the suburbs are the green forests. The
wind over the streets, fresh and soft, flows in from the Pacific.[23]

This reputation for natural amenities, combined with a strong economy driven largely by the postwar housing boom and the corresponding
demand for lumber, attracted many new residents to the region in the 1950s.
The increasing urbanization that marked the entire American West in this
period was evident in the Northwest as well, leading a few observers to
lament the impacts of growth, though the primary assessment was positive:
growth was good for the economy and thus good for the region's inhabitants. The compounded effects of this growth, however, began to produce
clear changes soon after the war ended. The transition from hinterland to
major manufacturing center, brought about by the wartime development of
shipyards, airplane plants, and the aluminum industry, reduced economic
dependence on timber and agriculture, helping to shift economic influence and population growth more completely toward the urban centers of
Seattle and Portland. The effects of this transition were noticeable in less
than a generation; as one observer put it in 1971, "The impact of progress is
strong and fresh here. . . . This landscape has undergone such rapid change
that, unlikely as it may seem, it is even possible for a regional inhabitant of
only four decades to have achieved a degree of historical perspective."[24]

The rapid pace of change in the postwar Northwest meant not only
shifting patterns of growth and economic development but an evolution
in the way residents viewed their collective past. At a time when daily
experiences in growing urban centers were beginning to diverge from the
natural resource–based myth of the promised land, delegates to the Pacific
Northwest History Conference in 1952 were debating just how to begin
writing a regional history that was more than a simple recapitulation of the
larger national story. Ironically, they turned toward a history that celebrated
the pioneer experience and the natural abundance of the Northwest at a

time when its dominance was just starting to be challenged in the main-stream culture, economy, and politics of Oregon and Washington.[25]

Previously, a group of regional authors, including Vardis Fisher, William Adams, C. E. S. Wood, Ernest Haycox, and H. L. Davis (who won the Pulitzer in 1936 for *Honey in the Horn*), had helped generate an increasingly complex portrait of the regional character in a series of novels, short stories, and poems that relied heavily on the environment of the Northwest as more than just setting.[26] Their work was perhaps the first response to the desire for a regional literature expressed by H. S. Lyman in 1901, when he opined that "if Oregon is to have a worthy future, it will first appear as a literary consciousness, uniting all elements of society that we have here."[27] Though some regional authors may have lamented the passing of certain elements of the male-centered resource-extraction culture of the old Northwest, none openly questioned the region's resource-based economy; these industries still defined the Northwest to most of its inhabitants in the 1950s.[28] To writers outside the region, the Northwest—and Oregon in particular—offered a convenient place that was at once a familiar setting, with its lush forests and constant rains, and yet far enough outside the mainstream that most readers could accept whatever shape it was given. The promised land proved quite malleable, at least in the hands of authors who built upon the popular image of the region in their work.[29]

In 1956 Richard Neuberger, Oregon's junior U.S. senator and a widely respected journalist, published a pamphlet on the Pacific Northwest entitled *Our Natural Resources—and Their Conservation*, which called for a conservation strategy to ensure forest resources would not be exhausted and wilderness would be maintained.[30] Supreme Court Justice William O. Douglas, a Washingtonian, spanned the decade with two influential works, *Of Men and Mountains* (1950) and *My Wilderness: The Pacific West* (1960), which argued eloquently for the preservation of the mountain and forest environments that he felt shaped his life.[31] Douglas's preservation philosophy was neatly captured in a 1960 essay on Oregon's Hart Mountain National Antelope Refuge, where he wrote, "Those who visit Hart Mountain next century will know that we were faithful life tenants, that we did not entirely despoil the earth which we left them. We will make the tradition of conservation as much a part of their inheritance as the land itself."[32]

Neuberger and Douglas were among the most prominent public voices calling attention to the decline of the region's natural resources and their importance in shaping the lives of its inhabitants. By the late 1950s such conservation messages began to find a receptive audience in the Northwest as the twin pressures of population growth and industrial development, long evident in other parts of the nation, made it clear that the nineteenth-century image of an agrarian Eden no longer reflected lived experience across the region. As one observer framed it for a Tacoma audience in 1957, by "selecting all that is best in the pioneer tradition" while recognizing that "we may have learned just in time how to preserve what is left," the Pacific Northwest offered the opportunity to "make man happy if he is capable of happiness."[33] If, it was implied, the right choices were made in time.

Despite the postwar prosperity and cultural expressions of faith in the abundant resources of the region, criticism of the impacts of growth emerged on the national scale at midcentury as well. Finding a new audience for its concerns in the expanding suburban middle class, a growing national conservation movement publicly questioned the conventional wisdom with regard to natural resources. This was manifest most obviously in high-profile conservation battles, such as that over Echo Park in Colorado's Dinosaur National Monument, which mobilized opposition to the actions taken by the federal government that would have been heralded as signs of progress in the 1930s or 1940s. The Echo Park struggle, an important victory for conservation advocates against the dam-building Bureau of Reclamation, helped recast John Muir's Sierra Club and Robert Marshall's Wilderness Society as political forces at the heart of a growing wilderness preservation movement.[34] Closer to home, the environmental impacts of suburban expansion were increasingly evident as farm fields were cleared, graded, and converted into subdivisions following the model pioneered on Long Island by William Levitt and Sons after the war. Some early critics feared the mass-produced suburbs would quickly become "the slum of the future," but residents' experiences of nature were more significant drivers of the nascent ecological awakening of the American public.[35] As historian Adam Rome explains, "In new subdivisions, children were often able to play in undeveloped land nearby—then one day the bulldozers would come to turn those playgrounds into lots for new houses."[36] A generation was thus educated directly about the conflicts between growth and quality of life in their youth and was prepared to participate in debates over regulating the impacts of growth as adults.

Of course, the ironic juxtaposition of newly settled suburbanites opposing the growth of suburbs was far from unique. In the Northwest, the task of preserving some version of the fabled Garden of Eden to which nineteenth-century immigrants had journeyed was complicated by countervailing economic factors, not the least of which was that residents of the region derived most of their economic activity from the land and its resources. Though Oregon's net agricultural acreage increased by 64 percent between 1920 and 1960, due substantially to increased irrigation east of the Cascades, nearly 20 percent of the state's richest farmland was removed from production between 1955 and 1965 as urbanization encroached on agriculture in the Willamette Valley.[37] Forest products and agriculture remained at the core of the Northwest economy through the 1960s, but the rising importance of tourism attached some degree of economic utility to the preservation of the forests, rivers, and open spaces that attracted the tourists, who were obviously drawn to neither clear-cuts nor alfalfa fields. Nature thus came to be seen as a marketable feature in its intact state, as well as a source of raw materials, just as preserving open space emerged as a sign of "smart" suburban development.[38] Indeed, at a time when California was attracting tourists with the artificial environment of Disneyland, which opened in 1955, tourism officials in Oregon began to advertise their state as an escape from urban pressures in campaigns depicting happy families on auto tours through the state parks, in national forests, and along scenic highways. Governor Mark Hatfield captured the core marketing message of the state perfectly in the official welcome for the Oregon centennial souvenir program in 1959: "Perhaps it is only fair to warn our visitors that they will face a challenge. The land weaves an enchanting spell. Oregon is no longer hard to reach, but it is hard to leave. It is a land to live in, a place to raise a family well, to nurture good ideas, to establish solid occupations. Our horizons are wide and our air is fresh. . . . You are welcome to stay with us a day, a hundred days, welcome to stay a lifetime."[39] If there was a down side to the popularity of western travel and recreational tourism in the postwar decades it was the increasing number of visitors to the region who subsequently decided to relocate there permanently.[40] By the 1960s the populations of Oregon and Washington were growing at rates exceeding the national average, primarily through in-migration, as the region's birth rates were historically below average; the general public attributed much of the growth to the impacts of tourism.

Fig. 1. Oregon Centennial souvenir program, 1959 (Original in author's possession)

These new migrants were often different from those of earlier periods, being drawn in not by economic opportunity but often by what they perceived as the "Northwest lifestyle" and attraction to the environment not for its potential consumptive uses but for its aesthetic and recreational qualities. By self-selecting for these values, new arrivals contributed to the formation of what geographer Wilbur Zelinsky calls a "voluntary region," a place characterized by the "spontaneous, selective migration of like-minded persons to places with desired qualities," such as perceived quality of life, environment, or cultural factors, as opposed to traditional pull factors such as economics, ethnicity, or religion.[41] The combination of these new regional perspectives, the growing economic importance of recreational tourism, and the fledgling national environmental movement challenged the utilitarian views of nature that had dominated the region since the arrival of the Anglo-European fur traders 150 years prior. Writing for a regional guidebook, Stewart Holbrook, the dean of Oregon journalists by the 1960s, expressed the popular suspicion that large-scale industrial development was incompatible with the quality of life that marked the Northwest as unique in his mind. "We have not been able to attract much industry since World War II, for reasons that are none too clear. Some say it's the rainy climate, others the cool attitude of many natives who hate belching smokestacks. But Oregon . . . is happily still free of the clutter of military installations and defense industries that have defaced much of the landscape in neighboring states."[42]

While some were puzzled by Oregon's lack of a major manufacturing base, especially compared to its more industrialized neighbors to the north and south, Holbrook saw this as a "feature" of the state. As growing tourism revenues began to offset the contracting timber industry in the 1960s, it became common to portray the shift as a conscious choice—a decision made to preserve quality of life by reducing economic dependence on natural resources. Even major corporate leaders viewed development with some concern; the chairman of the board of the region's largest utility, Pacific Power and Light, said of the 1960s, "In the Northwest for a while, everyone was hell-bent for development. But were we worshiping a false God at the expense of our environment?"[43] This growing concern for quality of life, or "livability" as it came to be called in Oregon, would be broadly associated with the state in the national media and even popular culture by the mid-1970s, but at the dawn of the 1960s most of the region's inhabitants had yet to accept the idea that the environments they inhabited were under threat.

That would change in 1962, due substantially to the efforts of a television news reporter named Tom McCall. Born in Egypt, Massachusetts, in 1913, McCall was the grandson of a famed copper baron on one side and a former governor and congressman on the other. The family divided its time between one grandfather's Boston estate, Dreamwold, and Westernwold, a more modest residence built for McCall's parents in the Crooked River country of central Oregon, where young Tom was raised among elements of his patrician heritage and the raw experience of a working cattle ranch.[44] He became a journalist after college, served as a military reporter in the Pacific during the war, and then settled into a broadcasting job in Portland upon his return, at which point he also grew interested in Republican politics, acting for a time as executive secretary to the governor. A deep concern for the environment, born in part of his experiences on the family ranch, led to his involvement in a 1962 television documentary called *Pollution in Paradise* that shocked many Oregonians out of their complacent views on unregulated growth and industrial development, challenging the belief that the region's natural resources could provide unlimited fuel for economic expansion while simultaneously absorbing its byproducts. McCall's exposé dispelled the popular belief that pollution occurred only in decaying eastern cities or California's booming south, undermining the widespread notion that Oregon's environment had survived a century of development with its core qualities intact. The documentary raised McCall's public profile significantly, but more importantly sounded an alarm that ultimately propelled Oregon to the vanguard of national environmental leadership.[45]

Timing, of course, was everything. Rachel Carson's *Silent Spring* was published two months before McCall's documentary first aired in 1962, exciting widespread public interest in environmental issues and driving national headlines over the impact of pollution on public health and natural systems.[46] The sudden realization in Oregon that "pollution was not something that happened only to rivers and lakes east of the Rocky Mountains" and McCall's emerging image as a pollution fighter helped him win the governor's race in 1966. A liberal Republican, McCall was elected governor the same year Ronald Reagan took office in California, but their records could not have been more different. While Reagan presented himself as a fiscally conservative law-and-order candidate, preventing the further decay of Oregon's environment became McCall's signature issue, leading to his proclaiming the eleventh commandment to be "thou shalt not pollute" and successfully seeing more than one hundred new environmental protection laws through the legislature during his first term in office.[47]

Quality of life—"livability"—became the defining political issue of Tom McCall's gubernatorial administration. His first priority in office was cleaning up the polluted Willamette River, a task to which he set himself with dramatic flair. He later fought famously to permanently establish the state's entire coastline as a public beach, declaring access to the sand a birthright of all Oregonians. Soon after, the state drew national attention when it banned single-use beverage containers in an effort to address the problem of roadside litter plaguing its highways. But McCall's most famous words, framing his own reputation and fueling the Oregon mystique in the 1970s, were delivered offhand in a national television interview in which the governor expressed his concerns over migration and population growth, proclaiming to viewers, "Come visit us again and again. This is a state of excitement. But, for heaven's sake, don't come here to live."[48] This was a far cry from prior governor Mark Hatfield's frequent repetition of "we welcome you to come visit us for a little while or a lifetime," and soon signs reading "Welcome to Oregon: Enjoy Your Visit" were erected on the state's southern border.[49] Since the majority of the new migrants came from neighboring California, the phrases "Don't Californicate Oregon" and "Oregon for Oregonians" appeared on bumper stickers as well, while "Native Oregonian" became a badge of honor often pasted on the rear of automobiles as a political statement.

Before long Oregon and the Northwest were being portrayed as a sort of anti-California in the national media, an image bolstered by photos of scenic northwestern vistas presented beside hazy shots of Los Angeles smog that appeared in magazine stories and air-quality campaigns. By the mid-1970s, according to one observer, a "cult of livability" had taken a vocal role in regional politics, demanding the preservation of the "Northwest lifestyle" at all costs. To McCall this meant challenging the nation's dominant philosophy—which he pejoratively labeled "growth for growth's sake"—and lead him to announce that while Oregon needed some development it was "not willing to take any industry at any price. The industry must come here on our terms, play the game by our environmental rules, and be members of the Oregon family."[50] Livability, in his formulation, required balancing growth against its impacts and would be acceptable only under certain conditions that fell increasingly outside of national norms.

In questioning the ideology of growth, McCall was reacting in part to the type of urban sprawl that had consumed much of Southern California over the previous three decades; he often used California as the rhetorical antithesis of his vision of responsible environmental practices, claiming that "unlimited and unregulated growth leads inexorably to a lowered quality of life." Responding to mounting concern over the loss of prime agricultural land and green space around the state in the early 1970s, the governor took a central role in the fight to establish statewide land use zoning, confronting a powerful coalition of business leaders, labor interests, developers, and property-rights advocates, during his second term in office. The resulting law was a unique reflection of Oregon's tradition of progressive politics, the maturing environmental movement, and the art of compromise politics: a new state agency, the Department of Land Conservation and Development, would establish a series of statewide land use goals to be implemented by *locally* written policies.

Debates over the land use bill in 1972–73 focused on the preservation of agricultural land that was rapidly falling to suburban development around Willamette Valley population centers and to the subdivision of rural land into small homesites or vacation properties. Clay Myers, Oregon's secretary of state, explained the issue in a 1972 speech. In claiming that increasing migration and the fact that "some of our best recreation land [is] being snapped up by out-of-state developers" represented the "greatest threat to our way of life," he appealed to concerns over declining quality of life that increasingly animated the public in this period.[51] McCall followed with an impassioned call for land use regulation that signaled his self-conscious grasp of the state's emerging status as a national environmental leader: "There is a shameless threat to our environment . . . and to the whole quality of life—[that threat] is the unfettered despoiling of the land. Sagebrush subdivision, coastal 'condomania' and the ravenous rampage of suburbia in the Willamette Valley all threaten to mock Oregon's status as *the environmental model for the nation*" (emphasis added).[52] The governor's appeal to Oregonians' emergent self-perception as environmental leaders is telling—only a decade earlier residents would have expected to hear their governor wax poetic about the timber industry, perhaps celebrating the state's dominant position in the production of forest products, but by McCall's second term in office political references to the state's newfound reputation as a leading environmental steward were more compelling, as they resonated with a broader cross-section of the population than did images of the fading logging industry.

Opposition to land use control came, of course, from developers and real estate interests, but also from traditional resource-dependent sectors

of the economy. The timber industry and construction trades were especially vociferous in their opposition to the initial bills. Popular support split
in part along urban/rural lines, reflecting the level of local concern over
growth issues, but fear over the loss of agricultural land prompted support
from some rural residents as well. The influx of migration to already developed areas of the Willamette Valley provided a constituency that strongly
supported preservation of the open space that remained; this was mobilized in part by the efforts of planning proponents, including a 1973 television commercial produced by the advocacy group Keep Oregon Livable,
in which the narrator announced, "Once upon a time we didn't have any
problem with space in Oregon. We had it all to ourselves, and it was beautiful. Then more and more people moved into Oregon, and today there are
more people per square mile in the Willamette Valley than in California,
Ohio, or Pennsylvania. We're not against growth; what we are against is bad
planning . . . because if we don't plan for growth now, we might be overrun by success." The imagery on the screen was not of pristine landscapes
or crowded cities; it was a close-up of a three-dimensional scale model
of Oregon with mountains apparently made primarily of sugar. The final
pull-back shot, synchronized with the delivery of the words "we might be
overrun by success," revealed the Willamette Valley swarming with ants
that appeared as giants on the model's surface.[53] In the face of such mes-
saging, the declining economic influence of resource-dependent industries
left opponents of land use controls outnumbered and without the overwhelming political power they once held. The eventual passage of the bill
is often credited to the support of farmers, who were ultimately convinced
it protected their interests by keeping agricultural land prices low, and to
McCall's ability to rally public support for the somewhat vague concept of
livability, which was malleable enough to incorporate the views of a spectrum of political viewpoints. McCall's role as the unabashed advocate of
planned growth drew national attention, enough so that he was spoken of as
a possible Republican presidential candidate in 1976. Following his death in
1983 he was memorialized as the savior of Oregon's quality of life, both for
sounding the alarm over environmental decline in the 1960s and for providing the template for what seemed to be a solution in the 1970s.[54]

Oregon's legislative accomplishments of the 1970s and the national reputation they garnered helped shape the perception of the Pacific Northwest
as a region where environmental quality was considered a central priority

by politicians and citizens alike. The utopian fantasy of Ernest Callenbach's popular 1975 novel *Ecotopia*, which portrayed a future in which the Pacific Northwest (and parts of Northern California) seceded from the union to form a nation of environmentalists, seemed to many to be a logical extension of the values underlying these new policies. The British magazine the *New Scientist*, in an article about urban planner Peter James's journey to experience the Oregon system in 1979, explained that Callenbach's selection of the Pacific Northwest as the location of his utopia was logical, as "'Ecotopian' attitudes have a long history in Oregon, beginning with the visions of a 'paradise on earth' carried by the early settlers struggling over the Rockies. So too does a concern with quality, rather than quantity, of life." James himself saw many parallels between Callenbach's ideals and practices in Oregon, concluding that "if an ecotopian society were to develop anywhere, then Oregon would be one of the most likely spots on the globe."[55]

When McGraw-Hill produced a series of educational films on the geography of the United States for the Bicentennial in 1976, the Pacific Northwest edition emphasized this tension between the use of natural resources and preserving the quality of life as a distinctive feature of the region. The film opens with a lighthearted narrator describing his subject: "Tucked in a corner created by the Canadian border and the Pacific Ocean, the Pacific Northwest might seem a bit out of the way to some people. It rains a lot and the terrain can be rugged. But most of us who live here like it that way." Scenes of the Pacific coast, Cascade Mountains, and Douglas fir forests fade to an urban waterfront, where a young woman on a boat remarks, "When I think of the Northwest I think of water, mountains, hills, and views. To me this seems like really one of the last unspoiled areas in the country." A cutaway to a similarly young man working a piece of lumber with a hand plane leads to his statement: "One of the problems is that a lot of people, I think, want to move out here, want to come here. A lot of interests are really concerned with bringing in more industry, and those things are in conflict, definitely, with what a lot of people want this area to remain." Written and directed by Jon Wilkman, an independent filmmaker based in Los Angeles, the eighteen-minute film concludes with the narrator's statement that "in the Pacific Northwest it's easy to take our natural resources for granted. In other areas of America time has taken its toll on such resources. We hope to learn from the mistakes of the past. It is a matter of survival." The final word is given to one of the residents from the opening urban scene, who explains, "People are questioning now what growth means, and whether it's good."[56] Even when distilled to its essence for classroom use, the region's primary identity had by the mid-1970s become framed as a battle between livability and growth.

Visitors to Oregon, both professional and casual, emphasized livability in their descriptions throughout the 1970s. Awards of such labels as "Most Livable City," won repeatedly by Portland in that decade, and "Most Livable Town," given to various smaller communities, underscored the state's emerging political and social commitment to environmental quality as a possible standard for the entire nation.[57] Oregon's greener-than-thou image was celebrated frequently, as in a 1976 feature article in *Atlantic Monthly* that devoted over forty pages to a description of the Pacific Northwest under the subtitle "God's Country: Please Keep Out." The article focused on Oregon's environmental record and its by then famous standards of livability.[58] Despite the widespread use of that term, however, *Oregon Magazine* noted in 1980 that while everyone seemed to be *for* livability, few seemed able to explain what it was—instead they preferred to define it in negative terms. It was not "the California mentality," not "eyesore condominiums, numerous fast-food franchises and ugly shopping centers," and not simply economics. Nonetheless, "Oregonians seem[ed] determined not only to keep using the word, but to base public and personal decisions upon it," the writer concluded.[59]

The close of the 1970s did not put an end to Oregon's—or the nation's—struggles over environmental quality; indeed, political conflict over environmental issues in the Northwest only intensified in the 1980s. The so-called Northwest timber crisis, which led to the listing of the northern spotted owl as a threatened species by the U.S. Fish and Wildlife Service in 1989, marked the culmination of years of wrangling over the use of the region's forests and involved a protracted political fight that sometimes bordered on cultural warfare. Communities were split, families estranged, and a good deal of property damaged in the struggle to determine the future of the region's timber industry, as competing concepts of livability collided directly with the economics of recession and declining employment in the forest products industry. Contrary to many media reports, however, it was not simply an "owls vs. jobs" economic issue.[60] A closer look revealed that people on both sides of the issue claimed to be environmentalists (even if they didn't use the term itself) and used the region's history to support their positions. Thus the tradition of livability and concern for the environment was mobilized in opposition to logging as well as in support of the industry. As the head of one small logging company noted in 1989, "I'm so [expletive] tired of this [expletive] debate. A big tree turns me on for a lot of reasons. It's neat that it's been there so long. Do I get a religious feeling from a big tree, something mystical? No, leave it to whoever. It don't do it for me. But those people who do have a religious experience need a place for it."[61] Less accommodating was an industry advertisement that mocked opponents by asking, "Suppose farmers found corn too lovely to pick? To be sure, the forest holds enormous beauty. But it also holds great promise. To realize that promise, we must remember that there is a time to sow, and a time to reap."[62] Modern industrial silviculture, or tree farming, is a product of the research programs of Northwest timber companies and the U.S. Forest Service dating back to the 1920s. Consequently, arguments in defense of the industry often cited historical precedent, claiming that logging was as much a part of the region's culture as fishing, camping, or any other outdoor activity. While everyone acknowledged that the "endless forests" of the nineteenth century had met their limits, the timber industry clearly believed that with some human assistance they could continue harvesting timber in the region forever. Not only was scientific forestry on their side, but they had a longer history than the environmentalists and a popular culture of their own to back them up. The "timber carnivals" that marked the height of summer in many Northwest communities celebrated the activities and lore of the logging camp, and of course folklore in the region is resplendent with logging stories. Even ads for logging trucks claimed their machines would "haul loads that would shock Paul Bunyan."[63] But many Oregonians, and particularly the more recent arrivals, felt that it was not the practice of logging but the trees themselves that contributed to livability and made the state a pleasant place to live. The forests were part of their sense of place that, once combined with the stewardship mythology of the 1970s, became a nonnegotiable issue for many who did not subscribe to the belief that the state's primary identity should be tied to the forest products industry.

After several years of conflict over the future of the forests, however, it became clear that some degree of compromise was needed to mediate between competing economic interests and mutually exclusive ideas of what life in the region was all about. In the community of Mill City, Oregon, representatives of the timber industry organized Earth Day tours of local mills and logging sites to help inform their opponents about the measures they were taking to reduce the impact of logging on the environment.[64] Banners appeared in the downtown districts of several small towns, declaring themes like "Dallas, Oregon Style" over outlines of green fir trees; these were accepted on both sides of the forest debate as symbols of their communities. Letters to the editors of local papers commonly cited "this is the way it's always been done in Oregon" as justification for *both* the preservation and continued logging of the region's forests.

Telling one side from the other was not always as easy as the media coverage suggested in the 1990s; indeed, it was clear that most of the people on either side shared common concerns about the future of the state's forests. They just disagreed on how the resource should be managed—as a reflection of Oregon's long-term reliance on natural resources, or as part of an environmental legacy that some felt made the state uniquely livable? A political compromise reducing but not eliminating logging on public lands, a result of the direct intervention of President Clinton in 1993, helped prevent the conflict from being decided in the courts, but the debate over livability and working forests was never permanently resolved.[65] The forest products sector of Oregon's economy subsequently continued its decline, with employment falling from a peak of nearly ninety thousand in 1950 to sixty thousand in 1990, then ultimately below thirty thousand in 2010. Timber was no longer king; by the turn of the twenty-first century wood products accounted for less than 3 percent of Oregon's overall economy and overall harvests were roughly half what they had been at the industry's peak in the 1970s.[66] But the trees remain part of the region's sense of place, and the logger remains as much a regional symbol as the environmentalist.

What was most interesting about this central political battle of the late 1980s and early 1990s is the degree to which it incorporated appeals to the concept of livability generated during prior environmental conflicts in Oregon, to the point that the struggles of the previous decades became part of a mythology of stewardship that helped shape residents' sense of place and political perspectives. The vocabulary of the debates, the historical claims, the links to tradition, and the public pleas made by both sides resonated with the assumption that Oregonians were concerned about their environment and that economics alone would not convince many of the need to continue logging at obviously unsustainable levels. This common vocabulary may in fact have allowed for some of the compromises that helped cool the timber conflict by providing a set of ideas and values familiar to those on opposite sides of the bargaining tables and to their constituents. The meaning of "preserving Eden" was mutable; it could feed a strong preservationist orientation in one place and a literally green, managed forest resource agenda in another, but both were rooted in a culture that reflected the mythologization of past battles over growth and environmental quality. These dual (and perhaps at times dueling) ecotopias shared the heritage of Oregon's postwar environmentalism and a common ground based in place and concern for maintaining livability, even if they interpreted the lessons differently when applying them to the future of the forests.

The development of a regional sense of place rooted in nature and bound together by a mythology of stewardship was not a process entirely unique to Oregon in the 1970s, but it was there that the process was most evident, most lasting, and had the greatest impact on public policy and personal behavior. The stories that make up this mythology are told and retold in the region, in the media and at backyard barbeques, to the point that they have become part of its cultural fabric. Unlike some popular environmental slogans—consider "think globally, act locally"—which have lost meaning as they have become ubiquitous, what Governor Tom McCall labeled "the Oregon story" has retained much of its power because the mythology remains supported by public policy. The legacy of the conflicts explored in this book contributes to a form of what rhetorician Anne Marie Todd calls "environmental patriotism," or "the belief that a country's greatness is defined by its environment." The incorporation of nature into cultural values and identity allows for a linkage between the global and local, the abstract and specific, which can provide a basis for political action on issues like growth that might otherwise seem too distant or overwhelming to be addressed.[67] While the nation as a whole "saw a decline of environmental patriotism after World War II" as economic expansion and rising standards of living redefined American lives around consumption, the story was different in Oregon and other parts of the Pacific Northwest. There growth came to be seen as a threat to livability earlier and efforts to regulate the impacts of the postwar economic boom were more effective because residents believed nature was at the root of the region's exceptionalism. As Todd notes, "Environmental patriotism is exceptionalism based on preservation rather than the unfettered exploitation of our natural heritage."[68] Regional identity and sense of place in Oregon were shaped by both the fear of losing valued natural amenities and the steps taken to preserve livability in response, a process that reinforced the existing belief in exceptionalism.

In marking the close of the twentieth century by stating that "Oregon showed the way" to an environmental awakening, the Associated Press was acknowledging the national impact of the state's policy innovations in the environmental era—the epitome of the local becoming global. The Eden residents enjoyed was little like the landscapes encountered by their nine-teenth-century forbearers; it was an ordered, simplified, and commercial-ized environment that had largely yielded to the yoke of capitalism by the turn of the twentieth century. By midcentury romanticized images of liv-ing on the "frontier" had given way to a modern, industrial society nestled within an abundant nature that offered aesthetic and recreational ameni-ties in which residents took pride; it informed a sense of environmental patriotism that differentiated them culturally from both Californians *and* New Yorkers. The pace of growth prior to the 1950s had been slow enough and its impacts modest enough that environmental decline could usually be overlooked or ignored. As a result, calls for restraint in the use of natural resources were seldom heeded and warnings of impending loss ignored. Eden, the majority felt, would provide both garden and working forest, river and sewer, space for recreation and for dumping garbage. There was room for everyone and growth, when it came, was good.

These sentiments would be challenged in the 1950s. As national conversations about the impact of development and the limits of growth began, few in Oregon responded. Attempts to mobilize residents to pre-serve or restore nature met with limited success; they were simply not yet ready to hear that their Eden *needed* preservation. When one of the region's best-known voices called for the preservation of a long stretch of the Pacific coast late in the decade he met with a disappointing reception. As it turned out, the potential for mobilizing environmental patriotism was limited by the lack of a widely perceived threat—people might celebrate their natural heritage, but taking action to preserve it required they be worried for its future. That level of concern would come with time, and the earliest efforts to awaken the public to the need to act in defense of livability would help speed the process along.

Chapter 2
A Dunes Park for Oregon?

> Our recent Pacific coast recreation area survey clearly showed that
> the Oregon Dunes area is one of the three or four finest remaining
> recreation areas on the Pacific Coast.
>
> —E. T. Scoyen, acting director, US National Park Service, 1959

Oregon's widespread association with progressive environmental policies is
rooted most deeply in the early 1970s, a period in which polling showed
that national concern over environmental issues was at its peak and the
state repeatedly made headlines as a place of both great natural beauty and
innovative efforts to preserve (or restore) environmental quality. Through
much of that decade, Oregon's reputation as an environmental haven was
both a powerful force in attracting new residents and a distinctive element
to be used in marketing the state to tourists, who were quickly becoming a
linchpin in the state's economy. Such had not always been the case, however; prior to World War II Oregon's economy was dominated by the timber
industry, which at one point employed well over half the state's wage earners. Suggesting that tourism would one day overtake logging in the race to
the top of the economic ladder would have provoked laughs in the 1930s
or 1940s, as would any demand to set aside significant amounts of natural
resources for such "nonproductive" uses as recreation. The first challenges
to this orthodoxy came in the 1950s, but not as literal voices in the wilderness; unlike California in 1900, Oregon had no John Muir. The loudest calls
for conservation and preservation at midcentury came, rather, from urban
boosters and politicians who believed the time had come once again to
establish a national park in Oregon—something that had not been seriously
attempted in several decades. Oregon, they believed, deserved a second
national park; it would serve as proof of the quality of its environment and
the wisdom of its people in preserving it when other states had not.

Oregonians welcomed the establishment of Crater Lake National Park in 1902 as the ultimate endorsement of their claim to scenic grandeur equal to that of Yellowstone or Yosemite. The nation's sixth national park, Crater Lake had been promoted by both local supporters and newspapers statewide; following its creation these same forces turned their efforts to promoting the lake as a regional tourist destination.[1] For most Oregonians, however, this taste of national recognition was enough to put the state on par with neighboring Washington (where Mt. Rainier National Park had been established in 1899) and to quiet any further demands for scenic preservation by federal action. Over the following decades an extensive state park system was developed in response to public calls for new recreation areas, leading to increased tourism and serving as a lasting point of pride for state boosters.[2] But in the late 1930s, soon after Mount Olympus National Monument in Washington was upgraded to national park status, Oregon's conservationists once again turned their attention to establishing a new national park within their state.[3]

In 1939 Richard L. Neuberger, a young reporter for Portland's *Oregonian*, drew national attention with a number of conservation-oriented articles in major magazines calling for the preservation of the unique natural resources of the Pacific Northwest. In an article entitled "Hells Canyon, the Biggest of All," written for *Harper's*, Neuberger staked the region's claim to having the deepest canyon on the face of the earth—Hells Canyon on the Oregon-Idaho border—against the common belief that the Grand Canyon was the deepest. He also noted that the National Park Service (NPS) planned to explore the area the following summer, a prospect that Neuberger feared would threaten the gorge with "professional tourists, junketing politicians, knicknack peddlers, and glamour girls" unbefitting its stature as a symbol of the region's grandeur and inaccessibility.[4] Within a few months, though, he began a series of more positive articles in the *Oregonian* exploring the state's options for a new national park and explaining some of the potential obstacles along the path to park establishment. Neuberger identified three possible sites for a second national park in Oregon: Hells Canyon; Mt. Hood, just east of Portland; and a forty-mile stretch of sand dunes along the southern Oregon coast, distant from any major city, all of which were under official review by the NPS as potential additions to the federal park system.[5] In the final article of the series he noted that a coastal park would be a first for the West and a rarity within the national system, further enhancing its attraction and the state's claims to unique scenic values. Apparently the prospect of an influx of "professional tourists" was less of a concern on the coast than at Hells Canyon.

What Neuberger could not have known at the time was that his articles foreshadowed a conflict over a dunes park that would drag on for well over a decade, pitting the interests of local residents against the conservation agendas of state and national leaders and prompting debates over whether Oregon needed another national park at all. That conflict stood twenty years in the future; in 1940 the prospects for a second national park for Oregon looked promising as Governor Charles Sprague announced his support for a new national park in the Oregon dunes, declaring that it would enhance the state's tourist appeal.[6] Coming on the heels of the 1937 authorization of the Cape Hatteras National Seashore in North Carolina, a site of similar size and arguably lesser quality, and amid "the most dynamic period of expansion in the history of the National Park Service," during the New Deal, park supporters were justified in their belief that the dunes could well become Oregon's next national claim to unmatched scenic grandeur.[7] Unfortunately for them, the turmoil of World War II and the corresponding decline in both visitation and funding for the national parks put the question of a new park for Oregon to rest until the 1950s.

The war years marked a period of intense change in the Pacific Northwest as the region was reshaped by industrial expansion and rapid population growth. The harnessing of the Columbia River, begun with the completion of Bonneville Dam in 1937, marked the beginning of fifty years of surplus hydroelectric capacity that led to the creation of new industries based on cheap electric power, while wartime contracts dramatically expanded shipyards and aircraft plants in Portland and Seattle and fed an industrial expansion that demanded new workers.[8] Portland alone attracted 160,000 new residents in the 1940s, mainly to jobs in war industries that represented a significant shift away from the region's traditional agricultural and timber economies. This industrialization drove hopes that after the war the region might escape its longtime role as a resource colony for eastern capital, an economy based on exporting agricultural products and raw materials rather than manufactured goods. But immediately after the war unemployment was widespread as government contracts were concluded or canceled; only a handful of major companies were able to successfully retool their assembly lines for consumer goods or develop other commercial markets by the late 1940s. While some of the newly developed industries were there to stay—notably aluminum production—the traditional economy regained its dominant position quickly after the war. By 1950, fully 60 percent of Oregon's manufacturing employment was once again in the forest products industry, though over the succeeding decade the diversification of the industrial base that had started during the war would make some progress toward overtaking that sector of the economy.[9]

Perhaps the more striking impact of the war years on the region, however, was population growth. A nearly 40 percent increase between the 1940 and 1950 census counts suggests that many of those who migrated to Oregon decided to stay, even after wartime employment opportunities disappeared; Washington's population similarly grew by 37 percent, bolstered by continued manufacturing work in the Seattle area.[10] The bulk of these new residents were concentrated in or around the urban centers west of the Cascade Mountains in Oregon and Washington—a total of 837,200 new residents settled in this area between 1940 and 1950—which gave them access to city-based industries, the agricultural centers of the lush western valleys, and the Douglas fir forests of the Coast Range and western slopes of the Cascades. In Oregon 92 percent of this population growth was concentrated in the nineteen western counties, locating nearly four hundred thousand new residents between the Cascades and the Pacific coast.[11] Quality of life was a strong factor in people's decisions to stay in the region; the climate was temperate, it was considered a good place to raise children (adults under age forty-five and children made up the bulk of the newcomers), it was seen as a place of great economic potential due to the abundance of resources and cheap power to fuel industry, and it offered unequaled access to outdoor recreation, which many expected to take advantage of in their leisure time. Indeed, making these recreational amenities available had been part of organized labor's regional agenda since the 1920s, when automobiles first put lakes, rivers, camps, and beaches within easy reach of even the working class.[12]

In keeping with postwar trends nationally, a rising interest in recreational travel was evident in Oregon by 1947, when an estimated 630,000 tourist automobiles traveled the state's highways, contributing $105 million in related sales to local economies. This represented a 300 percent increase since 1936, an early sign of a trend that would see tourism become the state's third-largest industry by the 1960s.[13] To accommodate existing demand for outdoor recreation, the acreage of the Oregon state park system had been expanded almost tenfold between 1930 and 1950, in part with revenues derived from a gasoline tax approved by the voters in 1942. Most of these new state parks focused on scenic preservation rather than recreation, though; overnight camping was not commonly allowed in Oregon's parks until the mid-1950s.[14] As the postwar boom in leisure travel sent visitation figures skyrocketing, the state's ability to provide enough campgrounds, picnic areas, and related amenities in addition to basic scenic preservation was quickly outstripped. Thus by the early 1950s, with a larger, younger population expecting to spend more active leisure time in the outdoors than a decade earlier, conditions were once again ripe for discussion of a new national park for Oregon.[15]

Similar forces were at work across the country. The national parks, largely idled during the war, enjoyed a rush of popularity after 1948 as the postwar economy recovered to make leisure travel accessible to more Americans and the baby boom drove the average age of the population lower, with many young families eager to visit attractions such as Yellowstone and Grand Canyon National Parks. The NPS watched visitation grow from just six million in 1942 to thirty-three million in 1950–a figure that would nearly double again by 1960.[16] The sheer number of automobiles entering the parks severely taxed the system's infrastructure and exposed the decrepit state of park roads, campgrounds, and visitor centers, leading Congress to approve the Eisenhower administration's Mission 66 program to rebuild the national parks in 1956. Over the following decade the ambitious program would allocate over $1 billion to the parks, primarily for the expansion of roads and visitor facilities to accommodate the dramatic increase in public demand for outdoor recreation and scenic travel.[17] But demand still surpassed the capacity of the nation's parks to provide recreation to all who wanted it, so private interests became involved as well. Grants from the Mellon Foundation in this period, for example, funded a series of studies that focused on water-based recreation in coastal areas and near major urban centers, resources that were tangential to the NPS's traditional missions of scenic and historic preservation. From these studies came the reports *Our Vanishing Shoreline* (1955), *Our Fourth Shore: Great Lakes Shoreline Recreation Area Survey* (1955), and *Pacific Coast Recreation Area Survey* (1959), all of which suggested that developing recreation areas near water would both address the need for more outdoor recreation and

preserve shoreline resources that were rapidly shrinking due to development pressures.[18]

The *Pacific Coast Recreation Area Survey* found that along the shores
of Washington, Oregon, and California "almost every attractive shore
area . . . that is accessible by road ha[d] been developed in some manner"
and noted that these areas represented a "limited and diminishing resource
of scenic and scientific interest for which there is no substitute."[19] The relatively pristine Oregon Dunes area was, not surprisingly, among the sites
receiving specific recommendations in the report, which judged the area
to be "of national importance" for both recreation and "the inspirational
worth of the resources to the American citizen" that "warrant permanent
preservation for the nation as a whole."[20] These dunes are representative of
Pacific coast landforms distinct from those of the Atlantic shore. A geological study published in 1958 found that 45 percent of Oregon's coast
bore sand dunes of some type, with some extending as far as 2.75 miles
inland. Of the three major dunes structures in the Pacific Northwest, the
"Coos Bay dune sheet," colloquially known as the Oregon Dunes, was the
largest, spanning over fifty miles north to south and constituting "the most
continuous and widest of the dune areas [with] the most comprehensive
display of forms and processes" on the entire coast. While dune structures
and processes had been subject to lengthy and focused study in Europe
and Africa, research on North American dunes was "meager" in the 1950s,
with even less attention paid to the geomorphology of coastal dunes than
continental ones; as a result remarkably little was known about the dunes
and the natural processes that built and sustained them.[21]

Government-funded stabilization projects, involving the planting of
nonnative European beach grass, had reduced the area of active dunes con-
siderably by midcentury in attempts to protect lakes, highways, and private
property from being overrun by sand.[22] This "battle against the sand," as
it were, was compelling enough to have inspired freelance writer Frank
Herbert to propose an article called "They Stopped the Moving Sands" to
his agent in 1957. Herbert, better known as the author of the enormously
popular science fiction novel *Dune* (1965), failed to complete his article
about "the small Coastal town of Florence . . . the scene of an unsung victory
in the fight that men have been waging since before the dawn of recorded
history. The fight with moving sand—with dunes."[23] But the writer's observations made it clear that the remaining dunes were, in a sense, the very

Fig. 2. Sand dunes slowly consuming a forest, Oregon Dunes, 1938 (National Archives and Records Administration, Record Group 79: Records of the National Park Service, LI 79-OC033)

essence of the at-risk sites of "scientific interest" the NPS was charged with protecting under the Antiquities Act of 1906.[24]

By the late 1950s state and national conditions were once again favorable to revisiting the question of preserving the dunes as a national park, and this time Richard Neuberger, who had advanced the idea in the *Oregonian* twenty years earlier, was in a much better position to promote the project—he had been elected to the U.S. Senate in 1954 in a campaign in which conservation had featured so strongly that he had distributed packets of grass seed to promote restoration of the state's public grazing lands in place of the usual election-year trinkets.[25] Attacking incumbent Republican senator Guy Cordon for "selling out Oregon's most precious heritage, its resources," Neuberger ran strongly against the Eisenhower administration's "give away" policies on natural resources and the views of Secretary of the Interior Douglas McKay (himself a former Oregon governor) in particular.[26] The junior Democratic senator quickly earned a reputation as a staunch conservationist through his opposition to private hydroelectric dams on the Snake River, his outspoken criticism of US Forest Service (USFS) timber management policies across the West, and the conservation essays he published in popular periodicals like *Progressive, Outdoor America*, and

Fig. 3. Senator Richard
Neuberger, official portrait,
1957 (Original in author's
possession)

the *New York Times Magazine*. Almost immediately following his election
he was being lauded by national figures for his positions on conservation;
for example, in October 1955 Howard Zahnizer, the executive secretary of
the Wilderness Society, forwarded to Neuberger a copy of a letter to the
New York Times written by famed wildlife biologist Olaus J. Murie praising
the senator's position on the Hells Canyon Dam as an example of "multilat-
eral planning" that accounted for wildlife as much as development.[27]

Though Neuberger's perspective on natural resources was firmly
rooted in the multiple-use conservation approach of the day, he was also
a strong proponent of wilderness preservation, telling the *New York Times*
in 1957 that "somewhere in this vast land of ours, we ought to retain a few
valleys or uplands just as they were when Lewis and Clark carried our flag
across a virgin and untrammeled region."[28] Near the end of his first term
in office Neuberger looked to the creation of the Oregon Dunes National
Seashore as a preservation project that would both extend Oregon's
national recognition as a scenic showplace and cement his bid for reelection to the Senate in 1960. Because the NPS had been quietly considering

the Oregon Dunes for designation as a potential national seashore since 1957, Neuberger rightly expected the agency's support for his proposal and assumed his constituents would welcome the bid for a second national park in Oregon.[29]

In March 1959, without fanfare or substantive consultation with the private landowners affected in Oregon, Neuberger introduced a bill in the Senate to establish the Oregon Dunes National Seashore. Given the national interest in recreation, the implied support of the NPS, and his home state's pride in scenic preservation (not to mention its growing taste for tourist dollars), he believed passage before the 1960 general election was reasonable. He foresaw few problems in Congress, as the dunes park could be created primarily from existing undeveloped federal lands within the Siuslaw National Forest at relatively low cost, which he felt made it a stronger candidate for national seashore status than concurrent proposals for Cape Cod National Seashore in Massachusetts, Padre Island National Seashore in Texas, or the Indiana Dunes National Lakeshore on Lake Michigan, each of which had already stirred controversy over questions of landownership and concern about their proximity to urban areas. Neuberger's S. 1526, "A Bill to Establish the Oregon Dunes National Seashore," then, was the first step in the process of preserving "for the benefit, inspiration, and use of the public certain unspoiled shoreline in the State of Oregon which possesses scenic, scientific, and recreation values of national importance."[30] The brief bill offered only an outline proposal and authorized the NPS to determine the boundaries, policies, and conditions for the establishment of the new seashore recreation area in keeping with its mission. The press was informed of the senator's intention to introduce the bill in advance, so when Neuberger took to the Senate floor on March 25 he was able to include some initial reactions from Oregon in his remarks, reflecting his enthusiasm for the project and his belief that the state needed another national park to validate its claims to scenic beauty.

Written by Neuberger and cosponsored by Oregon's senior senator, fellow Democrat Wayne Morse, S. 1526 set an upper limit of 35,000 acres for the seashore park, which was to include the dunes area and an additional 340-acre plot to the north that incorporated a site known as Sea Lion Caves. The only mainland sea lion rookery in Oregon, the caves had been operating as a commercial attraction since 1932 and were under consideration as a state park when Neuberger decided to include them in

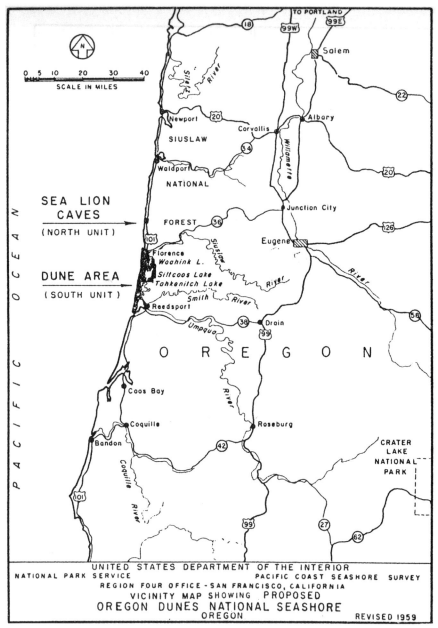

Fig. 4. Proposed Oregon Dunes National Seashore locator map, 1959 (US National Park Service)

his bill—not to preclude the possibility of a state park but to ensure they would be preserved for public access.[31] Saving these two coastal areas, the senator noted, was vital because while "much of man's destiny has been decided where the land meets the sea . . . many of these areas have been exploited or liquidated so that their recreational value is permanently impaired." The Oregon sites were of particular merit because of their striking natural features, described in Neuberger's journalistic style as including "lofty and massive ramparts of sand which tower above the sea. Behind the dunes lie gemlike little lakes. Native grasses and evergreen trees add to the wild beauty of the location. Birds and wildlife abound. The sea-lion caves combine rocky grandeur with the rookeries of these clumsy but fascinating mammals, which inhabit tossing reaches of salt water."[32] In accord with the mission of the NPS, the dunes were said to be of scientific as well as scenic merit. Included in the record with Neuberger's testimony was a text he had produced for the Oregon Coast Association that explained in poetic detail the drama and beauty of the area. The promotional material claimed that the mystery of forests buried alive by sand, the artful designs of the wind on dune slopes, the hidden lakes and streams all were part of a "geological wonderland" of great scientific interest as well as being nice to look at. Here visitors would "find fascinating beauty in tramping the gray Aeolian sands that reach from the wooded highlands to the smooth straight-line beach in an alluring series of ridges and hollows that hold an impelling touch of scientific interest in the cause of . . . the geologic and physiographic changes that have . . . forced transformation of this portion of the Oregon coast from a living forest to a sand dune exquisite under the implacable influence of the slowly rising Continental Shelf."[33]

Economic opportunity also entered into Neuberger's calculations. National parks were, in his estimation, "magnets for the attraction of visitors," and he was confident that "the establishment of the Oregon Dunes national seashore area [would] stimulate the economy of the entire Oregon seacoast" by drawing travelers to adjacent towns, stores, and hotels and through the national publicity such federal sites gained from organizations like the American Automobile Association.[34] Precedent was the final element in his case for preserving the dunes. The previous year Neuberger had successfully helped establish the Fort Clatsop National Memorial near Astoria, Oregon, marking the site where the Lewis and Clark expedition spent the winter of 1805–1806. That act of historic commemoration, he felt, should be complemented by an effort "to preserve scenic grandeur and out-door majesty" on the coast. Furthermore, he noted that "despite Oregon's substantial area and its wealth of scenery, comparatively few areas . . . have been set aside for permanent safekeeping under the jurisdiction of . . . the National Park Service [and] we of Oregon have not fared overly generously as national park reserves have been created during the past half century, despite the vast scenic potential within our state's boundaries."[35] It was, in his estimation, Oregon's turn for another park.

Neuberger's read of the political situation was also likely influenced by the company he kept in Oregon. As a former journalist, he maintained close relationships with many of the writers, editors, and broadcasters of the region, while his lifetime interest in conservation yielded friendships with the state's most prominent advocates for public control of and access to natural areas. Following his election to the Senate, Neuberger received a steady stream of advice from home, much of it reinforcing his beliefs about conservation, like this congratulatory letter sent by John Gribble of the Izaak Walton League in December 1954:

> Some of us oldtimers who know of the struggle made by Gifford
> Pinchot . . . really can be thankful for the outcome of the Oregon
> election. We can look back across a half to 3/4 century on thievery,
> waste and destruction of the people's heritage, and still see millions
> of acres of scorched earth, ruined watersheds, barren rock wastes,
> shifting sand deserts, caused by greed for quick dollars, and no
> care for anything or anyone else. . . . You will have hard fights Dick,
> but please feel assured that those who worked to get you elected
> will also work to support you in your fights for a better America.[36]

Similarly, Fred McNeil, executive news editor of the *Oregon Journal*, wrote, "You have a tremendous following in the position you have taken on conservation matters," while the superintendent of public schools in Warrenton, a small community on the northern coast, noted that "we have few enough places in the country where the natural grandeur of the North American continent still endures. I feel we have a genuine obligation to the next generation of Americans to preserve some of their natural heritage in the state in which we found it."[37] The freshman senator was even contacted anonymously by a "federal employee in conservation work" who signed his

Fig. 5. Senator Richard Neuberger and Secretary of the Interior Harold L. Ickes, n.d. (Oregon Historical Society Photo Collection, OrHi 72504)

correspondence only "Oregon conservationist" while urging Neuberger to "become the spokesman in Congress for all conservation programs." Writing four years before the Oregon Dunes bill was introduced, this anonymous correspondent proclaimed, "I feel confident that the [NPS] would look with favor on the establishing of a national seashore, similar to Cape Hatteras, somewhere on the Oregon Coast" and even enclosed a draft bill to help start the process.[38]

Much to Senator Neuberger's surprise, news of his park proposal met with a lukewarm reception in the metropolitan centers of Oregon's Willamette Valley—which accounted for a majority of his Democratic supporters—and with outright hostility in some of the small coastal towns adjacent to the proposed park. The editors of the *Oregonian*, the state's largest and most influential newspaper, immediately raised the question of whether a new *state* park would make more sense in the area, noting that "unlike the states on the Atlantic seaboard, Oregon has reserved its beaches for the public benefit" and suggesting a new state-run park would only "increase Oregon's stature as a state of many parks and playgrounds."[39] In the coastal town of Florence, at the northern end of the proposed park, Neuberger's bill was met with "violent opposition" and a list of concerns ranging from its impact on property values and the local tax base to the relationship residents had established with the Forest Service, which already managed much of the area in question.[40]

What had gone wrong? The bill proposed a park of modest size, approximately 35,000 acres as compared to Yellowstone's 2.1 million; it left the question of boundaries up to the NPS, allowing it to include only those areas that merited protection; and it would follow established procedures for acquiring title to private land within the area. Ironically, it was these very points—the proposed park's size, the lack of clearly defined boundaries, and the issue of property rights—that generated the most ardent opposition among coastal residents. Localized opposition to new national parks was fairly common, but Neuberger had expected strong support from inland residents (especially those who had called publicly for the expansion of parks and recreation areas within the state); instead their response was inexplicably tepid when the plan was first announced. Neuberger, it appeared, had badly misjudged the level of support for his plan at the outset and was forced into a defensive posture before the first hearings on the bill were even scheduled.[41]

At an appearance in Portland on March 28, 1959, Neuberger told reporters he was "shocked and dismayed" by the reception his park proposal found in Oregon, blaming the response on "special interests" and promising to "press intensively" for the project in a united efforts with Senator Morse.[42] It soon became evident that public opinion on the dunes park proposal was mixed, with coastal residents logically more polarized than their valley neighbors. Two days after S. 1526 was introduced the weekly paper in Florence published an article on the proposal that included coverage of a preemptive meeting of local business leaders who had passed a resolution requesting the park proposal be deferred because "local people have been given no voice and have been unable to get satisfactory answers to their questions."[43] The president of the Florence Chamber of Commerce telegrammed that his members were "extremely disappointed in . . . your announcement of impending legislation authorizing accuations [sic] of land . . . for national recreation facilities [having] tremendous impact on future of this area."[44] Later public meetings in coastal towns were characterized by confrontations between small numbers of park supporters, who commonly felt the region's economic future lay in tourism, and organized groups that wanted to maintain the traditional mix of forestry, commercial fishing, and recreation at the center of their economic life.[45] Inland the response was more muted, allowing Neuberger to point out to the press that "there has always been some bitter local opposition—everywhere in the country—to the creation of new national parks and refuges." Soon after, though, he suggested that the park "would result in marvelous advertising for Oregon and aid tourism" and asked the assembled reporters, "How can people be so short sighted?"[46]

In early April the Eisenhower administration began to distance itself from the plan. Despite Neuberger's cooperation with the NPS and that agency's support for new parks on both coasts, an "informed administration source" told a reporter from the *Oregonian* that rather than building new parks at that time, resources from the Mission 66 program would be directed toward improving existing parks. This may have been due in part to rising controversy over the proposed Indiana Dunes National Lakeshore, which Illinois senator Paul Douglas had been promoting for a year prior to the introduction of Neuberger's dunes bill. (In that case clashes between pro-development interests and park supporters had become central to the debate over how the southern shore of Lake Michigan would be used, and the administration may have wanted to avoid a similar blowup in Oregon.)[47] When representatives of the NPS arrived in Florence for a public meeting on April 9 they found opinion on the issue mixed. Dan H. Thompson, the chief of recreation for the park agency, answered questions about the proposal and made no mention of the Eisenhower administration's reticence. His presentation provided more detail than S. 1526 or any previously published stories had, including estimated budgets, staffing levels, and the assurance that "the recreation area should produce far more revenue than ever received from taxes." It was disclosed at the meeting that the chamber of commerce of the town of Reedsport, on the southern boundary of the dunes, favored the plan, while their counterparts to the north in Florence were among the more vocal of the opponents.[48]

Also appearing at the Florence meeting were members of the "Vine Maple Savages," a purported secret society that had been organized in 1944

Fig. 6. Vine Maple Savages protest Oregon Dunes park plan, Florence, 1959 (*The Oregonian*, Oregon Historical Society Photo Collection, OrHi 13151)

for a public power battle against the government-owned Bonneville Power Administration. The Savages, arriving with shotguns and dressed as mountain men, informed park officials they would need passports the next time they came to town, as the area would secede from the union if the proposal went through. They were not completely opposed to the idea of a new national park for Oregon and offered NPS officials a sarcastic counterproposal for a "Frog Bog National Park" that would include extensive private property in the scenic Columbia River Gorge near Portland.[49] In a letter to Neuberger, Karl Onthank, a well-known conservation advocate based at the University of Oregon, dismissed their message as part of "a more or less staged demonstration against . . . your bill. The appearance of the 'bush boys' in costume with a fancily prepared protest, for instance." The bulk of residents, Onthank believed, did not hold firm positions because they still did not understand the details of the proposal; once they did their objections were likely to quiet.[50]

From the outset individual property owners whose land fell within the proposed park boundaries were the most outspoken of the critics, even more so than the few corporations that held tracts of private timberland within the dunes or relied on timber from the surrounding Siuslaw National Forest. Foremost in their minds was the fear that their property would be seized by the government. Their position was expressed by a resident of Florence, who wrote in a letter to the *Oregonian*, "What needs to be preserved? The sand dunes? No. These large drifts of sand keep coming in from the ocean and will continue as long as the wind blows and the waves roll. . . . What then needs to be preserved? [T]he right of the individual citizen to live in his own home without fear of a government agency, such as the National Park Service, taking it all away from him."[51] A resident of the community of Westlake, a tiny community midway between Florence and Reedsport, echoed this sentiment and further criticized Neuberger for introducing "legislation without consultation." He charged that "to take over the holdings and home of private individuals without their consent and at a price set by the government is something that when done by one country to another is called aggression." The entire plan, he felt, was intended to "add laurels to the brow that was not satisfied with the accolade of the squirrels."[52] Though not a clear majority of coastal residents, the opposition of "a vociferous minority whose personal interests are at stake" presented a significant challenge to park proponents.[53] Neuberger's reputation as a conservationist and his arguments for the public good carried little weight with the landowners, who would prove to be the most tenacious of the park opponents over the following decade.

By mid-April 1959 local opponents in Florence and from across Lane County organized into the Western Lane Taxpayers Association (WLTA) and began raising funds to back a letter-writing campaign against the park; soon thereafter the Lane County Chamber of Commerce issued a resolution opposing the park as well.[54] Their actions helped convince Wayne Morse to call for local hearings on the matter, while Neuberger initially advocated holding hearings in Portland, nearer the bulk of the state's population and where the opposition was less intense and urban park supporters were more likely to attend.[55] Property rights were also on the minds of timber industry representatives, who collectively expressed concern over the potential loss of access to timber on the Siuslaw National Forest, restrictions on groundwater withdrawals for industrial use, and the possible condemnation of commercial tree farms within the boundaries of the proposed park. Their opposition, however, was purely a business decision; if suitable exchanges for public lands elsewhere were in the offing, they would not oppose the park. In May Representative Charles Porter, a Democrat representing the district the dunes were in, announced that he would not support any bill that lacked specific park boundaries due to the uncertainty this caused for property owners. Though a supporter of the park idea, Porter was responding to criticisms from local residents as well as "allegations that business would be stopped in the area."[56] Without Porter's support in the House, the chances of sending a dunes park bill to the president's desk before the 1960 elections were greatly diminished, as it was unlikely a park would ever be authorized over the objection of the local congressman.

The issue was further confused in June when representatives of a Native American council representing several tribes in the dunes area announced their opposition to any park plan, claiming that the land in question had been illegally seized in the nineteenth century when Congress failed to ratify the treaty transferring it to the federal government, thus denying the tribe compensation for their ancestral lands.[57] In July representatives of the business community in the two largest towns adjacent the proposed park met to discuss the plan and were told by WLTA leaders that the "impact would be disastrous," leading many to join the Chamber of Commerce in its formal statement of opposition.[58] By this point local opposition had crystalized into two major groups: property owners who feared losing their homes and cabins, and business owners who were convinced that a park would mean the end of growth for the local economy. Their arguments spread quickly in the press, no doubt contributing to the sentiment behind the *Oregonian*'s August editorial against the park, which stated that the paper was "by no means convinced" of the need for a coastal park in Oregon, where "the shoreline is not vanishing." Instead, the editors argued, it made more sense to "establish public reserves on the beaches in California, where population is much greater and private ownership has sealed off so much of the shoreline."[59] Though he had responded only briefly to opponents in the coastal press, Neuberger could not safely ignore the loss of the *Oregonian*'s editorial support. His immediate reaction was to point out that opposition to the Cape Hatteras National Seashore (established in 1953) was based on similar arguments and that "just as the local fears were proved unfounded in North Carolina, I am sure that they can be similarly discredited with regard to the Oregon dunes area."[60] He did not then recognize the depth of the opposition or imagine that the controversy would remain in the news for another dozen years.

Neuberger's official response to coastal critics was to schedule hearings before the Senate Interior and Insular Affairs Subcommittee on Public

Lands for October in the town of Reedsport, on the southern boundary of the proposed park and about twenty miles from the core of opposition in Florence. As the date of the hearings approached he announced that he would be willing to amend the park bill to stipulate specific boundaries for the seashore, addressing the fear that the NPS would be allowed to dictate the park borders over local objections; Neuberger also suggested that a provision to allow waterfowl hunting could be added to the bill to accommodate local hunters.[61] In a column written for the *Oregonian* the senator responded to what he viewed as the most valid concerns about the proposal—the loss of private homes, the potential negative impact on the local tax base, and the loss of hunting access—by noting that similar objections to the Cape Hatteras National Seashore had been forgotten in the years since the park was created and that tourism in the area had soared some 350 percent. He showed a hint of exasperation, though, in concluding that "I am not going to stuff this great national seashore park down the throats of the people of my native state if they do not want it. But I would consider myself a poor senator, indeed, if I did not express the claim of Oregon's majestic seacoast when our government is moving to reserve national shoreline parks . . . at places of far less beauty than where Oregon meets the Pacific's tide."[62]

Neuberger's belief in the attraction of a coastal park was seconded soon after by the Oregon State Highway Commission's Advisory Committee on State Parks, which issued a statement supporting the plan in mid-September.[63] This was offset a week later, though, when the State Committee on Natural Resources announced that it would issue a statement opposing the park at the upcoming hearing due to concern over the establishment of a "single-use" recreation zone in an area that was already developing other resources.[64] This report, representing not only the views of the heads of the state's twelve land management and natural resource agencies but that of Governor Mark Hatfield as well, was seen by the *Oregonian* as the death blow to the park. It prompted Neuberger to rebuke Hatfield publicly, stating in an open letter that "if an Oregon Dunes National Seashore is now rejected . . . your attitude will unquestionably have been a material factor."[65] The senator took his criticism a step farther just before the hearings began on October 7, telling reporters, "I can't understand why anyone would run down his own state, particularly when what he says isn't true," referring to criticisms of the dunes area's climate and recreational offerings contained in the report issued by the state Committee on Natural Resources but clearly aiming his comments at Hatfield.[66]

The final flurry of publicity preceding the subcommittee hearing did draw a number of park supporters into the papers, including former governor Oswald West (known as the father of the state's public beach access law), who claimed that "the people of Oregon would be crazy to turn down the gift proposed by the Neuberger bill."[67] The editors of the *Oregon Statesman*, the second-largest newspaper in the state, penned a long column defending the proposal and noting that "if we want tourist travel to become a bigger business in Oregon, we must turn our gaze from within our own borders," explaining that a state-run park simply could not match the attraction of a national park, especially for out-of-state tourists.[68] Endorsements from several conservation organizations were also publicized prior to the hearing, including that of the Izaak Walton League of Oregon, which played an advisory role in writing Neuberger's bill. These were added to private correspondence with Neuberger from a range of park advocates, including William Tugman, publisher of the *Port Umpqua Courier* in Reedsport and the chairman of the Advisory Committee on State Parks, who wrote, "I personally feel very strongly that we must have the National Seashore . . . to preserve public access forever" and explained that it was "beyond our present or foreseeable means to add much to what we have now at Honeyman [State] Park" to ensure that access via state administration.[69] Organized labor backed the park as well; the secretary of the Lane County Labor Council, AFL-CIO, wrote to Neuberger in September that following a "full debate" the council had voted to support the dunes proposal and that with "more mobility, longer vacations, and shorter work week[s] . . . workingmen and women are spending more time and money for outdoor recreation."[70] A new park on the western end of the county would provide just that.

The influential regional travel magazine *Sunset: The Magazine of Western Living* featured the Oregon Dunes in its October 1959 issue, describing the "dream-like quality" of the "tan, shifting hills of sand [that] stretch more than 40 miles in a bizarre, uneven emptiness interrupted only by occasional streams and patches of vegetation." Here visitors could take "roller-coaster like tours up and down some of the steepest and biggest dunes for 75 cents" or fish for "sea-run cutthroat trout and silver and Chinook salmon in the stream that runs by the camp" at Siltcoos. Hikers were warned, however, that "navigation sometimes presents a problem, particular[ly] in finding your original point of departure."[71] While not taking a position on the park proposal, the editors of *Sunset* were certainly endorsing its appeal to tourists as a unique natural feature, noting both the developed attractions (car rides and campgrounds) as well as the wilderness appeal of the open dunes themselves.

The Subcommittee on Public Lands convened its first hearing on the Oregon coast in Reedsport on October 5, 1959, with Richard Neuberger presiding and representatives from the NPS and the USFS in attendance, along with dozens of local residents, state officials, and other witnesses prepared to address the merits of the park proposal. Introductory testimony from the NPS stressed the need to preserve the nation's few remaining undeveloped coastal areas and introduced exhibits claiming that revenues associated with the proposed thirty-five-thousand-acre Oregon Dunes National Seashore would exceed $26 million within twenty-five years of the park's opening, versus $8 million if existing land uses were continued.[72] Management policies and the processes by which private lands would be acquired were also laid out in detail. Neuberger added that official estimates projected a $2–3 million initial expenditure to purchase private property and install basic facilities for the park and that much of that would go to support local labor. Copies of the report on the dunes produced by the NPS's Pacific Coast Seashore Survey were distributed and entered into the record, the first opportunity many had to see the details of the proposal in written form. While Ben H. Thompson, chief of the NPS Division of Recreation Resource Planning, explained that the agency did not in fact support Neuberger's S. 1526 (it preferred to authorize several seashore recreation areas at once), he felt the report provided a fair assessment of what NPS planners envisioned for the dunes. The dunes area, the report stated, was unmatched on the Pacific coast in terms of "inspirational qualities" and recreation potential, and though the state parks and existing USFS facilities provided some recreation opportunities they were filled throughout the recreation season by demand that "far outstripped" their capacities.[73]

A second document, entitled *Jensen Economic Report—Proposed Oregon Dunes National Seashore*, was also introduced by Thompson during the hearing. The economic analysis compared the potential revenue from the proposed park with projections based on maintaining current practices under USFS and private ownership over a fifty-year period starting in 1965. At the outset the report stated that while recreation had not yet been widely recognized as the area's central economic activity, income from recreation would eventually surpass all other local sources even if no changes were made in the dunes. By 1990, the midway point of the study, projected visitation numbers would reach 1.5 million *without the new park* and contribute nearly $8 million to the local economy; to this was added an estimated gross income from timber of under $300,000 and only $12,000 from agriculture, for a total of $8.2 million under the status quo. The park option, on the other hand, yielded visitation projections in excess of 3 million per year that would contribute $26 million in economic activity—$18 million, or 220 percent, over the status quo. To this was added a payroll of $6.6 million, as compared to just $2 million without the park.[74] These figures did not take into account expenditures prior to 1965, which would include the estimated $2–3 million needed to acquire private property and develop visitor facilities. The example of Grand Teton National Park was given to demonstrate the positive effect a new park could have on adjacent property values and nearby Jackson, Wyoming, as typical of a town enjoying rapid growth due to tourism at an adjacent national park. Certainly this data supported Richard Neuberger's claim that a dunes park would ensure the economic future of Florence, Reedsport, and the other communities in the vicinity.

Following Ben Thompson to the witness table, Herbert J. Stone of the Forest Service countered with a lengthy statement in opposition to the plan, claiming that the fourteen thousand acres of Siuslaw National Forest land included in the proposal were already managed for recreational purposes under the USFS's "multiple-use" policy and that ceding these lands to the NPS made little sense economically, as it would prohibit existing nonrecreational uses (primarily logging) that contributed to the local economy. Neuberger responded from the chair by pointing out that the Forest Service managed some fifteen million acres of land in Oregon alone and that the "loss" of fourteen thousand acres of that would be insignificant to the agency, suggesting that the NPS was more likely to be able to secure funds for the development of recreation sites, while the Forest Service, with its institutional focus on timber production, would face serious challenges in securing funds to improve its existing recreational facilities on the Siuslaw National Forest and could not be expected to build the kinds of new facilities outside the forest boundaries that could be established under NPS management.[75] If nothing else, the exchange underscored the ongoing dispute between the National Park Service, in the Department of the Interior, and the U.S. Forest Service, in the Department of Agriculture, over which would be the primary recreation agency at the national level. Though the Oregon Dunes proposal was a point of relative agreement in Washington, DC, any conflict over territory between the two agencies was likely to be complicated by this larger debate.[76]

As the hearing progressed, local opponents added their concerns to those of the Forest Service. Property owners with land inside the proposed park objected to any plans to condemn their land, claiming that the park would be of no benefit to them. "I believe no government should take private property from a citizen against his will," one area resident stated, while another emphasized simply, "We do not need a park."[77] The seasonal nature of the tourist trade was also raised by several witnesses. Others presented claims about the danger of the dunes environment; quicksand, high winds, and the uniquely hazardous "spruce chimney" (formed when a spruce tree is consumed by sand, then rots away, leaving a deep, narrow hole that cannot be escaped by anyone unfortunate enough to fall into one) were all raised as obstacles to tourism. Even Governor Mark Hatfield was on record as believing that "the climate conditions of the dunes do not lend themselves to recreation" and presented a danger to children.[78] In the end, the objections could generally be grouped once again into two primary categories: those of property owners who felt their interests were threatened and those of people who believe the park would have a negative economic impact on the coastal economy.

As the hearings progressed, accusations of self-interest and claims that developers and industrial interests were the primary backers of the antipark faction were frequent, as were charges of shortsightedness and lack of public spirit. An editorial introduced at the hearing asked the question "Who to Believe?" with regard to contradictory claims about the dunes park and quoted former governor Oswald West as saying, "If the people of Oregon do not back Neuberger . . . they are damn fools." West, who in 1914 had taken executive action to keep the beaches of Oregon in the public domain, was a powerful symbol of the state's public land history and the sense of entitlement many citizens felt with regard to the coastline; his opinion would likely be held in high regard by a majority of Oregon residents. In responding to West's proclamation the newspaper editor stated

that the people of Oregon were certainly not damn fools and indeed had
"a vision and imagination far greater than those displayed by their present governor." (A few days before the hearing Hatfield had publicly derided
the dunes as being simply "big piles of sand" with no recreational value.)[79]
For some park proponents the debate was becoming one of personalities,
though the majority were more concerned with the status an additional
national park would confer upon Oregon, the recognition they felt was due
the coast, and the belief that Oregon "deserved" more federal parks than it
had. As Neuberger pointed out for the record, California had over 4 million
acres of national parks and Washington 1.2 million, while Oregon had just
160,770 acres under NPS management.[80] Given the sense of competition
Oregonians felt with regard to their neighboring states, learning that the
Golden State had twenty-five times more parkland was likely a significant
factor in making up some citizens' minds.

A second hearing convened inland at Eugene, the Lane County seat,
on October 8 produced similar testimony from both sides. Governor
Hatfield's position was clarified somewhat by the testimony of Dan P. Allen,
the executive secretary of the state's Natural Resources Board. The author
of the board's largely negative report on the park proposal, Allen was sent
by Hatfield to represent his office and to clarify the state's position. After
offering a copy of his report for the record, Allen succinctly summarized
the objections of the governor and the state's resource management agencies, telling the committee that they were based on the belief that Senator
Neuberger's S. 1526 and related national seashore bills affecting the area
were "premature," that the dunes area was already assured of preservation under USFS and state management, that existing recreational facilities were sufficient to meet demand or could be expanded under current
management, that committing the local economies to tourism was "undesirable," and that multiple-use management (including logging) could
continue without harming the dunes resource.[81] Initial questions from
Representative Porter and Senator Neuberger were aimed at establishing
Allen's qualifications to judge the merits of the park proposal, his authority
to speak for the governor, and why exactly his committee's report conflicted
so dramatically with the assessment of the NPS and the Jensen economic
report. Their first exchange set the tone for the Eugene hearing:

Mr. Porter: I am sorry that the Governor isn't here, but I
   understand you are speaking for him today. Is that correct?
Mr. Allen: My testimony will show that, yes.
Mr. Porter: . . . you are familiar with the Governor's stand, so if we
   ask you other questions you can tell us something about what
   the Governor's view is?
Mr. Allen: I would be happy to attempt to answer them,
   Congressman, if they related to this testimony. Otherwise I
   don't feel obliged to engage in a verbal slugging match.
Mr. Porter: I did not suggest that. . . . I wonder if we could have for
   the record your qualifications as an expert in this field.
Mr. Allen: I have no objection to giving you that statement,
   Congressman, except that I have never touted myself as an
   expert in this field.
Mr. Porter: Well, let's hear what your qualifications are, because
   you are appearing—
Mr. Allen: My qualifications along what line, sir?
Mr. Porter: As an expert in the area of resource development.
Mr. Allen: I do not claim to be such an expert. . . . I was asked to
   gather all pertinent information and data and compile it in a
   recommendation, which the committee then considered.
Mr. Porter: Then your position is that you are not an expert in this
   area?
Mr. Allen: Those are your words.
Mr. Porter: Well, is that your position? Are you or aren't you an
   expert?
Mr. Allen: No, sir; I am not an expert.
Mr. Porter: Thank you. That is what I wondered. Now, what
   preparations did you take for this report? What did you do?
Mr. Allen: Mr. Chairman, Senator Neuberger, may I ask a question
   before answering that?
Senator Neuberger: Certainly.
Mr. Allen: I am here to represent the Governor in presenting this
   testimony, and that alone. Now, I would be happy, as I say, to
   continue this discussion throughout the day. I don't think that
   is particularly germane. The testimony is here. That is all I am
   authorized to present.[82]

The root of the apparent hostility between Allen, Porter, and Neuberger, though not immediately clear from the hearing transcripts, was likely a product of the senator's frustration with the lack of support from state officials and the confusion raised by press coverage of Allen's work on the committee report. Neuberger was not alone in his negative assessment of certain conclusions of the report; its fairness had been questioned in the press, particularly in inland areas, and had privately drawn the scorn of former governor West. Accusations leveled prior to the hearing charged that Allen had contacted only park opponents in researching his "exhaustive study" of the dunes proposal and that his negative conclusions were often based on one-sided appraisals. With Allen at the witness table, Neuberger methodically challenged the conclusions of his report, focusing particularly on the criticisms of the dunes area that Hatfield had publicly restated in the weeks before the hearing. Because the issue of climate had been repeatedly raised in the Reedsport hearing as mitigating against the park, and the press coverage of Allen's written remarks about it had been widely circulated by the opposition, Neuberger was especially aggressive in questioning the sources of information used in the report and what he felt was Allen's bias.

> Senator Neuberger: Now, let's talk about the weather portion of
> your report. You have said in your oral presentation that you
> did not intend to run down or belittle the weather in this area.
> Can I ask where you obtained your weather data?
> Mr. Allen: . . . the U.S. Department of Commerce Weather Bureau
> in Portland.
> Senator Neuberger: May I ask where you got the statement:
> "Winds of gale force strike the coast frequently during the
> summer and winter, making the beaches uninhabitable, and
> causing dangerous wave action on the inland lakes. During
> these periods the Siuslaw River bar is impassable." Where did
> you get that statement?
> Mr. Allen: That is from personal observation, Senator. I have spent
> many hours in that area on the dunes and on the rivers and on
> the lakes.
> Senator Neuberger: I thought that you had obtained this from the
> U.S. Weather Bureau at Portland?
> Mr. Allen: I said the statistics came from the weather bureau.

Senator Neuberger: The statistics came from the Weather Bureau, but did the factual material referred to in here?

Mr. Allen: The statistics are factual, yes.

Senator Neuberger: I am talking about the editorial content in your report. I asked about the statement that I read. Was that from the U.S. Weather Bureau?

Mr. Allen: I told you that was from personal observation.

Senator Neuberger: I was just going to point out to you that you made it seem as bad as you could for an area in your own State.[83]

At this point Neuberger introduced written testimony from the state climatologist that contradicted some of Allen's conclusions and made his summary of the climate issue seem unfair. Clearly, though, it was Allen's loyalty to the state that Neuberger wanted to call into question. Near the end of Dan Allen's three hours of testimony, Richard Neuberger initiated a final exchange in which he expressed his exasperation with the state's official position on the dunes and once again suggested that Allen lacked pride in Oregon.

Senator Neuberger: The reason I feel badly about the position taken by the Governor, and yourself, is this: I think we have a wonderful State. I think we should be honored that the U.S. Park Advisory Board recommended only four areas in this entire Nation . . . for establishment as national seashore parks and that one of them is in our own State. . . . In my opinion, your testimony contains every possible adverse comment on this proposed park, and many are possible, and scarcely anything in its favor. This is certainly disappointing to me, as the sponsor of the bill, as a native son of Oregon, and as a Senator from Oregon. I just wondered what comment you have on that.

Mr. Allen: I have no comment, Senator. I have been happy to be here. I ha[d] not anticipated I would be subjected to such a vicious cross-examination in an effort to discredit the Governor and my testimony. I regret it has evolved into that.[84]

And finally, when questioned about the state's potential support for alternative bills that might lead to the creation of an Oregon Dunes park (such as S. 2010, the administration bill that would authorize four unspecified seashore parks), Allen responded, "We can't speak on some nebulous plans in supposition of what might happen should such and such a bill pass." This led to the final rebuke of the morning session.

> Senator Neuberger: Do you regard existing plans as nebulous?
> Mr. Allen: Yes, I do.
> Senator Neuberger: Well, there was nothing that compelled you to testify against [them] at this hearing.
> Mr. Allen: Would you prefer that the Governor of Oregon and the committee on natural resources make an appearance at this hearing?
> Senator Neuberger: I would prefer that you made an appearance in favor of this great seashore park in our State. I am bitterly disappointed that you have not. . . . As a Senator from Oregon, as a resident of Oregon, as a native of Oregon, I am disappointed that we do not have the backing of the Governor and yourself for this great national seashore park which has received so much national support. Do you have anything further you would like to say?
> Mr. Allen: Let's adjourn for lunch.[85]

Throughout the second hearing—even more so than the first—Neuberger repeatedly emphasized his belief that Oregon needed a new national park to validate its claims to scenic grandeur. Though he was particularly aggressive in his questioning of Allen, Neuberger challenged every witness who questioned this basic premise. The conduct of the hearings was at times so confrontational that newspapers covered the fallout for several weeks afterward. Critics cited the Spanish Inquisition and former senator Joseph McCarthy as models for Neuberger's questioning of Allen, while Howell Appling Jr., Oregon's secretary of state, called Neuberger's conduct "unwarranted abuse . . . intended for the sole purpose of camouflaging . . . the specific details of the bill they are trying to ram down the throats of the people of Oregon." The hearings were "cheap and picayunishly partisan," according to another witness, while

Representative Porter's call for Hatfield to personally clarify his "attitude and positions" on the matter prompted Governor Hatfield to charge him with "using bamboozling blackmail" in an attempt to force him to testify. As Hatfield proclaimed to reporters, "I shall not subject my position to the indignities thus far inflicted by certain members of this congressional committee."[86] Former governor Oswald West was less critical of the tone and saw Hatfield's position as misguided, though, cabling Neuberger that the "Governor's side kick's [opposition is] a lot of bushwah. Governor's intentions are all right he perhaps thinks its good politics, but he will find eventually that Allen is leading him . . . up a sorrowful trail."[87] Neuberger responded two days later, "Your . . . support of our Oregon Dunes National Seashore Park will be extremely influential because of your great prestige as the governor who originally saved the beaches of Oregon for future generations. . . . A magnificent national park on our scenic seacoast will bring the national recognition deserved by an area whose scenic grandeur and majesty you recognized many decades ago."[88]

Although much of the testimony, and certainly the more exciting ripostes, of both the Reedsport and Eugene hearings involved government officials, experts, and the organized park opposition, the two meetings did serve to lay out the basic positions on both sides of the issue for the subcommittee. Park proponents based their arguments primarily on the rare scenic and scientific qualities of the dunes, the potential economic impacts of increased tourism, the need for additional recreation opportunities to match postwar population growth, and emotional appeals to sense of place and state loyalty. A significant number of them also believed establishing a dunes park would help reverse the trend toward commercial development along the coast. It also became evident that (contrary to the claims of some park opponents) there were significant numbers of supporters living along the coast, people who tended to believe in the positive economic forecasts more readily than their neighbors. For example, the Port Umpqua Chamber of Commerce, based in the town of Winchester Bay near the southern end of the proposed park, supported Neuberger's plan because they believed it would "stimulate the growth of th[e] area and provide for a more stable economy, in that national advertising will attract many tourists who are not presently apprised of the tourist facilities and attractions that are available in th[e] area."[89] But the most ardent support came from conservationists and those who pursued recreation along the coast. The Multnomah County Labor Council, an AFL-CIO chapter in Portland, presented a resolution to the committee that read, in part,

> Almost every local effort of farsighted men to preserve as part of the public domain unusual scenic and recreational areas of our country for the perpetual benefit and enjoyment of present and future generations has met unreasonable and obstinate opposition from shortsighted and selfish men. . . . Whereas time has demonstrated the wisdom of those who have sponsored legislation to set aside part of the public domain as national parks. . . . If these areas are dedicated now before the pressure of population becomes greater and before shoreline speculators can make a killing at the expense of the people . . . all of us and future generations can enjoy them in the natural beauty endowed by nature.[90]

This sentiment was echoed by a group of students from a Salem high school who spoke in favor of the park, noting that "the natural playgrounds of America are fast disappearing under pressure from growing populations and expanding commercial interests" and that "the citizens of Oregon owe it to the future generations of not only Oregonians, but all Americans, to save such naturally beautiful areas as the dunes area . . . from defilement for the enjoyment of all Americans for many years to come."[91]

Conservationists occasionally combined economic arguments with the idea that Oregon remained a rarity in a growing, industrializing nation. A spokesman for the Oregon chapter of the Izaak Walton League testified, "As California continues to cover their entire state with endless concrete and asphalt highways, buildings, and smog, and as the entire Nation east of the Rocky Mountains becomes more industrialized, Oregon through adequate planning could become the vacation land of the United States with areas of such size that resident and visitor alike could be provided elbow room." Preserving wild places from despoliation was urgent, he warned; if steps were not taken soon "those of you who live in this still lovely State may come to wonder what happened to your lovely outdoors if you fail to take action now."[92] The Sierra Club representative at the hearing offered similar cautions, noting that the "phenomenal population growth" of the United States was consuming recreation lands while it was also increasing demand for them.[93]

The opposite was suggested by park opponents, who frequently claimed that there was already adequate recreation on the coast as provided by the US Forest Service and state parks. There were, it was suggested, already enough campgrounds and other recreation areas on the central coast, and if more were needed in the future they would be best managed under the Forest Service's multiple-use system. The multiple-use philosophy of the USFS was also raised in suggesting that a national park would unreasonably (and unfairly) limit economic activity in the area. Why not have recreation and logging, it was argued? Furthermore, under the preservation mission of the National Park Service some existing activities, particularly waterfowl hunting and commercial use of fresh water from the lakes, would likely be prohibited. The underlying theory that the economic future of the coast lay in tourism and that population growth would drive a steady increase in the demand for recreation was simply not accepted by most of the park opponents. Wagering a stagnant but apparently stable economy against a promised influx of benevolent strangers generally did not appeal to residents of the dunes area; they clearly preferred to take their chances with the existing diversified economy, despite the declines in logging and commercial fisheries reported by the economists who analyzed the park proposal. Nor did the arguments based on state pride or loyalty sway them. As one resident of Florence stated emphatically, "I oppose national parks and what they take away from the area. They're beautiful, but by the grace of God you can't eat the scenery."[94] Although questions of climate, the danger of high winds and quicksand, and other natural unpleasantries were often raised, the fundamental objections aired in the two hearings were clearly economic. Landowners did not want to be forced to sell their property, and business owners feared a tourism-oriented development scheme would cripple the local economy and evaporate its tax base.

Critics' charges that the senator mistreated park opponents aside, the hearings clearly influenced Richard Neuberger, who returned to Washington to draft a new park bill addressing many of the substantive concerns expressed in an effort to make the plan more palatable to those living near the site. The revised bill would allow for lifetime leases of homes within the park boundaries, rather than forcing their sale, and provided exemptions from standard NPS policies to allow hunting and the municipal use of groundwater from the park. The most significant concession to local opponents was the provision of payment in lieu of taxes to municipalities affected by the seashore for a period of twenty-five years. All of these accommodations were intended to address concerns voiced at the hearings and were, Neuberger later claimed, as far as he could go and "still retain the character of a national park."[95] Park supporters were pleased to learn the potential boundaries would expand to incorporate Tahkenitch Lake near the center of the park and additional dunes south to Tenmile Creek, about ten miles beyond the original proposal's boundaries; these extensions were less likely to provoke local opponents, as they included little private property.[96] The chairman of Crown Zellerbach, the corporate owners of a large tree farm adjacent Tahkenitch Lake, informed Neuberger by mail, "You are terrific! Certainly appreciate what you are doing. . . . In an exchange [for our land] we would want lands contiguous to our present areas of operation which could be in Columbia or Clackamas counties," signaling a willingness to negotiate over the company's interests near the park.[97] Time was of the essence, though; as the editors of the *Salem Capital Journal* pointed out in endorsing Neuberger's revisions, 1960 would be a year of politics and "even such a normally sacred subject such as parks to soothe the voter will be in danger as the year progresses."[98]

Representative Charles Porter took a different tack and scheduled additional hearings in the coastal town of Florence in late October 1959. The House Subcommittee on Public Lands hearing was chaired by Representative Gracie Pfost of Idaho and focused on Porter's H.R. 6260, which differed from Neuberger's S. 1526 primarily in that it would require the Forest Service to agree to transfer lands within the existing Siuslaw National Forest to the National Park Service before they could be included in the park. At the outset of the hearing, however, Porter introduced a letter he had sent to Governor Hatfield in which he laid out the changes he felt the bill should include in light of testimony given at the earlier hearings conducted by Senator Neuberger. These modifications included,

1. The inclusion of specific park boundaries in the authorizing legislation.
2. The extension of lifetime leases to landowners and such children as resided with them.

3. Payment in lieu of taxes to support local schools and other public services.
4. Acceptance of federal responsibility for highway relocation due to park needs.
5. A fee-for-use system designed to pay off the costs of acquiring land and operating the park.
6. Continuance of traditional hunting and fishing activities within the dunes.
7. Consideration of industrial needs for water and pipeline easements for future industrial uses.
8. No restriction on the activities of existing river guides and boat rental operations.
9. Maintenance of sand dune stabilization projects in certain vital areas.[99]

Despite these proposed modifications, Porter told surprised witnesses at the hearing, "I support no bill at this time." and claimed he had introduced it only to further the information-gathering process.[100]

The House subcommittee hearings were both shorter and less fractious than the Senate hearings had been; the Florence newspaper characterized them as "fair and dignified."[101] The substance of the testimony was generally similar to that offered in the Senate proceedings, though Neuberger's proposed revisions to his park bill prompted an additional measure of comment from commercial timber interests, which feared losing their access to federal forests. Their gloomy forecasts were offset, though, by William M. Tugman of the *Port Umpqua Courier*. Tugman had frequented the dunes area since 1927 and was a well-respected member of the community, so his testimony carried some weight with the local populace beyond the editorials published in his newspaper. In response to the claims of the timber interests Tugman was most adamant, stating that he regarded the dunes park "as holding the ultimate economic salvation for this area" and noting that just eighteen months prior to the hearing Reedsport had suffered through a period of 38 percent unemployment as the local mills were idled. Florence, he believed, suffered less because of its proximity to Honeyman State Park and its more varied recreation offerings. The central coast, Tugman believed, needed "maximum recreational development to balance [its] economy."[102]

Generally speaking, the House subcommittee hearings under Representative Pfost lacked the fire of the Neuberger-chaired sessions three weeks prior. A more conciliatory tone from the chair likely played a role, but it also seemed clear that the lines had been drawn and there was little to be gained in further vilifying one side or the other. Little that was newsworthy happened, so the press did not cover the Florence sessions as closely as it had those earlier in the month, instead offering only brief stories summarizing positions and reactions to Neuberger's proposed revisions in his park bill. There was also a notable decline in testimony based on Neuberger's own positions, particularly the idea that opposing a park was somehow disloyal to the state. That may have been due to Porter's revelation that he did not support his own bill, to the fact that these hearings were chaired by a congresswoman from Idaho, or possibly to park proponents' realization that such arguments were ineffective when weighed against economic or property rights concerns. It seemed that the majority of the people of Oregon were simply not swayed by warnings about rampant development and population growth at a time when local economies had been growing and traditional ways of life seemed stable.

In the months following the 1959 hearings in Oregon the fate of the park proposal seemed to be in limbo. In early November Eisenhower's secretary of agriculture, Ervin L. Peterson, announced he was "flatly opposed" to any park plan that would remove land from the Siuslaw National Forest, reiterating the USFS belief that its multiple-use policies were better suited to the location, and stated, "I fail to see that there would be any public benefits in Uncle Sam taking off his forest service hat and putting on his park service hat."[103] An internal, confidential Forest Service memorandum was similarly direct in its assessment of the bill and the political cost of opposition: "You know we have approved an adverse position on this. There is going to be a fight on these bills. Our position is unpopular with many of our traditional conservation friends."[104] Dan Allen of the State Natural Resources Committee restated his opposition to the plan in a public meeting soon thereafter, but later in the month the committee voted to take no stand on the revised plan until after the first of the year, citing reservations about the proposal but noting that "contrary to some impressions the committee didn't oppose the national seashore program" in general.

Governor Hatfield told reporters in late November that the revised plan was "getting the same calm appraisal" as the first and that he was disturbed that "some persons should exploit natural resources for political gain."[105] Although Hatfield had requested that Allen's committee provide a response to the revised plan by November 24, it was announced on the twenty-sixth that only three of the eighteen agencies had studied the changes and that a report would not be issued until January 12, prompting the *Capital Journal* to question the good faith of the state agencies involved.[106] Neuberger then told the press he would not introduce a revised bill without Hatfield's support, while Charles Porter claimed he could not even begin writing a bill until he heard from the governor.[107] By mid-December park supporters were growing tired of the delays, while the *Oregon Statesman* noted that "important Eastern interests are willing, if not downright anxious, to help pay for the development of a major recreation area in Oregon" and that it "seems strange that the foot-dragging should be done in . . . the place which will benefit the most."[108]

Richard Neuberger's final salvo on the issue for 1959 came in the form of a letter to the editor of the *Oregonian* published on December 27. Writing in response to prior criticism, he asked,

Is there any reason to presume that the first national park proposed in Oregon since 1902 lacks popular support? . . . I am convinced that the overwhelming majority of Oregonians are not critical of me because I contend that one of the three parks to be established next year should honor and hallow our magnificent Oregon coast. There will be a referendum of sorts in 1960 on sentiment regarding an Oregon Dunes National Seashore Park, because I have been willing to stake my political future on the fact that I believe majority sentiment in Oregon approves creation of such a park. This faith remains unshaken despite bitter and unrelenting attacks upon me by a belligerent and vocal minority for my sponsorship of the park bill. I simply cannot countenance the idea that a national park . . . is not wanted on the Oregon seacoast.[109]

As 1960 dawned another political element was introduced into the debate over the Oregon Dunes: Senator Wayne Morse, who had up to that point played the role of silent cosponsor, was turning against the park. Morse, the state's senior senator, was so closely linked with Neuberger in the senate that *Time* magazine had referred to the pair as "Senator

Morseberger" in the mid-1950s. By 1960 the relationship had deteriorated as the two split on issues of foreign policy and civil rights, to the point that Morse announced he would campaign against Neuberger to ensure the junior senator's defeat in his 1960 reelection bid.[110] The exact roots of the conflict were not publicly known, but it was widely speculated that it stemmed from events early in their relationship when Neuberger was a student at the University of Oregon Law School, where Morse was dean in the 1930s. According to some observers, Morse was jealous of Neuberger's success as a journalist and politician. Though Neuberger penned a genial assessment of his Senate colleague's prospects for reelection for *Fortnight* magazine in 1955, three years after Morse had defected from the Republican Party over its growing conservatism, their relationship continued to decay in the wake of a successful 1956 campaign.[111] Morse's opposition to the national park proposal, though couched in concern over the park's impact on private property owners, was at least in part a function of this growing personal animosity.[112] In September 1959 Morse had issued a public statement on the collection of seashore bills pending before Congress (including those for Cape Cod, Padre Island, and the Indiana Dunes), expressing his concern over the "delegation of power to the Executive branch" and calling for a new process of advice and consent by which Congress would approve specific park boundaries proposed by the National Park Service, rather than providing general authorization to establish a park.[113] It was likely no surprise to Neuberger when Morse told a reporter in January, "I doubt if the [park] bill could be put into a form that I would approve."[114] Both men knew Morse's opposition would effectively block any bill from Senate approval, as it was extremely rare for a park authorization to proceed without the full support of both of the subject state's senators.

The next blow to the dunes park plan came from Governor Hatfield's office in the form of a list of "minimum" conditions under which the state would support a new park. Hatfield, stating that "the need for such a park is not clearly established," reiterated many of the objections raised in hearings the previous fall but added the committee's demands that state consent be required for any hunting and fishing regulations in the park, that the park be officially named the "Oregon Coast National Seashore Recreation Area" to reflect its recreational purpose, and that "Federal and State lands inside the park be acquired only after consent of the agencies involved."[115] This final condition would effectively give the Forest Service (which was by then on record as opposing the park) veto power over any plan that transferred fourteen thousand key acres of Siuslaw National Forest land to the National Park Service; that acreage formed the bulk of the area between the dunes and U.S. 101 that was needed as a buffer zone for the park. Although an editorial response in the *Oregon Statesman* claimed that if the governor's conditions held "we may kiss the National Seashore Recreation Area (dunes park) on the Oregon Coast goodbye,"[116] both Neuberger and Morse interpreted Hatfield's statement as supporting their respective positions, leading the governor to proclaim that he would "not become a party to the attacks and counter-attacks leveled by our two senators against one another in the matter of the sand dunes."[117] Neuberger's ultimate response, though, was to introduce a new bill largely meeting Hatfield's demands and to suggest that the Department of the Interior arbitrate the differences between their two proposals. "What they accept, I will accept," Neuberger offered. "My goal is not political warfare; it is to bring Oregon its first national park since Crater Lake was set aside in 1902."[118]

By all accounts Neuberger's overtures to Hatfield were successful; in early February the governor visited Florence and assured reporters that a national seashore would be established. Local opponents, who until this point thought they had the upper hand, were "completely stunned" by the announcement, charging that "the governor ha[d] deliberately acted in bad faith" and that local residents had been "sold down the river by an executive they ha[d] trusted, purely for reasons of political expediency."[119] Neuberger, who came through soon after on a brief tour, was labeled a "hairless Fidel Castro" in the Florence-based *Siuslaw Oar*.[120] Local reaction wasn't entirely negative, however; the *Coos Bay World*, representing the largest community near the dunes, editorialized against the "sputtered accusations of betrayal" from the Western Lane Taxpayers Association and proclaimed that "the dunes and lakes of Oregon's coast will be here when Governor Hatfield's feuding with Senator Neuberger ha[s] been long forgotten."[121] Local reactions notwithstanding, the National Park Service accepted the governor's proposals, feeling they could work around Forest Service opposition, and when Senators Lyndon Johnson and John F. Kennedy expressed personal interest in passing the legislation supporters felt certain the park was close to becoming a reality.[122] In early March Charles Porter commissioned a survey of over one hundred thousand Oregon residents that found a majority supported the park in each of the seven counties near the dunes,

bolstering his prediction that it was "likely Congress will act on this legislation during this session."[123] Even in Lane County, where the issue had been
the most contentious, the results were reported to be 1,454 in favor of the
park and 1,375 against.[124]

Porter's optimism was soon derailed, however, by Richard Neuberger's
sudden death from a cerebral hemorrhage on March 9; the senator was
just forty-seven years old. Without its chief proponent the Oregon Dunes
National Seashore proposal was set adrift in the political sea. Wayne Morse
formally notified the U.S. Senate of Neuberger's death in a speech the following day, ignoring their long political battle and praising Neuberger's
service, saying, "Oregon and the nation have lost a courageous leader. His
record will live on as his monument." Senate President Lyndon Johnson
noted from the floor that Neuberger was "a man of great heart and great
courage . . . totally dedicated to his convictions. You always knew where
he stood, hypocrisy was completely foreign to his nature."[125] Seashore ally
Senator Paul Douglas remembered him as "a true conservationist who,
with his love of the outdoors, labored unceasingly to prevent the beauties
of the land, its mountains, rivers, valleys and deserts from being debased
and despoiled."[126] Editorialists praised the young senator around the state.
Portland's *Oregonian* wrote, "His stature as a senator and as a man became
greater in each year of his service." The *Medford Mail Tribune* said he would
"go down in the state's history as one of the great public servants of this
generation," while the *Coos Bay World* noted, "He leaves behind a river of
ideas and a reservoir of principles [that will] inspire others."[127] The former
newspaper editor William Tugman, an influential figure even in his retirement, told the *Eugene Register-Guard*, "In my many years in Oregon, this
state has suffered no greater loss than in the death of U.S. Senator Richard
Neuberger. During the last year Senator Neuberger and I worked together
for the great Oregon Coast [Dunes] Seashore project—a farsighted program of restoration and conservation work which I can only hope will not
be impaired by his death."[128]

Neuberger's death, though shocking to the public, may not have come
as such a surprise to his intimates. He had fought a very open battle against
cancer in 1958, speaking out about his condition and the need to increase
funding for cancer research while maintaining an active work schedule. His
1959 *Harper's* article "When I Learned I Had Cancer" explained that the
experience had changed him politically, leading him to "doubt if ever again

I could be wholly partisan," and he had gone into the 1960 election year confident that he had been cured and with the approval of his physicians.[129] Though there was no clear link between the cancer and the fatal stroke, friends said Neuberger had been looking very weak and was in Oregon for an extended rest at the time of his death.[130] Indeed, just weeks prior to his death the *Eugene Register-Guard* ran an editorial giving Neuberger a pass on reelection, explaining that while he had done "a pretty good job in Washington" and was "widely regarded as a cinch to win," his heart was in Oregon. "He might just not run again. . . . The possibility, we think, is real."[131]

Despite the uncertainties of the pundits, Neuberger expected to be elected to a second term in 1960 and believed the Oregon Dunes national park was to be both a major campaign issue and, in his words, a "gift to Oregon" to mark his second term in office. Upon his death bickering over the dunes immediately ceased and memorials filled the Oregon papers, many of them citing the proposed park as a career highlight. According to his close friend Supreme Court justice William O. Douglas, his writings were his legacy and "he translated the Pacific Northwest to all the people of the nation."[132] Senator Henry "Scoop" Jackson of Washington spoke admirably of his conservation record, telling reporters Neuberger "led an unrelenting fight over the years to conserve and better utilize for all the great resources of our Northwest and our Nation. He was a conservationist not only of natural resources, but of human values."[133] The *Oregonian* recalled that Neuberger in recent years had "turned away from partisanship" and offered as evidence the assessment that he "went to extreme lengths to get the cooperation of the state administration" in his effort to compromise on the dunes bill.[134] Not long after his death a bill to create the "Richard L. Neuberger National Seashore" in the Oregon Dunes area was offered by Senator Mike Mansfield of Montana, but it and other attempts to establish a dunes park as a memorial to Neuberger failed for lack of support.[135] A tribute was eventually made by naming Mount Neuberger, a 6,749 peak in Alaska, after the senator who had played a major role in the territory's quest for statehood.[136] The senator was buried in Portland's Beth Israel Cemetery in the city he loved.[137]

As a conservationist Richard Neuberger combined a strong belief in the power of the federal government to do right with a heavy dose of regional pride. He was deeply attached to the landscapes of the Pacific Northwest and often commented on his desire to return to Oregon after serving in Congress. Indeed, he is probably best remembered today for coining the phrase "they never go back to Pocatello," his offhand assessment of western politicians who became accustomed to life in the East and remained there after leaving office. In his voluminous writings about his home state Neuberger frequently expressed the belief that the landscapes of the West offered both unique opportunities for conservation and a culture that recognized the value of nature—if only they could produce what writer Wallace Stegner once called "men to match the mountains." In the 1950 article "My Hometown Is Good Enough for Me" Neuberger explained that he had frequently turned down lucrative offers to move upward—and eastward—in the publishing world because "the compensations of living in one's native community cannot be measured in coin of the realm.... When I look out across the slanting ramparts of the Cascade Range to Hood's frosty peak I feel like Antaeus, the mythical giant who gained strength merely by touching the earth."[138] It is only in the light of this sentiment, a deeply rooted connection with his home state that went well beyond pride or simple boosterism, that we can understand Richard Neuberger's conservation politics. He saw the defense of wilderness, national parks, and forests as an integral part of his political life but also as an obligation to future generations in the Pacific Northwest. The great bounty of his home state called to him from afar, pulling him back to its rivers, mountains, and coast whenever he was in Washington, DC, for too long. "Oregon affects us that way," he wrote in 1959, "Whenever we are separated from our native state, we are unable to feel really content or satisfied."[139] Nature, Neuberger believed, had done well by the United States—it was man's part that needed work.[140] His advocacy for an Oregon Dunes national park reflected these elements of his personality quite accurately in both his poetic descriptions of the area and his passionate defense of the national park ideal. Oregon *deserved* a park, he repeatedly said, not because its politicians held the power to create it but because the landscape demanded it.

Richard Neuberger's vision for an Oregon Dunes national park, first expressed in his 1939 *Oregonian* article, appeared lost until November 1960, when voters elected his widow, Maurine, to fill the vacancy he left in the Senate. Taking up the charge, Maurine Neuberger reintroduced Richard's compromise bill in 1961, hoping to recapture the momentum lost the previous spring. Cut by nearly twelve thousand acres, the revised park would require the inclusion of only 10 percent of the private land the first bill did

Fig. 7. Senator Maurine
Neuberger and President
Kennedy, 1961 (Oregon
Historical Society Photo
Collection, OrHi 102863)

and made provisions for limited logging and water withdrawals from the area. It would still, Maurine promised supporters, preserve the dunes and avoid the "honky tonk" development that had occurred on the strip along U.S. 101 from Florence to Coos Bay. Wayne Morse, however, quickly reiterated his opposition to any condemnation provision and was able to keep the bill from the Senate floor throughout 1961. The conflict over the park proposal spilled over into the Kennedy administration in 1962, with Interior Secretary Stewart Udall and Agriculture Secretary Orville Freeman each wanting his respective agency to control the seashore area. Later that year one-term Fourth District congressman Edwin R. Durno, the Republican who defeated Charles Porter in 1960, proposed a novel compromise: a "dunes park" run by the Forest Service in the form of a national recreation area. Durno's plan, of course, received no support from either Maurine Neuberger or the National Park Service and was quickly rejected as ineffective by conservationists, who were skeptical of the Forest Service's commitment to anything but timber harvests. Park opponents along the Oregon coast, however, were more open to the idea, as they had already established relationships with the USFS and generally felt that their economic interests would be looked after under such an arrangement. Durno, however, was defeated in November 1962 by Democrat Robert Duncan, who joined Maurine Neuberger in once again promoting national park status for the dunes (complete with condemnation authority) to avoid what one reporter called the potential to "encounter undesirable honky tonks nestled unpleasantly within the park."[141] Interior Secretary Udall believed Duncan's election would revive the plan, saying it would be "right near the top of the list" of his department's proposals for the next Congress.[142]

After additional hearings in Oregon in the spring of 1963, Robert Duncan introduced his own bill in the House that reduced the park's area from the forty-four thousand acres included in Maurine Neuberger's senate bill to thirty thousand. This revision also shrank the number of private homes within the park boundaries from 264 to 15, granting lifetime occupancy rights to the remaining owners and their heirs. Within the administration the NPS-USFS rivalry was settled in favor of the NPS, and the state's Committee on Natural Resources also gave its blessing to the smaller park. The *New York Times*, noting the progress, quoted Secretary Udall as calling the dunes "one of the finest remaining opportunities for seashore preservation to be found anywhere in this country" and editorialized on July 4 that "the Oregon Dunes on the West Coast require protection as a national preserve—now."[143] Morse, however, held firm to his no condemnation position, a provision that several senators (including Public Lands Subcommittee chairman Alan Bible) refused to endorse for fear it would set a precedent for future park sites.[144] The proposal was shelved for another year when Morse threatened to filibuster the revised bill unless all condemnation authority was deleted. The power to establish a dunes recreation area, as a later law review article concluded, lay "largely in the hands of Wayne Morse. . . . If Senator Morse is determined to prevent any national seashore in Oregon, he probably will succeed."[145] Despite these challenges, the National Park Service placed the Oregon Dunes National Seashore proposal at the top of its list for the state in the ambitious national outdoor recreation agenda entitled *Parks for America* the agency released in 1964.[146]

During each congressional session from 1964 through 1966 Duncan introduced seashore bills in the House while Neuberger did the same in the Senate. After the House passed Duncan's bill in March 1966, both the Republican and Democratic candidates for governor of Oregon endorsed the plan in letters to Senator Bible's committee and even considered

Fig. 8. The Oregon Dunes National Recreation Area embraced off-road vehicles, contrary to the wilderness vision for a dunes national park, 2006.

releasing a joint statement to that effect, indicating that whatever the out-come of the gubernatorial race, the next governor would back the park pro-posal.[147] With Interior Secretary Udall on board as well, prospects looked good that spring until Wayne Morse once again refused to allow the bill to come to a vote on the floor of the Senate. With little chance of progress in the Senate, one park opponent commented in June that "it appears that the tiresome dunes fight will be ended one way or the other by the time Congress adjourns" and noted that the bill was unlikely to be reintroduced in the Ninetieth Congress the following year.[148] In one sense he was right; Robert Duncan was replaced by John Dellenback (a Republican) in the House the following term and Mark Hatfield won the Neuberger seat in the Senate after Maurine chose not to run for reelection. Once again the dunes park had lost its champions, and as a result Secretary Udall directed the National Park Service to stop pressing for the site due to a lack of support among the Oregon delegation.

Interest in the Oregon Dunes did not die with the park legislation, though. In early 1967 John Dellenback made a formal request to the Forest Service asking that the section of the Siuslaw National Forest in the dune area between Florence and Coos Bay (twenty thousand acres, or roughly two-thirds the area of the smallest park proposals) be administratively designated a recreation area. The so-called peace pact negotiated between the Agriculture and Interior Departments in 1963 had barred the Forest Service from planning a recreation area, but once Udall withdrew the NPS from the process the USFS was free to step in again.[149] In March the Oregon House passed a resolution urging Congress to create a recreation area under USFS jurisdiction, an idea that appealed to many Oregonians because, as one newspaper reminded readers, "Oregonians have learned to live with the Forest Service and vice versa."[150] Later that spring Dellenback began drafting a bill to create a national recreation area under Forest Service jurisdiction that was remarkably similar to the last park proposals; at thirty thousand acres it avoided most of the private property within the dunes area but extended the southern boundary to include more Forest Service land, on which limited logging was to be allowed.[151] His bill was introduced in the 1968 session but made little progress, as Senator Morse's approval was not forthcoming. The November elections, however, saw Morse defeated in his reelection bid by Robert Packwood, and with Republicans now in both Senate seats, the White House, and the Fourth Congressional District, the odds looked good for Dellenback's Forest Service recreation area plan going into 1969.[152]

In 1969 John Dellenback introduced an Oregon Dunes National Recreation Area bill in the House that condemned no private land, used commercial tree farms as scenic buffers, and left the adjoining state parks outside the boundaries. Hatfield and Packwood cosponsored the bill in the Senate and it met with little opposition in either chamber. By this time Oregonians had turned elsewhere with their hopes for a new national park (the Cascades and Hells Canyon were both under consideration), and even the outspoken opponents in Florence accepted the compromise. The Nixon administration announced its support for the plan in 1970, and as it became clear the bill would eventually pass, Oregon newspapers began running stories about the long battle over the Oregon Dunes, many of them unequivocally blaming Wayne Morse for the failure to establish the state's second national park. Most interesting, though, was the commentary on how conditions had changed over the years: "When Sen. Neuberger began his campaign it was important that the area receive national park or national seashore status in order to gain tourist attention. . . . The past 13 years has seen a transition from an intense desire to attract tourists to camping regulation[s] which discriminate against the tourists."[153] By 1970 many Oregonians, it seemed, were more interested in keeping the state's recreation areas to themselves than in attracting additional tourist dollars. The question of state pride, Richard Neuberger's central appeal, had also become muted. The recreation area bill stalled in the fall of 1970 as Wayne Aspinall's House Interior Committee was idled by election-year campaigning, and again in 1971 when Aspinall and others expressed concern over the mix of Forest Service, state, county, and private land that was included within the area's boundaries; multiple jurisdictions, they felt, could lead to trouble in implementing regulations. These objections were finally overcome in the spring of 1972, and Richard Nixon signed the bill creating the Oregon Dunes National Recreation Area within the Siuslaw National Forest on March 24.[154] The signing statement he appended singled out the dunes for their unique beauty that "may be preserved for all Americans for years to come" and praised the "careful blending of Federal, State, and private responsibilities for the public benefit."[155] The dedication ceremony on July 15 was attended by members of the Florence Chamber of Commerce, Congressman John Dellenback, the governor, and the chief of the US Forest Service.[156] The postmortem in the Oregon press mixed relief with criticism of the earlier failures. The *Capital Journal* called for a visitor's center to be named after Richard Neuberger, noting that his warnings that the area would be "bought up and messed up" had come true in the intervening years.[157] Disputes (and ultimately lawsuits) over mining claims in the recreation area remained in the headlines for years after its creation, and a battle over wilderness designation in the dunes began in 1974 as preservationists became concerned about the direction Forest Service management was taking. Even when things finally seemed settled the Oregon Dunes remained contentious.

Richard Neuberger's vision of a national park for the Oregon coast, first expressed in 1939, was never truly realized. Over the years between the introduction of his 1959 bill and the final resolution of the matter the state of Oregon became a national leader in progressive environmental regulation and a haven for those drawn to wilderness and undeveloped public lands. On the Oregon coast, however, the political forces aligning old-style multiple-use conservation and private property rights won a war of attrition against preservationists who sought to protect not only the dunes themselves but the undeveloped appeal of the coastal highway and rural areas adjoining them. In the end, the USFS-managed national recreation area lacked the authority the National Park Service would have held over local development, and of course its multiple-use mission meant activities barred from national parks were allowed in the recreation area. As a result the Oregon Dunes National Recreation Area is today a popular place for off-road vehicles and much of Highway 101 in the area has become— as Maurine Neuberger feared—a "honky tonk strip" of tacky commercial developments. Under Forest Service administration, logging, commercial tree farming, and water withdrawals continued and development of the private land in and around the national recreation area proceeded in the directions Richard Neuberger's 1959 bill sought to prevent as well. The legacy of the battle is not a coastal park attracting tourists from across the nation, as first envisioned, but rather a multiple-use area serving the recreation needs of people within the region.

Not long after Neuberger's death public perceptions of environmental conditions began to change. The publication of Rachel Carson's *Silent Spring* in 1962 helped awaken the nation to the fact that postwar industrial development had a negative side that was as sweeping as the economic expansion it propelled. In Oregon that year citizens were shocked by a television exposé entitled *Pollution in Paradise* that showed them that the Willamette River, which flowed past 75 percent of the state's population, was so polluted that it was no longer safe for drinking, swimming, or even as habitat for fish. Air quality was little better; industrial effluents were choking the skies over Portland and other major cities, killing trees and plants and making the air unfit to breathe. By the early 1960s the public began to realize that there was in fact something to Neuberger's warnings that Oregon's fabled natural environment was threatened by prosperity. Within the decade their concern grew so great that rather than fight over protecting thirty-five thousand acres of sand dunes, Oregonians began a struggle to protect the entire seashore, from the Washington to the California borders. In that fight Richard Neuberger's characteristic idealism, loyalty to his home state, and poetic vision of the Oregon coast would be matched by similar qualities in Tom McCall, the journalist behind the *Pollution in Paradise* broadcast. Another reporter turned politician, McCall would follow a path to Salem rather than Washington, DC, and in the process mobilize a generation of Oregonians against the growing threat of unrestrained growth to the state's environment. Concern for livability would become the driving force behind a new movement to "keep Oregon green" in ways that Senator Neuberger no doubt would have supported but simply could not have imagined in the 1950s, when traditional conservation politics meant focusing on public lands and federal legislation to advance an environmental agenda.

Richard Neuberger pursued a conservation vision that not all Oregonians were ready to accept during his lifetime. In 1959 the twin pressures of population growth and industrial development had left their marks on the state but were not yet pressing issues in the minds of a majority of citizens or among all the state's political leaders. Livability was not under obvious threat: there were still fish in the rivers and trees on the mountain slopes; cities were still relatively small and the air was breathable, particularly in comparison to California. While coastal campgrounds were packed with visitors in peak season, there were still lesser-known places in which to escape the crowds for a quiet walk in the sand. Most importantly, scenic conservation, as the dunes park plan would have been called in its day, still took a back seat to economic growth. The economic impacts of tourism were likely underestimated in the minds of most citizens; it was widely understood that Oregon was a timber state—the golden pioneer atop the state capitol still carried an axe, not a guidebook.

Twenty years after Neuberger's failed effort to establish a national park on the Oregon coast, Tom McCall referred to opponents of the plan as "the epitome of the narrowness and the backwardness of coastal developers."[158] They were, he believed, emblematic of those who sought personal gain in the short term without regard for the public good. McCall and Neuberger shared many of the same traits and ideals, despite being from different political parties. The Republican McCall would make his mark as an advocate for Oregon's groundbreaking environmental laws in the late 1960s and early 1970s, laws passed with the support of the general populace amid concern that quality of life was deteriorating so rapidly that something had to be done to preserve the state's livability even if economic development was slowed. Rising concern over air and water pollution, industrial and population growth, and maintaining the state's fabled quality of life would soon draw national attention to Oregon, while the fight over the Oregon Dunes was largely forgotten.

Chapter 3
Pollution in Paradise

> Without a doubt, Oregon's most precious resource is its livability.
> We must preserve it—we must enhance it—because if we don't we're
> going to be faced with an irretrievable loss. We can maintain it only
> by drawing the line on those who would defile our environment.
> —Oregon governor Tom McCall, 1967

On a Wednesday night in November 1962, Portland television station KGW broadcast a documentary that changed the way many Oregonians thought about their state. Called *Pollution in Paradise*, the hour-long program pulled no punches in depicting the Willamette River as a cesspool of industrial waste and sewage and suggested that Oregon's air quality was in a similarly unhealthy state. Challenging the common notion that the state's environment could sustain continued growth without suffering the ecological consequences evident in other parts of the country, the documentary appeared at a time when Americans in general were becoming increasingly aware of the costs of rising population and industrial progress. Reporter Tom McCall, the primary force behind the program, wanted to "ring an alarm for the people of Oregon" and by all accounts succeeded.[1] That success would eventually help propel McCall into the governor's seat, while the resulting public awareness set the state on the path to becoming a national standard-bearer for pollution control and a symbol of the emerging age of ecological concern to many Americans.

That McCall's alarm needed to be sounded at all is to some degree surprising; his was certainly not the first call for attention to the problem of pollution in Oregon, nor the first to express concern over the condition of the Willamette in particular. Draining an area of 11,250 square miles, just under 12 percent of the state's total land area, the Willamette River is the twelfth largest in the United States. More significantly, it flows past more than two-thirds of the state's population, which is concentrated on the valley floor between the Coast Range of mountains to the west and the Cascades to the east. Consequently, the river played an important role as a source of drinking water, a transportation corridor, and a waste sink. As was common practice nationwide, wastes were historically dumped into the river without any sort of treatment on the assumption that the river would dilute and purify the material as it passed downstream.[2] While the river was capable of doing just that in the nineteenth century, these discharges eventually outstripped the river's ability to purify itself, leading to impaired water quality in the lower reaches, particularly near the city of Portland. By the turn of the twentieth century municipal sewage and industrial wastes discharged into the Willamette had drawn the attention of authorities, including the Oregon State Board of Health, and as early as 1911 reports indicating that the water was unsafe for drinking were issued.[3] Soon after, the threat of pollution to aquatic life (and especially game fish) was raised by the Oregon Fish and Game Commission, which notified the public in 1914 that "many of our most beautiful streams are being transformed into public sewers."[4]

These and other warnings gave rise to calls for action to reduce water pollution in the Willamette, leading to minor legislation in 1919 and a more concerted effort toward addressing the problem in 1926, when the State Board of Health sponsored an Anti-Pollution League to draw a response from the legislature in the 1927 biennial session. No action was taken by the lawmakers that year, however, so the problems persisted. As more research was conducted it became evident that the primary threats to the river were declining levels of dissolved oxygen, required to sustain aquatic life, and increasing levels of bacterial contamination, a potential source of disease to those using the river for recreation. While high fecal coliform levels, products of untreated municipal sewage, presented a health concern to those who swam in the river, the decline in dissolved oxygen meant that the river itself might eventually die as oxygen levels fell below the minimum needed to support fish, plants, and beneficial bacteria. The more organic waste present in a body of water, the more oxygen is consumed in breaking it down, so the increase in organic pollutants was in effect consuming the oxygen necessary to sustain river life and taxing the river's ability to cleanse itself. In 1929 and 1930 detailed surveys were conducted to determine the condition of the river at eighteen different locations and found that the most significant declines in water quality appeared as the river flowed past major urban or industrial sites. Water quality declined markedly near the state capital of Salem, dropped again after the paper-mill town of Newberg, and then fell to its lowest point in Portland near the confluence of the Willamette and Columbia Rivers. The shocking conclusion was that dissolved oxygen levels near the mouth were scarcely 10 percent of the minimum needed to support a healthy fish population. The river, these results suggested, was in fact dying.[5]

By the 1930s water pollution had become a significant political issue. As municipalities struggled to finance sewage treatment plants, the obvious decline of the Willamette drew more public attention—the river even smelled bad on warm summer days, leading the state epidemiologist to proclaim that "the odor, the stench, and the filthy appearance of the river violate our aesthetic senses."[6] In 1933 a comprehensive study of the issue was conducted at the behest of Governor Julius Meier and determined that liquid waste from the pulp and paper industry was matched only by untreated domestic sewage as a cause of the pollution problem. Paper mills produced pulp from wood by heating the raw materials in large vats of chemicals and water to release the fiber, a process that yielded a liquid byproduct rich in organic elements that required oxygen as they decomposed. This complicated the cleanup efforts somewhat, as nobody was exactly certain of the composition of the so-called waste liquors from the papermaking process or of the economic impact of forcing the industry to find alternatives to the broadly accepted practice of pumping the wastes directly into the river. A report on existing regulations prepared for the 1937 legislative session found that a confusing overlap in statutes related to water quality and limited enforcement authority had crippled earlier efforts to address the problem. When the session ended without action from the legislature, citizens' groups, including the Stream Purification Committee, formed in 1935, took the matter into their own hands, placing an initiative petition calling for a new government authority to regulate water quality on the statewide ballot in 1938.[7] Support for the measure was generated by towing a basket of fish in the Willamette through Portland; when most of the fish died due to the lack of oxygen in the water, press coverage ensured voters knew about it.[8] The initiative, passed by a three-to-one margin, established a new State Sanitary Authority under which responsibility for enforcing antipollution laws would be consolidated.[9]

Fig. 9. Portland Mayor Joe Carson with youth river advocates, c.1938 (*The Oregonian*, Oregon Historical Society Photo Collection, OrHi 1253)

Despite the obvious public interest in cleaning up the state's rivers, little action was taken by the new Sanitary Authority in the 1940s. As it turned out, the new regulatory agency had little power to enforce standards; the strongest weapon it had against pollution was the ability to publicize the condition of the river and to shame individual polluters into compliance. During the war years public attention was diverted to more pressing issues, though a 1944 fish survey concluded that "pollution in the Willamette River system is a state of shame—this magnificent river is at present in part an open sewer [and] the people of Oregon have sacrificed a heritage in the aesthetic value of clean water." Subsequent tests, including some commissioned by the pulp and paper industry itself, indicated that the amount of dissolved oxygen in the Willamette at Portland had effectively dropped to zero—and conditions as far as eighty river miles upstream at Salem were declining as well. It was projected that a section of the river reaching as far as Newberg (fifty miles from the river's mouth) would experience total oxygen depletion under typical summer drought flows in the 1950s.[10] After the war an order from the Sanitary Authority restricting the dumping of pulp mill waste liquors to periods of high flow was issued, but a complete ban was rejected as too costly. The pace of the river's decline was slowed primarily through the release of water from U.S. Army Corps of Engineers dams and other storage projects upstream, which augmented flows during critical summer months. Though opposed by some sporting and conservation groups for their impact on migratory fish runs, these dams offered both flood control and the ability to release stored water in order to limit periods of low flow that resulted in heavy concentrations of pollutants in certain areas and contributed to the ongoing problem of downstream deoxygenation.[11]

In contrast to the modest improvements made by industry, municipal governments found themselves hard-pressed to raise funds for treatment plants in the 1950s and continued to discharge sewage directly into the river. Bond issues to improve sewer systems in Portland and other cities were repeatedly defeated by the same voters who approved the Sanitary Authority initiative, and it was only the limited power granted to the state by that petition that eventually drove cities along the river (with the major exception of Portland) to comply with a directive to install primary

Fig. 10. Waste oil fire on Willamette waterfront, Zidell Machinery and Supply, Portland, 1959 (*The Oregonian*, Oregon Historical Society Photo Collection, OrHi 13727)

treatment facilities—designed to remove solids through mechanical action—by the end of the decade. By that point, however, it was becoming clear that secondary treatment would be required to further reduce the impact of organic waste on water quality.[12] At the same time, gains in water quality achieved by increasing river levels in dry summer months were offset by increased agricultural runoff due to expanding irrigation made possible by the same dams that regulated river flow.

Expansion in the pulp and paper and food-processing industries further exacerbated the problem, which became so bad that a 1959 editorial in the *Salem Capital Journal* labeled the Willamette the "Ganges of the West" and proclaimed that pollution control was "strictly a matter of values," implying that Oregonians had misplaced priorities. Any gains made since 1930, the paper explained, had been quickly offset by growth of population, agriculture, and industry.[13] What was needed were stricter pollution controls, and they would be expensive—the sewage problem alone required an estimated $55 million to cure, according to state officials.[14] Governor Mark Hatfield saw the problem as a national one, with population growth at its core. "The more people there are, the more severe problems of our environment will become," he told a group of concrete industry representatives in May 1959. "At the present rates we will be producing in 1980 enough sewage and other wastes . . . to consume all the oxygen, in dry weather, in all the 22 [major] river systems in the U.S."[15] Despite some support for a federal cleanup in Congress, it was becoming increasingly clear that action would have to be taken on the state level, and soon, if the Willamette was to be saved.[16]

Although over two-thirds of Oregon's population lived in the valley of the Willamette in 1960, the health of the river was not as sweeping a concern as one might expect. Guidebooks for tourists and residents alike still spoke of the beauty of the green valley without mention of the sometimes fetid water.[17] Newspaper stories told of the actions of the Sanitary Authority, which continued its attempts to convince cities to treat sewage and to reduce industrial wastes, but were seldom very critical of its record. The strong economic and population growth of the 1950s carried forward into the next decade, perhaps distracting some from concern about the river through the benefits of a strong economy—certainly residents had no problem traveling to see clean rivers and streams outside the valley, and the increase in expenditures on outdoor recreation in the period suggests that many in fact did so. Indeed, the most prominent conservation action

Fig. 11. Boys fishing from
Portland sewer outflow
near Crown (Centennial)
Mills, Willamette River,
1960 (*The Oregonian*,
Oregon Historical Society
Photo Collection, OrHi
18142)

taken by the legislature in 1959 was the creation of an Interim Committee
on Natural Resources that was to examine the state's resource policies
and suggest improvements to be made in the 1961 session, an effort that
was neither directed at nor a response to the condition of the Willamette
but rather stemmed from the work of recreational interests that wanted
increased access to public lands.[18]

It is likely that some observers had simply written off the Willamette by
1960; given that pollution had been evident for at least half a century, most
adults had no memory of the river teeming with salmon and clean enough
to drink from. The rhetoric of the State Sanitary Authority, and the generally uncritical coverage it received from of the press, allowed Oregonians
to believe the problem was being addressed in a sensible fashion. Indeed,
the 1961 legislature saw the introduction of a bill, supported by the City
of Portland, which would *reduce* what little power the Sanitary Authority
had.[19] This aura of complacency would change for good in the fall of 1962,
though, when a Portland television station decided to make a major public
issue out of the embarrassing condition of the Willamette River.

A new tone in river coverage appeared in an editorial in Portland's
Oregon Journal on November 21, 1962, alerting readers to that evening's
special television broadcast of *Pollution in Paradise*, which it termed "a
remarkable hour-long documentary [about] the efforts to fight pollution
[that] will be something of a shocker for those persons who have been obliv-
ious to the scope of the problem. It has some bite. It steps on some toes. It
can rightly be called controversial."[20] Pollution in Oregon was not as bad as
in other states, the paper noted, but Oregon's growth and the ongoing failure to permanently address the problem threatened "our way of life in a land
which many people consider a paradise." Produced by Portland's KGW-TV,
the documentary was the brainchild of program director Tom Dargan, who
committed the station to a public service role, and Tom Lawson McCall, a
political commentator and reporter. McCall had broadcast a series of com-
mentaries touching on issues of pollution in 1960 and 1961, including com-
parisons of the Willamette to the Potomac and Cuyahoga, rivers so badly
polluted they had become national issues. Dargan responded by suggesting
that the condition of the Willamette merited more attention and that the
station should "get on the back" of the State Sanitary Authority, not only
about its failure to clean up the river but also about pollution in general. The
message was to be simple: "You think pollution is something that is happening someplace else. But here are symptoms of these afflictions right here in
Oregon. Let's get working on them."[21]

Pollution in Paradise was in every aspect a product of Tom McCall's
personal and professional interests. Though the idea had come from Tom
Dargan, it was McCall who wrote most of the script, provided the narration,
and sent the camera crew out to film chugging smokestacks, outfall pipes
pumping mill wastes into rivers, and domestic sewage running untreated
into the Willamette and across beaches into the Pacific Ocean. The background research offered a surprising revelation to the reporter, who discov-
ered that Oregon was "beginning to develop symptoms that in other places
had proved to be the basis of the disease that was destroying the environment," leading him to conclude that the state had done a less than adequate
job of addressing the pollution problem and that identifying major polluters
by name would help direct public pressure against their practices. As the
project's cameraman later recalled, McCall believed those responsible "had
to be portrayed as culprits for something to happen. Good guys and bad
guys. Tom felt there had to be an adversary relationship between us and

those that were polluting."²² Despite pressure from some of those identified
as polluters and the uncommon expense of the production's extensive location work, the station stood behind the documentary and McCall's message
that "cleaning up pollution should be looked at as a cost of doing business."²³

In its broadcast form, *Pollution in Paradise* opened with an introductory narration by KGW anchorman Richard Ross reflecting McCall's fundamental belief that while Oregon stood as a beacon to those who loved the
land, its very future was threatened by unregulated growth and pollution.
Appearing before the camera as an impartial observer, and occasionally nar-
rating over images of polluted water or belching smokestacks, Ross set the
stage for the documentary by unequivocally telling viewers what was at stake:
"There is still an America that is wild and clean and beautiful, but there is
also a dying dream of America where the waters are poisoned by the wastes
of man and the breeze is strangled by the fires and fumes of civilization. No
part of America still retains more of nature's original work than the state of
Oregon, a paradise for those who treasure the unspoiled in sight, in smell,
in sound. But who are these foul strangers in Oregon's paradise?" These foul
strangers, it was implied, had taken up permanent residence in other places
already and if Oregonians did not act quickly they might soon see their state
meet a similar fate. Although Oregon was a "verdant land where a thousand
streams . . . make possible a bounty that a nation must envy," the condition
of the Willamette and other rivers suggested that "the days of paradise may
be numbered." The Pacific Northwest still enjoyed an abundance of natural
resources that were once shared by other regions, places that had lost these
benefits "because their development was achieved without regard to the
spread of pollution." The object lesson was clear: Oregon was at a crossroads
and could choose to proceed as others had before, or it could decide to preserve the environmental qualities that made it unique. "You in Oregon have
a rich abundance of clean air and clean water. They were cleaner in the old
days than they are now. . . . Oregon and the nation stand at the threshold of
a new stage of industrial and general expansion, and your state's sizable volume of tourism will increase now by leaps and bounds. It may well be that
the program that you are about to see can do more for Oregon than perhaps
any other state. You have so much to preserve that others, unfortunately,
already have despoiled or lost." ²⁴

As McCall picked up the narration from offscreen, the viewer was
immediately confronted with images of polluted waterways and skies. The

complexity of the problem was apparent in the case of the rivers, which suffered not only from the obvious effects of industrial pollution but also from the sewage discharged by a "huge navy of pleasure-boaters," the commercial fleet docking in Portland, transient houseboat residents, and other nonpoint sources. The sixteen hundred cargo ships docking along the Willamette each year carried an estimated sixty thousand crewmen, "enough to populate a medium sized American city and all using the river as an open sewer." Improper domestic sanitation, organic waste from food-processing and logging operations, agricultural runoff, and a litany of other contributors to the water quality problem were itemized. The level of harmful bacteria in the river at Portland was said to be nearly three hundred times the safe level established by health experts; far upstream at Salem levels still exceeded the safety margin by a factor of eighteen. Perhaps the most compelling images of the segment, though, were footage of dead fish along the riverbank and live but obviously unhealthy fish struggling in nets. The accompanying narrative indicated that due to the decline in water quality, "only carp and other warm-water trash fish were able to survive" in the Willamette, a river that once carried salmon runs so numerous that it was said you could walk across the water on their backs. The loss of the salmon stood as a powerful symbol of environmental decline for McCall and for viewers previously unaware of just how dire the situation had become.

Air quality came next, first with examples of Portland's frequent inversions that held waste from "furnaces, smokestacks, dumps, and auto exhaust" close to the ground and "pushed Portlanders to the very threshold of our irritation," a problem more frequent there than at "any place on the West coast outside Los Angeles." Stark images of billowing stacks and brown smog were overlaid with strident music bordering on the melodramatic. McCall's script explained that the costs of such pollution were tallied not just in the discomfort of urban residents but in dollars spent repairing and repainting structures corroded by the caustic air, crops lost to chemical contamination, and other direct economic impacts totaling in the millions of dollars. These problems were not confined to the inland population centers either. On the coast in Newport emissions from a Georgia-Pacific pulp mill smelled so bad that the town became known as the "stink center of the Oregon coast," threatening tourism and property values. Ironically, at the same time residents there complained about the air pollution, their own municipal sewage was running across the beach, untreated, into the Pacific

Ocean. While industrial smokestacks were the most visible contributors to air quality problems, the film's narration made it clear that the lifestyle of the typical citizen was as much to blame for the crisis as industry. It was not only commercial activity destroying Oregon, viewers were warned, but their own daily routines. The problems were complex not only because solutions would be costly, but because the sources of pollution were so varied and disparate they would require sweeping changes to address.

Despite the building crisis, McCall informed viewers, Oregon had been far from inactive in combating pollution. He credited the establishment of the State Sanitary Authority to address water quality issues as a major step forward, as well as the 1951 passage of the nation's first statewide air pollution control law. Oregon in fact had laws as tough as any other state's, but "new pollution problems caused by urban growth and new industrial processes occur faster than our staff can keep up with them," the chairman of the Sanitary Authority stated on-screen. The agency had been "a catalyst for changing the old ways for the better," particularly in its demand that municipalities build sewage treatment facilities. The authority was also credited with helping convince Georgia-Pacific to spend $2.5 million to revamp its waste-processing systems to "free the Newport sea breeze of its stinking cargo." Unfortunately, the process of establishing and enforcing pollution controls turned out to be "awful damn slow work" and "a terribly complex economic, technical, and political issue." The public response to the water quality problems of the 1930s simply did not anticipate the scope of pollution challenges in the decades that followed.

Solutions to the statewide pollution problem would have to originate in Salem; there was clearly no way that hundreds of distinct municipal and county governments, and thousands of businesses and individual property owners, could be expected to clean up pollution on their own. However, efforts to create a metropolitan council of governments in Portland, as Seattle had done in 1958, were met with charges of communism from the right and apparent apathy from other quarters. Further compounding the problem was the issue of scale: while a single-family residence might have little direct impact on the Willamette, one pulp and paper mill used about as much water in a day as all of Portland's homes combined. Would it be adequate to force commercial operators to cease polluting without making cities comply as well? The complexity of the problem was well illustrated by the situation in The Dalles, a city of ten thousand on the Columbia River about eighty miles east of Portland. There cheap electricity from federal hydroelectric dams supported a large aluminum plant employing local residents at relatively high wages. Emissions from the plant, area orchardists claimed, were destroying the peach crops, though spokesmen for the Harvey Aluminum Company countered that crop yields had been at record levels the previous year and suggested that climate variation rather than their effluents was to blame for the declining harvest. There was little scientific evidence to support either side, so the issue became quite contentious locally, threatening to divide the town. Statewide emissions standards offered one way to address the problem consistently and fairly, at least in the minds of many observers, though it was assumed the focus of the regulations would be industrial rather than municipal discharges.

Pollution in Paradise went on to provide numerous specific examples of both industrial polluters—identified by name and shown in the process of pumping smoke into the sky or liquid wastes into a river—and municipalities that were inadequately treating their sewage. Footage of pollution was repeatedly presented with stirring musical passages intended to convey a sense of urgency. Taken collectively, the decaying environmental conditions not only impacted those who lived and worked next to the Willamette or by a pulp mill but threatened the very livability of the state, the one quality that Oregonians cherished above all else. This carried a serious economic risk, as was illustrated by Gerry Frank, a powerful Republican political operative and chairman of the advisory committee to the State Department of Planning and Development in 1962, who said, "One of the major advantages we have in selling the industrial development program of the state of Oregon is good livability. People like to live and work in our state." Unprecedented growth projected over the following decade would only increase pressure on Oregon's environment, but the livability factor might be used to attract cleaner industry if it could be preserved. If not, creating new jobs might prove troublesome. McCall pointedly asked viewers, "Are industry and taxpayer prepared to shoulder heavier responsibility?"

The documentary's conclusions were sweeping. The State Sanitary Authority and other public agencies needed additional staff for monitoring and enforcement and had to expand research to determine the full scope of the problem and develop potential alternatives for safer waste disposal. Despite these needs, the legislature had reduced the Sanitary Authority's budget in 1961 and defeated related proposals for specific research projects, including one slated for The Dalles that was strongly opposed by the Harvey Aluminum Company. Reliable funding for research and monitoring became the first need to address. A supporting antipollution campaign could not be financed by cities alone but would require state funding. Beefing up Oregon's antipollution laws was another necessary task; as McCall saw it, the existing laws "lacked teeth" and were particularly weakened by the inability to force regulatory compliance. It was a task everyone could join in at the direct invitation of Governor Mark Hatfield, who told the television audience, "I invite all who are interested in maintaining playgrounds and payrolls in this state . . . to join in the enforcement of anti-pollution, and thus we can keep the Oregon way of life." McCall provided the final voiceover, intoning sonorously over a series of images of polluted air and water no less striking than those at the beginning of the program:

So all the king's horses, all the king's men, and the king himself
are united. Yet pollution still marches in paradise. There can be no
compromise with this invader while hundreds are stricken with
waterborne disease. While scrap fish take over from trout and
salmon in once-pure streams. While outpourings of industrial and
human filth corrupt our waters from cities, from food processing,
from pulp and paper making. While industrial stacks betray
the cleanliness of our air, damaging fields, crops, orchards, and
livestock, soiling our clothes and homes, and attacking human
membranes. While in short our air and water are stained in
countless ways as we mistreat our precious heritage. And it could
be only the beginning, for how far pollution marches in Oregon is a
matter in final analysis of citizen responsibility.

　　All will be well if each of us realizes he may be a polluter as well
as a pollution victim. Oregon's future in terms of payrolls and a way
of life envied from afar rides on the major resources of water and
air, resources you and I must not permit to be engulfed, lest the
story of Oregon's destiny tragically be told in terms of pollution in
paradise.[25]

The message to viewers was clear, the challenge stated, and the stakes high. It was up to each individual to address pollution in his or her own home, neighborhood, and city and to demand action at the state level to address the larger crisis. McCall had shown them what was wrong, what was threatened, and what needed to be done. In producing "the first really dramatic message of its kind that local television had tried," he and Tom Dargan threw down the gauntlet before the people of Oregon and the industrial polluters threatening the state's environment.[26] Copies were distributed to public schools and a second broadcast was scheduled in January, just before the legislature convened, in an effort to influence public opinion and the legislative agenda.[27] The alarm bell had been rung, resoundingly, in Oregon.

Pollution in Paradise did not prompt an immediate solution to the problems of the Willamette River. Though an effective warning bell, it could not offer the kind of complex solutions needed to solve the intricate puzzle of growth, pollution, and economic vitality. What it did achieve was a broad new awareness of the basic issue of pollution in Oregon—as one KGW producer remembered, "When Tom blew the whistle it really made a difference for a long time to come."[28] McCall and Oregon were far from unique in that regard, as 1962 was also the year in which the entire nation was dramatically warned about environmental decline by Rachel Carson's bestseller Silent Spring. First serialized in the New Yorker in June and then issued as a book in September, Carson's account of the threat of pesticides to all living things was the work of a concerned scientist, not a journalist, but clearly had the same intent as Pollution in Paradise in sounding a warning to the public. That the two projects were produced almost simultaneously is indicative of the uncertainty with which some Americans regarded industrial progress in the early 1960s—or as Carson put it to a reporter, "our willingness to rush ahead and use something new without knowing what the results are going to be."[29] Such concerns became increasingly common as millions of citizens joined the ranks of the middle class in the 1950s and their priorities turned from meeting basic needs to achieving a higher quality of life, which logically led to demands for better health and a cleaner environment. Often left unstated, their worries were given voice and coherence by such high-profile media events as the publication of Silent Spring and the broadcast of Pollution in Paradise, which helped awaken the nation to a crisis that had been developing for generations but to that point had drawn minimal response from professional ecologists, much less the general public.[30]

Silent Spring was immediately controversial, sparking debates well before it appeared in book form. Its basic warning was presented in lay terms: the widely used insecticide DDT was building up in the food chain,

leading to a precipitous decline in the bird population and ultimately pos-
ing a cancer threat to humans. Like McCall, Carson presented her findings
in a resounding call to arms, asserting the public's right to know about
the chemical threat and, most importantly, the right to reject the marketing campaigns of the manufacturers and to "no longer accept the counsel
of those who tell us we must fill our world with poisoning chemicals."[31]
Because she had singled out a specific type of chemical—insecticides—and
even one company's particular product as the primary example of technological risk to the environment, she drew immediate opposition from the
chemical industry. Despite the exhaustive research and copious evidence
behind the study, her conclusions were assaulted as bad science, attempts
were made to block publication of the book, and Carson herself became
the target of a negative publicity campaign impugning her credentials and
character, even suggesting her gender was to blame for her positions.

   Labeled a communist, a "hysterical female," and, most outrageously,
a spinster who should have no concern for genetics, Rachel Carson stood
behind her work and made frequent public appearances to support its message despite her own private battle with the cancer that would kill her in
1964.[32] The frenzied efforts of industrial interests to silence or discredit
Carson were indicative of the fear they felt at the prospect of a populace that
might question the value of continued "progress" and potentially reduce
consumption of their products. The reception *Silent Spring* received from
the public—Americans bought over half a million copies its first year in
print—and the widespread demand for action that resulted were compared
to the social impact of *Uncle Tom's Cabin* even before Carson's death. By
the end of the decade the book was generally accepted as the catalyst that
brought environmental concerns into the mainstream of American politics
and culture.

   In contrast to *Silent Spring, Pollution in Paradise* drew much less
industry opposition and Tom McCall himself was never directly attacked
for his role in the project. The more muted response may have been due
in part to the incontrovertible visual evidence the documentary offered;
it was hard to argue against stark images of dead fish, billowing smokestacks, and raw sewage running across the beach. Rachel Carson, unfortunately, had to rely primarily on technical scientific evidence drawn from
the research of others in condemning a product many felt was safe. As the
most prominent of a series of environmental exposés that appeared in the

national news in 1962, *Silent Spring* helped trigger a public outcry against industrial chemicals that often could be traced only by scientists studying their long-term effects on the environment. McCall's work, on the other hand, showed viewers that they were themselves part of a problem that was evident in their communities, had obvious and visible sources, and might readily be addressed through existing institutions if adequate funding was made available. McCall, of course, was also male and a well-known broadcast journalist in the region, making him harder to challenge on the basis of credibility than Carson, who was not only a woman but a rare one in the life sciences with a national audience. The size of the stage alone may also explain the differing response; Carson's book took on major multinational industries wholesale and was singled out by Supreme Court justice William O. Douglas as "the most important chronicle of this century for the human race."[33] John F. Kennedy ordered the President's Science Advisory Committee to produce a response to *Silent Spring*, which it issued in the spring of 1963 in the form of a report that concluded directly that "until the publication of *Silent Spring* by Rachel Carson, people were generally unaware of the toxicity of pesticides."[34] McCall's documentary, in contrast, was not widely seen outside the Pacific Northwest, and since it blamed specific facilities and the general population for pollution, rather than targeting a single industry, it did not draw the coordinated, national counterattack that Carson's book experienced.

The most evident short-term result of McCall's exposé in Oregon came with the 1963 legislative session, in which lawmakers responded to public pressure by giving the State Sanitary Authority the power to bring legal action against polluters found in violation of regulations under certain circumstances. State Senator Ted Hallock, who sponsored the bill, told reporters the effort was a direct result of the documentary and was written to "give the governor and the Sanitary Authority the teeth they've asked for."[35] This change was only the first step in a process that would see Oregon's political leaders become increasingly involved with environmental issues as the decade progressed, a change that has since often been credited to the impact of *Pollution in Paradise* on public opinion.

Although McCall's documentary drew public attention to the crisis of the Willamette River, it did not lead to an immediate solution. The waste disposal practices criticized in the film continued into the 1960s, and certainly nothing was done about the underlying issues of population growth and industrial expansion. Municipalities fought state orders to build new sewage treatment facilities, claiming that the expense and the mandated timelines were unrealistic. Meanwhile, the State Sanitary Authority responded to public opinion by attempting to crack down on polluters that had ignored regulations for years. In early 1963 one city official accused the authority of acting in dictatorial fashion when it refused to extend a temporary permit allowing the operation of a substandard sewage system and claimed the deadline set by the authority was impossible to meet. Perhaps emboldened by its newfound public support, the authority noted that it had been ten years since the city was first informed of the need to improve its facilities and no action had been taken; the city was given six months to address the problem and was threatened with court action if it failed to comply this time around.[36] Despite the agency's expanded authority and the interest the public took in the cleanup effort, progress remained slow in the early 1960s, hampered largely by the cost of building the necessary sewage treatment plants and by foot-dragging on the part of industrial concerns that saw little potential return on the mandated investments in cleaner factories and antipollution technologies.

By 1965 criticism of the slow cleanup rate appeared in the papers regularly, sparked by a substantial drop in water quality that occurred during the summer. The Sanitary Authority's efforts to restore the Willamette yielded some success, not through substantial waste reductions but by artificially increasing dry-month river levels by releasing water from upstream dams. The practice was usually effective in diluting pollutants but failed in 1965 due to lower than average rainfall and a temporary increase in waste output from a single paper mill.[37] Salem's *Oregon Statesman* ran a six-part series on the decline of the Willamette that fall that reflected the viewpoint McCall had taken in *Pollution in Paradise*, noting in the first installment that the descendants of the Oregon pioneers were "in danger of losing their birthright" as the river died. Although $85 million had been spent since World War II to reduce the flow of waste into the river, the population living in the Willamette Basin had grown from 338,500 in 1938 to 729,600 in 1964, effectively negating any gains realized by previous efforts. The city of Portland was singled out by the newspaper for its lackluster efforts at reducing pollution; the state's largest city had spent only one-third the amount per capita on sewage treatment as other cities along the river, and most of that had gone toward a system that simply diverted sewage from the Willamette to the Columbia River. Meanwhile, the much smaller city of Salem had invested in excess of three times Portland's per capita expenditure in a new treatment plant that cut discharges by 50 percent over its prior facility.[38]

The final article in the *Statesman*'s series explained the fundamental challenge to saving the river in simple terms: "The long-range problem is . . . that while cities and industries expand, the river does not." Growth projections suggested that even the most comprehensive attempts to reduce the waste flow with the current technologies were bound to fail and that the only hope was for municipalities to adopt new techniques for *tertiary* sewage treatment—at a time when most had yet to implement *secondary* treatment—that yielded an effluent "purer than any river water and cleaner than much well water."[39] The fundamental problem was the cost; it had taken over twenty-five years for most Willamette Valley cities to build secondary treatment plants because voters were loath to approve the necessary tax increases or bond measures, and corporations were unwilling to invest millions in antipollution technology that offered no clear financial returns.

Public acceptance of "business as usual" with regard to the polluted Willamette was wearing thin by the mid-1960s. Lyndon Johnson's Great Society program had helped make quality of life a national priority, and awareness of pollution and other environmental issues had become widespread in the wake of *Silent Spring* and subsequent calls to action like Secretary of the Interior Stewart Udall's compelling examination of ecological decline in *The Quiet Crisis* (1963). There Udall pointed out the lifestyle paradox of postwar America, warning that "while our economic standard of living has become the envy of the world, our environmental standard has steadily declined."[40] Oregonians reflected the national interest in the environment by once again demanding action on pollution within their borders and particularly on the Willamette River. This was quite evident in August 1965, when State Treasurer Robert "Bob" Straub publicly accused Governor Hatfield of giving only "token lip service" to the pollution problem and said that Hatfield "must carry personal responsibility for the disgraceful, stinking mess of the Willamette River."[41] Four days later the State Sanitary Authority, which Straub believed was underfunded, understaffed, and largely ineffectual, released a report stating that 60 percent of the organic waste discharged into the Willamette came from just three paper mills. The authority had given these mills until 1968 to reduce emissions to acceptable levels but was now considering moving up the deadline.[42]

Straub's outrage, it seemed, was having an impact. It had certainly forced the pollution issue back onto the front pages of the region's newspapers.

The year 1966 would prove to be a turning point in Oregon politics and, as a result, in the state's approach to the emerging environmental crisis. Mark Hatfield, the two-term Republican governor, spent the year running for the U.S. Senate, thus leaving the gubernatorial contest open. After the primaries the match would be between State Treasurer Robert Straub, the Democrat, and reporter-turned-secretary-of-state Tom McCall, his Republican opponent. As McCall remembered the race years later, the two candidates were of similar mind on most environmental issues. Hatfield "was a grabber for payrolls at almost any cost," McCall said, while "Straub and I brought a more rational approach to economic development, putting the balance between economic development and the environment into focus."[43] As a liberal Republican, McCall had continued to make pollution a theme of his news reports after the *Pollution in Paradise* broadcast, and he carried that interest into office when he was elected secretary of state in 1964. Democrat Straub, also a liberal, lacked McCall's newscaster celebrity but was still a formidable opponent in a state with majority Democratic voter registration. The two men had worked together in their elected positions as members of the State Board of Control, so were familiar with one another's political styles and personal values. Both knew the voters wanted a solution to the pollution problem and each began the campaign with strong views on the issue and what should be done to address it. Consequently, the 1966 gubernatorial race was characterized by frequent episodes of agreement on issues of conservation and the environment, promising the electorate that regardless of who won, the pollution problem would be high on the agenda of the next administration.

The timing was certainly right. In 1966 public frustration with the lack of progress on environmental issues became a significant factor in statewide politics. In June, Chamber of Commerce leaders in Salem were warned that without "proper planning and conservation . . . Oregon stands the chance of inheriting some of California's population problems—pollution, lack of living space, crowded recreation areas. We're ruining the thing that we have been trying to sell—livability. We can no longer continue without plans for the future."[44] Population growth threatened to turn the Willamette Valley into one large "interurbia" running from Eugene to Portland, according to another projection.[45] The threat that Oregon might follow the growth path of its giant neighbor to the south was a frightening prospect to many. But the biggest environmental problem, one reporter declared, was that "it takes up to 10 years to get something done about cleaning up dirty streams and fouled-up air." Oregon law had not kept up with industrial development and population growth, and the Sanitary Authority was not using the limited power it had to force improvements. According to one editor, the state was "out of step with the Great Society emphasis on cleanliness and beauty" and the time had come for decisive action. Gubernatorial candidates McCall and Straub offered hope, "both saying that abatement of pollution is taking far too long . . . to clean up existing situations and forestall new problems."[46]

The keys to solving these problems were political: what antipollution advocates needed was help from the legislature in the form of appropriations and leadership from the governor's bully pulpit to steer public opinion. Both had been absent in previous years, due in no small part to Hatfield's own economic conservatism and support for traditional industrial development;[47] this was especially evident in 1965 when efforts to shore up funding for the Sanitary Authority were defeated in the legislature and Governor Hatfield's own Department of Finance further reduced the pollution control budget administratively. That was before pollution "became the state's hottest political issue" in the final months of 1965, leading Hatfield to give a November address requesting public support for an ambitious antipollution program that would not only address the existing situation but also move toward the prevention stage by planning for future growth.[48] Hatfield, of course, would no longer be governor when the legislature convened again two years later and expected no real response from lawmakers. The speech was an obvious part of his effort to build support for his 1966 Senate campaign, but it also reflected the growing public demand for action that would force the next governor to make addressing the environmental crisis a top priority.

Tom McCall wasted no time in making environmental quality the central issue of his campaign, telling a group of Republican activists that the party's progressive tradition in Oregon demanded action on "the matter of general livability," which made the state "the envy of the nation." The charge, he proclaimed, was not just to stop pollution but to enhance this livability. "Let's move . . . to see that open space is clean, the air unsullied, the water uncontaminated, the scenery unblighted." Doing so would not only make the state more habitable but would transform it into a "mecca for business and development."[49] To McCall, improving environmental quality was never a matter of halting development and industry but one of managing them wisely in the best tradition of earlier Republican progressives like Theodore Roosevelt.

As the 1966 campaign for governor heated up, it became increasingly clear that the two candidates were of like mind on many critical environmental issues. News stories continued to alert Oregonians of threats to their environment and reporters asked the candidates for the specifics of their antipollution plans. Bob Straub responded in July by offering a sweeping vision he called "Willamette River Rediscovered" that would establish a recreational greenway on both banks of the over four hundred miles of river between Eugene and Portland.[50] Obviously a riverside park of such magnitude would require cleaning up the river before anyone would support it; that Straub essentially took the recovery of the river for granted raised the standard for restoring the river. The Willamette would not just be made safe, he implied, it would be made desirable. Beyond cleaning up the water itself, the river's banks should be developed for picnicking, cycling, hiking, camping, and horseback riding. The first step would be to "excite the public about the vast recreational and economic benefits" of his proposal to develop "one of the most important conservation-recreation ideas in our state's history."[51] Ultimately the *Eugene Register-Guard* declared Straub's vision "a dream too thrilling for politics," important enough that "politics should not get in the way of the truth that future generations will thank this one for saving something, as we thank our grandparents for preserving so much of the Oregon Coast."[52]

According to McCall, the river restoration concept originated in a report sent to both candidates by Karl W. Onthank, a professor at the University of Oregon and a well-known conservationist; Onthank, however, credited Straub with the plan.[53] The greenway proposal was immediately attacked by the *Oregonian* as being too far out to consider, but the following day McCall told the *Register-Guard*, "I think it's a good idea too," thereby taking a potential campaign issue away from Straub but also reflecting the extent to which the two agreed—so much so that some in the press began referring to the campaign as the "Bob and Tom Show."[54] Both candidates supported Senator Maurine Neuberger's efforts to establish the Oregon Dunes National Seashore, wanted to clean up the Willamette and reduce air pollution, felt that future growth needed to be directed in environmentally friendly ways, and saw the need for more recreation areas for public use. Passionate rhetoric from each candidate called for changing the way Oregonians used their environment, but their shared views made it challenging to distinguish the candidates on what had become a central theme of the race: protecting the environment and the state's livability.

The one major departure from this mutual agreement arose in midsummer, over a plan to relocate part of U.S. 101 on the Oregon coast from its existing inland route onto a sand spit near the mouth of the Nestucca River. The State Highway Commission and its powerful Republican commissioner Glenn Jackson wanted to move the highway to provide a view of the ocean for motorists and boost tourism. Indeed, the Nestucca realignment was only part of a broader plan to relocate the highway along much of the coast. The sand spit, however, offered walkers a two-mile stretch of undeveloped beach that was in near wilderness condition, a relative rarity along the coast, where most long stretches of beach were adjacent to roads, houses, or other development. Reaction to the proposal was strongly negative in the adjacent community of Pacific City, where residents demonstrated their opposition to the plan by "hanging effigies of Jackson and Governor Mark Hatfield from telephone poles."[55]

Bob Straub heard of the protest and after visiting the sand spit determined he would use the case as a campaign issue by placing himself at the center of the controversy, further demonstrating his commitment to the environment through outspoken opposition to the project. Straub embraced the local opposition, joining the Pacific City–Woods Recreational Protection League for an event billed as "Sing Along with Bob" that featured a hastily penned "Battle Hymn for Conservation" with lyrics tailored to the Nestucca Spit dispute:

Mine eyes have seen the misery of the coming of the road,
It is blighting all the wonders and the joys that we have knowed,
The sand is being covered up with cement by the load,
And nobody gives a darn.

The leeches want our beaches and the county wants them too,
Although we fight with all our might they'll ram the highway
    through,
The beach is torn, our hearts are worn from all we've tried to do,
And nobody gives a darn.

Sandy beach we're going to miss ya,
Cements coming down to kiss ya,
We're here trying to assist ya,
But nobody gives a darn.

The final verse of the song served as an endorsement for Straub himself, noting that that the state treasurer was on the right side of the dispute: "At last we have a champion and his name is Robert Straub, he's going to save the beaches and we're all behind you Bob."[56]

Tom McCall found himself on the other side of the sand spit issue. Prior to announcing his campaign for governor, he had approached Glenn Jackson to ask for his support in the race, knowing that he needed the influential Republican's help in winning over Oregon's business community in the wake of his high-profile attacks on industrial polluters. Jackson agreed to back McCall, but with one caveat: McCall must support the Nestucca Spit highway plan. The candidate agreed without hesitation, thinking the promise negligible in comparison to gaining Jackson's endorsement and not quite realizing what was being asked. Later, McCall would publicly justify his position by claiming, "The spit route will afford a continuous majestic view of the ocean . . . where [now] the motorist scarcely sees the surf and beaches. [It is] without a doubt, the most scenic area on the Oregon coast."[57]

Despite his public defense of the project, one of McCall's aides recalled, "Supporting that highway ran contrary to every bone in Tom's body. The only reason he went for it was because Glenn Jackson wanted it." So when McCall announced his acceptance of the Highway Commission's intention to move U.S. 101 onto the spit it took some observers by surprise, not least of all Bob Straub, who later commented, "I had expected McCall to oppose the highway, and I just wanted to be to the first to do so. I was shocked when he did not oppose it. After that, I tried to beat McCall over the head with it. It was about the only thing I had."[58] Unfortunately for Straub, the Nestucca issue failed to engage voters from the state's inland population centers as it did coastal residents, so his one significant opportunity to prove himself a stronger advocate for the environment than McCall was rendered politically moot.

As the race carried into the fall, two things became clear: the environment had become the central political issue for the voters and Straub had no chance of winning the election. One month before the election, Salem's *Oregon Journal* declared the state "perilously close to losing its livability in a cloud of pollution and in a jam of unplanned growth" and endorsed Straub as a source of the "uninhibited, imaginative leadership...[necessary] to dramatize the need for prompt action."[59] Still, McCall remained well ahead in the polls, a fact likely due less to positions he had taken than simply to his familiarity to voters, who had grown accustomed to his voice from radio and television, and his reputation as a strong antipollution advocate. McCall was able to label his opponent a "late arriving crusader" on the pollution issue in an October debate by referring to a 1951 incident in which Straub, then a county commissioner, advised against taking action on a local odor problem when the owners of the paper mill in question assured him they would take care of it on their own. Admitting "I was naive then," Straub claimed he had since learned better.[60] While Straub was forced to take bold positions to establish his environmental credentials, McCall could simply agree with those positions and capitalize on his own celebrity. Leaving nothing to chance, though, McCall repeatedly emphasized the pollution issue on the campaign trail, putting quality of life and a cleaner environment at the top of his list of campaign promises. Straub continued his attempts to differentiate himself from the front-runner, promoting the greenway concept and urging voters to demonstrate that Oregon had the "vision, courage, and ability to move" on environmental issues.[61]

Warnings of looming environmental catastrophe appeared regularly in the media that fall, ensuring the public would remain concerned and both candidates would be compelled to keep speaking out on the issue into the final legs of the race. Two weeks before election day, readers of the *Oregon Journal* awoke to the headline "Pollution Perils Oregon's Health, Way of Life" over a story revealing that one of the Willamette's major tributaries, the Tualatin River just south of Portland, was effectively dead. Researchers at the University of Oregon also feared that the water quality decline on the Willamette was nearing the point of irreversibility, prompting the paper to declare that "pollution in Oregon now threatens every resident's way of life. The things that most people in Oregon hold dearest—clean rivers, lakes and clean air—are disappearing here as they have in many other parts of the country. The only thing that can reverse this destruction and stop pollution is the people's awareness of the problem, coupled with enough 'love of the Oregon way of life' to do something about it."[62] The thing to do about

Fig. 12. Governor Tom
McCall official portrait,
c. 1967 (Original in author's
possession)

it, in the minds of a majority of voters, was to elect Tom McCall governor. On November 1, 1966, they did so, choosing McCall over Straub 55–45 and thus putting the man who in 1962 wanted to "ring an alarm for the people of Oregon" on the pollution problem in the unique position of having to respond to his own call to action.

In the weeks after the election the press kept the environment in the public eye. The *Oregon Journal* ran a series of articles in November and December explaining the root causes of many of the pollution problems afflicting the state, opening with the claim that "there no longer is any question that polluted water is a threat to health, as well as a great economic loss to a state whose third-largest industry is recreation. [A]ir and water pollution . . . are a threat to the health and well-being of every Oregon resident."[63] At his inauguration in January Tom McCall quoted Oregon's first governor, John Whiteaker, who proclaimed the state "one of the most attractive portions of the North American continent," then went on to call for a variety of measures to ensure Oregon would "continue to qualify for Whiteaker's description." Bolstering the State Sanitary Authority topped the list, followed by Bob Straub's plan for a Willamette greenway. Among the new priorities McCall laid out was a program to extend state ownership of the beaches from the mean-high-tide mark established under former governor Oswald West's leadership in 1913; McCall feared development pressures would erode public access to the beaches if the state did not own more of the shoreline. The inaugural address ended with a reiteration of a campaign point: "The overriding challenge—the umbrella issue of the campaign and the decade—is quality, quality of life in Oregon!"[64]

Perhaps emboldened by McCall's rhetoric, the Sanitary Authority took its most decisive action in years a few weeks later, adopting a new "get tough" policy that would see the agency ordering air pollution abatement and leaving the burden of implementation up to the polluter, rather than allowing pollution to continue for years while an acceptable solution was found. In the past, polluters had effectively postponed sanctions by promising to upgrade facilities to reduce pollution without ever taking action, but under the new procedure the authority would issue cease-and-desist orders immediately after a deadline passed rather than waiting years for signs of improvement. The primary targets of the new policy were the so-called wigwam burners that lumber mills used to dispose of sawdust waste, pouring choking clouds of smoke into the sky in the process. Four years earlier the authority had labeled the burners unacceptable but then allowed the mills to continue using them while modifications to reduce emissions were developed. Now the burners would be banned outright and in short order; a hearing in April would set the date for the complete prohibition of wigwam burners. The State Sanitary Authority had not been granted any new powers, but it is likely that the knowledge that the new administration backed them helped the members "come to grips" with adopting this "new philosophy" toward pollution, as one reporter put it.[65]

The slow progress of the Willamette River cleanup effort drew national attention in February, when the Federal Water Pollution Control Administration proclaimed the Willamette "one of the most serious examples of water pollution in the Northwest" and proposed its own program to save the river. Requiring an expenditure of $105 million, the plan aimed to make the Willamette and two major tributaries free of pollution by 1985.

According to the federal study, about 90 percent of the oxygen-consuming pollutants in the Willamette came from the seven pulp and paper mills along the river. Officials from Boise-Cascade, the operator of a large paper mill in Salem, responded by stating that their plant was on track to meet targets mandated by the Sanitary Authority early the next year, eliminating the need for major federal investment.[66]

The State Sanitary Authority quickly advised Governor McCall that the federal report "represents an extremely biased and slanted evaluation of the state's water pollution control program" and was so "riddled with fallacies and falsehoods that it approaches professional dishonesty." According to Kenneth Spies, the chief engineer of the Sanitary Authority, the Federal Water Pollution Control Administration relied on outdated information that did not accurately reflect gains in water quality made since 1965. More work was needed, he admitted, but the situation was not as dire as the federal agency led the public to believe.[67] Oregon's newest senator, former governor Mark Hatfield, told the press the report was an "unfair evaluation" of the progress made in the cleanup effort under his administration and that the State Sanitary Authority had been "terribly abused" by those who did not recognize this, including Bob Straub, whom he singled out for criticizing the authority during the gubernatorial campaign.[68]

Governor McCall, meanwhile, was putting his own plan for the Willamette River into action. In March he held a press conference to introduce his version of the greenway plan, making good on a major promise of his inaugural address. Drafted in the first weeks of his administration, the release was likely timed to divert attention from the new federal report and to secure the governor's reputation as an aggressive environmental leader. As envisioned, the Willamette River Greenway would establish a system of boat ramps, campgrounds, parks, trails, recreation areas, and scenic drives along the river from Eugene to Portland, at a cost of approximately $15 million. McCall was joined by his former opponent Bob Straub, who explained to reporters that funding for the purchase of nearly seventy-five hundred acres of land would come in the form of state-issued bonds and grants from the federal Land and Water Conservation Fund, while conservation easements would be sought for an additional seventy-nine hundred acres from private landowners to help reduce the cost of implementation.[69] The governor later told the legislature the project would not "disrupt existing land uses such as residential, commercial, or agricultural" and farmers were assured that their land was not in jeopardy. Immediate reaction to the proposal could be characterized as of mild support, though many voiced concern over the cost.[70] Once the details became public, with the introduction of HB 1770 and SB 33 in the legislature, louder objections were raised, particularly from farmers and property-rights advocates.[71] For McCall, though, the proposal represented his first opportunity to show the public he was serious about the environment—that the vision and commitment he campaigned on were sincere.

Another opportunity presented itself to Governor McCall not long after. Although the greenway plan suggested a vision of the Willamette for the future, nothing had yet been done to place McCall at the center of the current cleanup effort. In late March 1967 the state Board of Health held a hearing on the Willamette in Portland, where it was revealed that the river had been polluted so badly for so long that "nobody really knew what its natural state should be." Bob Straub appeared to call for stronger antipollution regulations, while a representative of the Izaak Walton League reported that the river remained a "stinking, slimy mess" and recommended the state adopt the plan offered by the Federal Water Pollution Control Administration earlier that year. Paper industry officials testified that new proposals from the State Sanitary Authority were "unrealistic and impractical," but other witnesses argued the standards should be raised high enough to support fish life along the entire river.[72]

The Sanitary Authority, it appeared, still lacked the power (either real or perceived) to dictate improvements in water quality. The situation was due in part to leadership; the authority had been chaired since its creation in 1939 by Harold Wendel, a Portland businessman, who had never attempted to use the agency as a bully pulpit. McCall was considering replacing him when Wendel unexpectedly died, leaving the position vacant.[73] Seizing the chance to draw attention to the antipollution effort and to underscore "the importance of pollution control to the people of Oregon," McCall took the bold step of appointing himself to the Sanitary Authority, where he was immediately elected chairman. His first move was to "declare war" on the highly visible wigwam burners, agreeing with another member of the Sanitary Authority that they should simply "tell the operators to stop polluting."[74] In an earlier statement to legislators, McCall had suggested the agency "draw a line beyond which existing pollution cannot come and then work out rollback schedules between the Sanitary Authority and the industrial or municipal polluter. It will help Oregon now and benefit future generations of Oregonians if we can establish that Oregon has propounded—and enforces to the hilt—an 11th Commandment: Thou shalt not pollute."[75] By appointing himself to the Sanitary Authority, McCall was taking an initial step in that direction, though the move was called a "political blunder" by state senator Lynn Newbry, who thought it left McCall "wide open politically," implying that failure would be attributed to the governor personally, rather than the Sanitary Authority.[76] McCall, however, seized the opportunity to promote the authority and highlight its importance in addressing "the most significant long-range problem facing the state."[77]

Promoting the antipollution cause from both the governor's office and the Sanitary Authority proved an effective combination. The strategy revived public interest in the authority and gave McCall more opportunities to promote his agenda to the press. Most importantly, it placed him in a position to lead the Willamette cleanup directly, at least as far as the public was concerned, and that raised the stakes significantly—if the effort failed, he would take the blame as quickly as he could take credit for any success. As one reporter explained it, McCall "put his personal prestige on the line in attempting to carry out pledges made during the 1966 campaign when he . . . constantly pointed to problems of air and water pollution as among the most needful of early solution."[78] The governor's goals went beyond old air- and water-quality struggles, though; McCall wanted to mobilize the state's entire population in a total war against pollution. To that end he designated May 1967 "Beautiful Oregon Month" and challenged Oregonians to address environmental decay in their own communities by cleaning up litter, improving parks, and doing whatever else they could to "add to the attractiveness of each area of our state."[79]

While the Sanitary Authority was working in the background to develop strict new regulations for industry, and particularly to address the problem of paper mill wastes, McCall pushed legislators to move forward on the Willamette greenway plan. His proposal drew approving coverage from the New York Times, which noted both its origins in Straub's campaign and the similarity to Lyndon Johnson's call to turn the Potomac into a public attraction by similar means.[80] In May the governor signed a bill granting state agencies the authority to acquire conservation easements in support of the plan, but the $800,000 proposed budget for land acquisition drew opposition in the legislature.[81] Despite concerns over funding, the greenway was viewed widely as a symbol of the state's willingness to improve the decaying river, or as one reporter worded it, to prove whether or not "they are really serious about preserving or re-creating some of the outdoor wonders which are so much a part of the Oregon way of life."[82] McCall promoted the greenway with this in mind, just as he continued to hammer home the antipollution message as the chair of the State Sanitary Authority, proclaiming in June that "with constant pressure and unrelenting vigilance, the desecration of Oregon will someday come to a halt."[83]

Despite the political benefits of seizing control of the body, Tom McCall soon found the work of the Sanitary Authority "too tedious and detail driven for his tastes" and resigned his seat on July 10, 1967.[84] In doing so he reminded the public that his ten weeks as chair had "brought Oregon its greatest strides in managing air and water pollution."[85] In his short tenure he secured the passage of strict new water quality standards, moved toward a complete ban on wigwam burners, and opened negotiations with houseboat owners along the Willamette who still released their untreated sewage into the river. More significantly for the long run, he put the imprimatur of the governor's office behind the Sanitary Authority; it now had

Fig. 13. Sport fishermen landing a Chinook salmon on the recovering Willamette River near Oregon City, 1973 (National Archives and Records Administration, Record Group 412: Records of the Environmental Protection Agency, LI 412-DA-5673)

the teeth it had lacked since 1939, just as the Willamette itself was draw-ing national attention. Not long after McCall left the Sanitary Authority, Secretary of the Interior Stewart Udall penned an article for *National Parks* magazine that explained, "There is much more at stake in the cleanup of the Willamette than the cost of the cleanup bill itself." Its valley was, "as Oregonians like to point out, an intensely 'livable' land" but would continue to be so only if water pollution were addressed. Udall credited the Sanitary Authority and Tom McCall specifically with establishing new water quality standards, marking "the beginning of a new era in water management in this country" in advance of federal deadlines.[86]

In the formal announcement of the appointment of John Mosser as his replacement as chairman of the Sanitary Authority, McCall told Oregonians he expected the body to "hold, roll back, and prevent pollution" in the future. From here on, he pledged, businesses seeking to open in Oregon would "have to pass the toughest air and water pollution criteria of any state." A line was being drawn: Oregon's new policy was to place environmental quality over economic growth, at least as far as the governor was concerned. Turning over leadership of the Sanitary Authority freed McCall to work on other pressing tasks, and as Mosser soon found out, it also isolated the governor from what would prove to be the first major tests of his pro-environment policies. But the public now knew what their new governor stood for. Due in part to McCall's advocacy, "preservation of the outdoors [became] second only to state and local government financing as a concern to Oregonians." When the *Capital Journal* asked in a newspaper editorial "Who Protects the Outdoors?" the only answer it could offer was Tom McCall.[87]

In the short span of five years Tom McCall moved from reporter to secretary of state to governor on a platform of environmental concern. Once in office he continued to employ the reporter's keen sense of the news industry to maintain public interest in the cause, working in the background to ensure steady progress toward his goals while taking on high-profile tasks like promoting the Willamette greenway and strength-ening the State Sanitary Authority to keep these issues in the papers and on television news reports. His rhetorical emphasis on the "livability" of Oregon, the language of crisis, and the implication that residents had a duty to preserve their natural heritage as a legacy for future generations framed debates over environmental quality in a new way—no longer would economic impact be acceptable as the sole factor in either politics or policy.

"Without a doubt," McCall told a Salem luncheon audience in May 1967, "Oregon's most precious resource is its livability. We must preserve it—we must enhance it—by drawing the line on those who would defile our environment."[88]

McCall's approach was even adopted by industry. A full-page newspaper ad taken out by Pacific Northwest Bell in 1967 warning about the impacts of unplanned growth overtly adopted his language. Compared to conditions in other states, the copy read, "We have the livability. That's the precious commodity. Livability. We believe we can have new prosperity and still enjoy our livability if we plan it now. . . . This is our country. Good country. And we want to keep it that way."[89] Correcting the mistakes of the past and planning for future growth in Oregon were political issues that could no longer be ignored by politicians or industry; Tom McCall and Bob Straub both had seen to that from the early days of the 1966 gubernatorial campaign, and as governor McCall carried his pledge into office. Before his first term was completed, the Willamette River became a model for the rest of the nation—an example of "how to deal with extreme levels of pollution from sewage and industrial wastes" resulting from unchecked development.[90] While that would not be the final word on Willamette River water quality—the issue would arise repeatedly over the following half century—it was good enough to merit a declaration of victory at the time.[91]

Despite this focus on future growth and livability, in the late spring of 1967 one environmental issue rose above all others to consume the immediate attention of Oregonians: the traditionally public status of the hundreds of miles of beaches along the Pacific coast was being challenged by developers who were considering building private resorts that would close off access to the sand, much as their predecessors had done in California and other coastal states. To Tom McCall this represented "one of the most critical conservation questions ever faced by a governor" and a very real threat to a "great birthright of our people" that could not stand.[92] It would be his response to the beach crisis, more than any other action during his first year in office, that would cement McCall's reputation as the man "who protects the outdoors" and who helped establish the state's reputation as a national leader in environmental policy aimed at preserving quality of life—or "livability," as it was quickly becoming known in Oregon.

Chapter 4
The People's Beaches

> All Oregonians should be deeply disturbed over the fact that we well
> may lose our rights to freely use the beaches of our Oregon coast.
> —Ancil Payne, KGW-TV8 editorial, May 10, 1967

In his 1967 inaugural address, Governor Tom McCall promised Oregonians
an administration that would stand for quality of life and offered a legislative agenda that would, in his words, "further dramatize the significance of
that issue."[1] High among the legislative priorities he mentioned that morning was the need to pass a bill to ensure continued public access to the
state's beaches. This may have come as a surprise to some in the audience
for, unlike the Willamette River cleanup, the subject of beach ownership
had not drawn much attention over the previous decade. But while conservationists were preoccupied with pollution and growth-related issues
inland, a crisis of an altogether different nature was developing along the
coast, one rooted in law rather than ecology. Since 1913 Oregonians had
believed their traditional right of access to the Pacific coast was protected
by state law, policy they credited to Governor Oswald West, a progressive
Democrat who served a single term in office, 1911–15. By the mid-1960s
some state officials were growing concerned that the beach law was seriously flawed and that it was merely tradition, rather than a strong legal
footing, that protected public access. Tom McCall, who like most other
Oregonians regarded access to the state's beaches as a birthright, wanted
to see that tradition codified by the legislature and permanent protections
established.

In July 1966, while still serving as secretary of state, McCall learned
from concerned citizens that a motel owner at Cannon Beach, on the central coast, had erected a fence across the sand and posted signs reading
"Surfsand Guests Only Please."[2] As governor he later realized that fence

had been the first shot fired in a war for control of Oregon's beaches, and he understood that his own political fate rested on the successful resolution of a crisis most of his constituents did not even know existed on inauguration day. Within a matter of months, beach access "exploded into the hottest issue of the 1967 legislature," and McCall quickly defined himself as the chief defender of the "Oregon way of life," promoting quality of life for all citizens over the selfish interests of the few in a style that would come to define his administration.[3]

Of course, the tradition of open use of the ocean beaches of the Pacific Northwest was deeply rooted in history and culture. When the first European explorers reached the northwest coast of North America they encountered substantial Native settlements near the ocean shores. The common practice of the ceremonial potlatch, during which gifts were given as a demonstration of wealth and power, reflected the culture of abundance that had been built around the bounty of the sea and coastal forests. Trade between bands was extensive and relied upon a network of inland trails and open beaches as travel routes.[4] The journals of the Lewis and Clark expedition include observations of these coastal trails and the various uses made of the beaches by the Native Americans in the vicinity of Fort Clatsop, where the Corps of Discovery wintered in 1805–06.[5] As white settlers moved into the region, they typically adopted existing trails as the basis of their own transportation networks; the small, isolated communities established along the coast often had nothing more than foot trails and the beach sands for north-south travel until the late nineteenth century, well after roads had been established for east-west commerce with inland settlements.[6] When railroads reached the coast in the 1880s they brought tourists from the Willamette Valley to enjoy the beaches, which in some places were attracting large summer crowds by the turn of the century. By that point, Oregonians were growing accustomed to public beach access and generally believed the sands to be common property, a position not without some legal basis.

Upon Oregon's entry into the union in 1859, Congress granted the new state control over navigable waters within its borders, and, under the traditions of English common law, title to tidelands along the ocean shore and adjacent estuaries was assumed to accompany that grant. These lands were treated as any other state-owned lands in the nineteenth century, that is, they were offered for sale to the public by the State Land Board

Fig. 14. Governor
Oswald West campaign
portrait, c. 1910 (Oregon
Historical Society Photo
Collection, OrHi 642)

beginning in 1874. By the turn of the century approximately twenty-three
miles of tidelands had been transferred into private hands. The growing
popularity of the coast as a recreational destination and the continuing
use of the beaches as transportation routes, however, led the legislature in
1899 to set aside a thirty-mile stretch of the beach from the Columbia River
south "as a public highway . . . forever open as such."[7] Traditions of public
access to waterways inherited from Europe, stretching back to the Greco-
Roman concept of public trust and including Sweden's *allemansrätt,* or "all
man's right," undergirded the common assumption that while individuals
could own the land adjacent to the ocean, they could not prevent others
from using or accessing the sandy beach. In the United States a complex
legal history developed around these issues, based ultimately around four
legal concepts: prescription, implied dedication, custom, and public trust.[8]
Oregon's political leaders would eventually turn to all four in effort to permanently secure legal public access to the Pacific's beaches.

When Oswald West was elected governor in 1910 the beaches were in
a state of limbo, public by tradition (and in part by law) but still subject to

sale. Running on a reform-oriented platform, West embodied the political spirit of the Progressive Era in his support of the "Oregon System" of initiative, referendum, and recall and through his record as an effective opponent of land fraud during his tenure as state land agent. During the 1911 legislative session he forced a reluctant Republican majority to bend to his will by vetoing sixty-three bills and promoting his own progressive agenda via the initiative process. During his term in office laws were passed to regulate working conditions, banking, stockbrokers, and public service corporations, while the causes of women's suffrage and prohibition were advanced through the initiative process.[9] Conservation of natural resources was also high on West's agenda, attracting national attention to Oregon and to West himself, who was described by former president Theodore Roosevelt, the country's most prominent conservationist, as "a man more intelligently alive to the beauty of nature and more keenly appreciative of how much this natural beauty should mean to civilized mankind than almost any other man I have ever met holding high political position."[10]

Oswald West's experience as state land agent and his sympathy for the publicly oriented philosophy of the early conservation movement led him to fear Oregon's beaches would someday fall into private hands, thus preventing free public access to popular recreation areas, an eventuality that had already come to pass along much of the eastern coast of the United States. In an attempt to prevent the future sale of tidelands owned by the state, he presented to the legislature a short bill that declared the entire coast from the Columbia River to the California line a public highway. West backed his bill by promoting this "free highway" to the public, and the legislature "took the bait," amending the 1899 beach legislation to extend the beach protection from border to border.[11] The 1913 law described the new highway as reaching to the average high tide mark on the beach, a definition vague enough that by the time U.S. Highway 101 was completed along the coast in 1932 Oregonians had come to believe that they collectively owned the beaches along the entire coast. It had become part of their heritage, along with Mt. Hood, the Willamette River, and the vast forests of the Cascades.

During the 1930s the State Highway Commission and State Parks Engineer Samuel H. Boardman worked to expand the park system along the coast by buying up as much adjacent land as they could for new parks that would offer access to the public beaches.[12] Much of this expansion was funded by Oregon's pioneering gasoline tax, which had been established to support road building but could just as easily be used for parks, since they also fell under the jurisdiction of the Highway Commission. In the 1940s attempts were made to establish a management plan for the beaches, but the 1913 beach law had not elaborated on what activities were to be allowed on the new "highway" or how they could be managed. Growth along the coast had put pressure on the state to allow development of beach lands, and indeed much of the shore above the high tide line specified in the law had moved into private hands. In 1947 the legislature, responding to pressure from coastal interests, revised the "West law" to proclaim that ownership of the beaches was "vested in the state of Oregon" and declared them to be public highways but also permitted the removal of sand and rock from the beaches by private parties. This angered Oswald West, who felt the revised law threatened what was widely accepted as his legacy to future Oregonians and charged that such permits would lead to private ownership of the beaches.[13]

As individual cases arose on the coast in the following years, the matter remained in the public eye as competing interests sought to further protect or develop the beaches as they saw fit. Oregonians, one observer declared, had a unique resource in their public coastline, which stood in stark contrast to neighboring California's, where the "horrible example of private title to beach property" warned of the possibility of "unguided private promotion with its haphazard hodge-podge of honky-tonk[s], eyesores and misplaced roads rendering Oregon's beaches just like beaches everywhere else."[14] An effort was made in 1953 to legislate a sort of squatter's rights to tidal lands on which "permanent and substantial installations and improvements have been built or constructed at least ten years prior" by requiring the state to offer these lands for sale to the developer, but the bill was defeated.[15] Oregon's coast drew national attention later that year when *Holiday* magazine produced an entire issue on Oregon; not long after *Life*, prompted by the managing editor's proclamation that the state's beaches were the "most beautiful he had ever seen," sent photographer Eliot Elisofon to shoot a feature along the coast.[16] In 1957 the State Highway Commission asked legislators to consider turning control of the tidal lands over to the State Land Board, presumably to rid itself of an administrative headache, but once again Oswald West spoke out in defense of his vision, claiming that the Land Board's history tended toward disposing of public lands rather than stewarding them.[17] The proposal was rejected, and in the process it became clear that West had become permanently associated with the popularity of open beaches in the public eye, so much so that the legislature voted to celebrate him personally rather than modify the popular beach law that session. At the direction of the legislature, the eighty-five-year-old former governor was honored the following year with the installation of a bronze marker at Neahkahnie Mountain on the coast, which read, "If sight of sand and sight of sky and sea has given respite from your daily cares, then pause to thank Oswald West, former governor of Oregon (1911–1915). By his foresight, nearly 400 miles of the ocean shore was set aside for public use from the Columbia River on the north to the California border on the south. This marker is erected and dedicated by the grateful citizens of Oregon to commemorate this outstanding achievement in the conservation of natural resources."[18]

Oswald West's death in August 1960 deprived the state of its most vociferous defender of public beaches at the beginning of a decade that would see the biggest challenges yet to his legacy. Population and industrial growth in the Willamette Valley in the early 1960s, as well as a variety of out-of-state advertising programs, propelled an increasing interest in the beaches as tourist destinations, while the concomitant growth of coastal communities placed new pressures for commercial and residential development on adjacent areas. A portion of this new development was industrial as well, and the inevitable clash between competing uses for the beach arose quickly. In 1961 it took the form of a request by the International Paper Company for an easement across the beach to accommodate a waste pipeline for a new paper mill at Gardiner, near the Oregon Dunes. Responding to company requests for a speedy resolution, the state House passed a bill permitting the pipeline and also providing the State Land Board authority to grant similar easements in the future, or in the words of one critic, to "offer any section of Oregon's public beaches to any firm for commercial development."[19] The Senate quickly approved the bill, with the only dissenting vote coming from a legislator who feared granting this authority without oversight or means of review.[20] Representative Beulah Hand, a Democrat from the Portland area, called on voters to urge Governor Mark Hatfield to veto the bill, claiming it would threaten recreation values along the beaches in exchange for short-term economic boosts and could damage the expanding tourist industry in the process. Representative Hand also included the now mandatory reference to Oswald West in her plea to the public, but the bill was signed into law over her objections anyway.[21]

Demand for recreation also influenced state beach policy in the early 1960s. The 1962 *Oregon Outdoor Recreation* report, produced by the Parks and Recreation Division of the State Highway Commission, confirmed the need to provide additional public access points to the beaches as private development further eroded traditional routes between the highways and the publicly owned sands. Priority was placed on the acquisition of beach-front property for parking lots and new state parks, both of which could be developed for beach access. In 1964 the Parks and Recreation Division began a development program intended to offer access every three miles along the coast in order to "encourage public use of the beaches and prevent private owners from barring beach access."[22] The plan "to prevent losing the beaches to the public as has happened on the eastern seaboard" would ultimately evolve into a system of some eighty access points along 240 miles of "usable" beach, the remainder of the shore being cliff areas, at a cost of approximately $6 million in gas tax revenues.[23] The rising numbers of recreational users of the beaches diversified their activities as well; while beach-combing remained the most popular activity, new activities like surfing and dune-buggy racing attracted additional numbers to the coast, to the point that "a beach enthusiast of just a decade ago wouldn't know the place," according to some longtime visitors.[24] The growing interest in the beaches prompted the legislature to once again revisit the Oswald West law, amending it in 1965 to reclassify the beaches as public recreation areas rather than highways. The amendment also prohibited the sale of publicly owned beaches, with the exception of sales made under special provision of the legislature.[25]

Eventually concern rose among state officials, who determined that "the state's prime recreational area was in danger of exploitation by private interests," as there had already been "isolated incidents of private builders constructing fills onto the dry sand" of what were thought to be public beaches.[26] The event that finally triggered a rush to "emulate Os West" was a deceptively simple one. Bill Hay, the owner of the Surfsand Motel at Cannon Beach, decided in the summer of 1966 to fence off the dry sands in front of his property and declare the beach private. Local residents and tourists alike were taken aback by his action, for they had never seen a private beach on the Oregon coast and generally did not believe it permissible to prevent the public from using the beach—after all, that is what Oswald West had guaranteed them two generations previously. Or so they believed. Confronted with the fence, some visitors became irate and wrote to state authorities to complain, asking if it was indeed legal to block access to a "sandy beach which has been used by the general public for over fifty years."[27] The Highway Commission responded to these inquires by dispatching William G. Nokes to Cannon Beach to investigate the matter firsthand. Arriving on August 11, Nokes found the beach was in fact closed off over an area extending some forty paces across the sand from the north-south property lines of the motel toward the ocean, about half the distance to the surf line that morning. The "private" beach had been delineated by placing driftwood logs around its perimeter, marked with signs reading "Surfsand Guests Only Please."

Interviews with several local residents indicated that the motel was telling people the beach was private and asking intruders to leave, but in the words of a waitress at the Cannon Beach Restaurant and Lounge, "the signs were just a bluff and didn't mean the hotel owned the beach." The motel manager, though, had clearly been informed by Hay of the legal justification for the fence, as she explained to Nokes that "the beach belong[s] to the Highway Department but the frontage owners can claim up to the mean high tide line." In her opinion the Surfsand owned the dry sand beach and could close it to the public as it saw fit.[28] Another citizen wrote directly to Secretary of State Tom McCall, noting that he was "greatly disturbed by the situation," fearing that it "establishes a precedence which will lead to the eventual defacing of all Oregon beaches and the take-over by commercial enterprises which profit from the public use of the sandy areas of the beach." Tempers in Cannon Beach, he warned, were "presently running high among those who are aware of the situation."[29]

The Surfsand case confirmed a growing fear among state officials: under the terms of Oswald West's law it appeared that the state legally controlled only the beaches below the average high tide line—or what soon came to be known as the "wet sand beaches"—and that the dry sands between that point and the higher vegetation line commonly used for recreation lacked state protection. It soon became apparent there was a wide gap between what Oregonians thought of as a birthright and the true legal status of the state's beaches; nothing could be done to force the removal of the fence erected by the Surfsand's owner. The Highway Commission investigated Hay's claim to the beach and determined the real problem with West's beach law was that it did not clearly delineate "public beaches." The 1859 Admissions Act had given the state of Oregon title to "tidelands" along the coast but did not explain what that encompassed. The 1913 law defined the beach as going up to the "ordinary high tide" line, while the 1965 revisions naming the beach a "public recreation area" specifically stated that these public lands fell *below* the ordinary high tide line. None of these laws, however, explained what the ordinary high tide line was. Would it be calculated in summer? Winter? Over a period of years? The answer was important because tidal fluctuations meant that the ordinary high tide in some months ran quite close to the vegetation line; in others it could be a hundred yards or more down the beach.

The question of tidal demarcation lines was an important one. In Texas, the only other state to enjoy a tradition of full public access to the coastal beaches, a 1958 court challenge had legally redefined the "public" beach as extending from the line of vegetation to the mean high tide mark, rather than the traditional mean *low* tide mark. The decision effectively eliminated legal protection for public access to the wet sand part of the beaches along the Gulf Coast. In response, the Texas state legislature passed the Open Beaches Act in 1959, legally restoring the traditional mean low tide line as the seaward boundary of the public beaches. In Florida the state constitution reserves ownership of the beaches "below mean high water lines" to the state. There the courts had decided that access to those public parts of the sandy beach would be determined on an ad hoc basis to reflect customary use; thus public access was protected only where custom was documented and then only to the area below the high tide line.[30] This reflects reality in most of the coastal United States, where public access is generally piecemeal; in Florida access reflects patterns of historic "customary use" while in many states it is entirely dependent on formal easements granted or purchased in the public interest.[31] Oregon, however, would follow a different path in resolving the access question, drawing some inspiration from Texas but most importantly based on the broad perception that Oswald West had steered the state in the right direction decades before; Oregonians, it was believed, should have access to *all* the coast.

Bill Hay's 1966 property claims raised some basic questions about legal ownership as well, since titles were sometimes vague in defining seaward property lines and often did not explicitly include ownership of the dry sand. Even when they did, it was not clear if such deeds could legally trump decades of public access that may have established a right to ongoing use of private property. The situation prompted a study by the state Parks and Recreation Advisory Committee, which found that 42 percent of Oregon's beaches were included in private deeds extending to the high tide line, immediately raising the prospect of a costly effort to purchase land to ensure continued public access.[32] In the end, it was determined that a legislative remedy was the only possible solution and the committee set to work drafting a bill to be introduced early in the 1967 legislative session.

During January and February of that year a team of lawyers working for the Highway Department researched the beach issue and determined that the simplest approach to the problem would be to pass a new law defining who owned the dry sand beaches above the ordinary high tide line (below which the state already held clear title) and how the line of demarcation would be determined. At its heart, though, the fundamental purpose of the law would be to codify the tradition of public access to the beaches from the vegetation line to the water and to guarantee its future, as the public thought Oswald West had done in 1913. The initial draft of the bill was based on the Texas Open Beaches Act of 1959, a law that had been upheld by that state's supreme court based on the concept of "implied dedication." Simply put, implied dedication was similar to adverse possession in that if the public made use of the beaches over a long period of time without attempt by the adjacent property owners to stop them, a right to continued use would develop. Based on this legal theory a bill was drafted to recognize a right to recreational use of the beaches between the ordinary high tide line and the vegetation line along the entire coast. It also included a clause effectively prohibiting the state from releasing title to these lands in the future without a specific law authorizing the sale or transfer, thus eliminating the threat of easements for projects like International Paper's proposed waste pipeline at Gardiner. The draft was approved by the Parks Advisory Committee and the State Highway Commission in mid-February and forwarded to the legislature, where it was introduced by Sidney Bazett and Stanley Ouderkirk in the House and Anthony Yturri in the Senate.[33] Interestingly, all three of the original sponsors were Republicans, though only Ouderkirk, who was from Newport, represented a coastal district.

Although the general public paid little attention to the matter, the first hearing on HB 1601 before the House Committee on Highways on

March 7, 1967, attracted significant opposition from coastal residents and property rights advocates.[34] Proponents were well versed in the history of beach use, though, and made compelling arguments for the new law. Dave Talbot, speaking for the Highway Department, testified at the outset that the department supported the bill and indeed needed the legal basis it provided to continue its work in providing recreational access on the coast. Legislative history going as far back as the 1913 West bill manifested an intent to protect public access from the vegetation line to the water, he explained, thus protecting both the dry and wet sand beaches, but the 1965 revision of the beach law limited that protection to the wet sand area only. Addressing that concern was the primary purpose of the bill.[35]

Loren Stewart, the chairman of the State Parks and Recreation Advisory Committee, submitted written testimony that referred to the beaches as "Oregon's greatest recreational resource" and conveyed the committee's unanimous endorsement of the plan to cement tradition into law, but opponents of the bill greatly outnumbered the supporters at the first hearing. Their objections were based primarily, as one would expect, on concern over property rights. One real estate broker felt the bill would "allow the Parks Department to harass private individuals while acquiring property rights," while an attorney representing several oceanfront property owners pointed out that in some places along the coast there could be as much as a mile between the vegetation line and the high tide line, suggesting that in taking title to the dry sands the state would open itself to lawsuits under the Fifth Amendment.[36] Although news of the bill was received with "a tremendous wave of interest" on the coast, it received only minimal coverage in the press.[37] Portland's *Oregon Journal* editorialized in favor of the bill the following week, noting that while "strong opposition is developing among some property owners on the Oregon Coast . . . at stake is the people's right to play on the beaches in the manner that they have always done." While praising the "farsighted action of former Gov. Oswald West," it otherwise treated the bill as routine.[38]

At the bill's second hearing, on March 23, Loren Stewart appeared in person to reiterate the history of the beach law and once again suggested that fallout from the Surfsand incident would

jeopardize the public's rights and interests in the vast beach recreation resources and much of that area could be barred

to public use as it is in California. . . . If the Bill doesn't pass,
more people are going to put up no trespassing signs and build
structures on the dry sand area and a great recreational resource
will be gradually lost to the people of Oregon and the nation.
We have the finest beach recreation areas in the nation and the
Highway Commission . . . wants to keep it that way. In short this
bill maintains the status quo.[39]

There was clear disagreement among the witnesses on details of the status
quo. It was pointed out that many property deeds described lots as extending to "mean high water" and that in many cases the vegetation line was far
inland of that point. When asked if the bill "would allow present private
property owners to maintain ownership of their property as they know it
today," Stewart replied that they would retain ownership and that the public
would also retain its right to use the property—there would be no change
in title.[40] As did Stewart, other proponents of HB 1601 frequently cited
California as an example of what should not be allowed to occur in Oregon,
often noting that visitors to private beaches in that state were forced to pay
for what was free in Oregon and calling for the passage of the bill to prevent
such a future from developing in their state.[41]

Opposition once again came from oceanfront property owners and real
estate interests from the coast. Written testimony from Donn DeBernardi,
a Lincoln City developer, detailed his involvement in the construction of a
"million dollar motel" on the oceanfront and claimed the bill would "make
a playground out of our front yard and utterly destroy our property values."
He further noted that he had "a very serious erosion problem" caused by
"people walking up and down the banks and children digging in them," a
situation he felt would be exacerbated by passage of HB 1601.[42] Witnesses
and committee members argued back and forth on the topic for over two
hours but little was done to sway either side on the merits of the bill; developers and property owners feared losing the ability to determine what was
done with beachfront property, and public beach advocates feared traditional access would be lost.

Press coverage of the hearing was once again limited, with the *Salem
Capital Journal* noting Stewart's warning that "California developers are
eyeing Oregon's coast" and portraying the decision as a choice between
"no trespassing" signs and traditional public use, without explaining the

conflict over property rights.[43] Three days later the paper's editors wrote that while they would "zealously guard Oregon's state-owned beaches against the tiniest threat . . . the current threat doesn't get us too fussed up." No one had developed the beaches, they reasoned, because the rough surf of the Pacific prevented anything from staying on them for more than a few years, natural or man-made. That was why nobody had blocked Oswald West's beach law in 1913. The question of who owned the dry sand was one that "should be pinned down tightly in the law," but in their minds there was no immediate threat to public access.[44]

HB 1601 was on the agenda of four additional House Committee on Highways meetings in April but none of these hearings was as extensive as the two in March. At the April 6 meeting the committee revised the bill into a "statement of policy which preserves the status quo" in response to coastal critics and also struck the language defining the public property boundary at the vegetation line. The bill in this form did little more than attempt to bolster the legality of traditional beach uses and declare the preservation of any resulting implied easements to be in the public interest, but it was still controversial enough within the committee that efforts later in the month to forward the bill to the House with a favorable recommendation or to shunt it off to an interim committee both failed.[45] Representative Sidney Bazett, chairman of the committee and a staunch supporter of public beaches, became concerned that HB 1601 would die without a floor vote in the House, so the list of witnesses testifying at the May 2 meeting was packed with professors from the state's research institutions, many of them oceanographers and marine biologists, who could speak in support of the bill and might draw more attention from the press. These men all testified to the importance of the public beaches in their teaching and research and several related anecdotes that told of researchers or students who had been hampered by newly designated "private" beaches. Dr. Robert L. Bacon, a professor at the University of Oregon Medical School, told the committee that the apparent lack of public interest in HB 1601 was due to its being listed in the legislative calendar as "relating to public rights in land," a phrase he believed was "inadequate to convey the idea that the bill had anything to do with the shore" and thus explained why there had been fewer witnesses in favor of the bill at earlier hearings.[46] Dire forecasts in the newspapers of a future where "barbed wire fences will keep the public out of the area it has been using for years," making Oregon "just like the east coast" had finally begun to stir up public interest, but it was not yet enough to force passage of the bill.[47] The committee voted 5–3 against sending HB 1601 to the floor at that meeting, but Representative Bazett's effort to draw attention to the legislation paid off with increased coverage from the media and, most importantly, the outcome of the vote and a direct appeal from Robert Bacon convinced Tom McCall the time had come to join the battle.[48]

On May 4, two days after the last scheduled hearing on HB 1601, both Governor McCall and State Treasurer Bob Straub held press conferences in support of the bill. One newspaper account, while citing the recent appearance of "no trespassing" signs on the coast as evidence of declining public access to the beaches, noted that no further hearings were planned and implied that the bill was likely to die in committee.[49] McCall quickly penned a letter to Sidney Bazett in which he stated his support for the bill in language that would become typical of the governor's public positions on environmental issues:

> We cannot afford to ignore our responsibilities to the public of this state for protecting the dry sands from the encroachment of crass commercialism. . . . The bill has been misrepresented as a land grab by the state or usurpation of private property owners' inherent rights. Nothing could be further from the truth. Should the public have by long use developed some legal rights to the dry sand portions of the beach, the validity of such rights must obviously be determined in a court of law. . . . The bill merely authorizes the Highway Commission to protect for the public whatever rights may have evolved.[50]

This letter was of course leaked to the press (likely at McCall's order) and helped trigger a flood of media coverage on May 5 that propelled the beach legislation to the front pages of the state's newspapers almost literally overnight. "Beach Access Issue Mustn't Die" read one editorial, while another story exaggerated the tone of McCall's letter even further to state "McCall Slaps GOP's Tabling of Beach Bill." The news coverage suggested that the cause might already have been lost for the 1967 legislative session, often speaking of the bill in past tense and warning that the time to act was limited. "Free and convenient public use of as much as possible of the Oregon shoreline must be preserved promptly. The sad experience of other states shows that it can all too easily become too late" warned the *Oregon Journal*, in stark contrast to the *Capital Journal*'s declaration just a few weeks earlier that its editors were not "too fussed up" about the threat.[51]

Associated Press reporter Matt Kramer took a particular interest in the bill, writing articles that appeared in two papers on May 5 presenting the bill's defeat as a fait accompli and portraying McCall and Sidney Bazett in a struggle against intransigent legislators "who side with property owners in the public-private fight over Oregon beaches."[52] It was Kramer's headlines that awoke the public to the story and attached the moniker "Beach Bill" to HB 1601 permanently in their minds. Additional front-page stories by Kramer appeared over the weekend of May 6–7, explaining the issue to readers in some detail and reporting that Speaker of the House F. F. Montgomery planned to use his authority to get the bill out of committee and onto the floor. Positions on the bill were clearly attributed to individuals, with McCall quoted as stating the bill would only "designate a state agency to protect what we already have." Representative Paul Hanneman, offered as a counterexample, claimed that it would take private property without compensation despite the fact that "no other state in the nation has offered such a large proportion of its beach frontage for public use."[53] The opposition favored sending the Beach Bill to an interim study committee that would recommend action in the 1969 session if appropriate, but the public, once awakened, thought differently.

In the week following the May 2 House Committee on Highways meeting Representative Bazett's office was flooded with calls and letters from the public calling for passage of the Beach Bill, as was the governor's office. The impact of McCall's public statements and the expanded press coverage ensured that the issue would remain under public scrutiny and offered proponents the opportunity to stir up sentiment by proclaiming Oswald West's vision of public beaches in peril, which is exactly what they did, forcing legislators to work almost in a panic to craft a compromise bill. The result, in McCall's words, was that "every politician rode off wildly in every direction" to find a solution.[54] On Monday the eighth, House Democrats (abetted by two sympathetic Republicans) attempted to strip the Committee on Highways of its authority over the bill but failed; reports of their effort and related criticism of the committee's handling of the bill—one member of the committee told the press his colleagues had been "playing games" with it—further inflamed public sentiment.[55] Political reporters in Salem declared the Beach Bill "the hottest issue in the 1967 Oregon Legislature" and almost gleefully covered the struggle to force the bill out of committee, noting that there were likely adequate votes in the House to approve the measure and send it on to the Senate.[56] In Portland a group called Citizens to Save Oregon Beaches was established by Lawrence Bitte, who had first alerted McCall to the Surfsand situation in 1966, and threatened to take the Beach Bill to the public through the initiative process if the legislature failed to act in the current session.[57] Once an additional meeting of the House Committee on Highways was scheduled for Thursday the eleventh, pressure to pass the Beach Bill only increased.

One of the most effective efforts to stir up public support was an editorial commentary broadcast with the KGW-TV's evening news on May 9. Ancil Payne, the station's general manager, laid the threat out to viewers in simple terms.

All Oregonians should be deeply disturbed over the fact that we well may lose our rights to freely use the beaches of our Oregon coast. As every one of us who was born and schooled in Oregon know, in 1913 Governor Oswald West declared that the beaches belong to the people. . . . Now there's a real threat . . . that fences and barriers will bar you and your children from the present easy access to the water and clutter up and divide the beaches, ruining the magnificent view and penning up the people. . . . Private beach front owners are laying title to the beach right down to the wet high tide mark and are planning to fence it off for their own private use. This will happen unless the legislature takes positive action to prevent it.

Only an immediate response from the public, he felt, would save the bill.

There's a bill in the House Highway Committee which establishes state policy as being that the public has ownership to the vegetation line. . . . There is no room for compromise in this simple bill. . . . There's a real and present danger that our children will not enjoy the beaches during their lifetimes as we and our fathers have during the last half century. Do you want to save our beaches? You have but a few hours in which to act. Let your legislators know by letter, telephone, or telegram that you're angry about this and want House Bill 1601 passed with no compromise, no flimflam and no tricks.[58]

Much of the flood of calls and letters to Salem was later attributed to KGW's editorial stance. Meanwhile, various legislators responded to the "statewide uproar" by drafting new bills to address the problem, in particular by dealing with the sticky question of just how the dry sand beach was to be defined. It quickly became clear that a beach bill of some sort would make it to the House floor, given the level of public interest, but just how it would balance the competing demands of property owners and the public remained to be worked out.[59]

To keep pressure on the legislators, Bob Straub invited Lawrence Bitte's pro-beach group to the capitol to organize a march on the house committee's May 11 meeting. Some seventy-five people packed into Straub's office to hear him defend the Beach Bill against "a small group of commercial developers, mostly representing out-of-state financing, that are behind the efforts to defeat the legislation."[60] When a revised version of the bill sponsored by House Speaker Montgomery was given to the press that afternoon, public interest in the proceedings only increased. Montgomery's bill addressed the problem of defining the public beaches by demarcating them not at the vegetation line, as the original HB 1601 proposed, but at a compromise point two hundred feet above the mean high tide line, below which landowners would be prohibited from erecting structures or fences or otherwise blocking public access. It would also, of course, surrender any claim the state had to dry sands more than two hundred feet above the line, land that had been used for recreation by generations of Oregonians. Bob Straub pointedly called Montgomery's bill "the most scandalous giveaway of public rights this century in Oregon" and promised he would be the second person to sign an initiative petition to preserve access to all the dry sand area if the original bill did not pass—right behind Governor McCall, who had previously told reporters he would be the first in line.[61]

For the May 11 hearing Beach Bill proponents pulled out all the stops. The state's major newspapers once again announced to the public that the stakes were high and urged the legislature to take action. The *Oregon Statesman*, for example, editorialized the morning of the hearing that

the public good . . . requires that public access to the beaches, dry
and wet sands, be maintained. What might happen if the property
owners prevail in their attempt to cut off the public? The situation
along sections of the New England coast gives a clue. The private
property owner, in most cases, owns all the beach in front of
his property. The public is confined to the few publically-owned
beaches. Even there, not all the public can enjoy the beach. In
many instances, public parking lots are provided near the beaches.
When these are filled with cars, all other members of the public are
turned away.[62]

Bob Straub appeared at the hearing in person to testify, while McCall sent
aide Ed Branchfield in his place to deliver a written statement. Speaker
Montgomery's proposed amendment was introduced in his place by
Representative Lee Johnson, who claimed that the original HB 1601 was
unconstitutional in that it amounted to an uncompensated taking of private
property.[63] Straub's prepared testimony countered this position, claiming
that some Beach Bill opponents were "using it as a smoke screen to divert
attention from their real intention, which is to seize important sections of
the beach for commercial exposition. To them I say: 'You won't get away
with it.'" Oregonians all knew the beaches were public, he stated, but when
"shockingly faced with the fact of fences on the beaches and 'KEEP OUT'
signs being posted" it became clear that action was needed to preserve the
"precious heritage of open beaches" against "a take-over by private interests." Passing HB 1601 in its original form, he felt, would ensure future
public access to the dry sand beaches, even if it did rely on the troublesome
"vegetation line" in describing the boundary.[64]

A new twist was introduced, however, when Ed Branchfield revealed to
the committee that the governor's office had been working with a team of
experts from the Department of Oceanography at Oregon State University
to devise a scientific formula to define the property line along the coast.
McCall's intention was to eliminate any future debates over where the
line fell by basing the law on a consistent, scientifically determined definition that could not be questioned, as the phrase "ordinary high tide" had
been under the 1913 law. The idea had first been presented to McCall by
Kessler Cannon, the governor's assistant on natural resource issues, but it
was the former newsman who realized the proposal could be turned into a

Fig. 15. Governor Tom McCall and Representative Norm Howard approach stake marking high tide line, Cannon Beach, 1967 (Oregon Historical Society Photo Collection, Kessler Cannon OL 640, Fol.3)

provocative bit of political theater in support of the Beach Bill. To that end, McCall announced he would personally visit five beaches on the coast on Saturday, May 13, along with Dr. Fred Burgess of Oregon State University's Department of Civil Engineering and other scientists to test the formula the team had devised.[65] Extensive testimony about the potential unconstitutionality of the original bill and the probable results of Speaker Montgomery's alternative was heard by the committee but no action was taken on either the engrossed version of HB 1601 or the proposed amendments that day.

The House Committee on Highways met again on Friday, May 12, over the objections of Chairman Bazett, who did not attend, but adjourned without taking action on the bill, deciding instead to allow McCall his day at the beach. As the governor anticipated, the announcement of his intention to visit the coast and demonstrate the new formula for determining the boundary of the public beaches had generated a great deal of public interest and was portrayed by the press as a valiant attempt to "break the deadlock" over the Beach Bill.[66] While most of the attention was focused on the practical application of the formula, which would eliminate the need for debate over the original bill's vegetation-line demarcation and the two-hundred-foot line proposed by Speaker Montgomery, McCall planned to capitalize on the publicity his visit would attract to make it impossible for legislators to accept any definition of the line but his own. Brent Walth, McCall's biographer, relates the story of what happened that Saturday morning like a scene from a movie:

> The morning of May 13th broke bright and clear on the Oregon
> coast. Beachcombers near Seaside walked along the shore,
> accompanied only by the sounds of gulls and waves. Suddenly,
> the air snapped as two helicopters rose over the mountains with
> the sun. The helicopters set down on the beach, the wind from
> their blades whipping the dry sands into a storm. Tom McCall
> jumped out first, followed by scientists, surveyors, and reporters.
> He marched up the beach, giving orders. Within minutes, the
> surveyors pounded stakes between the dry sands and the water.
> "The politicians and the lawyers have got this beach situation all
> fouled up," McCall told the reporters. "Now the scientists are here
> to straighten it out."[67]

Crediting his natural resources advisor with the idea of going to the scientists for a solution, McCall told the assembled reporters that the experts had determined that the vegetation line would be found at a consistent elevation above sea level along the entire coast. That elevation was determined to be sixteen feet above sea level, a line simple enough for the surveyors to determine with their instruments based on accepted calculations of sea level and one that would not vary along the hundreds of miles of coastline. At McCall's direction the team placed a series of stakes at points on the beach marking intervals two, four, and six feet above the average winter high tide line—the extreme limit of the wet sand beach.[68] Widely separated by swaths of dry sand, the three markers then became McCall's visual aids in declaring his position on the Beach Bill. Once they were in place, accord to Brent Walth, McCall "walked to the stake highest on the beach. This stake, he said, marks where the public ownership should start. Then he marched to the second stake at the edge of the dry sand. 'This is where the state's ownership now ends,' he said. Then he took several long strides toward the ocean to a spot near the waves. This, he said, is where the Republicans want the line."[69] McCall and his group surveyed the sixteen-foot line of demarcation at five different locations along the coast, each time in front of a crowd of onlookers and reporters.[70]

The highlight of the day came when the group arrived at Seaside and the helicopters disgorged the irate governor onto the beach next to Bill Hay's motel. Again, Walth relays the story: McCall "stomped toward the private beach now blocked off with a log barrier. . . . Motel guests sitting inside . . . looked up to see the governor of Oregon peering down at them, muttering in anger. 'He wasn't talking to anyone in particular, he was just mad as hell,' said Donald Jepsen, a United Press International reporter at the scene. 'He was just talking to himself, swearing like hell at Hay and the people inside this area.'"[71] The public spectacle of McCall's coastal visit, and especially the dramatic arrivals by helicopter, fueled the ever-increasing public demand for a solution to the conflict. Public-beach proponents capitalized on the attention as well; reporters interviewed picketers outside the Surfsand Motel that day as well, noting that even other beachfront property owners were opposed to privatization. "Boycott. Beaches Belong to the Public, Not Motel Owners" read one of their signs. Motel owner Hay was unrepentant, however, telling the *Oregonian* that "whether the bill passes or fails that barrier stays there."[72]

Members of the House Committee on Highways, which met on Friday, May 12, without Chairman Sidney Bazett to quietly agree to a compromise

Fig. 16. Governor Tom McCall contemplates a newly-marked "private beach," Cannon Beach, 1967 (*The Oregonian,* Oregon Historical Society Photo Collection, OrHi 52610)

amendment adopting Speaker Montgomery's two-hundred-foot line, quickly realized the abbreviated definition could not stand in the wake of McCall's grandstanding for the more encompassing sixteen-foot elevation line as the boundary of the public beaches.[73] On Monday the fifteenth Representative Bazett announced his acceptance of the McCall proposal to the press, while the governor released a statement noting that "the prime movers of the 'beach bill' ironed out the remaining points of conflict" over the weekend and crafted amendments that "mark today as an historic day for Oregon . . . fulfill[ing] the dream of former Governor Oswald West.[74] The morning papers on Tuesday declared "Leaders Agree on Beach Bill," explaining that compromise amendments including the sixteen-foot line and a zoning program that would prohibit all construction, removal, and fill on the beaches below that line would be introduced in the committee that afternoon and were expected to pass. The result of the weekend's efforts was, according to McCall, "a much better—and much stronger—bill than had originally been proposed."[75]

When the House Committee on Highways met Tuesday afternoon to consider the amendments, however, conflict once again arose between those who supported McCall's broad definition of the public beach and property rights supporters who favored a more restrictive definition. In an 8–3 vote the committee decided to cut four feet off McCall's defining elevation, producing a bill that would protect the beaches west of a line twelve feet above sea level. This would effectively exclude the popular driftwood area at the upper reach of the dry sand beaches from public use, thus protecting the interests of adjacent property owners and ensuring their ability to continue building on or otherwise alter the beaches in the area above that point. The impact of this change was illustrated by Robert J. Schultz, a civil engineering professor from Oregon State University, who explained that in Seaside the sixteen-foot line would yield a public beach of some 470 feet beyond the high tide, while a twelve-foot line would protect only 300 feet for public use.[76] Indeed, the details of the amendment set the line as twelve feet above sea level or three hundred feet inland, whichever was less, thus placing a maximum limit on the amount of public beach in areas of gradually sloping sands. In addition to reducing the amount of protected beach, excluding the driftwood area from the public beach effectively negated any impact the prohibitive zoning proposal would have, as it was generally impossible to build on the beach below the driftwood line, where winter storms would require annual fortification or rebuilding of even the most basic structures.

The response to the committee's action was somewhat predictable. The loss of the driftwood area from the bill's protections made headlines and resulted in news stories warning that the potential for fences appearing on the beaches still remained. Representative Bazett, one of three members who voted against the amendment, said the new line would "take away the playground area of the beach."[77] Lawrence Bitte, the founder of the Portland pro-beach group, announced that "since some members of the Highway Committee do not seem to care what the public wants, I think the only way we are going to resolve this critical issue is by an initiative to the people" to secure the sixteen-foot boundary line.[78] There were hints that some members of the committee would accept a fourteen-foot line as a compromise in a final hearing scheduled for May 18, though, so debate that afternoon focused on the application of the line in estuaries and similar low-lying areas and just what would be included if the sixteen-foot line were adopted. In the end, a solution was reached when opponents agreed to the sixteen-foot line with an exception for estuaries, where the line would be drawn at 5.7 feet above sea level plus 300 feet, to eliminate many low-lying areas but still provide some public area.[79] The agreement was further clarified by issuing a statement of legislative intent from the committee, which made it clear that the solution was predicated on a coastal survey to be completed by the State Highway Department and was, in essence, a bow to the pressure of public opinion and the time limits of the legislative session.

It is the intention of this committee to extend zoning only to those areas of the ocean beaches that are appropriate to public use and enjoyment. The major problem besetting this committee has been to determine a line which clearly delineates between the ocean beach area, in which the people of Oregon have a vital interest, and the area eastward. Your committee . . . is not satisfied with the zoning line we have adopted but believe that within the time limits of the legislative session that this is the only feasible solution. We believe that it is imperative that the State Highway Commission conduct a survey of the entire coast so that a more certain zoning line can be established.[80]

Undoubtedly the committee was responding to public pressure generated by the air of crisis permeating much of the media coverage. That an emergency clause was attached to the final bill to allow it to go into effect immediately after being signed by the governor, without the usual waiting period, is another sign of the urgency with which it was handled. Evidence of the outcry was voluminous; Representative Bazett told the press his office had received over thirty thousand letters and calls in support of the Beach Bill, and the governor's office logged many additional comments. As a result of this influx of support, the intense coverage the bill received from the media, and the dogged efforts of supporters, HB 1601 was sent to the floor with a "do pass" recommendation on a 6–1 vote (two members who typically split their votes on the Beach Bill were absent) at the conclusion of the May 18 hearing.[81]

The Beach Bill's passage from committee was heralded as a victory for the public interest that would yield a law that was "much broader and provides much more protection of public beach use than its original sponsors ever envisioned."[82] The zoning of the sands west of the sixteen-foot elevation line would secure virtually all the dry sands from construction, fill, or removal that threatened to block access to certain popular beaches, and ultimately the public would see a vested right in far more beach area than the 1913 law provided for—although arguably no more than Oswald West had originally intended to protect. Also included in the final bill was a provision requiring that the State Highway Department represent the public in fighting any attempts by private parties to restrict access to the beach; this would allow the state to bring suit against adjacent landowners who built fences or other structures blocking trails and other access points. In essence, opponents had lost virtually every argument they made in favor of property rights to the overriding demand that traditional public access be preserved. When the entire House voted on the bill on May 22 it passed by a commanding majority of 57–3, the only votes against the bill coming from three Republican legislators representing coastal districts. In an hour of floor debate most comments were directed in support of the bill, while others criticized the House Committee on Highways for failing to act on the measure more quickly. A few opponents accused the media of "creating hysteria among the public" over the issue, but in general legislators reflected the public opinion that the bill was necessary and at least appeared to welcome the opportunity to go on the record in its support.[83]

In a postvote commentary, the editors of the *Capital Journal* indicated that their earlier lack of concern over the issue had been firmly overridden by the public and it was time they "ate sandy crow." No one had realized, they pointed out, that Bill Hay's attempt to give his Surfsand Motel a competitive edge over other beachfront lodging would produce such an uproar. But "the ensuing beach hassle has been something to behold. And one result has been to remind all concerned just how highly Oregonians value the right to meander across the sand—every bit of it."[84] Not to be deterred, Bill Hay immediately began the process of driving pilings into the beach at his hotel, intent on challenging the bill once it was signed into law. "I fought for my rights in World War II," he told reporters, "and I don't see any reason to stop now. The constitutionality of this law will have to be determined."[85] It was the prevailing of calm heads that saved the beaches from the likes of Hay, in the eyes of one capitol-watcher, when "personality conflicts, partisan potshotting, and political pontifications were finally discarded in favor of a return to statesmanship" to produce a good bill in the House.[86] All that remained was to see the bill through the Senate and onto Governor McCall's desk.

HB 1601 was taken up by the Senate Judiciary Committee on May 26. Representative Sidney Bazett appeared before the committee to explain the process his own committee had followed with the bill, in part to avoid excessive duplication of testimony, and noted that they had to date received a total of thirty-two thousand contacts from citizens supporting the bill. Willis West, a lawyer and the nephew of Oswald West, then testified that he had personally proposed an amendment to the state constitution in 1962 that would protect the beaches but it had failed to be adopted. The problem as he saw it was a legal puzzle of ownership that could be addressed by amending HB 1601 to clearly read that the state was not relinquishing any rights in the bill. It was time once and for all, he said, to settle the question of title to beach property and that should be the ultimate intent of the legislation. He also advised that, in preparation for the certain legal challenges, the state attorney general begin to collect evidence such as old photographs to support claims of long-standing public use of the dry sand beaches. Ultimately the courts would decide who owned what, in his opinion, and the state should be prepared to defend the public interest.[87]

Opponents of the Beach Bill were heard as well, including representatives of beachfront property owners and others who claimed they had not been given an opportunity to speak at the House hearings. No action was taken on the bill that day, but it was clear that public pressure would propel the bill through the Senate as it had in the final week of House proceedings. Three more meetings were held before the bill was passed out of committee by a unanimous vote and sent to the full Senate for the final vote. On June 6 the full Senate passed the bill, once again unanimously, sending back to the House, where the revised version passed 36–20 the following day and was forwarded to Governor McCall for his signature. While opponents in the legislature branded the resulting law "unconstitutional" and even "a Communist manifesto" over their concerns for property rights, and legal challenges would continue for many years, the foundation for public beaches was secured by the passage of the Beach Bill (which thereafter took on capital letters to reflect its status in law and popular imagination) in the summer of 1967.[88]

The key role of the public in passing the Beach Bill suggested that Oregonians did indeed feel very protective of their tradition of beach access. The level of public interest certainly caught legislators off guard, a point that was frequently mentioned in the days following the final vote.

A lot of Oregon legislators—and a lot of fast buck artists who felt they had a neat swindle going—got a rude awakening a few weeks ago when popular indignation suddenly exploded. The public has been so quiescent and seemingly so indifferent to the plunder of the public domain in recent years that the boys in the back rooms felt they could get away with murder. As a matter of fact, the way things have been going of late, they might have gotten away with murder. But when they tried to take over the Oregon beaches, they got a kick in the pants that made the windows of the state capitol rattle. Never in recent years has there been such an outpouring of public wrath in Oregon. . . . Thank God for such "public hysteria!"[89]

When Tom McCall signed the Beach Bill a month later, he proclaimed it "one of the most far reaching measures of its kind enacted by any legislative body in the nation" and once again turned to Oswald West for a quote to link their efforts in time.[90] "In the administration of this God-given trust, a broad protective policy should be declared and maintained. No local selfish interest should be permitted, through politics or otherwise, to destroy or even impair this great birthright of our people," West had said of the beaches, and it was a charge that McCall was clearly proud to be carrying out.[91] Privately, he thanked others for their leadership in the effort, including Ancil Payne, general manager of KGW-TV, whose station, he said, "deserves to be singled out and commended for the crucial role it played in focusing the attention of the entire State of Oregon on the beach bill. No other factor in the battle for our beaches equaled the impact of your editorial statements. . . . They alerted Oregonians to the vital necessity to preserve our beaches—and generated an unprecedented blizzard of letters and telegrams from every quarter of the state. The people of Oregon—and generations yet unborn—owe an immense debt of gratitude to the staff and management of KGW-TV."[92]

What McCall may not have realized at that point was that the fight over the Beach Bill would become a model for his administration's approach to environmental issues, a combination of political wrangling and public relations expertise that made as much use of the governor's background as a reporter as his political skills. He knew that the public cared about the issue and could be stirred up to his advantage. The unequivocal responses he made, both publicly and privately, to those who professed concern for property rights are evidence of his commitment to preserving the public beach tradition regardless of partisan ideologies or the potential influence of money or power. McCall received hundreds of letters in opposition to the Beach Bill, most of them from beachfront property owners, and to all of these he replied with a standard letter stating that he supported both property rights and continued public access to the beaches for future generations—and that his primary interest was certainly on the side of public access.[93] To one of his more vociferous critics, a Republican political activist and insurance agent, he typed a personal addendum at the bottom of the form letter his staff sent out, revealing more of how his own reading of the Beach Bill debate influenced his advocacy: "Oh, man of little faith, it's your kind that has led the GOP away from Teddy Roosevelt and Gifford Pinchot—from a majority party to the 27% party. I saved the GOP from *disaster* on this one."[94]

In retrospect, the battle over the beaches can be seen as the first successfully coordinated effort to mobilize public opinion for the environment in Oregon in the 1960s. Unlike the case of the polluted Willamette River, a situation that was drawn out over several decades, the Beach Bill drew fervent attention from across the state and generated thousands of letters to public officials within the space of a few weeks. Even more so than the river that flowed past their homes, the tradition of public beaches was an integral part of the sense of place of many Oregonians. When that resource was threatened people were bound to respond. But it was the nature of the threat itself—or at least as it was portrayed by Tom McCall, Bob Straub, and other pro-beach advocates—that really set them off. The beaches represented a source of recreation that was accessible to anyone with the time to travel to the coast, and as such they were used by a representative cross-section of citizens that included rich and poor, working class and middle class, urban and rural residents alike. Those who threatened their access, however, were not portrayed as being like everyone else. Indeed, they were commonly characterized as outsiders, elites, or self-interested businessmen who cared little for tradition while looking to preserve their own right to use the beaches at the expense of everyone else. Motel owner Bill Hay made an ideal media villain because his actions so grossly offended Oregonians' idea of what the beaches were. Bob Straub repeatedly hinted that "out of state" funds were behind the anti–Beach Bill forces, a shorthand reference to the Californians who everyone understood had destroyed their own coast and were assumed to be looking for others to develop into more private homes, tacky shops, and "honky-tonk" motels.

The public responded to these threats as one might expect them to—by defending their traditions against perceived outsiders and selfish elites bent on revoking a privilege Oregonians considered a birthright. As one resident put it in a letter to Governor McCall,

> I was born in this state of Oregon as my mother before me also, and it has been with a great deal of pride I could travel the length and breadth of this country and "brag" about how we did things legislatively, tax wise and the scenic grandeur that was ours by right of birth. Now we have the last massive assault by money and people from other states that would have us conform to the modes and mores of California . . . it certainly doesn't seem right that I will be foreclosed from wandering th[e] beach as I have done all my life.[95]

The element of class conflict that appears in some of the letters and media coverage is somewhat misleading, though; many of the pro–Beach Bill forces were in fact wealthy individuals who owned beachfront property themselves, while some of the staunchest opponents were persons of limited means who lived on the coast and were bothered by the litter and noise associated with public access. The tradition of public beaches and the mythology that had grown up around Oswald West were widely accepted and cut across class lines. The real conflict fell instead between those who wanted to see the beaches remain just as they were and those who for various reasons foresaw a future in which they could be turned to economic advantage. In that respect, the conflict was no different than those over other resources in other places—a significant forest, a pristine lake, or even an historic building might just as well become the focus of public interest.

What was strikingly different about the case in Oregon is more apparent in hindsight. Yes, it demonstrated the power of the public to sway legislation in their favor, something that is far from uncommon in Oregon's political history. The public contributed critical cultural, political, and legal support to efforts that would ultimately lead to the preservation of "Oregon's coast [as] one of the most dramatic and undeveloped in the lower forty-eight states."[96] But the battle for the Beach Bill is more significant for what came after. In many ways it provided a model for a series of environmental disputes that carried into the next decade and led to the state developing a reputation as a national leader in the field of environmental regulation. It was the first significant victory of the conservation-oriented McCall administration and as such established a standard by which future conflicts would be managed and judged. It also demonstrated the potential for rallying the public around perceived quality-of-life issues, particularly if they could be linked to a sense of place—what it meant to be "Oregonian"—in the popular mind.

The cast of characters for future environmental conflicts was also established in the spring of 1967; the greedy developer, the destructive Californian, the tacky tourist, and the wealthy big shot all became stock characters in describing those who opposed progressive environmental legislation, regardless of the facts of the case. At stake was not only quality of life in the present, but the legacy left to future generations. "Beaches are for kids!" proclaimed advocates of a 1968 gas tax proposal intended to raise funds to purchase additional public access sites along the coast; Bob Straub helped lead that effort and later cited "thinking of future generations" among his chief qualifications for higher office.[97] As the twin

Fig. 17. Children rally
in support of Ballot
Measure 6 to fund public
beach access, Portland,
1968 (*The Oregonian*,
Oregon Historical
Society Photo Collection,
OrHi 534)

pressures of population growth and industrial expansion mounted in the
Pacific Northwest, the potential for future conflict grew apace. But unlike
the situation in 1959, when Richard Neuberger struggled in vain to convince people of an indistinct but approaching threat, in 1967 people were
beginning to see the products of change in the rivers, forests, and cities
around them. Drawing a literal line in the sand over property rights was
simply the first step taken toward placing limits on what society in general
thought of as progress.

A decade after the Beach Bill was signed into law—and after it survived
a series of legal and political challenges—the Oregon Parks and Recreation
Branch published a history of the public beaches that looked back on the
fight as a turning point for the state: "The state emerged from the experience with its first truly significant landmark environmental legislation. The
Beach Law focused public attention on the vincibility not only of Oregon's
beaches, but of her other resources—historic, agricultural, forests, rivers,
and air. The events thrust a relatively young and environmentally vulner-
able state through an emotionally and politically wrenching experience . . .
that intensified the need for compatible balances between conservation
and development."[98] As public awareness of that need grew, politicians
like Tom McCall found themselves able to mobilize public opinion in
support of actions deemed impossible only a few years before. Cleaning
up the Willamette River became a real possibility, but so did raising hard
questions about the limits of growth and the extent to which quality of life
should be subordinate to economic activity. Even the rights of individuals to

determine the use of private property would come to be questioned under what can only be described as a new environmental paradigm, one that emerged in the spring of 1967 with the Beach Bill and would be revised and expanded in the years that followed until it became part of a new Oregon tradition in its own right. Governor McCall, perhaps emboldened by the success of the Beach Bill, would take the lessons learned in the struggle and apply them as strategy in the years that followed to support his own vision of Oregon's future.

McCall's rhetorical approach to the conflict between development and livability took shape as a product of the Beach Bill debates. Going forward, he would become increasingly outspoken in his defense of the "Oregon way" against all others. The text of his address to a regional air pollution conference in the fall of 1967 captures McCall's emerging style and substance quite clearly.

The Pacific Northwest is much more fortunate than any other section of America. "Fortunate" because we have something that neither the East nor any other quarter of our nation has. . . I refer to *time*. The Northwest has the time to plan the orderly development of its burgeoning industry. If we want to, we can learn from the mistakes of the industrial titans of the East and to the south. We can learn valuable lessons from the smog of California . . . from the filthy Hudson River . . . and the black umbrella that strangled Pittsburg.

California stands as a sterling example of industrial development run wild. Our sun-tanned neighbors watched their industry grow at a cancerous pace . . . and now they're paying the penalty, in a myriad of ways. We can maintain our liveability [*sic*] and build our economy, but only if we are willing to give that extra measure of effort. . . . Unless we encourage others to take up arms and join us today, we're liable to wake up some morning, take a breath and find out that time has run out.[99]

Here McCall's passionate defense of livability and call for collective action stand out, as does his use of counterexamples from other states and the Californian boogeyman most prominently. It was in this role of "spokesman for the Oregon environment" that the governor would be most effective in office, though his behind-the-scenes political wrangling was often just as important. Indeed, in a 1968 press release listing his administration's "accomplishments in conservation" the Beach Bill was ranked ninth of twenty-one items, and then noted only that McCall "provided leadership" in the legislature and in "securing the technical assistance of Oceanographers and Oregon State University which broke the logjam on the bill."[100]

As Tom McCall settled into the role of governor, rather than reporter, his ability to connect with citizens through appeals to their love of Oregon's environment proved to be a powerful weapon against a wide range of opponents. First industrial polluters, then "Californian developers" drew his ire. Before his first term in office was over, however, McCall would attract national attention to Oregon once again by declaring war on an entire industry—and calling his own constituents out for their behavior along the state's highways. Billboards, bottles, and the blight of roadside litter became his next target, and with their governor at the helm Oregonians would lead the country into a debate over consumption and individual responsibility. Environmental decline was ultimately everyone's fault; to stop it Americans would have to change their ways. Livability, in that context, would come to incorporate aesthetics as well as natural resources, and regular citizens would be called upon to do their part in its preservation.

Chapter 5
Billboards, Bottles, and Blight

> Oregon, a most beautiful state, had much to lose to pollution—and was
> losing it. Oregon got tough. The first five years of the cleanup roused
> much resistance, triggered some riots. Let's see if it was worth it.
> —Paul Harvey, 1972

Soon after *Silent Spring* awakened Americans to the threat of chemical toxins in their communities in 1962, Rachel Carson was joined by a chorus of
others who shared her fear for the future. Scientists warned the public that
pollution was making it unhealthy to breathe in major cities or to drink the
water in small towns. Wilderness was being lost to development and the
American bald eagle was approaching the brink of extinction. Cold War
tensions were high in the wake of the Cuban Missile Crisis, driving concern over the possibility of atomic warfare. Meanwhile, global population
growth threatened the very future of the planet, at least according to Paul
and Anne Ehrlich's *The Population Bomb*. By the end of the decade, attendees at the American Newspaper Publishers Association convention ranked
the environment as the "big story" of 1970, trumping the war in Vietnam,
the civil rights movement, and Vice President Spiro Agnew's attacks on the
press. "Everybody is against pollution now," one publisher opined, "instead
of sin."[1] The sense of crisis that characterized national environmental
discourse in the 1960s contributed to the urgency surrounding Oregon's
Willamette River cleanup and the beach protection battle of 1967, both of
which drew on public concern over basic needs like clean water and opportunities for recreation to garner public support for government action.

But as Stewart Udall warned in *The Quiet Crisis* (1963), some postwar environmental worries were the result of affluence instead of industry,
problems that could be traced not to a single chemical, polluter, or ill-
formed public policy but rather to the lifestyles promoted by commercial

and social standards increasingly directed toward consumption and convenience rather than need. These problems were pervasive and could not be addressed by simply banning a chemical or assembling a panel of experts to devise a new policy but instead would require creative leadership to promote change in public attitudes toward the environment. Udall worried that the consumer appetite for convenience would lead to complete erosion of aesthetic standards, particularly along public roadways and on public lands, as continued economic growth became the only standard that mattered to Americans.

> Most state and local governments [in the 1950s] faced so many
> growth problems that they had little time for foresight in planning
> their over-all environment. It was a sad fact, also, that the men,
> women, and children of America the Beautiful became the litter
> champions of the world. . . . Aided by industries that produce an
> incredible array of boxes, bottles, cans, gadgets, gewgaws, and
> a thousand varieties of paper products, our landscape litter has
> reached such proportions that in another generation a trash pile or
> piece of junk will be within a stone's throw of any person standing
> anywhere on the American land mass.[2]

A byproduct of the emerging disposable society, litter consequently became a central focus for a segment of the nascent environmental movement, concurrently with the pollution scare triggered by Rachel Carson's pesticide exposé. The challenge to those concerned about aesthetic issues like litter was to capitalize on the attention generated by chemical, air, and water pollution to mobilize public support for their livability concerns, for while environmental toxins were a growing health worry to many Americans, roadside trash was not. The expansion of the conservation agenda to include such quality-of-life issues represented an important departure from the traditional focus on wilderness and public lands, while also extending the umbrella of potential supporters to include those not directly exposed to the kinds of industrial or urban pollution that made headlines on a regular basis. As Udall noted, the litter problem was apparent everywhere and offered a common basis for worry over declining livability nationwide.

Analogous to the problem of roadside trash, and more insidious in the minds of some critics, was the visual intrusion of commercial advertising along highways. In the absence of regulation billboards had proliferated across the nation in the postwar years, leading poet Ogden Nash to reflect in his 1945 poem "Song of the Open Road" on the logical extension of this sort of progress:

I think that I shall never see
A billboard lovely as a tree.
Perhaps, unless the billboards fall
I'll never see a tree at all.[3]

For aesthetic conservationists, billboards represented nothing less than commercial pollution, visual litter that distracted drivers and detracted from the experience of nature one might otherwise have while traveling a rural highway or that simply made urban driving unpleasant. Backed by a major industry, supported with the advertising budgets of the nation's largest corporations, and seen by many as examples of free expression, billboards came under fire regularly but opponents repeatedly failed to get control schemes through Congress or state legislatures. Billboard opposition was commonly led by women's associations like garden clubs, whose political access and impact was limited, leaving the billboard lobby free to dismiss their arguments as insubstantial or unworthy of serious political consideration.

The historic roots of billboard opposition in Oregon mirrored those in other states. As early as 1923 attempts were made to restrict outdoor advertising along Oregon's highways in favor of natural scenery, culminating in a modest bill that was accepted by Foster & Kleiser, the largest billboard concern in the region, but avidly opposed by a coalition of sign painters, billboard salesmen, and advertisers who felt themselves targets of the plan. Billboards of that era typically fell into two categories, the larger and more elaborate constructions erected by the major commercial advertisers (like Foster & Kleiser) and the smaller slap-dash ads painted on the sides of barns, nailed to fence posts, or otherwise tacked up along rights-of-way, often without the landowner's permission. It was this latter type of advertising that the bill sought to restrict, but the proposal failed to move beyond a "do pass" recommendation from the state House committee conducting the hearings. News coverage of the topic was exemplified by an editorial supporting "our friends the club women of Oregon" that appeared in the *Oregon Voter* in 1924, noting that women were "up in arms over the billboard evil along the state highways" but trusting they would make a distinction between "billboards—and billboards." The distinction referred to the differences between larger commercial signage and the tacky "Chew Mail Pouch" type of ads popping up along roads and highways across the state.[4]

As billboards proliferated in the late 1920s, so did the abuses that riled opponents: fake "danger" signs intended to slow travelers down long enough to turn them into customers, placards blocking views at railroad crossings, and numerous hot dog ads all added to "noisy displays" that were "antagonizing the aesthetic public."[5] Anger at the continued appearance of "poorly-painted boards, fence-smearing, barn disfigurement, and tawdry directions signs" in popular areas coalesced into the "roadside beautification" movement of the 1930s and was given an economic as well as aesthetic rationale by the president of the Oregon State Motor Association in 1931: "So far as the tourist is concerned, beautification of Oregon roads is an absolute necessity, to say nothing of the value to the home people who travel our highways. They themselves appreciate the beauty and cleanliness of the highways as much as anyone else. It is something of which they feel proud, and it naturally attracts the attention of the tourist coming into the state." Attracting that attention was an important factor in differentiating Oregon from other states in the minds of tourists, so restricting billboards could be presented as an economic necessity. If "by every bit of advertising that is put out on the roadside she is lowered to the class of the other states," then "how would she stand out . . . when there is intense competition for

Fig. 18. Roadside billboards lined highways across the Pacific Northwest, 1929 (*The Oregonian*, Oregon Historical Society Photo Collection, OrHi 9954)

the tourist dollar?"[6] A direct link between aesthetic conservation and tourism was logical to those seeking to promote economic development and livability in the prewar years, though it was a marriage that would not last through the 1960s.

In addition to regulation, alternative remedies like voluntary zoning of the "billboard evil" were proposed in Oregon in the 1930s, but the continued ineffectiveness of such industry-backed measures led to an attempt in 1941 to ban virtually all billboards placed more than twenty-five feet from the place of business they advertised. That bill (cosponsored by then–state representative Richard Neuberger) failed by a vote of 51–7, however, leaving the situation unchanged.[7] A decade later a proposal to remove billboards within five hundred feet of roadways was considered by the state Senate, including a novel provision that would authorize any citizen to remove an offending billboard after a two-year waiting period had expired. Despite enthusiastic support from the Oregon Roadside Council, which endorsed the approach of limiting "irrelevant" signs in part to preserve scenic views, this plan too failed to pass the legislature.[8] Some minor reforms were passed by the 1955 legislature, including a ban on posting signs without the permission of the landowner, but other attempts to address the issue at the state level were regularly defeated by industry opponents and a widespread lack of interest among politicians, despite growing popular support for new restrictions on roadside advertising of all kinds.

It was not until the issue jumped to the national stage with the passage of the National Defense and Interstate Highway Act of 1956 that hope for major progress on the billboard issue appeared. When Senator Richard Neuberger introduced a bill to tightly restrict billboards along the new highway system in 1957, he derided the industry for suggesting that people would prefer to "look at billboards advertising whisky, cigarettes or gasoline than at lakes, trees or mountains as [they] drive along the highways."[9] Despite significant support in the Senate, the *New York Times* suggested there was "little evidence of great interest in the billboard controversy among the public as a whole" that year.[10] When federal billboard legislation was finally passed in 1958, it was in a dramatically weakened form due to intense lobbying from the advertising industry and congressional disinterest in what was often seen as a women's issue by male politicians.

Aesthetic arguments against billboards and claims that scenic roadways provided "peace of mind" were easily countered by industry claims that motorists needed information and might welcome the occasional distraction from the monotony of highway travel. Consequently, the only substantial provision of the final bill was the promise of a 0.5 percent bonus on federal interstate highway construction appropriations to states that controlled billboards themselves.[11] This led the Oregon state legislature to consider a plan designating billboard-free scenic highway corridors that would include the entire lengths of the two newly designated interstate highways, but this attempt at regulation was also defeated. In both the federal and state cases, efforts to pass substantive billboard restrictions met with political and legal opposition, the latter strengthened by a history of court decisions limiting the scope of billboard-regulation laws to such requirements as licensing or permitting the companies that erected them or restricting size and location. There was little in the case law to suggest that an all-out ban would survive the legal challenge that was certain to follow the passage of any wide-ranging antibillboard legislation.[12]

Although Richard Neuberger told the press late in 1958 that he hoped Oregon would "take the lead in showing what a really good state program . . . should be . . . to make possible the complete elimination of all conventional, full-sized billboards along limited access highways," the weakness of the federal highway act and the power of the advertising lobby in Oregon prevented his vision from becoming reality.[13] Antibillboard forces, frustrated with lawmakers, resorted to an initiative petition in 1960 to achieve what the legislature could not. Sponsored by the Oregon State Grange, the Oregon Federation of Garden Clubs, the Oregon State Motor Association, the Izaak Walton League, the Oregon Association of Nurserymen, and other grassroots organizations, the petition sought to secure the 0.5 percent federal bonus by prohibiting all roadside advertising within 660 feet of the state's freeways and to "provide for public safety and more enjoyment of travel, attract visitors to [the] state by preserving the state's natural beauty, and . . . insure that necessary public information be presented effectively."[14] The industry's pledge to police itself had not significantly improved the sign problem, and the editors of at least one major newspaper felt there was little doubt that the petition would succeed, recalling that there may have been "some pretty decent pastoral scenery behind the billboard walls lining the Salem-Portland freeway" at one time.[15] Perhaps amused by their urban counterparts, the wags at the Prineville-based *Central Oregonian* suggested that drivers crossing the "monotonous" landscapes east of the

Cascades needed occasional diversions and that if billboards were to be banned, "farmers farming hillsides adjacent to highways could be paid to sow different crops spelling out an advertising message. Flowers in season would lend a more esthetic tone to hillside commercial messages, and provide a colorful compromise."[16]

As the petition drive heated up, proponents warned the public that the billboard industry and its allies would not take the threat lying down. "There will be violent opposition to this measure from the billboard interests, often coming through devious channels, as there has been all over the country when effort has been made to protect the public highways from the intrusion of needless and distracting ads" proclaimed the *Oregon Grange Bulletin*.[17] To combat this opposition the Highway Protection Committee, a group formed to back the initiative, named popular former governor and newspaper editor Charles A. Sprague honorary vice chairman of the effort.[18] By May 1960 the committee had gathered over half of the 33,712 signatures needed to place the measure on the ballot, while supporters predicted victory due to "a great backlog of resentment at the abuse of our state's beautiful highways by the billboards advertisers" and the realization that "controlling billboard advertising on our highways would be a real boon to the tourist business."[19] Two months later the drive had netted over forty thousand signatures in total, evidence of widespread support for what would become Ballot Measure 15.[20] But the opposition had yet to rally to the defense of billboards.

As the November vote approached, the billboard initiative looked to be the only controversial one among fifteen that would appear on the ballot. Industry supporters organized behind a Committee on Highway Regulation and pulled out all the stops in an effort to convince the public that restricting billboards was a bad idea. They attacked the bill as "confusing," claiming that the measure was "too technical" and that "the voters couldn't understand it," while also warning that eliminating roadside advertisements would adversely impact the tourist industry.[21] Frantic pleas to preserve jobs for sign painters and billboard erectors were issued, and ultimately even scare tactics were applied in the form of the suggestion that "women and children will be assaulted by desperadoes lurking behind informational signs the state would have to erect near city approaches" when the billboards came down.[22]

Antibillboard forces were bolstered by support from Governor Mark Hatfield, who declared that ground rules for billboards must be established before "our wonderful landscape [can] be enjoyed to the utmost along Oregon's scenic highways." Celebrities were lined up to support Measure 15 as well, including actress Ginger Rogers, who owned recreational property in Oregon and told reporters that she was "glad to work for Measure No.15 because the beautiful Oregon scenery is being taken over by the billboard industry."[23] On the Friday before the vote the *Oregon Statesman* editorialized once again in favor of the measure, remarking that the pro-billboard lobby had waged "one of the most costly campaigns ever conducted on a measure" and accusing them of distorting the truth about both the measure and the positive benefits of billboards to the traveling public. Industry claims that Measure 15 "would set Oregon's economy back 20 years" and "mean the loss of tens of millions of dollars" were labeled "ridiculous" by the editors, who further declared that "the tourist industry in this state depends on our scenery, not our signs."[24]

Despite widespread public support, the "intense, expensive and misleading campaign by billboard operators" was effective; Measure 15 was handily defeated at the polls on election day. The postmortem coverage noted that as the vote approached, leaders of the industry group, the Committee on Highway Regulation, had promised billboard opponents they would assist in drafting alternative legislation regulating roadside advertising. After its defeat industry representatives reiterated their commitment to improving existing laws (which were, of course, ineffective largely due to industry lobbying in earlier years), if only to head off a costly fight against a second ballot initiative.[25] The following spring the group made good on its word, compromising with opponents to produce two bills that would tighten regulations on roadside advertisements. The first was intended to take advantage of the 0.5 percent bonus offered by the federal government to states banning billboards along the newly established interstate highways, while the second would establish a seven-member Scenic Area Commission empowered to designate certain stretches of highway as scenic and forever billboard-free. Governor Hatfield, a supporter of Ballot Measure 15, signed both bills into law that May, ending the billboard battle for a time in Oregon.[26]

The restrictions adopted in Oregon in 1961 were, as elsewhere, only small steps toward the outright bans on billboards envisioned by activists who had been fighting against their proliferation for decades. While a few states (notably Alaska, Connecticut, Hawaii, Maine, and Vermont) had successfully passed stringent billboard restrictions, the industry lobby won many more battles nationally than it lost. Significantly, even the weak 1958 federal law failed to achieve its modest goals; the 0.5 percent of highway funds promised to states in exchange for local controls was so mired in red tape that it took five years for the first of these payments to be made. Worse, an amendment added by New Hampshire senator Norris Cotton, who felt it appropriate to restrict billboards along the new interstate highways but did not believe signs predating the Interstate Highway Act of 1956 should be removed, meant that as much as half the mileage of the new freeway system would be exempt. Everywhere existing rights-of-way were used or the interstate crossed an older highway (including almost all of Interstates 5 and 84 in Oregon) billboards remained unregulated.[27] Nebraska's Highway Department, frustrated by the slow pace of federal reform, took matters into its own hands and ordered a screen of poplar trees planted in the public right-of-way along sections of the interstate to block billboards from view, but this costly "green curtain" was little more than a novelty considering the thousands of miles and tens of thousands of billboards remaining along highways across the nation.[28] In places where the 660-foot prohibition was applied the industry simply created larger billboards, including the so-called jumbos that ran as large as five thousand square feet, over twice the size of the largest standard billboard used before the law took effect.[29]

It was in this context that Stewart Udall's condemnation of the appearance of the American landscape was delivered in 1963, at a time when the conservation movement was just beginning its evolution into a broader-based environmental movement that would capture public attention and command votes a decade later. As noted earlier, the emerging public concern for the "everyday environments" surrounding their homes and cities was in part a response to the negative impacts of affluence—the disposable consumer society—but it was also enabled by that same affluence. Postwar economic expansion and rising standards of living gave many Americans the freedom to be concerned about livability issues to a degree most had not experienced before. Once there was food on the table and two cars in the garage, it became easier to worry about the availability of parks and the appearance of public spaces in local communities. Quality of life became an increasingly significant factor in Americans' decisions about where to live, where to work, and where to raise the children of the baby boom. As suburbanization moved more middle- and working-class families out of decaying urban centers, they turned increasingly to outdoor recreation in their leisure time and became critics of the environment they had left behind in the cities, staunchly defending the "natural beauty" (however artificial it may have been) of their new suburban communities.[30] More time for leisure, more money for automobiles, and the growing institution of the mobile family vacation meant Americans were spending more time on the road, seeing more of the country, and visiting their national and state parks in ever-increasing numbers.

Concurrent with the rise in concern over quality of life—livability—was a growing critique of consumer culture in America. While *Silent Spring*, *The Quiet Crisis*, and *The Population Bomb* drove fears over environmental degradation and the use of natural resources, others criticized the "throwaway society" that developed around convenience products amid postwar affluence. Planned obsolescence and mass advertising, warned Vance Packard (in *The Hidden Persuaders* [1957], *The Status Seekers* [1959], and *The Waste Makers* [1960]), were required to drive economic growth but came at significant social cost in lost leisure time and quality of life. Consumers' rejection of the culture of consumption, based in part on feelings of unease at their role in the cycle of production for want rather than need, drove some to opt out of the consumer race and others to question its purpose. Thus the consumer protection movement developed alongside the environmental movement, simultaneous with an expansion of consumption that led inexorably to reduced livability through the use of natural resources and the production of waste.[31] The blighting impacts of "progress" were no longer necessarily taken as givens; critics of growth, advocates of appropriate technology, and anticonsumption "simple life" promoters alike helped transform the traditional conservation movement into the modern environmental movement, bringing quality-of-life issues to the forefront in the process.[32] These and other factors combined in the early 1960s to produce an audience more receptive to calls for aesthetic conservation than in previous decades, a situation those opposed to roadside advertisement would eventually turn to their advantage.

This emerging focus on quality of life and aesthetic conservation was evident at the highest levels of government. Lyndon Johnson's Great Society address, delivered May 22, 1964, established environmental protection as one of the three priorities of his ambitious reform agenda. "We have always prided ourselves on being not only America the strong and America the free, but America the beautiful," Johnson declared. "Today that beauty is in danger. The water we drink, the food we eat, the very air that we breathe, are threatened with pollution. Our parks are overcrowded, our seashores overburdened. Green fields and dense forests are disappearing. A few years ago we were greatly concerned about the 'Ugly American.' Today we must act to prevent an ugly America."[33] For billboard opponents the critical step toward preventing an ugly America was securing substantial regulation of roadside advertising, and in 1964 it seemed that even the president was interested in doing more for the environment than the traditional conservation agenda had previously included.

A timely and scathing critique of the impact of highways, billboards, and trash on the American landscape helped reenergize the antibillboard movement as well. Appearing first as an article in the *Saturday Evening Post* in 1963, the material collected for Peter Blake's *God's Own Junkyard: The Planned Deterioration of America's Landscape* (1964) offered compelling evidence that the process of uglification was already well underway. Blake pilloried the billboard industry for its impact on highway safety (he concluded that there were three times as many accidents per mile on highways lined with billboards) but reserved even more space for his condemnation of billboards' aesthetic impacts. The 1958 antibillboard bonus program was inadequate, he argued, not only because of its loopholes but because it applied only to the interstates—just forty-one thousand miles of the eight-hundred-thousand-mile federal road system—and not to state or county roads at all.[34] While American culture celebrated the open road, quite literally in the case of Jack Kerouac, Blake believed "the American highway [had] become the prime symbol of a nation frantically running around in circles and, in so doing, scattering debris in all directions of the compass."[35] The addition of nearly $1 billion worth of new billboards to those roads in the five years following the 1958 act surely signaled further action was needed, but how could concerned Americans overcome the industry that had defeated them so handily in the past?

The key turned out to be not the president but rather the First Lady. As was common practice with the wives of presidents in her era, Lady Bird Johnson expected (and was expected to) have a favorite issue to which her energies would be devoted when not needed in her capacity as hostess at the White House. She decided that "conservation and beautification" would become the foundation of her work and soon after the 1964 election began to promote a beautification agenda to her husband. In cooperation with Stewart Udall, she set out early in 1965 to remake the city of Washington, DC, into what Udall envisioned as "a 'garden city' whose floral displays and plantings would make it a handsome model for America."[36] Mrs. Johnson quickly assembled a group of influential women to develop a set of priorities intended to shine the spotlight of the Great Society into the darkest, dirtiest corners of the capital city, beginning with a program to clean up the monuments, memorials, and office buildings of official Washington and then expanding into urban renewal and public housing. But on her list of beautification projects the First Lady reserved the highest priority for the nation's highways, targeting the visual pollution of billboards and junkyards as environmental ills that affected all Americans and yet might be effectively corrected through government initiatives promoting natural beauty.

President Johnson offered his support for beautification in the 1965 State of the Union Address, in which he asked Americans to "make a massive effort to save the countryside and to establish as a green legacy for tomorrow, more large and small parks, more seashores and open space, than have been created during any other period in our history." Lady Bird's program of roadside improvement received special notice as the president called for "a new and substantial effort . . . to landscape highways to provide places of relaxation and recreation wherever our roads run."[37] Weeks later he delivered a second address on natural beauty in which he suggested specific areas for action in creating a "new conservation" that would include highway beautification. Soon after, in an interview published in *U.S. News and World Report*, the First Lady expressed some concern about taking on the billboard industry but believed that "public feeling is going to bring about regulation so that you don't have a solid diet of billboards on all the roads."[38]

Soon after Lady Bird Johnson, her staff, and her cadre of advisors began a well-organized effort to publicize a beautification agenda that would help shift the focus of conservation politics from remote wilderness areas to the nation's urban centers and highways. By the early spring of 1965 Lady Bird had already taken the role of First Lady well beyond the boundaries established by her predecessors, deciding to take a stand on beautification not only as a public advocate but as a private political actor as well, working directly with Congress and through the president to advance her agenda. She did this realizing she was setting a new precedent and carefully chose to focus her work on the two areas in which she felt her leadership could have the most positive impact: the beautification of the nation's cities and highways.[39]

The First Lady's beautification agenda was fully developed by the time the White House Conference on Natural Beauty convened in May 1965. Coordinated by Laurance Rockefeller, the conference brought some eight hundred conservation leaders, citizen activists, and government officials from across the nation together for meetings and panel discussions intended to frame goals for the Johnson administration's conservation agenda. At the meeting on billboard control Phillip Tocker, a lawyer for the Outdoor Advertising Association of America, offered a promise that the industry would work with the White House to restrict billboards to commercial and industrial areas voluntarily, but Oregon senator Maurine Neuberger explained that Congress to that point had "legislated piecemeal by offering a carrot instead of a stick to induce States to come into the billboard control orbit" and that it was time "to introduce a bill that has no more of this hanky panky." The general approach of those in attendance was captured in the remarks of J. Lewis Scott, who proclaimed, "Highway billboards constitute a menace to our life, liberty, happiness, and sight. They should be classed as sight blight or air pollution."[40] Ultimately the billboard control panel would recommend funding for scenic beauty amounting to 3 percent of each state's federal highway aid package, prohibition of all billboards within one thousand feet of both the new interstate system and the existing federal highways, and prohibition of all off-premises advertising in those same areas.[41]

On the final afternoon of the conference the president addressed the attendees, proclaiming that 1965 would "set new records in conservation in America" and that a new kind of conservation was needed to advance the agenda beyond the park and wilderness preservation of previous generations. "I believe in, and I fought all my life for, more national parks and rivers and forests and wilderness," Johnson stated. "But beauty cannot be a remote and just an occasional pleasure. We must bring it into the daily lives of all our people. Children, in the midst of cities, must know it as they grow.

Adults, in the midst of their work, must find it near. All of us, in the midst of increasing leisure, must draw strength from its presence. All of this must be true if we are to ever really have a Great Society." Toward the end of his remarks to the assembled guests, Johnson revealed that the very next day he would "send to Congress four new bills to help make our Nation's highways sources of pleasure and sources of recreation . . . [by requiring] the use of some of our highway funds for landscaping, beautification, scenic roads, and recreation along our road system" and by "eliminat[ing] outdoor advertising signs and junkyards from the sight of the interstate and primary highway system."[42] Certainly this was good news to the billboard opponents who had just recommended such legislation, but from the moment the conference ended they began to criticize the proposed highway beautification program. In his remarks about the bills being sent to Congress, Johnson had noted that the billboard regulations being offered would not apply in "areas of commercial and industrial use," a major concession to the billboard industry obtained by Phillip Tocker in the weeks preceding the conference. A secret deal had been reached before the panel on roadside control had even met, and this weakness would cost the plan the support of the very activists who had demanded such action for so long.[43]

Lady Bird Johnson campaigned tirelessly for the beautification legislation before Congress in 1965, and when it became evident that lawmakers were reluctant to offend the advertising industry forces providing them with free campaign billboards, the administration pulled out all the stops to secure passage of what was dubbed "Lady's Bill." That fall she participated in White House strategy sessions and directly lobbied for critical support for the bill in the House, activities that stretched the boundaries of the role of First Lady by extending her influence to new areas. The political pressure applied, both public and private, was essential, as there was limited support for billboard regulation on Capitol Hill; Senator Patrick McNamara, chairman of the Senate Committee on Public Works, which would hear the bill, remarked early on that he was "not bothered by billboards."[44] His position may in fact have reflected that of a majority of Americans, for despite the outcry for regulation from certain regions of the country there were many more that remained silent. Indeed, a study conducted in Missouri the following year found that only 40 percent of respondents felt "the beauty [lost] is worth more than the information" provided by advertising billboards along that state's highways.[45]

The bill reported out of the Senate ultimately included a clause requiring "just compensation" to billboard owners whose signs were removed, a critical handicap that would place a high price tag on removal and further invite the scorn of antibillboard organizations that felt the administration had sold them out. In a final push to get a bill approved by both houses before the fall recess the White House increased pressure on legislators, expending a great deal of political capital to win a bill—any bill—on beautification.[46] What ultimately emerged from the conference committee in mid-October was a bill that was at best imperfect, a product of effective lobbying by the larger commercial billboard companies at the expense of the smaller, rural advertisers, who would see the signs they erected in scenic areas removed while existing industrial and commercial corridors in urban areas received an exemption from the bill's restrictions.

Although the Highway Beautification Act of 1965 stated an intent to "protect the public investment in . . . highways, to promote the safety and recreational value of public travel, and to preserve natural beauty," antibillboard groups viewed the law as "a triumph for the billboard lobby, which engineered adoption of the compensation amendment. . . . Billboard removal has been impeded by the Highway Beautification Act instead of being assisted."[47] In practice they were correct; the compensation and the industrial and commercial zone exemptions made the law only marginally better than the 1958 bonus act, but it was all that could be wrung from a reluctant Congress. Lady Bird Johnson understood that the Highway Beautification Act was weak by any standard but accepted it as the best that could be passed that year. Despite its shortcomings the law did draw public attention to the matter and to the First Lady's broader beautification agenda, helping to set the stage for other environmental campaigns that followed as the public became increasingly willing to regulate activity and allocate tax dollars to restore or protect the nation's natural beauty.

Despite the limited impact of the Highway Beautification Act of 1965, Lady Bird Johnson's beautification program in general (and the public support it received) marked an important transition for the conservation movement. The passage of the Wilderness Act in 1964 was a triumph for traditional parks and wilderness conservation groups like the Sierra Club, the Wilderness Society, and the Izaak Walton League. In the years that followed such groups would either change the focus of their advocacy as quality-of-life issues took center stage in environmental politics or they would fade from the scene to be replaced by organizations more in tune with the public's interests. This was not an abrupt transition, but given the almost glacial pace with which the old guard moved it likely seemed that way to many participants. Regardless, by 1970 the majority of the traditional conservation organizations had embraced new environmental agendas, drawing in new supporters who were younger, more urban, and more likely to be female in the process.[48] Unlike the wilderness debates of the 1950s and 1960s, the new environmental movement was less about preservation of unique natural places than it was about cleaning up the more common spaces inhabited by most Americans. As such it reflected the broader engagement of Americans across class lines, for while the traditional wilderness agenda was driven significantly by those with the means to travel to and enjoy leisure time in wild places, the environmental movement would be embraced by a broader coalition of citizens concerned about quality-of-life issues often literally evident in their own backyards.

One image that came to characterize the public understanding of environmental issues in this era was the face of the Hollywood actor Iron Eyes Cody, who was featured in antilitter public service announcements sponsored by the nonprofit Keep America Beautiful beginning in 1971. In the soon to become iconic television and print campaign, Cody, an Italian American who typically portrayed "traditional" Native Americans and was adorned in stereotypical Plains Indian dress for the role, looked sadly upon an urban scene dominated by garbage and litter while he shed a silent tear. The television tag line was "People Start Pollution. People can stop it."[49] The message was far from subtle, employing what historian Shepard Krech III calls the "ecological Indian" to shame Americans into picking up after themselves, but it was very effective.[50] Beautification programs originating in Washington might have had some impact on roadside advertising, but as Cody's commercial suggested, it was the casual habit of throwing garbage out the windows of cars that more seriously degraded the quality of American highways. That interpretation was, of course, exactly what the Keep America Beautiful campaign intended; the sponsors of the "crying Indian" spot were in fact funded by the beverage container industry and wanted the blame for litter placed on individual behavior rather than their products. Litter would be defined as a social problem, not an environmental issue like other forms of pollution, if the industry had any say in the matter.

Ultimately the most innovative and effective attempt to deal with the problem of roadside litter would come not from Congress but from Oregon, where the tenacity of a single activist and the support of scores of concerned citizens met with the political ambitions of a governor determined not only to improve quality of life in his state but to make it a national leader in environmental legislation. At the time Oregon politicians were attempting to restrict billboards in 1961, state highway officials were simultaneously posting new signs of their own reading "Don't Litter Highways: $100 Penalty" in an attempt to reduce roadside litter. Although State Highway Engineer W. C. Williams felt Oregon's roads were "among the cleanest in the nation," many others felt they were a disgrace and in fact were growing worse day by day.[51] The Salem *Capital Journal* noted in 1964 that some stretches of highway were fine "until you round a bend and pass the many scatterings of civilization. Car bodies, tumbledown sheds, unpainted, jerry-built shacks with rusty oil tanks wired to their sides, piles of old car tires and a couple of decades of abandoned litter affront the eye." The problem was due in part, the editors speculated, to the fact that "most of us in Oregon are zero, one or two generations away from the hillbilly country of the lower Midwest or South, and we're slow to change slovenly habits."[52]

Whatever the root of the behavior, it was clear that the state's roadways were a mess, enough so to raise concern about the impression they would make on tourists, leading Governor Mark Hatfield to initiate a statewide campaign in 1964 encouraging Oregonians to voluntarily clean up roadside litter. A single cleanup program would prove inadequate as a solution to the problem, though; what was needed was a plan to stop litter at its source. As one observer noted a few years later, things in the "Land of Litter" would not easily be improved, because "many Oregonians make mass littering a habit" and they often would haul trash "out past the edge of town and dump it along the county roadsides."[53] This behavior could be prevented, some thought, by expanding garbage pickup service to include more homes. A bill was introduced in the state legislature in 1967 to ban private garbage dumps in an attempt to force citizens to use approved sanitary landfills, but even if it succeeded such a plan would likely reduce only the dumping of household garbage, which happened primarily in rural areas. The larger problem was along the busiest stretches of the state's road system, especially near the urban centers in the Willamette

Valley, where there was a larger concentration of habitual litterers who thought nothing of tossing their trash out the window of the car as they drove. The largest single component of this window-ejected waste stream was beverage containers: glass bottles and metal cans of drinks consumed in the car and then left to slowly accumulate along the nation's highways. As Americans became more convenience-oriented through the 1960s the percentage of beverage containers in roadside trash steadily increased, drawing attention from those who sought to improve the appearance of highways as well as those concerned about the impacts of litter.

The origins of the beverage container litter problem were much more recent than that of the billboards cluttering the nation's roadsides. Prior to World War II most beverage containers were of the returnable glass variety that generally carried a deposit and were picked up, washed, and reused until they were lost, broken, or worn out. The beer industry was the first to adopt the "disposable" metal can for widespread use in the postwar period; by 1958, 42 percent of the containers used for beer were of the nonreturnable metal variety. Soft drink producers were slower to adopt the cans (less than 2 percent of soft drinks were canned in 1958), in part due to the high acid content of their products and the deeply rooted traditions of the southern companies that dominated the market. But as the aluminum can became a viable option for soft drinks and beer, companies that made glass bottles felt threatened and introduced the "disposable" glass container as an alternative. Retailers preferred disposable containers, as they eliminated the need to sort and store returnables and their lower cost allowed producers to sell their products cheaper than competitors using glass returnables could manage. In fact, a returnable container had to be reused a minimum of eight times to break even with a disposable on a cost basis.[54]

Once the soft drink industry accepted the aluminum can as an alternative to bottles it was widely adopted, accounting for 13 percent of soft drink containers by 1968, while the disposable glass container accounted for another 9 percent of the national market. Simultaneously, Americans were dramatically increasing their consumption of soft drinks, with industry estimates rising from 10.9 gallons per capita in 1952 to 20.7 gallons in 1968. Beer consumption figures were relatively steady in this period, but as the malt beverage industry had adopted cans earlier, disposable beer containers had become a significant part of the waste stream by the early

1960s. By 1969, the President's Council on Environmental Quality estimated, from one to two billion disposable beverage containers (from a
total production of approximately forty-four billion) would end up along
the roadside as litter in the United States every year.[55]

In 1953 the Vermont legislature, in an attempt to prevent the expansion of disposable glass bottles and stem the rising tide of litter along the
state's highways, passed a law banning the sale of beer in nonreturnable
glass containers. Unfortunately, the ban coincided with the adoption of
metal cans by many beer distributors, so its restrictions served only to
accelerate the transition from bottles to cans in that market, with minimal
impact on the litter problem. Four years after the law's introduction a study
by the Vermont State Litter Commission concluded that the act had failed
to reduce litter and it was repealed in 1957.[56] A decade later a broader
ban on nonreturnable containers was debated in the province of British
Columbia, again with the primary goal of litter control. Coverage of those
efforts in Oregon newspapers in the summer of 1968 may have been overlooked by the vast majority of people concerned about the litter problem
there, but the story was noticed by a man named Richard Chambers, who
quickly decided that British Columbia had found the solution to the piles
of bottles and cans he had seen building up along the roadsides, trails, and
beaches of his state.

Like the famous wilderness advocate Bob Marshall a generation
before, Chambers was a man always willing to walk a bit farther to see
something new, wandering around Oregon on foot, sometimes for days
at a time. Unlike Marshall, however, he did something more than just
explore: he picked up litter along the way, sometimes bags full. "Litter
drove him wild," his daughter remembered. "He'd come back with these
bags and wave them and say 'Why do people have to do this?'" When
Chambers read of British Columbia's plan to reduce litter he immediately
took action, contacting state representative Paul Hanneman and convincing him quickly that Oregon needed a nonreturnable container ban of its
own.[57] Hanneman agreed to introduce a bill in the 1969 legislative session,
which was all Chambers needed to get started. From that day on he was a
one-man lobbying machine dedicated to passing what came to be called a
"bottle bill" to stem the primary source of litter he had observed during his
recreational walks.

Convinced by the data Chambers presented, Hanneman and two cosponsors drafted HB 1157 for the 1969 legislative session to do just what he suggested: stop the flood of bottles and cans at the source by prohibiting disposables. Their brief bill simply stated that "no person shall distribute, sell or offer for sale [soft drinks], beer or any other malt beverages in non-returnable containers."[58] The idea intrigued the *Oregon Statesman*, which expressed interest in the bill but pointed out that a ban on nonreturnable containers was possible "only if it would not pose an unacceptable burden on container makers and distributors." At the bill's initial hearing testimony was offered about the extent of the litter problem and the major role such containers played in it, but opposition from industry representatives led Hanneman to suggest a deposit system as an alternative to a ban, which the paper said "might allow young people to perform a salvage function for profit at no cost to the taxpayers. . . . [But] whether today's breed of youngsters will work for such small, tenuous remuneration is open to question. Perhaps today's volume of discards would make up for the small return per bottle."[59] Industry representatives doubted this was true, with the manager of a Portland bottle factory going so far as to say that he was "positive it would have no effect on the litter problem." "Products don't litter, people do," he told reporters, and added that people would continue to throw bottles away rather than return them for deposit due to the inconvenience involved.[60] Many of the state's traditional conservation organizations supported the bill, including the regional chapter of the Sierra Club, the Oregon Environmental Council, and local chapters of the Grange, among others.

By the end of the initial hearing Roger Martin, the chair of the House State and Federal Affairs Committee, had bowed to the pressure of the bottle lobby and expected the bill to die in committee. He was surprised when Paul Hanneman convinced another member to vote in favor of the bill, sending it to the floor on a 5–4 vote. There Martin both attacked the bill and requested that it be sent back to his committee for study, where he could presumably keep it tied up for the rest of the session. In a last-ditch effort to save the bill Hanneman called Tom McCall to solicit his support, hoping the governor would offer the same sort of Sturm und Drang he had employed to rescue the Beach Bill from legislative oblivion two years before. But McCall refused to back the bottle plan, as he had already privately committed his support to an antilittering campaign promoted by the bottling industry for the following year.[61] Soon after, the Bottle Bill was killed in a 33–27 vote on the House floor, disappointing Chambers and Hanneman and leading the *Oregon Statesman* to editorialize under the headline "Litter Growth Assured" in support of the new approach and against the only alternative litter plan passed that spring, an increase in the penalties for littering. "The House rejected a new method of 'treatment' of the 'litter disease,' a plan to require sale of beer and pop in nickel deposit containers," the editors wrote. "This would have offered a positive incentive to keep the state clean. At the end of another two years when the can and bottle level will be even higher on Oregon's beaches and riverbanks, perhaps the legislators will be willing to try an innovative approach instead of burrowing themselves deeper in one which has proved all over the nation that it won't work."[62]

Meanwhile, the *Oregon Journal* interpreted the debate over the bill as a sign that "increasing numbers of citizens, including legislators, are becoming fed up with the littering of our streams, lakes, ocean beaches and other recreational places" and saw some hope in the sudden willingness of the packaging industry to sponsor public education and cleanup projects to combat the problem.[63] But at the end of the year the Glass Container Manufacturers Institute, a national trade organization, announced a $7.5 million publicity campaign aimed at promoting no-deposit no-return bottles directly to consumers, "the largest single coordinated promotional effort ever undertaken on behalf of any consumer package," according to their notices. In response the *Oregon Statesman* revisited the Bottle Bill issue, recommending that "the all-out campaign to flood the country with no-return bottles should be met by [a] renewal of efforts to legally prohibit the sale of soft drinks and beer in such containers." Stopping potential litter at its source, it was argued, was "the only realistic way" to win the litter battle.[64]

Tom McCall's refusal to support the Bottle Bill in the spring of 1969 appeared to many observers to be at odds with his outspoken defense of the Beach Bill and the ongoing campaign to clean up the Willamette River. As related in his autobiography, the 1969 bill was "near approval" in the legislature when the bottling and brewing industry requested a delay to allow them to develop their own program to address the litter problem.[65] In July the governor attempted to launch his own antilitter campaign, revealed at a meeting with industry representatives, by proposing a diversion of tourism-promotion funding from the Highway Commission to support a "Keep Oregon Clean" initiative targeting "litter, vandalism and bad manners in our outdoors."[66] But interviews conducted by Brent Walth for his 1994 biography of McCall revealed the situation was more complex than that. As Paul Hanneman explained to Walth, McCall supported the Bottle Bill in concept but felt the timing was bad in 1969; he wanted to reintroduce the bill in the 1971 session, after the bottling industry had become complacent from promoting its own efforts to reduce litter. (There was also the possibility that McCall did not want Hanneman, who as a coastal representative had opposed the Beach Bill, to secure a victory on the Bottle Bill so quickly.) In fact, UPI reporter Don Jepson told Walth that McCall had fumed in the spring of 1969 that the high-profile debate would "blow the cover" off his plan.[67]

McCall may have expected the bottle issue to disappear quietly at the close of the 1969 legislative session, but news of the bottling industry's promotional plans angered legislators who had accepted the plea for time to create an industry-based litter reduction program as sincere. Within weeks of the December announcement Representative Gordon McPherson, from the coastal town of Waldport, told reporters the legislature had been "double-crossed" by the bottlers, while several newspapers editorialized in support of reintroducing the Bottle Bill in the 1971 session. Many were angered by the maneuvering of the industry and responded with calls for action, as did the Pendleton *East Oregonian* in proclaiming that "Oregonians should fight this and the way to whip it is in the legislature." The *Eugene Register-Guard* went even further, declaring that an expanded bill covering even more container types was in order: "What the country needs is a law even stronger than the one proposed last year. It ought to cover cans as well as bottles. And it ought to cover more than just beverage bottles. Mayonnaise jars, peanut butter jars and other containers should also be returnable. And the deposit should be high enough—say 5 or 10 cents—that it would be worth the user's while to return them."[68]

The day after McPherson's remarks appeared in the papers in January 1971, Tom McCall tipped his hand in a speech on conservation given at the Salem City Club. "I want to make it very clear," he said, "that there will be no relaxation of my commitment to put a price on the head of every beer and pop can and bottle sold in the United States." Without a

Fig. 19. Governor Tom McCall joins Mrs. Joe Rand of the YWCA in women's protest against nonreturnable bottles, Portland, 1970 (*The Oregonian*, Oregon Historical Society Photo Collection, OrHi 12697)

bottle bill, he predicted, "our environment simply cannot withstand the avalanche of non-returnable bottles and cans that these plans of the beverage industry make inevitable and inescapable." The Bottle Bill offered Oregon an opportunity, as McCall saw it, to "act as a pilot and guide for the rest of the nation" on environmental issues.[69] In an earlier speech that same day, McCall had predicted that Oregon would win the litter battle. "There is an awful lot to do, but attitudes are changing. You can see it. . . . The judges have been too lenient, the people too indulgent, but the times are changing," evidence of which he found in the environmental concerns of young people. "It will be their world we're sullying" he warned.[70] There was no longer any doubt that the governor backed the Bottle Bill idea. Indeed, he was well on the way to taking the issue from Hanneman and making it his own, as part of the crusade for livability that would mark his administration and bring Oregon to the national stage as a leader in environmental policy and regulation.

The bottle issue was expected to reappear in McCall's legislative agenda for 1971, but after he revealed his support for a disposable container ban in January 1970 it became a popular topic among reporters and consumers alike, remaining in the papers and generating mail to legislators throughout the year. One result of the attention was a spate of studies, both formal and informal, of the bottling industry and its impact on the waste stream. Data for 1968 revealed that Oregonians had purchased 210 million beer bottles, 112 million beer cans, and 30 million additional bottles of wine or spirits. These numbers were available because state liquor laws mandated careful tracking of sales; comparable figures for soft drinks were a closely guarded secret, but the bottling industry did report that 1968 had seen a 39.4 percent increase in sales of nonreturnable soft drink containers over the previous year.[71] If the number of soft drink containers was even close to that of alcohol, it meant some seven hundred million beverage containers were sold in Oregon annually, a significant portion of which ended up as litter. Determining just how many cans and bottles were being improperly disposed of in Oregon was a daunting task. Litter surveys reported wide-ranging results, often due to variations in methodology, but suggested in aggregate that beverage containers accounted for at least 30 percent and possibly as much as 60 percent of roadside litter, and as much as 95 percent by volume (most of the remainder being paper).[72] One individual's count in rural areas near Salem found two hundred cans per quarter mile.[73] Beverage containers, and glass ones in particular, were labeled "the most visible component of litter, the most durable component of litter, and the most hazardous element of litter" by another study, which estimated 1.7 billion glass containers had piled up along the nation's highways in 1966 alone.[74] All that could be said for certain in Oregon was that there were lots of cans and bottles being purchased and more of them seemed to end up as litter every year.

By February 1970 "the country's first great bottle battle" was shaping up in Oregon. While a legislative interim committee looked at the bottle problem and Tom McCall called for a literal price on their heads, industry representatives missed no opportunity to have their say in the matter, particularly through antilitter educational programs and parroting slogans like the National Soft Drink Association's "hands alone cause litter."[75] Working through SOLV (Stop Oregon Litter and Vandalism), the antilitter organization formed by McCall in 1969, bottling interests donated money for educational campaigns and cleanup projects and claimed the voluntary program should be given a chance to succeed. Ironically, one way the industry hoped to address the litter problem was by posting billboards carrying antilitter slogans along highways.[76] SOLV had been perceived by some Bottle Bill proponents, including Richard Chambers, as a way out for the industry that wanted to undermine the bill. But McCall actually intended the opposite—the organization would occupy the bottlers' energies while he and others worked to build support for the Bottle Bill among the public.[77] His strategy was ultimately revealed when McCall spoke out strongly for the bill in January 1970, but by that point the industry had no alternative but to support SOLV and hope they could convince legislators and the public that education, not regulation, was the solution to the litter problem. By early spring opponents were tossing out any objections they could conceive of, including the fear that scrounging for bottles along the roadsides might have a negative effect on children. "Could be disastrous," one grocer warned. "Could make a hippy out of him, and we've got enough of them already."[78] The YWCA responded to the industry's attacks by organizing a coalition of twenty civic groups to promote a voluntary boycott of disposable containers, hoping to turn citizens against them by dramatizing the volume of nonreturnables amassed by a typical family in a single week.[80]

Throughout 1970 the bottle issue remained in the papers while legislators worked on a revised bill. At the hearings held by the Legislative Interim Committee on Rules and Resolutions, which had been directed to study the issue at the end of the 1969 legislative session, industry representatives continued to promote education as the solution to the problem and object to the deposit plan as unfair or unworkable. But as one reporter put it, "If people can't be educated to quit killing themselves with cigarettes and automobiles, how are you going to educate them to quit littering the countryside?" The fact that SOLV was backed by industry money limited its credibility, and the governor frequently reiterated his intention to see "a price on the head" of every bottle and can, regardless of the impact of the educational campaign.[80] That fall the bill took shape along the lines that McCall desired, placing a five-cent deposit on all beverage containers and including an important innovation: a complete ban on pull-tab cans. The latter provision was in response to the sudden proliferation of discarded sharp metal tabs appearing "on just about every beach, trail, mountaintop, and campsite in the state," where they threatened injury to human and animal foot traffic alike.[81]

By the time the new proposals were approved by the full committee in October, lawmakers had been subjected to one of the most intensive lobbying campaigns ever seen in the Salem capitol building. Industry pressure and appeals from union representatives who feared jobs would be lost if disposables were banned failed to convince legislators to back off from a complete ban. "There is no compromise," announced Representative Gordon Mcpherson. "People are hell bent on eliminating non-returnable cans and bottles." He predicted easy passage for the bill in the House but was less confident about its prospects in the Senate. If the legislature failed to pass a bottle bill, however, he was certain that the public would take the matter into its own hands and do so by initiative petition.[82] Indeed, McPherson claimed such an initiative would win by a six-to-one margin![83]

The initiative approach was in fact tried almost simultaneously in neighboring Washington State, where political science students from Fairhaven College at Western Washington University began a petition drive to put a bottle bill on the November 1970 ballot. Initiative 256 would require a five-cent deposit on all beer and soft drink containers, and polling showed a large majority supported the idea going into the election. In fact, polling data showed 82 percent in favor in July and 79 percent in September, leading most observers to expect easy passage. The popularity of the initiative frightened the bottling industry, though, and its response was a coordinated attack orchestrated through the Washington Committee to Stop Litter and the Citizens Committee Against 256, both of which were funded with industry money. With the assistance of a professional public relations team hired in Seattle, these two associations were used to both attack Initiative 256 and offer an industry-supported alternative in the form of the Model Litter Control Law. The model law had been proposed as an alternative to the deposit by a third group, Industry for a Quality Environment, and would establish a program of education and enforcement of litter laws as well as require the free distribution of trash bags and other receptacles.

The industry-backed groups employed a variety of tactics to fight Initiative 256, including an effort to convince the petition's backers that passing the Model Litter Control Law instead would make Washington a national leader on the issue, boosting state pride and helping other states address their litter problems as well. When that approach failed, the attacks on 256 and its supporters began in earnest. When pro-256 forces ran a publicity campaign that included industry slogans supporting recycling such as "Pepsi Costs Less in Returnable Bottles," which Pepsi-Cola had previously used in its own advertising, industry officials accused them of attempting to "deceive the voting public and weaken the democratic process." These confrontations were just the beginning of what came to be known as the "Nix 256" effort. As the election approached, the antideposit groups repeatedly pointed out the failure of the 1953 Vermont bottle bill, though they conveniently failed to mention that it was rendered ineffective because bottles were replaced by cans that were not covered by the bill. They also fostered fear over the economic impacts of the bill, claiming that "1,700 lost jobs, $55 million in lost sales, and a $1.14 million reduction in state tax revenue" would result if 256 were approved. A final advertising assault in the weeks prior to the election provided the death blow for the bottle initiative, which was defeated 51 percent to 49 percent at the polls. The industry spent an estimated $2 million on its campaign to defeat the initiative, including in excess of $171,000 to its Seattle advertising firm alone.[84] The battle was won, but just as Tom McCall had tipped his hand on the Bottle Bill in January, Bottle Bill proponents in Oregon now knew what to expect going into the 1971 legislative session based on what they had seen in Washington that fall.

When the legislature convened in January 1971 everyone involved expected a protracted fight over the bottle issue. The public, which already supported the idea, according to polls, had been turned even more strongly toward the bill by the negative campaign waged by the bottling industry in Washington. New groups were formed to back the bill, including the People's Lobby Against Nonreturnables (PLAN), while existing organizations like the Oregon Environmental Council also lined up in favor of the plan.[85] The state's bottlers, brewers, distributors, container manufacturers, unions, and other interests opposing the bill were concerned about the threat to their economic interests and mobilized their resources accordingly. National representatives of the bottling and beverage industries were also quite concerned that Oregon might set a precedent for other states to ban nonreturnables, so they were committed to the bill's defeat at any cost.

When the first hearing on HB 1036 (now colloquially known as "the Bottle Bill") before the House State and Federal Affairs Subcommittee was held on March 3, the witness list included nearly two dozen legislators, activists, and citizens supporting the bill while only one person testified in opposition. Paul Hanneman restated his concern over the amount of litter appearing on beaches in his coastal district and Gordon McPherson pointed out that the industry was spending $7.5 million to promote throw-away containers while underfunded litter education programs were having little effect. They set the tone for the remainder of the hearing, and their arguments were echoed by witnesses from a wide variety of occupations and perspectives on the issue.[86] Richard Chambers, who had conceived the original Bottle Bill, was there to urge its passage and to offer the extensive data he had collected on the industry in support of regulation. He argued, in part, that the trend toward disposable containers would lead to the loss of 80,450 jobs and over $511 million in payrolls nationally due to consolidation and automation, countering forecasts by union representatives that a ban on nonreturnables would result in massive layoffs in the affected industries. He also pointed out that fully 96 percent of the beer sold in Oregon was produced in the three Pacific coast states and delivered by trucks that "run both ways and could easily carry the returnable beer bottles back to the breweries."[87]

One of the most convincing voices supporting the bill was that of John Buckley, a representative of the government of British Columbia, who came to testify about the performance of his province's Litter Act. After outlining the details of the act, Buckley testified about its specific goals: "We visualize some 400 million units per year from the beer and soft drink trade which, left to its own devices, could in a few years have forced the reusable returnable bottle out of existence and left society with 400 million pieces of hard garbage to dispose of. We see no necessity for this and history alone will tell whether or not public support is sufficiently strong to halt the trend of ever-increasing piles of garbage requiring disposal. We believe it can be done—this is our objective."[88] The British Columbia experience was an important factor to cite in support of the bill, as the Vermont attempt at banning nonreturnables (and its subsequent repeal) had already been used against the Washington bottle bill by industry lobbyists. Buckley's matter-of-fact presentation on the law, followed by his statement on its potential impact, would prove harder to counter. Just days after the first hearing, John Piacentini, the owner of a large chain of convenience stores in the state, took out a series of ads in favor of the Bottle Bill in the states' major newspapers, a significant setback for the industry lobbyists, who claimed that grocers were uniformly opposed to the plan. In one prominent bold-print ad, Piacentini stated, "Selling only returnable containers will be a hardship on certain industries [but] the fact that Oregon, the most beautiful state in the union, will become the cleanest state in the Union is well worth any hardship."[89] The businessman was so certain a bottle bill would work that he personally offered a temporary half-cent bounty on cans and bottles as a trial; Piacentini's Plaid Pantry stores expected to collect 120,000 containers but ended up with 3.5 million.[90]

At the second hearing, held on March 11, industry representatives dominated the witness list. One of the first people to speak, however, was Kessler Cannon, Tom McCall's advisor on environmental issues, who told the committee that the governor backed both the idea of a container deposit and the way it was implemented in HB 1036. He was followed by the presentation of a petition carrying eleven hundred signatures in favor of the bill collected by high school students in Klamath Falls, a small town in southern Oregon, and the endorsement of Oregon Environmental Council executive director Larry William, who represented a coalition of sixty-one conservation and planning organizations. Then spokesmen for the Glass Bottle Blowers Association, the Oregon Soft Drink Association, Continental Can Company, and brewer Blitz-Weinhard all testified against the bill, claiming variously that action against cans and bottles would not solve the litter problem, that jobs would be lost as production of disposables ceased, that people did not return the existing reusable bottles, that the bill would only shift the litter problem from the streets to the grocery stores, and that it singled out their industry unfairly. As alternatives they suggested the SOLV program be given a year or two to prove its worth and that voluntary recycling programs could capture most of the containers currently ending up as litter if the public were well enough educated on the matter.[91]

The debate intensified at the next hearing, on March 23, as the two sides were clearly arguing from opposite positions and both were unwilling to compromise. PLAN presented the results of a litter survey completed on March 20, which included the fact that along a single mile of highway near Salem volunteers had collected 679 cans, 198 nonreturnable bottles, and just 24 bottles that could have been returned for deposit. Overall, 56 percent of the litter collected was in the form of beverage containers. The group's leader, Don Waggoner, also pointed out that had HB 1036 been in force, the total amount of cans and bottles collected by the volunteers over the weekend would have netted $880 in refunds. Instead, they earned just $11 from the returnable bottles and the value of the metal collected.[92] An alternative bill supported by the industry representatives, HB 1949, was then offered as a solution to the litter problem; it would levy a quarter-cent tax on all nonreturnable containers and use the revenue collected to subsidize recycling and pay for litter cleanup. The plan was attacked imme-diately by Attorney General Lee Johnson, chairman of the group Citizens Against Litter, who felt it "would not even pay for the litter it would create, let along [sic] clean up the other litter." Instituting a tax rather than a ban on disposables would simply give bottlers "the right to continue to market non-returnables which will scourge the countryside."[93] Richard Chambers said HB 1949 would "short change" Oregon's citizens, and he was followed by several other witnesses who shared the opinion that the industry bill was too weak or even failed to address the challenge completely.

The writing was on the wall by the conclusion of the March 23 hear-ing. When the subcommittee held its final hearing on the Bottle Bill on April 1 the action taken was straightforward; the industry bill, HB 1949, was tabled in a 4–1 vote, some discussion of the unwillingness of the opponents to compromise ensued, and then HB 1036 was sent to the full committee with a unanimous "do pass" recommendation.[94] Ten days later it was approved by the full House 55–5, leading the *Oregon Statesman* to speculate that the politicians "were convinced the public has seized upon this anti-litter measure as a means of dramatizing the growing concern over preserving the quality of livability in the state."[95] In two short years the Bottle Bill had become symbolic of Oregonians' desire to clean up their state and to reject the culture of convenience in favor of environmental quality; the bottling industry had just lost round one in the House by an overwhelming margin.

The stakes were even higher when the Senate Consumer Affairs Committee held its hearing on HB 1036 on April 28. The failure of oppo-nents to stop the bill in the House, a success they likely anticipated given their relatively easy defeat of both Paul Hanneman's 1969 bill and Initiative 256 in Washington State, lent an air of crisis to the industry's side of the debate. The witness list for the three-and-a-half-hour hearing totaled nearly forty people, while an additional dozen opponents were unable to speak due to time constraints. Representatives of grassroots organizations like Begin Recycling in Natural Groups (BRING) were joined by leaders of student groups like the Johnny Horizon Club and the Pro Environment League in speaking for the bill, while teachers and high school students once again presented lengthy petitions to the committee.

Against these proponents were arrayed Dr. Robert F. Testin, director of environmental planning for Reynolds Aluminum; Paul B. Ennis, a lawyer from Washington, DC, representing the United States Brewers' Association; Norman Dobyns of the American Can Company in Washington, DC; Herbert Harrison, vice president and general manager of the Coca-Cola Bottling Company of Vancouver, BC; and William W. Wessinger, chairman of the board of the Blitz-Weinhard Brewing Company.[96] The presence of witnesses representing concerns outside of Oregon reflected their fear that Oregon would pass a precedent-setting bill that other states would mimic. To fend off that possibility they admitted that their industries "had been slow to react to ecological concerns," but as Norman Dobyns of American Can put it, "because our minds haven't been working right doesn't justify our destruction."[97] The somewhat frantic tone of his statement may have been due to the fact that this single afternoon was the only public hearing scheduled on the bill before it went to the Senate floor for a vote.

The behind-the-scenes lobbying that followed was indeed intense for Oregon's part-time citizen legislators. Opponents focused their efforts on killing the bill in the Senate, but the overt effort from out-of-state interests to influence the body was poorly coordinated and not well received by legislators. As Betty Roberts, chairwoman of the committee that had sent the bill to the Senate floor, recalled, "They did the most awful job. It was like 'Here we are from back in the East, and this is little dinky Oregon.'" Realizing that legislators were less than awed by their pedigrees, lobbyists tried anything they could to sway votes, reportedly even attempting to bribe Roberts and other senators to turn against the bill.[98] On May 21 the Senate voted 17–13 to return the bill to committee, where opponents hoped for an opportunity to kill it, but it was almost immediately sent back to the full body, where its fate was uncertain.[99] The national importance of the bill was becoming clearer by this point, with the *Capital Journal* informing readers that the Bottle Bill deliberation was "the big national test" of the concept and that Oregonians were "weary of the double talk of some of the lobbyists" and "just aren't going to put up with bottle and can litter any longer."[100] The competing Salem paper, the *Oregon Statesman*, saw the debate in a national context as well:

Oregon sits on the verge of an opportunity to demonstrate to the nation it is willing to put action behind all the words which have been spoken about cleaning up the environment. The battle being fought over the "bottle bill" is not just over whether all such containers must require a deposit. It is over a far bigger principle, whether a first, important step can be made to back away from overuse and misuse of our resources. It is symbolic because the litter with which it deals is so visual that it is a constant reminder of our polluted land.[101]

When the full Senate convened to vote on the Bottle Bill May 27, Betty Roberts told the assembly about the bribe she had been offered for her vote, further undercutting the opposition. When the vote came the bill was passed 22–8, a crushing defeat for the industry and a landmark in conservation legislation for Oregon and the nation. The importance of the vote was immediately recognized by the press, with one editorial featuring the bill as a sign that the entire nation was changing: "The hope of anti-litter workers is that Oregon's program will be the pilot for all 50 states. [The bill's passage] must indicate to [the industry] that there's enough support to doom any effort at repeal by popular vote. Their battle is lost, if only they see it. And so—we think—are many of the battles of industries in other sectors of the environmental field, if only they knew it. Passage of the bottle bill is just one more indication that there's more to the ecology bit than faddism. The fight for a clean world is here to stay."[102] The bill's importance was not lost on Tom McCall either. Although he had not played a direct role in its passage, at the signing ceremony he proclaimed it "one of the most significant acts in the nation to turn us away from use and waste to a positive program of reuse and save."[103] It would also prove a critical step in the process of establishing Oregon as the national leader in progressive conservation at a time when issues of livability were becoming more important to Americans than ever before. McCall was well aware of the bill's significance in this regard; a speech he gave before the Oregon-Washington Bottlers Association in February 1970, just weeks after he first spoke in support of the Bottle Bill concept, reflects this clearly.

Oregon again is in a bellwether position. What happens in Oregon is going to set a precedent for the rest of the nation. We are the key state in what I feel will be a domino reaction—and, as the key domino, the way we move will set-off a chain reaction. It is a fitting and traditional role for Oregon. Oregon pioneered against the exploitation of women and children in labor; Oregon pioneered in the direct election of United States senators; Oregon led the way in the initiative and referendum; Oregon invented the gasoline tax as a means of creating suitable highways; Oregon has been a leader in pollution control and in all forms of environmental legislation. . . .

That is the kind of confrontation the one-way container faces in the State of Oregon; that is our climate of firm resolve in the protection of our livability; that is the kind of determination Oregonians have shown time and time again. We are dogged in our dedication to the preservation of our environment![104]

Observers outside of Oregon recognized the precedent established by the bottle legislation as well. Just weeks after the signing ceremony, a story on the bill the *Torrington (CT) Register* opined, "It is to devoutly hope that the surge will spread eastward and we will soon be picking up nickels rather than refuse from our highways." In response, the editors of the *Oregon Statesman*, which had backed the bill from the beginning as an antilitter program, suggested it may have gone beyond its initial purpose to become "a first legislative step in turning this country from a profligate waster of natural resources to a recycler and conservator of resources."[105] Indeed, by the fall of 1971 plans to introduce a federal bottle bill were in the works, nearly a year before the Oregon bill would even take effect. William D. Ruckelshaus, the director of the Environmental Protection Agency and Richard Nixon's environmental point man, spoke out against a ban on nonreturnables in November, arguing that deposits would not prevent people from discarding bottles. The price had to be high enough for people to bother, he claimed, but if it were enough to make collecting the bottles worthwhile it could lead to fraud. To bolster this position he cited a federally funded study in California that tested an eleven-cent deposit on bottles but found that "if you put the price high enough, people start making bottles and turning them in" fraudulently. When the *New York Times* investigated Ruckelshaus's claims it revealed that no such study had been done, that the EPA director had only "thought he had been told that such a study existed."[106] Apparently the tactics that had failed in Oregon were still being applied by industry lobbyists in Washington, DC, in an attempt to fend off any expansion of the Bottle Bill before it had a chance to prove its worth in Oregon.

Bottle bill debates quickly spilled over into other states and Oregon became the prime example in support of banning disposable containers. New Jersey, for example, held hearings on a ban in September 1971, intended to "mark the beginning of a legislative drive to prevent urban America from being buried under the billions of tons of garbage it produces every day."[107] The bottling industry continued to argue vociferously against deposits and returnable bottles, having gone all-in with the push for disposables. The nation watched to see what would happen on the ground in Oregon, generally with high expectations for success.[108] Many of those taking the longer view read the bill as a sign of significant social change, with one analyst arguing that voluntary recycling without deposits (the industry's claimed solution) was an "exercise in fantasy" while "the popularity of the Oregon measure may well signify a shift in consumer preference from 'convenience' packaging to a type which is more 'environmentally acceptable.'"[109] If convenience packaging could not be banned or boycotted, at least consumers could be encouraged to reduce litter by putting a price on the head of every unwanted bottle and can. For everything else marring the roadsides, a bill was introduced to require all new cars sold in the state to come equipped with a "litter receptacle" from the dealer.[110]

While the outcome of Oregon's Bottle Bill experiment had yet to be determined, it was apparent upon its passage in 1971 that the "new conservation" that Lyndon Johnson had called for in 1965 had finally arrived. The Bottle Bill was a perfect example of the combination of quality-of-life (aesthetic) concerns and the need to address pollution issues, in this case solid waste disposal. Although some of its support came from traditional conservation organizations motivated by the impact of litter on recreational areas such as beaches, streams, and trails, the bulk of support for the Bottle Bill came from the general public's desire to confront something they lived with every day—the trash piling up along the state's roadsides. Although they had been unable to overcome the billboard lobby in attempting to improve highway vistas in 1960, a decade later the citizens and politicians of Oregon defeated not just a regional, but a national lobbying effort opposing

Fig. 20. Cub Scouts from
Harvey Scott Elementary
School in Portland
picking up litter on Sauvie
Island, 1973 (National
Archives and Records
Administration, Record
Group 412: Records of the
Environmental Protection
Agency, LI 412-DA-5704)

the Bottle Bill. The fight brought new activists into traditional conservation organizations, led to the formation of scores of new advocacy groups,
and demonstrated convincingly that Oregonians were willing to inconvenience themselves in exchange for ensuring the continued habitability of
the environments in which they lived. To Tom McCall the bill was even
more significant; it marked a sea change in the way people thought about
the environment and their desire to take positive action on its behalf. "[The
Bottle Bill] symbolizes the switch society has to make everywhere from
profligacy to husbanding diminishing resources," he declared. "It is a practical first bridge for this most wasteful of all countries to cross, in reducing
a life-style often bordering on opulence to a level of relative affluence."[111]
In the months and years that followed—as the Bottle Bill was tested and
proven a success—McCall would make the bill his trademark and use it
to catapult himself and the state to prominence on the national stage.
Meanwhile Richard Chambers, the man who had conceived Oregon's
Bottle Bill and fought for it behind the scenes, quietly faded back into the
woodwork. His family recalled Chambers repeatedly refusing to accept

credit for his efforts or even to give interviews on the topic, believing he "accomplished what I set out to do." Just before his death from cancer in 1974, Chambers's friends convinced McCall to honor him with the Clean Up Pollution Award, but shortly after the ceremony he told a reporter, "I am in no way qualified for this."[112] By that time Tom McCall had moved on to even bigger things than the Bottle Bill—an attempt to address the fundamental question of the environmental crisis: how long could human society continue to expand before it exhausted the limited space and resources nature could provide? Defining the limits of growth would prove the hardest task Oregon's environmental leaders had yet faced, and their efforts would set the state even further apart from the rest of the nation, as the environmental bellwether became an iconoclastic questioner of the gospel of growth at any cost.

Chapter 6
The Limits of Growth

> I'm not a fascist. I believe the public should be heard, but where they
> won't be, we move ahead. And then if they get volatile enough they'll
> use the initiative, referendum, or recall, Oregon's gifts to mankind, to
> get rid of the idea or get rid of us.
>
> —Oregon state senator Ted Hallock on the Land Conservation
> and Development Commission, 1997

The *Oxford English Dictionary* traces the use of the word *livability* as it
relates to "suitability for habitation or the capacity to offer comfort" back to
an English novel from 1872. It took another century, though, for the term to
take on the meaning it assumed during Oregon's environmental era, when
an article in the *American Journal of Agricultural Economics* in 1972 noted
the birth of "a nationwide propaganda campaign against air and water pollution and the general degradation of the livability of the earth for mankind
and other creatures."[1] The adoption of livability as an environmental metric
corresponded with the gradual decline of *conservation*, a concept that had
dominated environmental politics and policy in the United States for three-
quarters of a century. Credited to Gifford Pinchot, the first chief of the U.S.
Forest Service and Theodore Roosevelt's most trusted advisor, *conservation*
meant "the use of natural resources for the greatest good of the greatest
number for the longest time."[2] In practice, it was a top-down philosophy
that relied on expert managers to make resource allocation decisions for
the good of the country rather than for private interests.

   Environmentalism, in contrast, stemmed significantly from grassroots
initiatives based in concern over quality of life—livability—and recognized
a utility in natural resources that went beyond potential consumptive uses
to include such factors as aesthetic and recreational values.[3] The explosion of interest in environmental issues in the 1960s was associated with

a younger, better educated, and more gender-diverse population than conservation. This form of environmental concern became a complicating feature of middle-class participation in a culture of consumption that encouraged Americans to spend their leisure time and disposable incomes in pursuit of higher quality of life while simultaneously raising concerns about the sustainability of those pursuits. Middle-class Americans enjoyed the benefits of consumption but became increasingly anxious over declines in livability that they understood were due in part to the economic and technological systems that made their lifestyles possible.

The shift from traditional conservation to modern consumer-oriented environmentalism was evident in Oregon in the 1960s, helping to drive such initiatives as the Beach Bill and the Bottle Bill to success and establishing the state's reputation as a pioneer in forward-looking environmental policy. Despite these groundbreaking successes, however, those seeking to cement Oregon's growing role as an environmental leader in the 1970s ultimately found themselves facing a challenge far greater than litter or access to open spaces as they prepared to challenge the seemingly unstoppable forces of population growth and economic expansion, both of which threatened livability in the region. In 1961 the Conference on Metropolitan Area Problems, sponsored by the Institute of Public Administration, examined the public addresses of U.S. governors and found many deeply concerned about patterns of future growth.[4] The issue was framed even more directly for Oregon by the *Saturday Evening Post*, which ran a feature in the fall of 1961 titled "Oregon Dilemma" that asked, "Can this green and timbered state keep its natural beauty—and prosper too?" While Governor Mark Hatfield told the author "We've got to sell, sell, sell Oregon!" in an interview, the piece went on to argue that Oregon "is more than a state: it's a way of life." One feature of that way of life was a reluctance to embrace all growth as progress, which manifested itself in resistance even to common boosterism; the chairman of the 1959 Oregon Centennial Commission explained that "some of the old-time Oregonians whose 'Uncle Charley' came here in a covered wagon don't want anyone else looking over the back fence." Hatfield countered, "I don't share the feeling that we can't get new industry without losing recreation and livability."[5] Without question, the impacts of growth in Oregon were on the radar for both citizens and politicians alike by the dawn of the decade.

By the late 1960s bestsellers such as Paul and Anne Ehrlich's *The Population Bomb* and gloomy forecasts related to impacts of the increasing human population burden upon the Earth elevated population growth high on the list of primary concerns for people around the globe. While industrialized nations had followed a typical pattern of falling birth rates and lower infant and adult mortality rates as they developed, a demographic transition driven in part by the declining need for labor as agriculture was replaced by manufacturing and consumer economies, many developing nations had not yet made the transition by the mid-twentieth century and were still growing at two to three times the rates of industrialized nations. The trend was accelerated by technological exports from developed nations, including medicines and fertilizers, which helped reduce mortality from disease and expanded the food supply. Consequently, in the decades following World War II a substantial portion of the world's population moved from a demographic regime of high birth rates and high death rates to one of high birth rates and low death rates, with the dramatic impact of doubling the net growth rate of the global population between 1950 and 1960 and setting it on a pace to expand even more rapidly in the decades that followed.[6]

The ultimate fear of demographers and ecologists was thus no longer simply a contraction of the human population as resources were gradually exhausted but rather a complete collapse of global ecosystems triggered by human alterations of natural processes beyond the planet's capacity for self-repair. As Barry Commoner, one of the most prominent scientific critics of the business-as-usual approach, warned, humanity faced a "question of survival" in which "the present course of environmental degradation . . . will destroy the capability of the environment to support a reasonably civilized human society."[7] Although the population of the United States was not growing at such an alarming rate, the proportionally greater consumption of resources by its affluent population led many Americans to conclude they were in greater danger of land shortages, water and air quality problems, and declining resource stocks than some developing nations.[8] Some of the more pessimistic critics believed the United States would outstrip its resource base even before the trend toward global ecological destabilization became clear to policy makers. Indeed, Tom McCall himself warned student audiences on his 1970 Earth Day speaking tour that "it will take drastic and continuing efforts to stave off mankind's suicide."[9]

The quality-of-life issues that drove the nascent American environ-mental movement of the 1960s were often seen as reverse functions of pop-ulation growth. Expanding populations, in other words, produced growing problems in waste disposal (diminishing landfill capacity, air pollution, and water pollution), in resource management (shortages of energy, miner-als, timber, and other raw materials), and in declining space for housing, recreation, and food production. The postwar economic expansion in the United States was not, however, a universal one—as Michael Harrington's *The Other America* (1962) so dramatically pointed out, there were exten-sive pockets of poverty among the plenty, accounting for as much as 20 per-cent of the American population. Regional economic variations invariably led to migration as people sought better job opportunities, thus driving up population in areas thought to have stronger economies (i.e., California in the 1930s). When economic migration was compounded by other factors, such as perceived differences in quality of life, the influx of new residents to an area could present a significant challenge to existing residents as they adjusted to an increasing population and to correspondingly smaller shares of the limited resource pie.

Sustained population growth typically proves a challenge to the social and physical infrastructure of a community, but it also taxes the land, particularly on the subdivided margins of urban areas in "the greed belt, where the farmer sells land rather than crops," as one landscape architect put it in 1970.[10] By the first Earth Day, in April of that year, it was appar-ent that a certain segment of the population considered quality-of-life factors as or even more important to their decisions about where to live than the economic factors that had once driven scores from the Dust Bowl to California in search of work. For many Oregonians in the early 1970s population growth was perceived as a serious threat to the very landscapes that drew nineteenth-century pioneers to their region; the perception of environmental degradation and decline motivated their defense of livabil-ity against the industrial pollution and resource abuses they blamed for declining quality of life in other states. Ironically, it was in part their success that attracted the attention of the prospective migrants whom they feared threatened everything Oregon celebrated.

In 1970, the year Tom McCall was elected to his second term as gov-ernor, the decennial census counted 1.9 million residents in Oregon, an 18 percent increase over the 1960 figure and 37 percent above the 1950 count.[11] This compared to national population growth of 13 percent for 1960–70 and 31.5 percent for 1950–70, so the state was gaining population at a rate substantially higher than the national average.[12] Not surprisingly, this growth was concentrated within the state as well, with 86 percent of new residents in the 1960s settling within the Willamette Valley, a region that accounts for just 14 percent of Oregon's land area.[13] Most shocking for those charged with planning for growth in the state, however, was the finding that over a quarter of a million people—254,823 in total—had migrated to Oregon from another state *since 1965 alone*.[14] As one study succinctly put it, "Oregon is attractive to people from other states." But more darkly, the same study also concluded that these interstate migrants "consumed more energy and products" and thus "place[d] a burden on environmental quality which is greater than might be expected were one only to consider their numbers."[15]

According to economic logic, migration into Oregon should have slowed with the economic downturn of the late 1960s, especially as declines in the national housing market reduced demand for wood products, one of the state's core industries.[16] That it did not suggested that something other than jobs was attracting people to the region; many observers thought it might be the quality of life made possible by the relatively low population density of even western Oregon and the abundance of fairly pristine natural areas offering recreation, inspiration, and related values not available in other states. "Now at last Oregon, less known than many other of the world's great beauty spots, for better or for worse is gaining national recognition as one of the dwindling number of places where getting away from it all is still possible" is the way one editorial interpreted the situation in 1968, with a mixture of pride and concern.[17] Although one local development official celebrated Portland's achieving a population of one million residents in 1969, claiming it was "ironic that one of the most beautiful cities in the world . . . is relatively unknown," others were less sanguine about the impact this growth would have on their cities and the state's celebrated environment.[18]

Governor Mark Hatfield saw the writing on the wall in 1966 when he identified the population influx and rising numbers of tourists as potential conflicts for the future of Oregon's resource-dependent economy, but he also believed there was "nothing incompatible between economic growth of the state and preservation of its natural resources."[19] Indeed, he argued in his 1968 book *Not Quite So Simple* that "a total expansion of our economy" was the solution to Oregon's economic and social challenges—that diversification and growth of industry were "the best way to deal with the job needs of our people."[20] Not all business leaders agreed, though, and some took surprising positions on growth that reflected concern over things beyond the bottom line. Pacific Northwest Bell telephone, for example, ran advertisements in local papers during the spring of 1967 promoting regional planning and warning of the dangers of unplanned growth. "Blight isn't planned," one ad explained. "It sneaks up on you. One moment all seems green and peaceful—the next moment, the countryside is gone. Sometimes it happens on a frightening scale when population booms. Witness the supersprawls in the Midwest, on the Atlantic Coast, in California. Is this what we want in Oregon? [L]ike you we live and work here. This is good country. And we want to keep it that way."[21]

Expressions of concern over the impacts of growth were not limited to political and industry leaders. Indeed, a concerted but decidedly tongue-in-cheek effort to dissuade people from moving to Oregon had been launched by Portland author Stewart Holbrook in the 1950s in the form of the James G. Blaine Association (later the James G. Blaine Society), an amorphous group whose sworn mission was to spread misinformation about the Pacific Northwest as widely as possible. Named for the nineteenth-century secretary of state from Maine because Holbrook liked the sound of the name, the mysterious association had no membership rolls or constitution but gained a reputation by the mid-1960s as a defender of a region threatened by growth. In 1962 a fifty-page feature on the Pacific Northwest in *LOOK* magazine paired an article titled "Why Aren't We All Living There?" with Holbrook's own "Yankee Go Home," in which the Blaine Society founder proclaimed, "We believe that the Pacific Northwest is the Promised Land, and we mean to protect it from the steadily mounting hordes of Goths and Vandals who have been touring our blessed region in increasing numbers." The sardonic writer went on to proclaim the success of the society's efforts, noting that "I alone was responsible that a few more than two hundred home-seeking families did not settle, as they had planned, in Oregon but chose California instead."[22]

Holbrook and the Blainers (many of whom were writers) frequently circulated tales of constant rain, giant mosquitos, and moss-covered homes in a sort of antipromotional campaign aimed at tourists who, it was feared, might like what they saw and decide to settle in Oregon.[23] When Ralph

Friedman, author of a popular guidebook called *Oregon for the Curious*, began to get frequent letters from people saying his book had convinced them to move to the state he wrote an open reply in regional newspapers addressed to "Dear Residents of the Other 49 States" in an attempt to steer the immigrant hordes away.

> Oregon is a lovely place to visit, but it is a mess to live in. After the tourists have left it rains like crazy here. Mosquitos are big as Sherman tanks. The people are unfriendly, they cheat each other, and most of us are starving. . . . There are no fish in the streams here, the lakes are full of silt, trees don't flower, and nobody has seen a rose around here for years. Actually, what happens in the summer when the tourists come is that we paint our hills green, put up false-front silhouettes for mountains, borrow a few lakes from Washington and California, and hire some actors to look cheerful. So stay home. And spread the word. Oregon is a great place to visit but no place to call home.[24]

Friedman's letter was typical of the ironic tradition of Oregon-bashing in which the Blainers engaged, but more direct solutions to the migration problem were proposed as well; Stewart Holbrook himself had once found tourists such a threat that he suggested the state post "armed vigilantes in the mountains to 'hold 'em off at the pass.'"[25] When the shadowy quasi organization endorsed the storage of military nerve gas in Oregon in 1969, the *Oregon Statesman* called for keeping a closer watch on the Blainers, noting that while they had traditionally emphasized keeping newcomers out this was the first time the group had "endorsed a measure which has the potential of eliminating some of those [who] already are here."[26]

The linkage between tourism and population growth was not actually that clear, but in the minds of many Oregonians concerned about growth tourism was likely the most visible contributing factor. After all, advertisements financed by public and private investment attracted large numbers of vacationers to the state every summer and it seemed there were more of them each year. It was not unreasonable to assume that a percentage of these visitors were impressed enough with Oregon to relocate there later. So while public officials celebrated the expanding tourist trade along with the motel and campground owners, segments of the public grew increasingly concerned about the impact all the new visitors would have on the livability of their state. When data was collected on these out-of-state tourists the numbers were impressive; estimates produced by the Oregon State Highway Department (based on surveys of passenger cars with out-of-state plates) found that over seventy-five million visitors entered the state between 1960 and 1970 by automobile alone.

According to the department's data, over forty times as many people visited Oregon from outside the state over the course of the decade than actually lived there in 1970. Whatever the result of these visits was for the tourists, their economic impact on the state was unquestionable, with an estimated total in excess of $2.1 billion spent by tourists during the same period.[27] Indeed, a 1967 study commissioned by the federal Bonneville Power Administration identified tourism as the Pacific Northwest's fourth-largest industry and projected it would rank number one by the end of the century, leading the *Oregonian* to editorialize that "the Northwest industry with the greatest future—tourism—depends on keeping our air, streams, lakes and other natural resources free of pollution," suggesting the rising tension between tourism and industrial expansion.[28]

Year	Cars	Passengers	Expenditures
1960	1,934,500	6,383,850	$154,425,195
1961	2,208,250	7,066,400	$168,090,990
1962	2,804,660	9,255,378	$168,055,227
1963	1,944,979	5,445,941	$161,747,289
1964	2,149,683	6,019,112	$177,231,062
1965	2,192,584	5,788,421	$181,959,000
1966	2,383,000	7,029,850	$184,200,000
1967	2,502,000	8,656,920	$190,982,000
1968	2,696,400	7,819,560	$215,645,000
1969	2,847,100	7,829,525	$260,964,000
1970	2,815,200	8,445,600	$272,761,000

Table 1. Out-of-State Passenger Cars Visiting Oregon, 1960–70 (*Source: Oregon State Highway Department*)

Fig. 21. "Oregon...Cool,
Green Vacationland,"
promotional campaign
c. 1967 (Original in
author's possession)

Oregon...cool, green vacationland

The undeniable popularity of Oregon among tourists fed speculation that the flood of visitors was also the source of the state's population growth, which made some people uneasy about the pace of expansion evident in the tourist industry and the role state government played in fostering that growth. In the mid-1960s Governor Mark Hatfield had created Oregon Welcome, Inc., as a privately financed adjunct to the Travel Information Division to promote tourism outside the state. Oregon Welcome operated primarily through support from banks, utility companies, the tourist industry, and local chambers of commerce interested in promoting Oregon vacations in a carefully targeted fashion, selecting advertising markets and offering packaged tours intended to attract more middle-class tourists, who were thought to be bigger spenders and more likely to relocate.

Not long after he took office in 1967, Tom McCall created his own Governor's Committee for a Livable Oregon and charged it with examining the tourist industry, which by that time had become the state's third-largest economic force and was on pace to surpass agriculture and timber in the not-too-distant future. A report produced the following year proclaimed Oregon a pioneer in tourist promotion, having adopted the nation's first gasoline tax in 1919 to support road construction and then in 1935 creating the Travel Information Division within the State Highway Department with the express mission of promoting tourism and attracting new residents to the state. By 1968 the budget for that office had grown to nearly $750,000, about half of it spent on advertising campaigns run in other states and much of the rest on the production of tourist information materials mailed in response to individual inquiries. Unsurprisingly, the largest single target of these promotional efforts was the state of California, which produced about 45 percent of the out-of-state tourists visiting Oregon each year and received a substantial percentage of the approximately three million maps, brochures, and guides distributed annually by the late 1960s. The theme of the 1968 promotional campaign, "HELLO," an acronym for "Help 'Em Linger Longer in Oregon," offers a good sense of the nature of these materials.[29] McCall's committee, however, also raised concerns about the "quality" of tourists attracted by the state's promotional materials, noting that just "15% of tourists were a 'better class' who arrive by plane, train, or bus," as compared to the car-traveling majority, who were assumed to be predominantly campers or "tin-can tourists" who were "prone to littering."[30]

The combined efforts of Oregon Welcome and the Highway Department put Oregon in the middle of the national range of spending on tourist promotion in the postwar decades. However, McCall's committee determined that tourists who visited the state tended to spend a third less than the national average on food, lodging, and related items compared to visitors to other states, most likely due to the large number of Oregon's visitors who engaged in outdoor recreation (camping, hunting, and fishing) rather than staying in urban centers or at resort properties. This is, perhaps, unsurprising; *Sunset* magazine's travel guide to Oregon, published in 1968, opens with the observation that "there is an unspoiled quality about Oregon that is refreshing to the traveler. . . . Endless miles of untouched forest look almost the way they did when the first settlers wrested them from the Indians more than a century ago."[31] Most of its pages feature scenic vistas and note the proximity of urban areas to outdoor recreation. The Committee for a Livable Oregon could do little to fight the state's image as a recreation destination. Ultimately it recommended that state and regional land use planning be intensified in order to direct development of tourist and recreation facilities in a manner consistent with the values that attracted visitors to the state, offered a general endorsement of the existing industry, and further suggested the public should be made better aware of the positive economic impacts of tourism.[32]

Public attitudes toward tourism and population growth were mixed in the 1960s, though most Oregonians were likely aware of the mounting evidence demonstrating the importance of tourism revenue to the state's economy. However, as a livability issue there were certainly pockets of resistance to tourism development around the state (witness the local opposition to the Oregon Dunes National Seashore proposals as early as 1959), and a general concern over the impacts of growth was evident in such phenomena as the James G. Blaine Association and the frequency with which concerns about growth appeared in the media. Some of the complaints were the product of frustration with crowding in recreational facilities and competition for limited space in campgrounds. For example, in the wake of several seasons during which campers were turned away from overflowing state parks, officials in 1968 proposed a reservation system that would not only secure spaces for campers in advance but would give preference to Oregon residents over out-of-state tourists, who, it was believed, were taking up the bulk of the sites available during the summer camping season.[33] Frustration was aimed at Californians in particular, which is logical given they made up the largest proportion of visitors, and it sometimes reflected an element of class envy as well. As one Oregonian wrote,

> I don't believe any Oregonian has a dislike for individual
> Californians, but I do believe they dislike having them come here
> and buy up our state for retirement, a playground, and building
> those monstrous condominiums all over our coastline and state.
> . . . I also feel our Oregonians have a squawk coming when they get
> to their own camps and can't get in because early-bird tourists got
> there first. Working people don't usually get off work until 5 or 6
> p.m. My solution is to have one or two camps at the north end of
> the Coast, in the middle and at the south beaches for out-of-staters,
> and if they can't beat each other to those camps let them go to the
> motels. Leave the rest of the camps to Oregon campers only.[34]

In 1969 Glenn Jackson, the powerful chairman of the Oregon Highway Commission, decried the fact that while Oregon was absorbing a disproportionate share of California's recreational travelers, it received limited federal funding to support state facilities. Expanding tourism and industry brought in revenues but could also lead to environmental decline, raising the question of whether the economic impact was "high enough to justify the loss of this environment which is the greatest asset Oregon has."[35]

Despite the reluctance of some to accept the rapid expansion of the tourist industry and the influx of migration it presumably abetted, growth-related issues ranked relatively low in a 1970 survey of the public's environmental worries, with 13 percent identifying "planning needs" and just 9 percent listing overpopulation as significant environmental problems in Oregon. The catchall category of "pollution," in contrast, was selected by 98 percent of respondents as a statewide worry.[36] This echoed an editorial that appeared in the *Oregon Statesman* late in 1969 suggesting that Oregonians "still tend to think of preserving livability largely in terms of eliminating or reducing pollution." Planning, however, was considered by the editors as the key to future livability, and regional planning in particular was promoted because "regional authority [is necessary] to solve regional problems."[37] For Tom McCall's economic development team, this meant being selective about growth; as his chief economic advisor put it in 1970, "Our industrial growth policy is changing from a shotgun to a rifle approach. We are going toward the concept of preserving quality of life rather than growth." In response to questions about the expanding population, he explained, "We really can't prevent population growth. We can't shoot people trying to come into the state." But statewide planning via zoning, he believed, would be necessary to steer growth in the right direction—the challenge would be to "convince people they will have to give up some rights in order to preserve their environment," such as "the right to have an abandoned car in their backyard."[38]

The first attempts to establish a statewide land use planning program in Oregon date back to a 1947 law authorizing counties to plan and zone within their boundaries, though that authority was seldom used. The pace of growth in the Willamette Valley in the 1950s precipitated a dilemma experienced across the nation: property taxes on farms were skyrocketing as the value of the land was driven upward by demand for residential subdivisions, prompting some farmers to sell out as their farmland became worth more as lots for homes than for planting crops. As a result, limited farmland was rapidly being converted into subdivisions to make room for an expanding population, a process that happened more rapidly the closer the farms were to urban or suburban areas but was also beginning to leapfrog over existing developments into what had previously been almost exclusively rural farm country. The emerging problem of urban sprawl received national attention by the late 1950s, as home construction and urban expansion consumed in excess of one million acres per year, much of it farmland, giving rise to a new movement of "open space" activists concerned about the loss of green space and the services it provided: agricultural potential, recreational opportunities, aesthetic value, and habitat. Agriculture in particular was deemed to have cultural value as well as economic; mass migration from the farm to the city might signal the end of an agrarian, rural past.[39]

Oregonians attempted to address the problem of "farmland conversion" in 1961 through a proposal to establish a category of "exclusive farm use" (EFU) zoning that would limit property taxes on farmland; in the 1965 legislative session the so-called Greenbelt Law, which based taxation of farmland on its rental value instead of its sale value, was passed. From initial concern over the conversion of farmland to subdivisions (and the loss of green space in general) an effort eventually arose to require zoning in all counties. In support of a program of statewide zoning, Tom McCall appeared at the opening of the 1969 legislative session to declare that "an urban explosion of environmental pollution is threatening the livability of Oregon in such a manner that effective land use planning and zoning have become a matter of statewide, not merely local, concern." In his own inimitable fashion the governor laid out the stakes involved in controlling urban sprawl, telling legislators that "the steady scatteration of unimaginative, mislocated urban development is introducing little cancerous cells of unmentionable ugliness into our rural landscape whose cumulative effect threaten to turn this state of scenic excitement into a land of aesthetic boredom."[40] The governor was backed by a range of allies, including the recently formed Oregon Environmental Council, who felt a statewide zoning mandate was the next logical step in the state's efforts to manage growth.[41] Quality of life was predicated on quality of environment in their collective view, and action was needed to preserve both for Oregon. Land use regulation and livability thus became inextricably linked.

The legislation passed that spring, Senate Bill 10, went beyond the 1947 zoning authorization to require all counties in Oregon to engage in comprehensive planning and to produce zoning plans by December 1971 or face the prospect of the governor's office doing it for them.[42] It drew considerable attention nationally, including praise from Interior Secretary Walter Hickel, who wrote to McCall, "I wish you every success in this pioneer effort—for the sake of both Oregon and of the rest of the nation, which I hope will soon emulate Oregon's example."[43]

Unfortunately, legislators were unable to agree on specific goals for the program and refused to provide funding from state coffers for the work. The resulting unfunded mandate was unpopular with local officials, many of whom saw little benefit to be gained from the work required; it also triggered opposition from property rights advocates, who felt zoning would infringe on their ability to determine what was done with private land. Compliance with the zoning requirement was therefore minimal, and an attempt was made to repeal the law by initiative petition in 1970. McCall remained outspoken on the need for planning, though, telling voters, "Repeal SB 10 and you might as well throw me out too. I refuse to preside over the deterioration of Oregon's quality environment." The failure of the repeal initiative on a 55–45 vote signaled public support for statewide planning and heralded "a new kind of land use politics in Oregon in which economically minded farmers and foresters, aesthetic quality-of-life preservationists, and ecologically minded environmentalists could find common ground," even if the commitment appeared half-hearted to those who advocated more stringent planning as the key to preserving future livability.[44]

At the same time he was defending SB 10 against repeal, Tom McCall was also defending his own record as he ran for a second term as governor. When asked in early 1970 what the greatest accomplishment of his first term was, McCall replied, "visible leadership in reflecting the popular will toward environmental quality," a theme that would dominate his campaign strategy that fall.[45] Days before confirming that he would indeed stand for reelection, the governor's office issued a six-page press release detailing the environmental accomplishments of McCall's first three years in office. Among the forty items listed were major successes such as the Willamette River cleanup initiative and the passage of the Beach Bill, but lower-profile achievements were also included in the report. McCall's service as the only governor on President Nixon's Citizens Advisory Committee on Environmental Quality was highlighted, as were the formation of the Governor's Livable Oregon Committee, the creation of SOLV , and the passage of SB 10 with its statewide zoning mandate. Item number twenty-four, "secured passage of legislation officially naming the beaver as the state animal," was one of the few that might not be read as a major environmental victory elsewhere. McCall was indeed setting a new standard for political leadership on environmental issues, a quality that the *Oregon Statesman* highlighted in its endorsement prior to the election. The editorial also served as a rejection of the initiative to repeal SB 10 by highlighting the importance of the planning and zoning process that was just beginning to be implemented:

> We endorse Gov. McCall's re-election because he personifies the growing determination of Oregon people not to let the problems which have overwhelmed other sections of the nation overcome us. . . . Elsewhere, regions are unable or unwilling to enact the zoning and antipollution legislation necessary to preserve the livability of their land. In Oregon, McCall has led the way to statewide land zoning, preservation of river greenways, and pollution controls.
>
> In the future, the Mid-Willamette Valley may be especially grateful for Gov. McCall's willingness to go out and meet the issues. A million-dollar planning program to preserve the livability of the Valley is being generated by his administration. This type of comprehensive planning may be difficult to sell politically. But McCall is willing to tackle the unpopular now in order to preserve the future. We need him for another four years.[46]

Though the *Statesman* endorsed McCall as the candidate of livability, his opponent Bob Straub ran on a very similar pro-environmental platform. Both men were passionate defenders of Oregon's quality of life, and in challenging a popular incumbent Straub's strategy was to push for even greater protections. Because the two men respected one another and shared common values, according to Straub's biographer, they "managed to avoid the nasty, name-calling, tit-for-tat political spiral that was tearing the rest of the nation apart" in 1970. Instead, their friendly competition pushed both men to "forge a new vision for Oregon" that led to "the most fruitful period of environmental policy making in Oregon's history."[47] Although Straub's allies repeatedly advised him to go on the offensive against McCall—state senator Thomas Mahoney privately warned the Democrat, "Do not repeat the 'McCall is a nice guy' stuff. He is definitely not a nice guy; he is a cold-blooded, selfish, childish, mean bastard"—the challenger chose to stick to the high ground.[48] Ultimately he campaigned on the theme of a bolder future and a more aggressive governorship; on environmental issues he pledged to "stop the scolding of polluters" and to recognize "the fine line between yelling industry right out of Oregon and letting people keep on dumping filth into our environment."[49]

Throughout the gubernatorial campaign the issues of growth and tourism remained linked in the public consciousness. In the fall of 1970, just weeks before the election, the Oregon State Highway Commission Travel Advisory Committee issued a report entitled *Tourism in the Seventies . . . Is Oregon Ready for It?* The opening sentence of the report underscored a significant characteristic of the ongoing debates over growth: "Oregonians seem to be divided on the subject of tourism in their state." Indeed, a strong majority appeared to support expanding tourism (fully 70 percent, according to one study) and had the power of the motel, restaurant, and tour industries behind them. But the remaining fraction of the electorate opposed to increasing tourism was a vocal lot and enjoyed a disproportionate influence on the state's policy makers. Tourism's outsized impact was evident in myriad reports, underscoring its undeniable importance to the state's economy; the rate of growth for tourism in the 1960s alone was triple that of agriculture and far outpaced the stagnant timber industry. Oregon's rising popularity as a vacation destination in this period was driven as much by external forces as internal promotion. For example, in 1969 *Reader's Digest* profiled the Beaver State in its influential Armchair Travelogue column, which described Oregon as "a place of dream-like peace and beauty" where "the people match the land" and live "unplagued by many of the problems that harass the rest of the country."[50] The Blainers' efforts to "keep Oregon for Oregonians" may have backfired as well; the *Oregon Statesman* reprinted an editorial from a Michigan newspaper that observed, "Oregonians are dead serious about their anti-tourism campaign" and pointed out that the state had "passed more bills on the environment in 30 months than all the other state[s] together have passed in 30 years." Concluded the *Statesman*, "We can't think of anything, in this overpopulated world, more likely to attract people to Oregon than a campaign to keep people away so we can enjoy the place ourselves."[51] A similar report in the *Oregonian* summarized the Blainers' impact as a "reverse psychology of elbow room under the clear skies of Oregon" that likely attracted more outside attention than it deflected.[52]

The ambivalence some expressed toward tourism in the 1960s, regardless its economic impact, turned to outright hostility in 1970, and as a consequence the state's policy of promoting tourism drew criticism from many who previously allowed tourist-dependent industries to steer public policy in that area. In July the Highway Department reported a 3 percent increase in tourist inquiries at the California border and a 15 percent increase at the primary Columbia River crossings from Washington over the previous year. But these visitors were spending less; the *Oregonian* speculated that this was because they were camping and preparing meals over campfires rather than staying in hotels and eating in restaurants.[53] One response was the development of promotional materials aimed not simply at attracting tourists but at attracting specific *types* of tourists who would stay longer, spend more, and engage in activities that would direct them away from overused facilities such as state parks and campgrounds. The Travel Advisory Committee recommended developing private resorts as an alternative to public recreation areas, which they felt would both reduce some of the crowding problems (particularly along the heavily traveled coast) and encourage visitors to stay longer and spend more money on lodging than campers typically did.[54] But moving visitors from campgrounds, where they competed with residents for space, to hotels would be a daunting task given the degree to which outdoor recreation and scenic vistas were drawing tourists in the first place.

In November 1970 the majority of Oregonians signaled that Tom McCall was doing the job they wanted him to do; the governor was reelected with over 55 percent of the vote, which he took as an endorsement of his policies and goals for the future. When asked about his priorities for the new term in January 1971, the governor singled out school funding as the most pressing issue on his agenda (public schools relied on a much-hated property tax set by local levies at that point), but the complex of issues surrounding tourism, population growth, and planning would dominate the year to come, once again raising McCall and Oregon to the national stage in the increasingly familiar role of environmental bellwether.[55] Changing the way tourism was promoted to solicit a "better class" of tourists was one way to approach the issue, but shortly after his second inauguration McCall touched off a controversy that had Oregonians considering a complete ban on publicly funded tourism promotion, assessing new transient taxes on visitors, and levying "hiking fees" on out-of-state users of state park facilities to discourage them from displacing residents who were tired of competing for campsites and other amenities. "Oregon for Oregonians" would become their rallying cry.

This response was unintentionally triggered by a remark McCall made to CBS News correspondent Terry Drinkwater during a special report on Oregon's environmental achievements in January, shortly after his second inauguration. While explaining his philosophy of responsible growth to the reporter, McCall exposed the tension between tourism and population growth in what became the defining statement of his career. Oregon's message to the nation, he said, was "Come visit us again and again. This is a state of excitement. But for heaven's sake, don't come here to live." Drinkwater interpreted this for the audience, telling them that the environment was the first priority in Oregon and that the state would swear off both tourism and economic development in order to preserve it. Almost overnight the quote became famous, and then infamous, as an exhortation for people to simply leave Oregon alone. Reporters from around the country called seeking clarification from the governor—did he really mean to turn people away from his state? He did not, reporters were assured, and it was pointed out that tourism was rapidly becoming the state's most important industry and that while the promotional strategy had been changed to attract more affluent visitors, the invitation was still open to all.[56]

The tumult surrounding McCall's remarks revived interest in the James G. Blaine Society, which had been advocating its "no tourists" stance for years and recently had become more serious in its pronouncements on the ills of growth. In 1970 Blainers celebrated the 140th anniversary of the birth of James G. Blaine by releasing a satirical tour guide to Oregon's "must-see" sites, including paper mills, polluted sloughs, and the new nerve-gas repository at the Umatilla Army Depot, urging visitors from California in particular to save time for the "Ronald Reagan Forest Preserve," a four-thousand-acre tract that featured only a single tree.[57] That fall *Smithsonian* magazine published an article on the organization and Oregon's incipient antitourist atmosphere. Although Stewart Holbrook had died in 1965, the Blaine Society was better organized in 1970 than ever, thanks to the work of a freelance writer named Ron Abell who appropriated the name

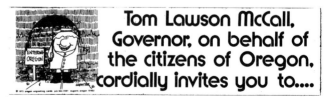

Fig. 22.   Oregon
"Ungreeting"
bumper sticker, 1972
(Original in author's
possession)

and began soliciting paid memberships from like-minded Oregonians and selling such items as bumper stickers reading "Oregon for Oregonians."[58] (This was a tip of the hat to James G. Blaine himself, who often used the phrase "America for Americans" in his political attacks on immigrants in the 1880s.) The state needed an organization like the Blaine Society, reporter A. Robert Smith wrote that year from Washington, DC, because among politicians the need to preserve Oregon's "unique splendor" was "often forgotten unless there is a watchdog group standing by to remind the decision makers that progress is not always measured in terms of population increases, or miles of highways built, or new shopping centers erected where cows once grazed, or more motels dotting the coast, or small towns becoming big towns, when these developments made every Oregonian's personal life a little more crowded and polluted with the various wastes of contemporary urban living. The James G. Blaine Society has earned a great reputation. Now it's time for it to deliver by organizing to make the good fight."[59]

The acclaim was not universal, however. In response to Smith the *Oregon Journal* editorialized against organizing the Blainers more formally, explaining that "the unique beauty of the James G. Blaine Society is that its membership is limited only by the number of people who love their region and its program only by the subtlety of their imaginations. . . . In disorganization there is strength."[60] *Sports Illustrated* reported that "there really are some hostile natives—the Blaine Society—who would like to build barbedwire fences along the state borders, keep tourists and industry out and let Oregon go its own way."[61] Still, some feared the lure of exclusivity would serve to attract growth, rather than slow it down so planning could be completed. Governor McCall's economic development advisor later confirmed that the Blaine message had a "boomerang effect" that was leading corporations interested in livability for their employees to consider relocating to Oregon to join others that "put preserving the environment ahead of industrial growth because they like to go fishing too."[62]

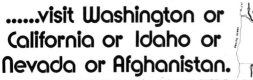

It was in this context of growing antitourist sentiment that McCall's 1971 comments on growth, typically shortened to simply "visit but don't stay" by the press and public alike, were delivered and immediately drew national attention to the state that eschewed what many others appeared to want—growth for the sake of growth. Letters from around the nation arrived in the governor's office, most of them supporting his positions on livability. "I wanted to tell you," wrote a woman from Tennessee, "how refreshing it was to learn that there is a politician in this country who has his priorities straight." Over 97 percent of the letters received in the weeks immediately following the interview were positive; many expressed hope that McCall and Oregon would become a model for their own states. "I can (as a native of Vermont) sympathize with your predicament, for we here in Vermont are currently under siege from New York, Connecticut, Massachusetts, New Jersey, and other assorted uninhabitable places," one wrote. McCall had clearly touched a chord that resonated with those concerned about growth in other regions. "How refreshing it is—at a time when most other states still compete in the insanity of quantity—to hear the head of at least one state speak of quality and stability. . . . We will all be in your debt if you stand by your views," wrote an Indiana conservationist. Only a few of these letters indicated concern over the implication that Oregon was "closing its doors" to visitors, including one that objected, "The personal freedom to live where we choose . . . remains a cherished privilege," and another that warned, "I remain interested in moving there, you'll be unhappy to know."[63]

Within Oregon the response was less than universally positive, with many in the tourism and real estate sectors expressing alarm that the governor would so openly attack their livelihoods. In some parts of the state, most notably the sparsely populated counties east of the Cascade Mountains, it was made clear that McCall did not speak for everyone. Jack Steiwer, a real estate broker from the tiny town of Fossil in Wheeler County, pointedly stated, "We're not James Blainers" in explaining the need for new residents in his part of the state and the programs developed to lure them in. He did add one caveat, though, explaining that "we don't want to talk about hunting. We get all the hunters we can handle now."[64] Nevertheless, news items with headlines like "Quality of Life Diminishing in State" were appearing in ever-increasing numbers, raising concern about the direction of state planning and drumming up opposition to growth that multiplied the impact of McCall's statement by alarming some who may have not previously considered the issue all that pressing.[65] Backtracking from the implications of "visit but don't stay" almost immediately after the January broadcast, the governor spent much of the spring clarifying and defending his position on growth. Planning, he emphasized, was key. "If we could deploy population growth judiciously we could stand quite a lot of growth. We have to do the planning and the zoning that makes sure people are put in the right place, that they don't crowd out the open space which makes life livable."[66]

Following Nobel laureate Norman Borlaug to the podium at an Oregon State University planning conference in February, McCall felt compelled to clarify his position at the end of an address that focused primary on planning for orderly growth, concluding that "so far as Oregon is concerned, as much as perhaps some would like to build a fence around it, this is not realistic. A sobering thought creeps in: that as we improve our livability, we also increase our attractiveness and thereby add to our environmental burden. . . . The continued awareness of our citizens that protecting the priceless asset in Oregon's natural surroundings must be our first objective. . . . We've made progress, more than just about any other jurisdiction in the nation. There is more to be done."[67] The *New York Times* picked up the story in March, featuring Oregon at the top of an article on states that were reconsidering tourist promotion and debating policies intended to slow growth. While McCall's now-famous "visit but don't stay" quotation led the piece, it incorporated similar sentiments from a range of officials in other states, notably Florida and California, including a former chamber of commerce director from San Jose who lamented, "We unfortunately have gone for growth's sake and have forgotten the consequences. . . . We are victims of our own success."[68] Writing for the *New Republic* that same month, Peter Barnes contrasted Oregon with California, describing the former as "the kind of place where people come not in search of instant riches or sun or glamor, but simply of room to work and think and live." He lauded McCall and his allies—including Ron Abell and the Blainers—for their efforts to slow growth and preserve livability. Ultimately, "it may well be that no state can long remain uncluttered when all around it there is overcrowding and urban sprawl," Barnes declared, "but it's reassuring to know that somewhere the fight is being made."[69]

In April McCall spoke at the Oregon Travel Industry Conference, where, after being introduced as "Oregon's Number One Un-Tourist," he reassured those in attendance that tourism was "the most exciting prospect on our developing horizon" because it was a clean industry that attracted money from outside the state and brought with it "no smokestacks or ecological imbalance." But visitors should be discouraged from moving in permanently, he said, because "we can't handle that kind of growth and keep Oregon, Oregon. We insist on exercising the greatest care with this precious environment."[70] The governor also reaffirmed his stance against polluting industries, a position he had been promoting in public appearances around the western United States in the wake of the Drinkwater interview. As he told the tourist industry representatives, "Oregon has been wary of smokestacks and suspicious of rattle and bang. . . . Oregon has wanted industry only when that industry was willing to want what Oregon is. When you live in Oregon, you realize how carefully the public watches its heritage. Let any speculator attempt to move in the shadows and the voice of the people thunders through the governmental halls. . . . Oregon people place a high premium on livability: They fear pollution of all kinds, they give top priority to the special environment which they are blessed to have."[71]

Despite the governor's repeated attempts to clarify his message and to focus attention on his policy of inviting temporary visitors and clean industrial growth, tourism remained a contentious issue both within the state and without through the spring. The national tourism industry felt the impact; one representative at a Minneapolis travel show reported that "the Oregon image has taken a considerable setback," noting that 40 percent of visitors to his booth refused literature on Oregon destinations because "Oregonians don't want us to visit."[72] Nevertheless, in May the legislature debated removing all public funding for tourist promotion from the budget, including a $1 million appropriation for the Highway Department's advertising program. Although the funds survived by an 8–5 vote in the Joint Ways and Means Committee, the House later voted 43–17 to send the bill back to committee with the recommendation that the tourism budget be deleted. As one representative joked, cutting the Highway Department appropriation meant that "the money will be available to the James G. Blaine Society."[73]

As word of the state's lukewarm welcome to tourists spread, the *Los Angeles Times* ran a front-page headline in September asking the question "Oregon—A Paradise Lost for California Immigrants?" The answer, "at last report, none has been turned back at the border," was underscored by stories of endless rain, lack of jobs, limited "city comforts," and "skyrocketing" land prices, combined with residents who were openly hostile to Californians.[74] Days later, Portland's *Oregon Journal* reported on the *Times* piece under its own headline, "Oregon Hostile, Papers Tells Californians," repeating the claim that "suspected Californians are sometimes charged double or triple the usual price for lumber to build a house" due to a "growing feeling among many Oregonians that discontented Californians should move east, not north."[75] Tom McCall expended significant energy in redirecting the public conversation away from California's tourists and toward planning for growth, capitalizing on the national attention his "visit but don't stay" comment generated by increasing the stakes. Oregon, he felt, should be the model for the nation. As he told the Portland League of Women Voters at a luncheon address in the fall, the stakes were higher than just one state's future: "What if we save Oregon and lose the rest of the nation or the world? If everything around us goes, we go. . . . Our avowed plan is this: we will save Oregon contagiously. Whatever we do here must be a model for everywhere. . . . If we can get a hand-hold on the slippery cliff of environmental breakdown then we can extend a foot-up for the next one below us."[76] Vilifying Californians served more than a rhetorical purpose; it offered a warning of what could happen everywhere if the Golden State's postwar model of essentially unregulated growth was not altered to reflect the environmental and social costs it imposed. Tourism and its impacts were simply the most obvious examples of the growing disparity between Oregon, which had developed slowly, and its neighbor, which had experienced rapid industrialization and explosive population growth following World War II.

Though occasionally leavened with humor, the panic over tourism was of course a byproduct of deeper concern over the broader issue of population growth, not only in Oregon but nationally. When the Citizens' Advisory Committee on Environmental Quality, a group established by the Nixon White House's own Council on Environmental Quality, issued its first formal report in May 1971, population and land use were given as much weight as air and water pollution in the recommendations. National land use standards were viewed as a means of leveling the playing field between states, and population growth, it was suggested, could be managed through building new towns near existing urban areas. The committee's recommendations were lent significant weight by its members; chaired by Laurance Rockefeller, the group included biologist Rene Dubos, Arthur Godfrey, Charles Lindbergh, California assemblyman Pete Wilson—and

Governor Tom McCall of Oregon.[77] McCall carefully parlayed his growing national reputation as an environmental leader into opportunities to
spread "the Oregon message," not as a traditional booster but in fact as
more of a doomsayer on the impacts of environmental degradation and the
need for coordinated responses on the local, state, and national levels.

In this context Oregon's crowded campgrounds were an inconvenience, to be sure, but the deeper threat clearly lay in unregulated growth;
by the early 1970s planners were warning that without intentional man-
agement the future of the Willamette Valley in particular looked bleak.
Under a 1971 headline reading "Is It Too Late to Save Our Valley?" the
Capital Journal reported that some officials felt it *was* already too late.[78]
Tom McCall felt otherwise. That fall his office, working in cooperation
with local officials in the valley, launched an operation called Project
Foresight that was given a daunting charge: to take the recently completed
Willamette Valley Environmental Protection Plan and develop a process
for implementing it across the myriad agencies with authority over the
region, nearly twelve hundred units of local, state, and federal government
in all.

Establishing baseline data and projections of future growth were
among Project Foresight's initial undertakings, and in the process one of
the fundamental dichotomies of the growth issue became clear: urban
areas were growing faster than rural ones. In fact, though the population
density in the valley had doubled since 1940 and would likely double again
by 2000, the reality was that people were clustering around urban areas
with strong economies in ever greater numbers while depressed rural
areas were sometimes losing population.[79] This realization meant that any
programs aimed solely at restricting growth might do irreparable harm to
struggling rural areas in order to preserve aesthetic qualities demanded by
urban residents, a political nightmare for anyone seeking to get a planning
program through the state legislature. But every confirmation of continued
population growth received front-page attention in urban areas, such as
a December 1971 story reporting that the city of Salem had grown by 4
percent in the previous nine months alone, further stirring local demand
for planning and controls on growth. Immediately below the body of the
Salem story ran a second item that allowed little room for doubt about
the widespread antipathy toward growth; it was simply headed "Northwest
Is Getting Too Many People."[80] By fall Oregon's antigrowth position had

spread to the congressional delegation in Washington, DC, where Senator
Robert Packwood announced,

> I would be happy if Oregon had no more people 20 years from now
> than it has now. I see no advantage in Oregon with slightly over
> 2 million people today having 3 million people in 10 years and 5
> million people 30 years from now. . . . We can make a choice in
> Oregon. The question is, "How is it going to affect those of us who
> live in Oregon now?" We can have outsiders come in and dam our
> rivers and pave our farmland. But 20 years from now will those
> of us who are in Oregon today be any better off? I really doubt it.
> We have approached something close to a paradise in Oregon,
> compared to the rest of the nation. . . . I don't want Oregon to
> become a West coast Ohio.[81]

Of course, Ohio was not the model most Oregonians who worried
about growth feared—California was. California not only offered a convenient example of poorly managed growth, it also carried the substantial
threat of a burgeoning population of nearly twenty million people who, it
was thought, were simply marking their time before flooding across the
border into the promised land. The reality was stark: Oregon's population was 10 percent of the size of California's, which by itself accounted
for approximately 10 percent of the 203 million enumerated nationwide
in the 1970 census.[82] That year 44.5 percent of the tourist cars entering
Oregon came from California, over 1.25 million automobiles crossing the
border northward in just one year. Given that the average number of pas-
sengers per car ranged from 2.2 to 3.8, it can be assumed that a minimum
of 2.75 million Californians visited Oregon in 1970, a full 31 percent above
the total population of the smaller state.[83] Furthermore, though no direct
correlation had been proven between tourism and immigration, data
did exist to establish that 39 percent of immigrants to Oregon between
1965 and 1970 originated in California, 2.3 times the percentage coming
from Washington State, the second-largest source of new residents.[84] Of
course, in politics perception was even more important than data, and
substantial numbers of Oregonians were convinced that California represented everything that Oregon did not want to become as well as the
source of many of the negative impacts associated with growth. In an open

letter to the *Sacramento Union*, one Oregonian shared his thoughts with his Californian neighbors: "I think we'll see a lot more Californians up here this year and every year. You've cluttered and littered your own state. You've almost ruined the Big Sur, you've let your beaches be sold for private use (all ours are public) and you've over-crowded, over-commercialized and you don't want to stay home. Barring any extreme measure on our part, you'll keep on coming. I know that. So all I can say is please don't ruin Oregon. If you treat my state like you have yours, then none of us will have a nice place to enjoy."[85]

That California had been adversely affected by the pace of its growth (the population nearly doubled between 1950 and 1970) and the lack of planning behind it went without saying. Among Californians themselves a substantial number were extremely critical of the way their state had developed, some of whom published books decrying the loss of the qualities that had once made California a land of dreams. These included such titles as Samuel E. Wood and Alfred E. Heller's *California Going, Going: Our State's Struggle to Remain Beautiful and Productive* (1962), Raymond F. Dasmann's *The Destruction of California* (1965), and William Bronson's *How to Kill a Golden State* (1968). Bronson's book was a particularly passionate study of the impacts of growth that captured the fear expressed by Oregonians toward their larger neighbor, observing in its introduction that "California has led the rest of the world into the age of mass affluence and has become standing testimony to man's infinite capacity to befoul and destroy in the quest for an ever-higher standard of living."[86] The hundreds of photographs he presented as evidence offered a chilling portrait of what might become of Oregon—choking smog, burgeoning garbage dumps, sprawling developments of identical homes, farmland carved up for freeways, subdivisions, and shopping malls, and perhaps above all else the constant presence of an almost mind-numbing aggregation of automobiles. To Bronson, California's major cities had become little beyond parking lots, their shape and function dictated by the needs of the automobile rather than their human residents.

By the 1960s the orange groves and other agricultural foundations of "old" California were fading; what was left frightened Oregonians who visited there or saw pictures of it on television, because they had witnessed the first stages of the same process taking place in their own state. Perhaps the changes had come too fast for Californians to realize what was happening to them, or possibly the newly emerging environmental consciousness had equipped Oregonians with a way to express their concern that had not been available a generation or two previously when growth became California's mantra.[87] All that was clear to many in Oregon was that right next door was a striking example of what not to do and their Californian neighbors appeared to want an easement on Oregon's backyard, at the very least.

That Californians and the Californian model of development were perceived as threats is evident in both the public and private statements of people from all parts of Oregon and from across the socioeconomic spectrum. Such concerns were certainly not limited to Oregon; around the West people pointed to California as the worst-case scenario for growth, coining new words like "Californication" to describe the process of destructive sprawl and crowding that had seemingly consumed the Golden State in a few short decades.[88] Opposition to growth appeared in many places that shared characteristics with Oregon, including relatively low population densities, limited industrialization, heavy reliance on tourism, and discomfort with the rapid pace of change seen in the postwar decades. In New Mexico an Undevelopment Commission that sounded much like the James G. Blaine Society directed its ire toward Texans. Coloradans sported bumper stickers reading "Don't Californicate Colorado," and Governor Richard Lamm sounded not unlike Tom McCall when he announced that his state was "beginning to overcome a whole heritage of mindless Chamber of Commerce promotionalism." Even sparsely populated Montana was feeling the pressure of immigration as low land prices and mountain views drew the attention of wealthy vacationers from elsewhere.[89] Whether it was the relative abundance of Californian tourists or the symbolic role of Los Angeles as an environmental antilesson, residents of other western states felt threatened, a phenomenon played upon by the drivers of a car with California plates seen traveling south on Interstate 5 with a sign in the rear window reading, "Don't Worry Tom, We Are Going Home" at the peak of the 1972 tourist season.[90]

Oregonians often manifested this fear in concern for stewardship of their home state's livability and frequently expressed it in letters to Governor McCall, the symbolic guard at the borders. A pair of Oregonians serving in the military in North Carolina wrote of their concerns to McCall after a visit home, sharing their worries about what they had left in his care.

We went home to Oregon on leave early this month and what we
saw made us both wonder what is happening to our state. We saw
California license plates in such abundance that we wondered what
state we were in. . . . Somewhere, at some seldom patrolled portion
of the border, there must be a hole in the wire, because there sure
are a lot more people in Oregon than there used to be.

Certainly we were once all immigrants. Certainly we should
share this beauty. Certainly we have no real authority to stake it off
in front of God and everybody and say "You can't come any farther
because you're from California and you carry the plague that kills
land." But just as certainly Governor McCall, we are the caretakers
of some of the most magnificent country left in the adjacent 48
and it is our responsibility therefore, to maintain that heritage. . . .
What are you going to do about it? What can we do about it?[91]

One suggestion the men offered was for a system of zoning that would
concentrate development and tourism into limited areas. Combined with a
moratorium on the sale of land in parcels smaller than ten acres, a coordinated development system, they felt, might alleviate some of the negative
impacts seen under the current market system. Many others wrote the governor out of frustration that crowded summer of 1972, often sharing their
observations and pleading for action before it was too late.

My wife and I are average Oregonians, what you would call
members of the silent majority. We have just completed an
extensive tour of our beautiful state and have concluded that we
all have one giant problem—the Californian invasion. Everywhere
we went, the natives that we talked to had the same views—what
can we do to curb this destruction of our state? We are all suffering
from the invasion but we seemingly are defenseless. It is a sad state
of affairs when our farmers can no longer afford to farm because it
is more profitable to sell out to Californians. It is also sad that our
school budgets can no longer be passed mainly due to the retired
Californian "No" vote.

Personally, Gov. McCall, I am willing to work in any legal way
possible to stem the invasion. My fellow natives are equally aroused
to the point where they are also willing to work. What we need

Fig. 23. Governor Tom McCall receives "SNOB: Society of Native Oregon Born" t-shirt, n.d.
(Oregon Historical Society Photo Collection, OrHi 64676)

are guidelines as to what can and should be done. This is what we
would like to get from you, Gov. McCall.[92]

As the debate over public funding of tourist promotion carried into
the fall of 1972, McCall and other political leaders were in fact planning a
coordinated response to the growth problem.[93] Part of the plan involved
stirring up public support before the legislature even convened for the 1973
session; this was coordinated via Project Foresight and the circulation of
materials produced for the Willamette Valley Environmental Protection
Plan, including a series of panels illustrating two different possible futures
for the valley that were displayed in towns across western Oregon. The
exhibits related to the growth study became "the most universally accepted
dog and pony show to hit the Willamette Valley since the barkers unloaded
their cure-all elixirs 70 years ago," according to one reporter describing
the presentation of a scenario depicting the valley floor as it would look
in 2002 if development continued at its current pace. A second prediction
based on model environmental regulations and careful planning for growth
and resource use offered a beguiling alternative. The point of the exhibits
was not to present a plan (for there was not yet any plan to present) but
rather to prompt the public to accept planning in general as an alternative
to unregulated growth. "We're going more . . . for mood than legislation,"

said Secretary of State Clay Myers. "We're trying to set the tone to create an environmental awareness."[94]

Awareness of the problem was certainly apparent in the flood of news stories decrying suburban sprawl that assailed Oregonians that fall, but the tone of the coverage was often fatalistic, presenting the division between the politically powerful developers and the unorganized opponents of growth as an insurmountable gap. Questions about property rights were raised in response to any suggestion that land use might be regulated, and the idea that some sort of regional body might be given veto authority over local land use decisions was considered so wildly experimental that opponents felt it would never be considered seriously by the legislature.[95] Industry leaders were less certain, however. Fred Weber, writing in Portland General Electric's *Area Development and Research Forum*, explored the connections between growth, public policy, and livability in historical context, noting that "Chamber of Commerce syndrome" drove what passed as planning in the 1960s, as the region was focused on improving standards of living by increasing consumption. Oregon's widely envied livability, he argued, was a product of its historic patterns of slow growth relative to other states; for the future, "planning . . . is the key word to the enhancement of livability." Zero growth was not the answer, but organized, intentional planning could be.[96]

Developers had cause to be skeptical of these paeans to planning, as land use regulation was still in its infancy in 1972, having grown slowly from its legal roots in municipal regulations of the early twentieth century. The impetus behind some of the earliest American zoning plans was the City Beautiful Movement, part of the Progressive Era agenda to improve living conditions in urban centers that was best characterized by the 1901 McMillan Plan for Washington, DC, which sought to use public spaces and memorials as tools for social control. Influenced by the French Beaux-Arts style, planners there designed a space (the National Mall) that combined the order of the Greco-Roman foundations of the country's political philosophy, the style of European castles and gardens, and the vision of the city's original designer, Pierre L'Enfant, into an area of monuments and thoroughfares intended to evoke the power of the federal government and the democratic culture of the nation.[97] At the same time, slums were cleared or divided by new avenues replete with fountains and sculptures intended to lift the impoverished from their wretched state though exposure to aesthetic beauty, a practice that led critic Lewis Mumford to comment that the City Beautiful Movement's great achievement was to "provide gran-diloquent stones for people who have been deprived of bread and sunlight and all that keeps man from becoming vile."[98]

The most common tool of land use regulation was zoning, which first appeared in substantial form in the New York City Zoning Ordinance of 1916. From these origins grew the practice of "Euclidian zoning," which regulated the use of private land, the density of development, and the size of buildings. The term "Euclidian" in this context stemmed not from geometry but from the U.S. Supreme Court decision in *Village of Euclid v. Ambler Realty Co.*, a 1926 case that upheld the constitutionality of public regulation of private land.[99] In the half century following the *Euclid* deci-sion, zoning emerged as the most powerful land use control available to municipalities and was often used to direct housing and commercial devel-opment into socially beneficial patterns by isolating industry from residen-tial neighborhoods, limiting the size of apartment complexes, and similar measures. More darkly, zoning was also used to contain ethnic, religious, and racial minorities as well as the poor in urban neighborhoods away from the suburbs; the most common device for this sort of discrimination was exclusionary zoning, which dictated low population densities (and thus large, expensive lots) in new developments.[100] Regional planning advanced in the 1920s, notably in Los Angeles and Chicago, but met with limited success outside the realm of transportation.[101]

In the years before "urban sprawl" came into widespread use as short-hand for uncontrolled growth, efforts to preserve open space focused on preserving the countryside from expanding cities. William Whyte, author of the suburban social critique *The Organization Man*, was at the forefront of such efforts in the 1950s. As historian Adam Rome explains, Whyte dis-counted the desire to impose government-enforced zoning as land use pol-icy, considering it impermanent and an affront to property rights. Instead he called for public ownership of green space through direct purchase and conservation easements. Government funds should be used to buy open space and preserve it in the public interest, Whyte argued, a concept that was both enacted directly through government grants and echoed in the expansion of parks budgets throughout the 1960s.[102] Other voluntary or market-based strategies, including cluster development, were adopted in some cases as well. The pace and impacts of growth seemed inexorable, though, and calls for increased regulation persisted.

Prior to 1970 land use zoning (and land use regulation in general) was typically restricted to municipalities; few states exercised any authority over land use outside of state parks and similar reserves. But in a 1971 report entitled *The Quiet Revolution in Land Use Control*, the federal Council on Environmental Quality indicated that growing environmental concern and the pace of urban growth had begun to challenge the states' traditional deference to local government on land use policy: "The 'ancient regime' being overthrown is the feudal system under which the entire pattern of land development has been controlled by thousands of individual local governments, each seeking to maximize its tax base and minimize its social problems, and caring less what happens to all the others. The tools of the revolution are new laws . . . sharing a common theme—the need to provide some degree of state or regional participation in the major decisions that affect the use of our increasingly limited supply of land."[103] The laws at the forefront of the revolution—zoning in Maine, Vermont, Massachusetts, and Hawaii, municipal regulation in San Francisco and Minneapolis–St. Paul, and wetland protection programs in Massachusetts and Wisconsin—were presented as models for broader adoption. Critically, this new approach to planning required the redefinition of "land" itself; no longer just private property holding an economic value determined by the market, "land" in the future would be expanded to incorporate nonmonetary public goods, including aesthetics and what would come to be called "ecosystem services," such as the filtering action of wetlands or wildlife habitat provided by trees and brush. Proponents of this revolution were involved in drafting a Model Land Development Code to be published by the American Law Institute as a template for new state laws to regulate growth and expand zoning beyond municipal boundaries. Begun in 1968, the drafting process drew significant attention from the planning community as well as from developers. Long before it was completed in 1975 the concepts it promoted—including statewide zoning—were being considered by those on both sides of the growth debate.

In Oregon, developers and planners alike were following this "quiet revolution" in the late 1960s, and in fact they played a part in the battle themselves with the passage of SB 10 in 1969, which vaulted the state to the national forefront in land use planning by requiring all counties to establish their own zoning programs. Unfortunately, many counties failed to comply and others chose not to enforce the plans they produced, leaving the law little more than a token gesture toward increased regulation. The ultimate indictment of the 1969 zoning law came from Lincoln County on the central coast, where officials simply ignored their own zoning plan in approving several new subdivisions that, rather than connecting to city services, conveniently ran their sewage from pipes onto the public beach and ultimately into the ocean without any treatment whatsoever.[104] The failure of SB 10 to affect the growth rate or slow the conversion of farmland to subdivisions prompted calls from some quarters for a new, stronger regulatory response, coincident with the growing demand by the general public for action on growth and migration.

Attempts to revisit the zoning law in the 1971 biennial legislative session were blocked by conservative Republicans who controlled both houses, leaving the issue ripe for debate as the 1973 session approached. A variety of plans were under consideration by the fall of 1972 as a host of legislators, planners, developers, citizens groups, and lobbyists prepared themselves for battle in the upcoming session. Among these was an ad hoc committee chaired by Senator Hector Macpherson, a dairy farmer from outside Albany in the central Willamette Valley who had run for the state senate in 1971 with the intention of representing farm interests on issues like field burning, opposition to which he felt threatened the state's agricultural industry.[105] In his words, Macpherson "knew the planning problems first hand as a dairy farmer threatened by city folks moving down the Peoria Road near to my operation," and though he "didn't expect to take the lead in proposing a solution" as a freshman senator, he quickly found that nobody else would, leaving him to cobble together resources and political support for what would ultimately emerge as one of the most important issues in the 1973 legislative session.[106]

Macpherson's efforts to persuade Senate leaders to fund an interim study of land use regulation in 1972 were rebuffed, leaving him to make his own way in preparing a land use bill for the next session. He then thought of approaching Tom McCall's executive branch for support, leading him to the Local Government Relations Division in the Executive Department, where he met an administrator named Robert Logan and immediately found the backing he needed. As Logan recalled it, "Macpherson just walked in here one day. Hell, we were delighted!" Working in tandem with Logan, the senator quickly formed the Land Use Policy Action Group, bringing together planners, citizen activists, legislators, business leaders,

Fig. 24. Burning grass-seed stubble impacts air quality, Willamette Valley, 1972 (National Archives and Records Administration, Record Group 412: Records of the Environmental Protection Agency, LI 412-DA-2558)

farmers, and other interested parties with the intention of producing a land use package to replace SB 10 and address the constellation of issues surrounding the growth debate. Divided into two teams, one working on statewide zoning and the other on rural land protection, the group spent 1972 hearing testimony and beginning the hard work of drafting what would become the most stringent package of land use planning regulations in the nation.[107] Macpherson chaired the main committee himself, later recalling, "The wonderful part of the Senate Bill 100 for the committee [is] I was the only legislator so I had veto power over everything. And I loved that, that part of it—there was nobody that could tell me what went into the bill."[108] By the fall of that year reporters were writing stories about various antigrowth bills to be introduced in the upcoming session, with Macpherson's group receiving the most coverage for their "missionary zeal" and commitment to maintaining environmental quality.[109]

Governor McCall frequently expressed support for revamped land use regulations as well, calling the task "the most important work left in Oregon's environmental protection movement." As he explained it those assembled for the Governor's Fifth Conservation Congress in November 1972 in Portland, "The issue this year is whether we can morally justify forcing the next generation to pay the price of a failure of this generation to properly respect the land." The solution, McCall advised, was to support Hector Macpherson's land use planning bill, which he felt would put an end to the "buffalo hunter mentality" of developers and maintain local control of land use decisions in 90 percent of cases.[110] Soon after, he proposed the creation of a state Department of Land Conservation and Development to coordinate state and local land use plans, for which he included a $300,000 line item in his budget request for the 1973 legislative session to serve as seed funding.[111] McCall was laying the groundwork for the political struggle he knew was on the horizon, and through his bold pronouncements and calls for action he hoped to kindle public support for land use reform just as he had for the Beach Bill and the Bottle Bill in previous sessions. He was not, however, directly involved in drafting any of the proposed legislation. Hector Macpherson sent the governor periodic updates on the progress his committee was making in the interim, but he never received a response. "The impetus to get started was entirely at my end, to begin with," Macpherson recalled, "after I started working on it I found [others] were interested . . . but I never directly talked to Tom McCall. When I approached him about working on it he said, 'I don't have time to work on it, but when you come up with something we'll get together.' I think he thought that probably I never had much chance of getting it passed."[112]

As the 1973 legislative session opened and the bills produced by Macpherson's working group took center stage as the most credible among the land use proposals, McCall pulled out all the stops in support of the general idea of land use regulation. Appearing before a joint session on January 8, the opening day of the legislative session, he gave an address that came to be known as the "grasping wastrels speech" for a phrase that took second place only to his earlier "visit but don't stay" remark as a defining oration of his career. In response to those who had asked him for guidance, McCall offered hope as well as declaring that while Oregonians had a right to be proud of their environmental record, they had to continue to innovate to remain a national leader in environmental policy.

> Over the years [we] have brought about imaginative change that will be warmly received by posterity. But modern society permits us no time to savor our successes. Society is not static, and

government must be able to respond promptly, capably and fairly to emergent crises. The people of Oregon have high expectations. They look to us for fulfillment.

Key evidences of our reverence for quality of life abound. . . . [They] mean that after earning a living we have a living that is worthwhile. But there is a shameless threat to our environment and to the whole quality of life—unfettered despoiling of the land. Sagebrush subdivisions, coastal "condomania," and the ravenous rampage of suburbia in the Willamette Valley all threaten to mock Oregon's status as the environmental model for the nation.

We are dismayed that we have not stopped misuse of the land, our most valuable finite natural resource. The interests of Oregon for today and in the future must be protected from grasping wastrels of the land. We must respect another truism: That unlimited and unregulated growth leads inexorably to a lowered quality of life.[113]

In supporting land use planning McCall offered an answer to those who expressed concern about the rate of population growth, the impacts of tourism, the perceived flood of immigration, the loss of open space, and the declining livability that had marked the previous decade and appeared to be accelerating into the 1970s. Here, in one step, Oregonians could forever preserve critical elements of their land base and "Keep Oregon, Oregon" as the bumper stickers read. In a subsequent message on land use widely reported in the press, the governor warned that there was "a very real danger that uncontrolled development will clear-cut the state of its livability." The public had spoken loudly, he felt, "not saying 'no growth' but saying 'planned, controlled growth that is both environmentally acceptable and compatible with the livability of Oregon.'" To achieve that end, McCall presented the story of Hector Macpherson's efforts and carefully explained (for public consumption) how the resulting legislation, now named Senate Bill 100, would work.[114]

As SB 100 emerged from the Macpherson committee's draft, the central idea was to provide for local land use planning within a framework of state-enforced goals. The mandatory (but practically unenforceable) zoning requirement of 1969's SB 10 had produced such a haphazard system of county and city ordinances that subdivisions were being approved in floodplains, on rich farmland, and often without regard for future needs; few restrictions were placed on overall levels of growth at any level of government. Consequently, the dual intentions of SB 100 were to address the most glaring problems of the existing order while simultaneously preparing for future demand for development land and green space to be preserved to bolster quality of life.

The proposed system would coordinate statewide goals under an appointed seven-member Land Conservation and Development Commission (LCDC) that would hold review authority over local ordinances, ensuring that critical needs like mass transit and habitat protection would be included in all zoning plans but also giving local officials the ability to adapt the planning process to their particular situations. No longer would municipalities be able to sprawl independently or rural counties be allowed to proceed with the wholesale conversion of farmland to subdivisions. Instead, the various levels of government involved would be combined into planning districts that would be overseen by both LCDC (working through a new state land use agency called the Department of Land Conservation and Development, or DLCD) and a Joint Legislative Committee on Land Use in the legislature. The DLCD would retain authority over certain resources designated "areas of critical state concern" (wetlands, coastal zones, scenic areas, interstate highway corridors, etc.) and land uses labeled "activities of state concern" (airports, power plants, landfills, etc.), to be managed at the state level in keeping with planning goals to be set in the commission's first year. The scheme represented a substantial shift of control from local government to the state, as well as the first restrictions on private property rights that some rural areas would have seen.[115] McCall expected significant opposition from the day the bill was introduced, which explains the dramatic tone of his "grasping wastrels" address and the care he took in presenting land use control to the public as not another way to increase government control over their lives but rather the most critical step in Oregon's efforts to maintain a quality of life that had become the envy of the nation.

As its proponents expected, SB 100 met with substantial opposition and was greeted by such headlines as "Land Use Bill Hasn't Much Chance" upon its introduction in January 1973.[116] The initial hearings drew negative testimony from developers, real estate brokers, construction companies, property rights advocates, and a host of others who variously felt the plan was a land grab, an unconstitutional taking of private property, an unwar-ranted expansion of state authority, or even communistic. The inclusion of councils of governments (COGs), the mechanism used to combine local governments into regional planning districts, drew especially heated criticism as it was seen as establishing an unnecessary (and unelected) third level of government. When the governor's chief environmental advi-sor, Kessler Cannon, presented the bill to the Governor's Committee for a Livable Oregon he described it as "the most explosive issue before the 1973 legislative session," and for good reason.[117] It quickly became clear that the bill would never be passed in its original form and that signifi-cant revision and compromise would be required to make any meaningful progress.

Hector Macpherson's partner in shepherding SB 100 through the leg-islature was Ted Hallock, a liberal Democrat from Portland and the chair-man of the Senate Environment and Land Use Committee. With years of legislative experience, the professional public relations consultant was quick to recognize that his own committee had been loaded with plan-ning opponents by Senate president Jason Boe, who represented a coastal district that many considered to have failed at land use planning; Hallock also understood that the bill would have to be amended to have any hope of passage. Convinced the proposal was doomed without action to address the deep-seated opposition to the COGs and to giving the state any overt authority over local land use decisions, Hallock decided to bring together planning advocates and opponents in an ad hoc committee to work out some of their differences and produce a passable bill. The key to the plan would obviously be the committee chair, who would have to mediate between the competing interests. Hallock chose a union official and for-mer head of the state Department of Environmental Quality named L. B. Day for the task, knowing his commanding personality and strong support for land use planning offered the best chance to wring something useful from the group. Described by Macpherson as "a hulking Teamster Union leader and DEQ director with . . . black, patent leather hair, a laugh that could penetrate hearing room doors and a snarl that could make bureau-crats tremble," Day took command of the disparate group of people rep-resenting the timber industry, real estate developers, mining companies, farmers, local government, and environmental organizations and in the course of ten days hammered out a compromise bill that one observer tagged a "minor miracle."[118]

Though they made the bill much weaker than the one originally drafted by Hector Macpherson, L. B. Day's revisions to SB 100 yielded ground to both sides in the debate over land use and thus, as a true compromise solution, gave the bill a much better chance of passage than any statewide land use legislation previously considered. The two biggest changes in the bill were the deletion of the councils of governments and the removal of state authority over the "areas of critical concern." While both of these provisions were seen as important strengths by the backers of the original bill, they drew the staunchest opposition from opponents and were jettisoned in hope of gaining support for the broader goal of statewide zoning. As a result, responsibility for the zoning process would remain in the hands of county officials, who would act under goals set by the state Land Conservation Development Commission, which would also serve as the ultimate enforcement authority. The tradeoff for planning proponents was the retention of state regulation of critical *activities*, including infrastructure such as highways, sewage systems, and airports. A final, crucial element was the inclusion of financial support for counties to complete the zoning process, a stumbling block that had helped render SB 10 ineffective.[119] L. B. Day also realized the importance of citizen support for the process, so he envisioned a planning process "that basically comes from the bottom up, not from the top down" by requiring counties to include proposals for citizen participation when preparing their land use plans.[120]

When the revised bill was introduced before the full Environment and Land Use Committee in March 1972, Tom McCall spoke of the importance of providing state funding to give counties the means to create their own land use plans. The failure of SB 10 to accomplish its goals, he felt, was due to its provision for state-imposed zoning in counties that failed to adopt plans of their own, since without adequate funding it had proven hard for the majority of counties to complete any plan at all. McCall recognized that SB 10 had the "stick—although not a very forbidding one—but not the carrot." One strength of SB 100 was that it was "based upon the premise that the carrot—the money—will be furnished to local government, as necessary, by the state."[121] Although McCall groused about the loss of the COGs, which he felt were important in bringing regional officials together and had been deleted not because of their function but rather as a "result of personalities, jealousies and the smallness of people," he expressed his unqualified support for the revised bill. Of course, as L. B. Day explained it, the loss of COGs and proposed limitations on state authority were only modest compromises. In his words, "The counties are going to be given the responsibility to carry out a mission. . . . If they can't do it, the state will. There's no use sugar-coating it."[122] Realistically, there was little chance a bill including the COGs would have passed; Hector Macpherson recalled that "counties were certainly terribly opposed to it when we had councils of government in there," but their removal quieted opposition from that level significantly.[123] Given the public support for planning in urban areas of the state, gaining the favor of county officials from rural areas (or at least limiting their opposition) was crucial to winning enough votes to pass the final package.

The sugarcoating may well have contributed to the bill's success in the Senate the following month, when the revised SB100 was approved on an 18–10 vote on April 19 with virtually no amendments, a victory that planning proponents had viewed as unlikely a few months prior. A companion bill would appropriate $3 million to fund the initial planning effort, two-thirds of which would go to support the counties in their zoning work. The fact that SB 100 did not include its own funding provisions stirred some debate, which Ted Hallock quashed by pointing out to opponents that "we've got things a little turned around here. If the Senate and the House determine that they want a land use bill, we'll find the money. We'll tell the Ways and Means Committee what the hell to do."[124] Immediately after the vote, Hallock rushed to the office of Representative Nancie Fadeley, who chaired the House committee that was considering the bill, and told her that a conference committee would spell doom for the bill. To avoid that fate, he appeared before Fadeley's committee and warned them directly, "If you guys change one comma, that calls for a conference committee, [and] we're dead. It's through."[125] The committee listened, and on May 23 the full House passed SB 100 without amendment after just two hours of debate, sending it to the governor for his signature.[126]

Though McCall was concerned about the compromises that weakened the final bill, he saw it as the only chance to address growth issues in a concrete way that was also moderate enough to survive political opposition. SB 100 proved the value of its moderation that fall, when backers of an initiative petition to repeal it failed to collect enough signatures to authorize a special election, prompting the editors of the *Capital Journal* to comment, "We've never been happier about the failure of a referendum before."[127] It was an important victory for McCall as well, who was constitutionally limited to just two terms in office and thus had little time remaining to make his mark in land use practices in the state.

Creating the state Department of Land Conservation and Development (the agency that would back up the Land Conservation and Development Commission) and implementing SB 100 became the next challenge in Oregon's land use drama, leaving the McCall administration with the task of both appointing the group of commissioners to establish statewide planning goals and staffing the agency to support them. L. B. Day, the man Hector Macpherson considered the "savior of SB 100," was appointed to chair the LCDC and Portland lawyer and environmental activist Stephen Schell was named vice chairman. Meanwhile, Arnold Cogan, McCall's planning director, was picked to head the new zoning agency. The immediate problem facing both bodies was the refusal of the Ways and Means Committee to appropriate operating funds; only through support from the governor's office did they manage any progress in the early days, when, as Cogan remembered it, "We were a beleaguered agency with a small staff, an inadequate budget, no place to call home, and little help and support." When the legislature finally appropriated operating funds, only $100,000 was approved; land use planning would have to progress through the critical goal-setting process in 1974 without the level of support its crafters had envisioned.[128]

Despite the passage of SB 100, the battle over land use had just begun, as McCall explained in January 1974:

Ensuring the presence of a statewide planning process does not guarantee that Oregon will develop as its citizens wish it would. A plan cannot be an end in itself, as a look at the thousands of plans now gathering dust will attest. The true test of whether Oregon can, over the years, preserve the quality of life, rests in Oregonians being able to formulate the elements of the lifestyle they wish to enjoy and to then translate these goals into policies to be implemented now.

Therefore, it will not be the Oregon Land Conservation and Development Commission that will be able to keep Oregon, Oregon. Oregon's future can only be determined by its citizens.[129]

The connection between population growth and land use planning remained at the top of the agenda for Arnold Cogan in the early months, reflecting the basis of popular support for zoning. It was critical, he said, for Oregon to plan for a mobile and growing population and to do so with citizen participation. Accordingly, a series of twenty-eight public meetings was scheduled across the state in 1974 to begin the goal-setting process.[130] As the governor had suggested, citizens would indeed play a major role in determining the future of land use in the state.

It was no coincidence that less than a year after Oregon legislators approved SB 100 a national land use program was under consideration in Washington, DC. Tom McCall, as a visible public proponent of land use controls, was called to testify before Congress on the matter as something of an expert. At hearings chaired by Representative Morris K. Udall of Arizona, a Democrat who shared McCall's environmental sensitivities, the Oregon governor offered his support for a bill that would look not unlike his own state's new law, claiming that other states needed to be raised to Oregon's standards for environmental values.[131] When the federal bill was defeated on a 204–211 vote in June 1974, McCall publicly rebuked Representative Sam Steiger, an Arizona Republican who had commented that killing the bill would get the politicians home quicker. "Should this thinking in Congress and a few statehouses be allowed to prevail," he stated bitterly, "there won't be any home to come home to in a very few years, the way many states are permitting their prime lands to be raped."[132] Later that year McCall expressed the fear that land use planning in Oregon might in fact have the opposite effect on migration than some supporters had hoped, particularly in the absence of a federal land use law. "This is going to have such a perceptible impact that if only a few other states have it, people are really going to want to move here," he told reporters during an appeal for public participation in land use planning.[133]

The process of implementing SB 100 would prove to be a long one, fraught with legal and political challenges, including petitions to repeal the entire law, efforts to limit funding to carry out the planning process, and lawsuits from property rights organizations. Happily for planning proponents, Oregon's court system at the time was supportive of the concept of subordinating individual property rights to the public interest. Indeed, a zoning-related case that went all the way to the state supreme court in 1973 established the public welfare as a legitimate consideration in planning decisions, a precedent that would undergird the land use planning effort for years to come.[134] Once again acting as pioneers, Oregonians would have to make up the rules as they went along, determining how to best balance the rights of individuals and the need for economic development with the desire to preserve livability and to conserve scarce resources across the state. To the questions of growth and the puzzle of tourism no immediate answers were offered; instead citizens would have to trust their representatives to develop policies that reflected their values. It was a delicate balancing act, because anything done to improve the state's quality of life also made it more attractive to others and thus encouraged migration. Even the distant *Wall Street Journal* noticed this, resulting in a 1974 headline that read, "Try as They Might, Folks in Oregon Can't Deter New Residents."[135]

What Tom McCall did not know in 1974 was that Oregon's new land use planning system would remain among the state's most contentious political issues for decades, though it would also attract the envy of other states unable to summon the political will to address the issues that he and others had pushed into the spotlight in the late 1960s. Population growth, loss of open space, urban sprawl, migration, and related issues would occupy the attention of politicians and citizens across the nation for the quarter century that followed, surviving Watergate, the Cold War, economic recessions, and other pressing matters to regularly resurface in one state or another, and every time that happened people would look to Oregon and SB 100 as a model. The governor himself would become a symbol of Oregon's willingness to say no to unregulated growth in hope of preserving livability for its citizens; more than any other issue the state's land use planning program would form the bedrock beneath a national reputation for environmental innovation, leadership, and uncompromising standards that would carry into the twenty-first century. But in 1974 that was in the future; for McCall and Oregon the immediate task was to figure out how to turn the new law into policy, and then to turn the policy into action that would literally help keep Oregon green.

Chapter 7
Keeping Oregon Green

> Oregon, so far, seems to be infested with fewer of the rapists of land
> and befoulers of air who have done such grievous environmental
> injury to other parts of the United States and the world.
>
> —Paul M. Lewis, 1977

In the fall of 1999 Portland's KGW-8 TV assembled a panel of historians
to produce a list of the five most important "Oregonians of the Century"
to mark the passing millennium. The historians' picks were set against
those chosen through an unscientific poll of the general public in a series
of broadcasts presenting brief biographies and assessments of the lumi-
naries. Despite some differences between the two lists, both groups overwhelmingly selected former governor Tom McCall as the "Oregonian of
the Century." Reporter Walden Kirsch opened his story on the results with
the declaration that "Tom McCall's image still looms over Oregon like
Paul Bunyan," a sentiment echoed by historian Stephen Dow Beckham,
who agreed that the governor was "a remarkable figure; he stood tall, he
spoke boldly." But beyond his commanding figure and political skill, it was
McCall's signature environmental agenda that was singled out as notewor-
thy: the broadcast of *Pollution in Paradise*, the Beach Bill, the Bottle Bill,
and LCDC's land use planning program were presented as the core of what
the report identified as "the Oregon myth."[1] Lauded in the final newscast
of the series as "a man whose fame has faded only briefly and whose ideas
have guided Oregon for more than a quarter century," McCall's selection
reflected his impact on the state's political history and the central role environmental quality continues to play in the formation of regional identity.

The environmental achievements of the McCall era continue to reso-
nate in the public imagination in Oregon. Despite the passage of time and
significant changes in the state's population and economy, the key elements

of the fight to "keep Oregon green" are now irrevocably linked in the public imagination with the image of Tom McCall declaring an "Oregon way," framed in the language of livability and stewardship, to form an enduring element of the region's sense of place. The craftiest politician to wield the concept of livability thus himself became part of its mythology, informing an identity that imbues place with meaning and provides a common narrative for understanding what is unique about Oregon. In the national consciousness, Oregon became green on McCall's watch and today enjoys a reputation substantially based on a relative handful of high-profile victories that marked the state as an early leader in environmental policy and practice, while within the region the governor himself remains an iconic symbol of the values he promoted.

Despite Tom McCall's central role in the process, the development and application of the concepts of livability and stewardship as rhetorical tools did not occur within clear chronological, topical, or geographical boundaries. Though evident in Oregon politics by the early 1960s, they were not fully formed by the end of the decade; nor did they become static following the events of the 1970s. Instead, their roots predate the environmental era and they remain active and evolving components of the political and cultural landscapes of Oregon today, decades later, adapted by those who advocate stewardship to maintain livability in the environments they inhabit. Richard Neuberger called for stewardship of Oregon's—and the nation's—natural heritage in his writings well before World War II, but stewardship was not yet part of the common vocabulary of the region at that time. When the senator made a concerted effort to convince Oregonians to preserve some of their coastal dunes as a national park in the 1950s, he was surprised they did not leap to his support. While local opposition to the establishment of new federal parks was not uncommon, Neuberger clearly expected the vast majority of his constituents would welcome his proposal and would see in its preservation goals a reflection of their sense of place, a pride in the state's natural features and associated livability. He was sure enough of this that he first sent word of the plan to the editors of the state's major newspapers, just days before he introduced the first park bill, in a telegram that closed with understated confidence: "Trust you will regard the idea favorably."[2]

Though supporters shared Neuberger's vision of a dunes park that would, as one expressed it, bring together coastal resources "like the surviving possessions . . . of the pioneers scattered here and there in the attics of the homes of their descendants" in a plan "worthy of Oregon and her citizens," the senator's inability to mobilize overwhelming support for the park reflected the population's uncertainty about the need for such projects as much as it did his own political failings.[3] While opposition on the state and local levels appeared formidable, as noted previously it was easily dismissed by former governor Oswald West as "a lot of bushwah" and could have been overcome by an outpouring of public support, something Neuberger hoped to generate through his appeals to Oregonians' sense of stewardship and pride in their coastline. That support never materialized, however, and Senator Wayne Morse's protracted opposition ultimately doomed the proposal.[4] One observer later described this period in the state's environmental politics by claiming that Oregon "predictably . . . always had a land ethic" due to its heavy reliance on natural resources; when a stronger *environmental* ethic developed in the late 1960s it was based in a form of environmental populism not yet evident in Neuberger's time.[5] If that was true, of course, then any initial land ethic was almost entirely utilitarian— calls to *limit* economic development in the 1970s in favor of preserving quality of life were thus more revolutionary than evolutionary, despite frequent political rhetoric to the contrary.

Today, nearly sixty years after Richard Neuberger first proposed an Oregon Dunes National Seashore, the U.S. Forest Service manages the Oregon Dunes National Recreation Area in a fashion that reflects the compromises from which it was born in 1972. The $5 million initial investment projected in the national park plan never materialized, nor did the large annual budgets for visitor services and interpretation; appropriations for the Forest Service–managed national recreation area remained steady at around $1.2 million from its creation until 1994, when Congress slashed funding by nearly half. At the same time, timber harvests were also reduced, leading to a budget shortfall that was reversed only by the passage of the Recreation Fee Demonstration Program in 1997, which allowed some federal recreation areas to retain a percentage of their fee revenues for local reinvestment, and ultimately by the 2005 Federal Lands Recreation Enhancement Act, which made that program permanent.

Annual visitation levels at the Oregon Dunes remain close to the 1959 projections for a Forest Service recreation area, around 1.2 million per year or about half the number expected if a national park had been established in its place. Of these visitors, one-third are off-road vehicle users, a form of recreation that would likely not have been allowed under National Park Service management.[6] One wonders how an Oregon Dunes National Seashore would have fared after fifty years—would the fiftieth anniversary celebration have generated national attention? The NPS marked the golden anniversaries of Cape Cod, Padre Island, and the Indiana Dunes with a range of special events, and each saw increased visitation numbers throughout the celebratory years.[7] One thing that is certain, however, is that very little about the modern dunes recreation area embodies the calls for stewardship and livability that characterized Richard Neuberger's campaign for national park status. There is in fact little to suggest even a basic awareness of past hopes for a national park in the dunes, now relegated substantially to a form of recreation antithetical to the wilderness vision of the park's proponents. By the Forest Service's own admission, the site remains among area residents and visitors primarily "famous for its OHV [off-highway vehicle] riding opportunities."[8]

Richard Neuberger's concept for a dunes national park embodied a style of conservation that was both ahead of and behind the times in 1959, reflecting a politics based primarily among elites in Washington and state officials with a traditional focus on wilderness preservation. This was the form most conservation battles of the period took, with only a scarce few issues "going national" in coordinated appeals to the general public, as was the case with Colorado's Dinosaur National Monument in 1955.[9] However, Neuberger also employed the language of stewardship and livability in his dunes efforts, using the threat of future environmental degradation as a warning to generate support for preservation out of both moral obligation and enlightened self-interest. He remained convinced to the end that the public overwhelmingly supported his plan, and he would simply not accept the possibility that "a national park . . . is not wanted on the Oregon seacoast."[10] What he lacked was the ability to mobilize that support, a shortcoming likely due not to his personal political limitations but to the fact that Oregonians were not yet ready to embrace the notion that their state was in less than pristine condition or to accept that the environmental decay seen in the urban East might soon threaten their own quality of life. Without a sense of crisis among the public to bolster his claims about the future, Neuberger's appeals for stewardship, while based on an amalgam of state pride and obligation to history, did not produce the widespread response needed to sway decision-making elites or mobilize the masses in support of his plan to bring a second national park to the state.

A few years after Richard Neuberger's death the situation in Oregon looked markedly different. Tom McCall's *Pollution in Paradise* broadcast awakened Oregonians to the environmental problems around them in 1962; in amplifying growing unease over the impacts of growth in the Willamette Valley it generated a level of public support for environmental action that Neuberger could not have imagined. This was due in part to changing issues; fear of declining livability raised by environmental threats in or adjacent to population centers was obviously more compelling politically than the preservation of remote wild areas. Just as importantly, these emerging environmental concerns were linked from the outset to a stewardship obligation by McCall and others, who offered historical contrasts to both shock and shame the public into action. "How could you let the salmon die?" *Pollution in Paradise* asked those who lived near the Willamette. "Were they not part of the legacy your ancestors handed down?" it rebuked. The shocking images of carp and other "trash fish" clustered in a sewage-choked Willamette were the most powerful of the documentary, and it is not surprising that cleaning up the river became the central environmental issue of the 1960s in Oregon. The documentary and the political momentum it generated helped propel Tom McCall into office and launched Oregon onto the national stage, a position reflected well in *National Geographic*'s 1972 cover story declaring the Willamette River "reborn." The Willamette cleanup itself soon became part of the mythology of stewardship, a story and a symbol of what Oregonians could achieve when they set their minds to an environmental challenge. They actually *saved* a river, the story goes: they brought it back to life.

National Geographic placed the Willamette in stark contrast to contemporary coverage of Ohio's Cuyahoga River, a waterway so polluted it became a symbol of environmental decay when it famously appeared in *Time* magazine after catching fire in 1969.[11] What was missing from the *National Geographic* story, and is still absent from the mythology that grew around the Willamette cleanup in subsequent decades, is the fact that while the improved condition of the river first drew national attention in 1971–72, Oregon's Department of Environmental Quality had found that by the state's own standards the cleanup goals had largely been met in 1968, when according to official records "past efforts culminated in water quality

Fig. 25. *National Geographic* cover featuring the Willamette River cleanup, 1972 (Original in author's possession)

meeting standards in a major portion of the river." By 1969 only a few short stretches of the river near major pollution sources failed that basic test.[12] Public impressions to the contrary, none of the initiatives promoted by Tom McCall's administration could have impacted river quality to such a degree so shortly after his taking office—he was in some ways simply the man on watch when the good news came upstream in the form of the returning salmon migration. The hard (and costly) work had in fact been done by the municipalities that had been slowly installing modern sewage treatment plants since the early 1950s and by industrial polluters that were investing in new, cleaner technologies (or simply closing down) to reduce effluents from paper mills and other major point sources of pollution. While McCall certainly pushed for stronger regulations and increased compliance from both groups, the groundwork for the return of the salmon had been laid years before he became governor in 1967. In the end the long-beleaguered

State Sanitary Authority had accomplished the task it was created for in 1938—it had just taken three decades to do so.

That Tom McCall received most of the credit for the river cleanup in the public eye is not surprising, but it is problematic for several reasons. That decades of work to clean up the river prior to McCall's involvement were largely ignored by the media (*National Geographic* located the beginnings of citizen concern in the mid-1960s) is certainly cause for concern among historians. Perhaps more troubling, though, is the suggestion that complex environmental problems that take decades to develop can be solved simply with bold leadership and a few years' time. A series of such quick, easy victories could give rise to a sense of complacency over environmental issues as citizens and politicians alike choose to postpone costly reforms into the indefinite future. But at its heart, the most damaging element of the popular story of the Willamette's recovery is that the solution it held up as a model—a quick technological fix made possible by popular political support and the commitment of enlightened leaders—overlooked the fact that the full spectrum of conditions underlying water quality problems in the Willamette was never directly addressed. In 1959 Governor Mark Hatfield proclaimed pollution a byproduct of population growth and called for a national solution, but the mythological "quick fix" in Oregon suggested that better regulations could make growth benign and that individual states were up to the task of saving the nation's waterways from the compounding ravages of unchecked industrial and urban expansion.

Since 1967 regulations on industrial pollution signed into law by Governor McCall and the water quality standards imposed by the federal Clean Water Act of 1972 have further reduced the impact of factory wastes on the river, just as advocates hoped they would, but the Willamette's waters today remain under threat of chemical and biological contamination from nonpoint sources such as urban and agricultural runoff, much of it a direct product of continued population growth in the Willamette Valley.[13] Though the state Department of Environmental Quality itself produced a documentary titled *A River Restored: Oregon's Willamette* in the 1980s, which suggested the future challenge would be to maintain the water quality improvements made in the 1970s, it has become increasingly clear in recent years that the 1972 victory was a temporary one.[14] Near its Waldo Lake headwaters the river remains relatively clean and pure, but by the time it reaches the Columbia River near Portland it has flowed through

a federally designated Superfund site (the Portland Harbor). Ongoing studies have found high levels of toxic contaminants such as polychlorinated
biphenyls (PCBs) and dioxin along the river bottom in multiple locations.[15]
Most surprisingly, until the completion of a twenty-year replacement project 2011, the city of Portland continued to employ an outdated "combined
sewer outflow" system that poured untreated sewage directly into the river
during periods of heavy rain, making stretches of the Willamette unsafe for
human contact for weeks at a time.[16]

Despite the inadequacies of the original solution to the Willamette
River problem, the impact of *Pollution in Paradise* and the first campaign
to restore the river remain a fundamental part of Oregon's stewardship narrative and are often recalled by proponents of new cleanup campaigns to
justify the expense of continued action on water quality. The worst industrial polluters and point sources of sewage contamination were largely
contained by 1972, but today the hard work of treating over a century's
worth of contaminated sediments—at estimated costs in excess of a billion
dollars—looms over the river as darkly as the threats of the 1960s.[17] "We
took care of the easy stuff," Don Francis, founder of the advocacy group
Willamette Riverwatch, told a reporter in 2000. "We looked at a handful of
industries and said, 'Clean up or go away.' We restored oxygen levels, but
we didn't look at the whole problem to begin with."[18] The original effort to
restore the river failed to protect it from perils unforeseen at the time, but
the legacy of the public outcry over the river's condition is as evident in
the existence of groups like Willamette Riverwatch as it was in the return
of the salmon celebrated, albeit a bit prematurely, by *National Geographic*
in 1972. That initial victory suggested that solutions to the environmental
problems plaguing other states could be found in Oregon and proved that
the political will was there to carry them out. The story of the river's first
cleanup is still frequently retold as part of the effort to develop political
support for the costly investments required to maintain the Willamette's
health in the face of these most recent threats.

Unlike the effort to restore the Willamette River, the plan to secure
Oregon's beaches for public use in perpetuity has been an unquestioned
success. Subject to legal challenges that culminated in hearings before the
state supreme court in 1971, the Beach Bill survived intact to become a
national symbol of Oregon's penchant for livability and environmental
protection. In a unanimous decision the court then declared a proposed

road to be in violation of the 1967 law and "an unsightly blemish upon an otherwise natural area of considerable scenic beauty" in affirming the public's right to access beaches below the vegetation line.[19] The following year the *Capital Journal* editorialized on the law, noting the remarkable contrast between Oregon and East Coast states where public beaches were few and far between. "We know of no state which approaches Oregon's degree of public ownership," the paper noted with considerable pride, concluding that "Oregonians are lucky that people like Governor Os West more than half a century ago took firm steps to prevent squandering of the beachland."[20] This recognition of West's early role in preserving the beaches aside, it was Tom McCall who would be most associated with the Beach Bill in public memory. While relatively few Oregonians today might recognize Oswald West through association with anything other than the state park that bears his name, McCall's enthusiastic grandstanding in support of the Beach Bill assured the legislation would be forever tied to his image as Oregon's environmental governor. When the bill's thirtieth anniversary was marked in 1997, television coverage focused on its results—public access to beaches along the entire coastline—and McCall's role in securing its passage. KATU-TV's report included a visual of the governor signing the bill and segments of the press conference following the ceremony, ensuring that those who did not already link McCall to the beach issue would not fail to do so again.[21] A new generation learned the story in detail when Oregon Public Broadcasting produced an episode of *The Oregon Experience* history series on the Beach Bill to celebrate the fortieth anniversary in 2007, and the legislative battle was remembered at a celebration of the law at the Mark O. Hatfield Marine Science Center in Newport.[22]

Despite Oregon's unique success in preserving public access to its beaches and the attention this drew from other coastal states, there was no rush to duplicate the law elsewhere. While the federal House of Representatives held hearings on public beach access in 1973 at which Oregon's attorney general testified at length, only Hawaii followed Texas and Oregon in legally protecting public access to the entirety of its coastline.[23] Rather than the Beach Bill, another piece of legislation became the central element of the state's reputation as a source of progressive environmental ideas: the 1971 Bottle Bill. Unlike the beach legislation, which logically interested only coastal states in which beach access was at issue, the Bottle Bill drew national attention not only because it represented a response to a recognizable national problem but also because its proponents secured victory against a well-funded, national industry lobby.

Universally viewed as groundbreaking, the passage of Oregon's beverage container law was celebrated as "a break in the dam which has been holding back national action" that might ultimately "be recognized nationally as more than pioneer environmental legislation. It may be realized [as] a first legislative step in turning this country from a profligate waster of natural resources to a recycler and conservator of resources."[24] The Bottle Bill survived several legal challenges even before it took effect, with one circuit judge refusing to intervene in part because, as her opinion stated, "This bold and forceful action . . . reflects and is, I believe, a major response to the concern that citizens in Oregon feel and have demonstrated concerning their environment."[25] When an initial impact study found a 75 percent reduction in bottle and can litter along a series of randomly selected test sections of highway, the governor declared the bill a "rip-roaring success" in 1973.[26] As these results were confirmed by subsequent studies, environmental advocates from other states turned to Oregon as a model, just as proponents had suggested they would when the bill was first introduced.[27] Never one to miss an opportunity to speak out for Oregon, McCall accepted invitations from around the nation to explain the function of the new law, becoming a de facto spokesman for the national antilitter campaign while simultaneously promoting the state. As he told attendees at the 1972 National Symposium on State Environmental Legislation in Washington, DC, "Oregon is the state with a bottle bill, and if there is a state representative here that has not asked for a copy of our law requiring a refund, you represent a minority."[28]

When a federal bottle bill was finally introduced in 1975, its chief sponsors were Oregon senators Mark Hatfield and Robert Packwood. Despite the support of the Environmental Protection Agency the effort failed by a wide margin, due in part to what the *Capital Journal* called the "astounding lies" about Oregon's bill spread by its industry opponents.[29] Bottle-return proponents responded to this defeat by pressing forward in state legislatures across the country, and each time a bill was introduced elsewhere Oregonians reacted with a mixture of pride and glee. "Follow Oregon's Lead, U.S. Told" declared one headline. "Connecticut Joins Oregon's Crusade" stated another. The tone became almost smug when California legislators killed a deposit bill in the face of intensive industry

Fig. 26.   Overflowing trash at a Portland International Airport viewing area illustrates distinct lack of bottles/cans in wake of Bottle Bill, 1973 (National Archives and Records Administration, Record Group 412: Records of the Environmental Protection Agency, LI 412-DA-5644)

lobbying: "Californians may be ahead of the nation with their fascination over chain letters, cocaine snorting and Transcendental Meditation, but when it comes to such heady stuff as enlightened legislation, they rank on a par with Arkansas," one Oregonian sniped.[30] Only Vermont succeeded in passing a similar bill close on the heels of Oregon, in 1972.

To industry leaders it was Oregon that was out of place. William May, the president of American Can, explained in one state that such legislation "may work in Oregon, but it won't work anywhere else. They're a bunch of woodsy weirdos out there."[31] Ultimately it was not just the "woodsy weirdos" of Oregon and Vermont who approved bottle bills, however; Michigan, Maine, Iowa, and Connecticut followed suit in the 1970s, as did the municipality of Columbia, Missouri. Massachusetts, Delaware, New York, and even California got on board in the 1980s. Hawaii is the most recent state to have implemented a bottle bill, in 2002, while both Delaware and Columbia, Missouri, have since shut down their deposit systems.[32] Tom

McCall was pointed in his condemnation of the bottling industry, telling an audience in 1981 that "the bottle bill ought to be the keystone of a conserver [*sic*] society, but big business won't let it."[33] By the mid-1980s those who had conceived of and sponsored Oregon's Bottle Bill, Richard Chambers and Representative Paul Hanneman, were largely forgotten by the public, while McCall's association with his administration's environmental focus ensured he would continue to play a central role in what he called "the Oregon story," a narrative accepted by most residents as an element of what made their state unique.[34] Once again, McCall's livability agenda had taken on a life of its own as part of the mythology of stewardship he popularized.

The crest of Oregon's tidal wave of innovative environmental legislation was of course the 1973 land use planning law, commonly referred to by the acronym for the commission established to oversee it, LCDC (for the Land Conservation and Development Commission). The completion of a statewide zoning scheme to preserve open space and farmland became one of Tom McCall's highest priorities as governor (the other, the passage of a sales tax to fund public schools, was never realized). A pragmatic conservationist at heart when it came to natural resources, his vision for Oregon involved not preserving nature for its intrinsic value alone but protecting livability—which meant the continued utilization of natural resources for economic production as well as the provision of amenities like green space and recreation. Politically pragmatic as well, the governor realized that a top-down, state-level program imposed on local governments would not work in Oregon, so he supported the unique planning model that became SB 100, designed to establish state-level goals and review authority but to place responsibility for developing and implementing plans with local government. Despite the fact that the initial idea, the original bill, and most of the political wrangling that won its eventual passage were the work of others, McCall personally accepted national acclaim for LCDC on Oregon's behalf and devoted significant time after leaving office to its defense.[35]

Indeed, legal challenges and repeal efforts were expected from the outset; in 1974 attorney Henry Richmond warned the governor that his land use program would require an active defense and proposed a model for a "non-partisan, non-lobbying organization with a first year budget of $50,000" to play that role.[36] Richmond soon cofounded an organization called 1,000 Friends of Oregon by initially seeking the support of one thousand donors, including McCall, who publicly announced its formation shortly before leaving office in 1975.[37] As public discourse and political values shifted away from environmental protection and toward economic utility in the later 1970s, LCDC would come under repeated fire from both ends of the political spectrum, proving Richmond's warning prescient.[38]

The power of the citizen's ballot initiative (the heart of the "Oregon system" of initiative, referendum, and recall) can be wielded as a blunt instrument to repeal entire laws over disagreements of any scale; the initiative process offered opponents of land use planning an avenue of attack on LCDC that was exercised frequently after 1973. In 1976 a repeal attempt was defeated 57–43 percent, with nearly a 75 percent voter turnout. Two years later, Ballot Measure 10, a follow-up proposal to end LCDC, met with coordinated opposition from a coalition of land use planning defenders, including the state AFL-CIO, the League of Women Voters, and Associated Oregon Industries. Their pro-LCDC campaign was waged under the banner "Uncontrolled Growth Will Kill Oregon" and featured appeals that went right to the heart of the mythology of stewardship and claims that Oregon was unique:

> We have what the rest of the country has been trying to put
>   together for years.
> The whole country looks to us as leaders.
> Reasonable people, living sensibly with planned growth.
> Let's not let it all get away from us.
> Our land.
> Our jobs.
> Our way of life.
> Don't let Oregon become like California.[39]

Tom McCall, by then retired, returned to the political stage in 1978 to warn voters that Oregon had just become the sixth-fastest-growing state in the nation. LCDC was needed because "good planning is the only weapon—the only shield—we have to protect ourselves from the[se] enormous growth pressures." The planning process was by then almost complete and "it would be suicide as far as quality of life in Oregon goes to let Ballot Measure 10 pass."[40] This time repeal was rejected by an even larger margin, 61–39 percent, with only five predominantly rural counties voting in support of the initiative.[41]

One of the closest calls for LCDC came in 1982, when a third repeal initiative made the November ballot. Hector Macpherson formed an organization called Citizens to Defend Your Land to oppose what became Ballot Measure 6, warning that if it passed "Oregon's carefully drawn system of land use planning, which has taken 10 years to put into place, will be destroyed."[42] As election day approached things looked grim for the zoning law, but 1,000 Friends of Oregon and other supporters worked tirelessly to turn public opinion against the initiative. Their greatest weapon was Tom McCall, who came out of retirement once again to wage a public defense of what had become his signature environmental legacy. McCall, though, was also fighting a private battle with cancer, and as the election approached it became clear to observers that he was in decline. He appealed to the citizens of Oregon to preserve the law, explaining that he badly wanted to win this last political contest: "You all know I have terminal cancer—and I have a lot of it. This activist loves Oregon more than he loves life. . . . If the legacy we helped give Oregon and which made it twinkle from afar—if it goes, then I guess I wouldn't want to live in Oregon anyhow."[43] Hector Macpherson remembered the former governor being "very supportive . . . right when he was dying" during the fight to save LCDC in the fall of 1982.[44] Tom McCall celebrated his final political victory when Measure 6 was defeated at the polls. He died just two months later, on January 8, 1983.

As Oregon's land use planning law passed its ten-year anniversary and the original deadlines for completing its county-by-county planning documents, even Governor Victor Atiyeh, an ardent opponent of SB 100 in the legislature, remarked on the achievement, reflecting in his 1985 legislative message that "historians will detail our singular efforts in concluding a statewide land-use plan that stands as a national landmark."[45] When planners gathered in 1998 to celebrate the twenty-fifth anniversary of Senate Bill 100 and LCDC they lauded Hector Macpherson as its author and driving force. But Tom McCall's presence was inescapable, evident in quotations on event programs and in recordings shared at meetings, never yielding center stage but seizing it in a voice from the past, reminding celebrants that "it is the place of Oregon that means the most. We must, first and foremost, cherish the place. All other good things will follow if we recognize the special beauty of Oregon first in all our planning; if we revere the magic; if we protect the quality."[46] Poet Kim Stafford captured the almost reverent spirit surrounding LCDC in the minds of its supporters in a poem written for the anniversary:

OLD 100

They call it "Land Use Planning." I call it our shimmer of camas blue.
They call it law. I call it what we saw and will see—what we tasted, and will taste
as we move upriver through time. What we loved in Oregon, and will.

This is where we decided to be together.
Now we choose how to live as one.

Bill One Hundred, be our friend to old ways. Our teacher
as we practice to be here gently and long. Our ambassador.
Our way to meet this place, and be the people of this place.[47]

It takes a remarkable piece of legislation to inspire a poet, but SB 100 and the stories that have grown up around it are remarkable. Not surprisingly, Tom McCall remains at the center of those stories told most often, even though Macpherson lamented in 1999 that "Tom's getting a lot of credit that in some ways he doesn't deserve . . . because he was the one that would really rouse the people with his eloquence."[48] While the reverential air surrounding LCDC may have been limited to a segment of the Oregon population, within the broader planning community the law did indeed serve as a model by which "Oregon . . . influenced heavily and in more or less direct ways the content of growth management systems adopted [by other states] during the 1980s."[49]

LCDC's association with McCall did not lessen after his death. In October 1999 two dozen graduate students from the University of Oregon's master's degree program in community and regional planning attending an annual tour of the Department of Land Conservation and Development offices in Salem were greeted with the McCall saga the moment they arrived. These students came from around the country to study land use planning at the place best known for it and so were already steeped in the history of SB 100. At the opening session of their morning orientation, however, the first thing they heard was not a speech from the DLCD director (his deputy was second on the agenda) but an audio recording of Tom McCall's grasping wastrels speech, which ended with the familiar declaration "We must respect another truism: That unlimited and unregulated growth leads inexorably to a lowered quality of life."[50] The graduate students nodded in understanding as the recording played, while DLCD staffers, many of whom had been with the agency since its beginning, beamed at them in appreciation. These were people who shared a common perspective, one reflected in McCall's vision as much as in the policies they worked to implement. This attitude was even evident in official publications of the Department of Land Conservation and Development at the time, including the primary information brochure on LCDC, which prominently featured quotations from Tom McCall (on the first and second pages) and closed with Aldo Leopold's advice that "when we see land as a community to which we belong, we may begin to use it with love and respect."[51] A recording of McCall's 1973 warning to the legislature about the "unfettered despoiling of our land" appears on the DLCD website in 2016, over forty years after it was delivered.[52]

While support for LCDC was certainly never unanimous, the national attention the law continued to attract decades after its passage, such as its number-one ranking in a Sierra Club study on preventing urban sprawl in 2000, offered frequent opportunities for proponents to revive the story of its passage and share the quotations from Tom McCall that have come to characterize its spirit and intent. Such opportunities have been frequent, for LCDC continued to weather attempts at modification or outright repeal well into the twenty-first century. A November 2000 ballot measure requiring the state to compensate property owners for land value lost to regulation (by defining it as a "regulatory taking") was passed with limited attention from the press and public, establishing the "most restrictive language on the subject of government 'takings' in the nation."[53] Criticized as a "stealth measure" by opponents for its failure to even mention LCDC, the initiative appeared with over two dozen others on one of the most complicated ballots Oregon voters had ever seen. Ballot Measure 7 was immediately challenged in court by 1,000 Friends of Oregon and Audrey McCall, the governor's widow, who were concerned it would effectively invalidate SB 100 by making it impossible to enforce due to the cost of compensation.[54]

The Oregon Supreme Court ultimately overturned Ballot Measure 7 on technical grounds in 2002, finding that it violated a prohibition on changing more than one part of the state constitution in a single act. Opponents successfully passed a similar initiative, Ballot Measure 37, in 2004 with enough alterations to survive the expected court challenge; that measure provided an alternative to payment for regulatory taking of property value in the form of a grandfather clause that would allow landowners to develop property under the laws in force at the time of original purchase.[55] Voters demonstrated their mixed feelings toward land use planning just three years later, when they approved a ballot referendum to significantly limit the impacts of the 2004 initiative by a 61 percent majority. Soon after, the state legislature established a new Oregon Task Force on Land Use Planning (nicknamed the "Big Look") to undertake a broad review of the implementation of SB 100. The Big Look recommended a range of modest changes but concluded that "despite its flaws, Oregon's land use planning program had largely achieved its goals of protecting farm and forest lands and containing urban sprawl."[56] As the prominent Oregon historian William Robbins put it, "The effects of Senate Bill 100 are visually scripted across Oregon's landscape."[57]

The stewardship agenda that arose in the 1960s helped propel Oregon to the forefront of the national environmental movement by providing a framework that embraced progressive legislation as a way of maintaining or restoring the environmental qualities that were central to the state's livability. Rooted in nineteenth-century visions of the region as an "Eden at the end of the Oregon Trail," this mythology of stewardship presented an idealized past that suggested Oregon's Euro-American settlers had learned lessons about the wise use of resources from the landscapes they inhabited. Those lessons, it was believed, were passed on in the form of farsighted laws, such as Oswald West's 1914 beach law, or through informal traditions on which commercial and recreational practices in nature were supposedly based. This form of stewardship represented a departure from the common tension between "environment as Eden," which embodies a utilitarian view of natural resources as gifts for use, and "the aesthetic of the sublime," which demands preservation of creation.[58] Instead, Oregon's approach conceived of a middle ground in which nature provided both the resources and amenities that yielded livability simultaneously; striking this balance was the primary goal of good stewardship. If it were practiced, the past mistakes of other regions (such as the cutover of the Great North Woods, the privatization of the New Jersey shoreline, or the pollution of the skies over Pittsburgh) would not be repeated in the Pacific Northwest. The myth conveniently ignored the reality of sweeping changes wrought upon the environment, first by the pioneers and then their descendants, as aboriginal peoples were eliminated or relocated and ecosystems modified for primarily utilitarian purposes. Instead of marking these changes, the dominant culture celebrated a static nature, idealized in images of pristine rivers, heavily forested mountains, and picturesque valleys teeming with wildlife. In reality, of course, Oregonians followed the pattern of most human cultures, altering their environment to the extent their technologies and population allowed. The sheer scale of these landscapes, however, allowed them the luxury of ignoring most impacts and pointing to remnants of the presettlement environment as evidence of their collective wisdom.

As the pace of environmental change became more rapid following World War II, due in particular to increasingly rapid urbanization, industrialization, and population growth, the effects became more immediately noticeable in the places where the bulk of the population resided. Once the public's attention was drawn to the signs of decay evident in their midst—Tom McCall's television exposé was just part of a process that was going on across the nation—they needed a way to make sense of the situation; explaining it in a declension narrative undoubtedly reinforced people's misgivings about the pace of progress as much as it reflected their naïve vision of "the good old days." Whatever its roots, the phenomenon allowed conservation advocates to make broad appeals for action based on the very real and concrete problems anyone could see, such as the dying Willamette River, and to justify the costs of their solutions as a debt owed simultaneously to the past and the future. It was both their duty and their desire to keep Oregon green.

Tom McCall was the most successful defender of livability and employer of this mythology of stewardship because he believed in both sincerely. That truth, combined with his natural eloquence and commanding personality, made his appeals broadly convincing. When he spoke of Oregon's natural heritage and the importance of preserving it for subsequent generations, audiences knew he shared their concerns about the future. While Richard Neuberger employed similar tactics, he was less successful in motivating Oregonians to support his cause. This was due in part to the issues he chose to pursue—topics of traditional conservation (i.e., wilderness preservation) rather than the quality-of-life issues that more directly touched people's lives—but it also stemmed from Oregonians' unreadiness to hear such appeals in the late 1950s. Change, much less environmental decline, was simply less evident then than it would be a decade later. Of course, by McCall's time in office the national conversation on environmental quality had shifted as well, helped along by Rachel Carson's warning bell and the Great Society's emphasis on natural beauty. As a result, when Tom McCall spoke of the "foul strangers" polluting Oregon's air and water, people listened; they could see it happening outside their homes and smell it as they drove past the fetid Willamette River. McCall continued to employ the rhetoric of livability and Oregon's exceptionalism into the final months of his life, reviving the central character of his favorite myth and noting that "we've kept faith with Governor West [and] protected the birthright that he first recognized" in a speech given in the fall of 1982.[59]

Ironically, McCall himself was in the process of becoming part of Oregon's mythology of stewardship even before his death, a fact that he recognized. When asked about "the burden of the McCall legend" by a reporter in 1978, he replied, "The legend is bigger than I ever was."[60] Indeed, the governor had struggled to find direction after his second term ended in 1975. He was a frequent guest speaker for environmental organizations around the country, telling "the Oregon story" to adoring audiences who wanted their states or regions to follow Oregon's lead in protecting livability.[61] He was direct in his message to a *New York Times* reporter just days after leaving office, proclaiming, "I promise everyone 'You can do this in your own state'. The Oregon story is innovative, regenerative. We've reversed the tide of pollution here. We've shown that the future can be made to work. The question isn't 'Can it be done elsewhere?' It's 'Do we have the commitment?'" McCall was emphatic about the need for others to follow Oregon's lead as well: "Damn it, when I was elected not many people, even in Oregon, believed we'd be able to pull off what we have, in fact, we've passed more ecological bills here in eight years than all the other states have done in fifty."[62] This role as environmental spokesman was clearly one McCall relished; his personal files are filled with his hand-annotated copies of speeches delivered around the country between 1975 and 1981, and while the audiences ranged from industry groups to the Audubon Society, the messages were strikingly consistent in their condemnation of business as usual in the face of environmental decline. The future, he believed, demanded action from everyone—and Oregon's path provided the best available example of how to proceed.

In addition to the speaking circuit, McCall flirted with returning to politics. In 1974 he had considered, then rejected, a run for the US Senate against fellow Republican Robert Packwood. When a reporter asked about his future political ambitions late in 1977, he replied, "I'd be perfectly requited if I were governor again and got to keep Oregon on the map just the way I did."[63] Though his top advisors were set against it, McCall ran again for governor in 1978, hoping to recapture the magic of his previous service and build upon the Oregon myth. But the state had changed since he left office; the environmental governor was an undisciplined candidate who some said appeared to expect a coronation rather than a hard primary fight. Hammered in debates for his "anti-growth" policies, McCall responded by pushing a middle ground that alienated his environmental allies, some of whom turned against him openly at an Earth Week address in April.[64] A loss to the probusiness Victor Atiyeh in the May primary ended his formal political career.

Academia called almost immediately after McCall left office as well; in 1975 he was offered the presidency of Linfield College in McMinnville, Oregon, which he ultimately declined with the recognition that "my careers as newsman and politician have produced no sign whatever of any ability on my part to succeed at the kind of fund-raising the school needs."[65] Whitman College, the University of Oregon, and the University of Vermont were also interested in the possibility of McCall entering academia. A faculty position at Oregon State University was ultimately more appealing, but the former governor stepped down from the Tom McCall Chair of Communication and Public Affairs after teaching a single course, finding the dynamics of the classroom less fulfilling than those with the reporters and politicians with whom he was accustomed to dealing. He served as executive chairman of the Rene Dubos Center for Human Environments until it closed in the wake of Dubos's death in 1982 and returned to journalism as well, writing for the *Oregonian* and offering regular political commentary on radio in Oregon while attempting to secure national syndication to reach a broader audience. Without the attention afforded a rising political star on the national stage nor the daily support and guidance of a professional staff to keep him focused, McCall seemed unable to capitalize on his national reputation in the late 1970s, ultimately settling for a role as an elder statesman willing to speak his mind from the sidelines and defend his record against all comers.

At his funeral on January 12, 1983, McCall was eulogized by Governor Vic Atiyeh, former governor Bob Straub, and Tom Dargan and Ron Schmidt, two members of McCall's personal staff.[66] Straub, who had run against McCall for the governor's office twice and worked beside him on multiple environmental campaigns, remarked on what it was like to play a political second fiddle to the popular governor and reminded Oregonians of the connections between McCall and what had become the best-known legislative components of the state's environmental identity:

> My own political life had to be under his political shadow. But it was a shadow of sunlight and hope and optimism. Tom McCall was a mentor to the soul of Oregon. . . . So I say, goodbye Tom McCall.
>
> Because of you the Willamette River runs clean with life. Salmon spawn in her tributaries where a few brief years before no fish could breathe.
>
> Because of you the windswept beaches are quiet with shifting dunes, freed from concrete and steel with open access to all.
>
> Your heroic fight with the last ounce of your strength for land-use planning in Oregon will help keep the beauty and abundance of our land unscarred.
>
> [You] will endure, inspire, and symbolize Oregon.[67]

Win McCormack, writing for *Oregon Magazine* soon after McCall's death, categorized him with leaders like Winston Churchill and John Kennedy, men "who are remembered—and missed—more for the sense of greatness they inspired in their followers and constituents than for the greatness of their own actual executive or legislative accomplishments." McCall, he believed, would be remembered for his legislative victories on environmental issues but would have a greater long-term impact "for the sense of pride and moral purpose he instilled in the people of Oregon. McCall worked a transformation in the Oregon psyche, convincing the citizens of this state that they had an almost ethical duty to preserve their natural heritage against the potential ravages of modern technology, and that their greatness as a people lay in doing so. He created an image, or myth, for Oregonians to live up to."[68] That myth was based on an understanding of the power of history and the environment as elements in a sense of place, the idea that landscape and culture could be combined to offer common meaning to people with sometimes dramatically divergent political views and socioeconomic backgrounds. Tom McCall turned it into a powerful political force and in time was incorporated into the myth himself. This is nowhere as apparent as in the small collection of official portraits in the state capitol; there McCall's portrait stands out strikingly for both its subject and style (it was also the first such painting of the modern era, many older ones having been lost in the 1935 fire that destroyed the capitol building). Painted by Henk Pander, a young Dutch immigrant who arrived in Portland in 1965, the image is not a typical one of a politician posed in a study or library. Instead, McCall is portrayed in the midst of perhaps his most famous action, walking across the beach after disembarking from a helicopter in 1967, the great publicity shot of the Beach Bill battle. The subject is in midstride, his hand reaching out to the viewer as "both a handshake and an offer to help lift you off the floor and up to his level. His hand is an invitation to join, to be an Oregonian" in the words of one art critic.[69] At the formal unveiling ceremony on statehood day in 1983 Thomas Vaughan, director of the Oregon Historical Society, shared a poem by Yakama Indian poet Luella Jean Azule that McCall himself had read at the memorial service for famed Oregon legislator Grace Peck following her death in 1979.

> Do not stand at my grave and weep.
> I am not there: I do not sleep.
> I am a thousand winds that blow.
> I am sunlight on a glistening snow.
> I am a pastel rainbow in the misty rain.
> I am golden wheat on a rolling plain.
> Do not stand at my grave and cry.
> I am not there; I did not die.[70]

The most prominent memorial to the former governor is Tom McCall Waterfront Park in the heart of Portland, stretching along the west bank of Willamette River in place of a freeway that was removed in 1974. Dedicated in 1978, the park offers both a high-profile thirty-acre downtown green space and a visible symbol of the city's prioritization of people over cars, made possible in part by the actions of a task force appointed by the

Fig. 27. Henk Pander portrait of Governor Tom McCall celebrating his role in passing the Beach Bill, Oregon State Capitol (Photo by Tim Thayer)

governor to study the area in 1968.[71] Tom McCall is buried in Redmond Memorial Cemetery, where his headstone reads simply "Governor of Oregon, 1967–1975" over the epitaph "He Cared."

The broadcast of *Pollution in Paradise* in 1963 may well have marked "the birth of enlightened Oregon," as Brent Walth called it; the death of the same is somewhat harder to trace, but Oregon's status as the nation's environmental bellwether did not long outlast Tom McCall.[72] The timing of the birth was perfectly aligned with the emergence of the national environmental movement; a series of events ranging from the publication of *Silent Spring* in 1962 to the famous "spaceship Earth" images of 1969 unquestionably challenged Americans to reconsider the impacts of resource extraction, consumerism, and population growth on the planet's ecosystems. This was particularly true in the western United States, where the environmental decay marking eastern urban centers was not yet as evident. Tom McCall thus became "the one Western political figure who more than any other single individual symbolized the new era."[73] The media abetted this process, helping launch the "environmental decade" with an Earth Day bang of coverage in 1970 and then slowly losing interest over the following years—but never reverting to the benign neglect of the early 1960s. This was evident, for example, in a study of *New York Times* references to the key concept of limits to growth in a world of finite resources; the number of stories incorporating this idea grew by a factor of ten between 1962 and 1970, then fell 50 percent by 1977 to remain at a level still six times the initial baseline.[74] Oregon's own environmental arc followed a similar trajectory, and as the nation's attention moved elsewhere in the late 1970s—toward "stagflation" and the Middle East in particular—the Oregon story became one of many more quotidian concerns. While the McCall-era accomplishments would still be celebrated on occasion, Oregon's governors of the 1980s would not be called to lead the nation in responding to the environmental crisis.

When *Earthwatch Oregon* asked a group of regional leaders about the state's environmental future in January 1980, the most telling response was that "by the late '70s the environmental movement was on the defensive everywhere" due to backlash from industry and the declining economy. Much of their future work, it was predicted, would be defensive—fighting to preserve the gains of the prior decade, not necessarily moving forward. While Governor Victor Atiyeh pledged "I will keep Oregon livable" to members of the Associated Oregon Industries business lobby that winter, state officials "made clear that there must be some areas where regulation may be softened in order to promote economic growth." All this signaled that "the '80s may not bring the environmental victories scored early in the '70s," a prescient prediction in hindsight.[75] By the spring of 1980 the *Economist* would write of "Oregon's new bias towards economic growth" under Atiyeh, who approved a sixteen-page advertisement in *Forbes* magazine declaring the state "open for business."[76] This new tenor would come to characterize Oregon in the eighties; as early as 1982 stories with such contradictory headlines as "Lumber Industry Woes Dim Good Life in Oregon" and "Living the Ecotopian Ethic" were appearing in the media as the state's economic decline undermined support for continued environmental innovation.[77]

The death knell for environmental Oregon most likely rang quietly sometime in 1983. By then, according to Brent Walth, "the courageous charge at building a better, smarter state turned to retreat as Oregon's leaders . . . worried about keeping the state out of bankruptcy."[78] Kelly Ross, a former aide to Senator Mark Hatfield, offered a grim prognosis in *Reason* magazine that year in which he decried the negative economic impacts of Oregon's antibusiness image, including a number-thirty-six ranking for "business climate" in a 1982 survey and a near-bottom ranking on a *National Industrialist* magazine scorecard of industrial growth. The state's economic slide, driven particularly by reduced demand for forest products during years of high mortgage rates, was taking its toll, and consequently efforts to roll back environmental regulations were gaining steam. SB 100's land use planning requirements drew particular fire from areas of the state where the health of the economy was at its worst—rural areas dependent on timber and agriculture—and Ross felt they needed to be curtailed. He condemned Tom McCall for his tactics in fighting against the Ballot Measure 6 effort to repeal LCDC in 1982 and excoriated the media that "gobbled up the maudlin exhibition," believing the former governor's emotional appeal narrowly saved a law that was hurting Oregon's chances to grow out of its economic decline. Just a year after the *Almanac of American Politics* had written positively that "going to Oregon is almost like traveling to English-speaking Canada," the Oregon story seemed to no longer be sacred myth, but simply something in the way of economic development.[79]

The following year, *Inc.* magazine explained that while in the 1970s "Oregonians weren't particularly concerned about catering to industry," that changed in the long recession of 1979–1982, when the state's unemployment rate hit 11.5 percent. Afterward, "Oregonians, who once led the nation on environmental issues . . . and land-use planning, no longer feel they are leading in anything."[80] Even the James G. Blaine Society was declared dead in 1986, remembered for "symbolizing Oregonians for a few years" when "the state was defined to the rest of the country by the things the James G. Blaine Society stood for." According to organizer Ron Abell, in the intervening years the role of government in Oregon had changed from being "concerned with social issues and the well-being of the environment" to focusing on business development. "If someone were to stand up today and say no growth, he'd really be a pariah," Abell lamented.[81] This was a far cry from the peak of the environmental era, when environmental advocates received frequent positive media coverage and their business-minded opponents were treated as extremists. By the early 1980s environmentalism's critics had only to cite economic indicators to make their case, and the bully pulpit of the governor's office had handily switched sides in the debate.

Fig. 28. "Oregon. Things Look Different Here" promotional campaign materials, c. 1989 (Original in author's possession)

The Oregon Tourism Division revealed a new slogan, "Oregon. Things Look Different Here," in collaboration with Portland advertising firm Wieden + Kennedy in 1988 in an attempt to merge tourism and economic development into a single brand.[82] One of the first promotional pieces developed for the campaign carried the title "We've Been Saving a Place for You" and featured the Beach Bill on its first page, described as "the greatest expression of our respect for nature." The law was presented as evidence that "ensuring that future generations, and those who visit, will always be able to enjoy the quality of life Oregon offers, is something of a habit with us."[83]

The 1990s did not bring a rebirth of Oregon's environmental optimism, but they did usher in an age of nostalgia for the 1970s, as is evident from the new tourism slogan ("Things Look Different Here" would serve throughout the decade). In 1991 Governor Barbara Roberts invoked the Oregon story's most celebrated victories—the Beach Bill, the Bottle Bill, and LCDC—in her opening address to the Public Interest Law Conference in Eugene. Oregon, she claimed, was "still the envy of the nation, [b]ut now is not the time to rest on our laurels. . . . As Governor, I can either accept the slippage of Oregon as the Nation's most creative conservation leader, or I can help move Oregon center stage once again with responsible, long term environmental programs and policies."[84] On the ten-year anniversary of Tom McCall's death in 1993, the *Oregonian* reminded readers of his legacy, citing the public beaches, returnable bottles, improved health of the Willamette River, and land use planning regulations alongside the "sometimes provincial nature of native Oregonians who remember, often with fondness, his admonishing people to visit Oregon 'but for heaven's sake don't move here.'" Indeed, the inclusion of the modifier "native" in describing those Oregonians who recalled the former governor was telling; as one of McCall's speechwriters then explained, "So many things have changed here. There's such an influx of people from out of the state who don't really know the background."[85]

Each of these anecdotes illustrates an interesting evolution in the use of the Oregon story in the 1990s, as its core elements were interpreted increasingly as a blend of history and mythology, similar to the role Oswald West's accomplishments played for McCall in the 1960s. The state's long economic slowdown, driven substantially by the decline of the timber industry, combined with rapid population growth and seemingly intractable debates over the management of critical natural resources like old-growth forests and salmon to leave many nostalgic for an era of assumed environmental consensus. Telling stories about past environmental successes helped long-term residents and newcomers alike place the current conflicts into a larger context, for as Kim Stafford put it, "The problems of our time are political, economic, and environmental, but their solutions are cultural."[86] While surveys in the mid-1990s found majorities in favor of conservation-oriented policies toward both forests and salmon, the cultural drive to maintain environmentalism as an element of Oregon's identity no longer held center stage.[87]

In 1998, thirty years after national attention was first drawn to Oregon's environmental agenda, Salem's *Statesman-Journal* ran a series of feature reports revisiting the McCall era as a model for the future. Over the course of a month these reports appeared under the headline "Paradise Lost: Searching for Tom McCall's Oregon," emblazoned over the profile of the former governor. The series proved so popular that it was reprinted and given away to meet public demand for copies. The state had experienced a 56 percent population increase between 1970 and 1995, and the feature was in part a reframing of the Oregon story as an important element in orienting new residents to events that occurred well before their arrival. It ultimately questioned whether Oregonians were in fact living up to McCall's standards. The familiar tales of environmental triumph were of course retold; combined with information about changes in the state since the governor's death, the package served as a primer on Oregon's modern environmental history and an exhortation to remain worthy of its legacy. One included editorial went so far as to claim, "Two decades after Tom McCall died, it's clear that Oregon is slipping, and it's just as clear that the reason is since Tom McCall, there haven't been any other Tom McCalls."[88] The result of the cultural and political focus on the environment during the 1960s and 1970s was just as evident, though, in the polls of current residents that appeared as sidebars to the report. The most telling was a survey of new residents (nonnative Oregonians), who were asked why they chose to move to Oregon. Fully 86 percent selected either "environment" or "quality of life" as a primary motivating factor, confirmation that Oregon was indeed what geographers label a "voluntary region," a place where people migrate out of choice rather than necessity.[89]

Though the Associated Press lauded Oregon for its environmental legacy at the turn of the twenty-first century, it was barely two years later that the *Oregonian* ran a multipart series under the headline "The Oregon Dream Vanishes." The economic divide between urban and rural communities had become so pronounced that Democratic governor John Kitzhaber (who had vetoed a record number of Republican-backed bills in the 1999 legislative session) proclaimed the state to be "ungovernable," while antigovernment conservatives had taken over the Republican Party, in the process turning it into something Tom McCall would not have recognized.[90] The state that was once heralded for "showing the way" to the rest of the country was being mocked for its failures, including a Doonesbury strip that drew attention to dramatic reductions in the public school calendar made necessary by funding cuts triggered by a 1990 property tax limitation measure.[91] Political polarization along the urban-rural divide became de rigueur, while a series of antigovernment ballot initiatives undermined any remaining faith in the ability of public institutions to address the state's needs.[92] These divisions were so deep that little hope of any solution was evident; when a team of the *Oregonian*'s reporters asked in 2003 if the newly elected governor, Ted Kulongoski, might be able to bring the sides together, a former secretary of state responded, "It's the 'Tom McCall on a white horse' phenomenon," concluding that the political culture was so damaged that no one leader could offer salvation.[93] That fall one of the same reporters argued the state was not divided in two but rather into nine regions with incompatible interests, while a new history of Oregon was published with a final chapter titled "A Polarized State, 1975–2003," underscoring the fracturing of consensus politics under a quarter century of adverse economic conditions.[94] The increasingly diverse economy and the broken political machinery in Salem drove the loss of a sense of common identity and purpose as the Oregon story and appeals to livability failed to carry the political weight they had a generation prior.

The darker, almost xenophobic side of the McCall era ultimately retained its currency much longer than the stewardship myth. In the face of unprecedented population growth in the 1990s, Oregonians were quick to dust off the governor's "visit but don't stay" exhortation, and it was often said that more recent migrants were among its loudest proponents. Californians were once again a favorite target, drawing ire on talk radio and in letters to the editor in communities across the state, and became victims of vandalism (aimed at cars with California plates) and scapegoats for virtually anything that was wrong with the region, including traffic, litter, suburban sprawl, gangs, and a general decline in civility. In the 1999 legislative session, Republican senator John Lim introduced a bill to erect official signs at the state borders proclaiming, "You're welcome to visit Oregon, but please don't stay." In the face of criticism from the tourist industry, Lim claimed the signs would promote the "Oregon mystique," citing McCall's original statement as evidence. The proposal was defeated in committee, but the fact it was advanced at all suggests that the currency of McCall's memory and the mythology surrounding Oregon's environmental era were far from exhausted.[95]

The extent of vitriol reserved for Californians, long symbolic of unrestrained growth and other excesses, clearly had not lessened over the decades; in the words of one 1990s migrant from the state to the south, Oregonians' feelings toward them were worn on their sleeves: "It almost causes them physical pain to see these Californians coming here."[96] This exclusionary attitude appears in the stories told about Oregon's nineteenth-century pioneers, the most often repeated of which is the tale of the crossroads at Pacific Springs, where the Oregon and California trails diverged. As Oregonians liked to tell it, the trail to California was marked by a pile of gold-bearing quartz, the other simply with a sign reading "To Oregon." Those who could read chose the latter. Though mythic in origin, this story stands as a prime example of the efforts on the part of Oregonians to establish an identity distinct from that of their cousins to the south; its frequent *retelling* a century and a half after its setting suggests that maintaining their unique identity is still a priority among Oregonians.

Another story widely circulated in Oregon in the 1990s captured this air of exceptionalism particularly well, as it played off the stereotypical disdain for Californians in a manner that combined one of the region's oldest brands of beer and the Bottle Bill for both its humor and its point:

An Oregonian, a Californian and a Texan were out camping. They were sitting around a campfire when the Texan pulled out a bottle of tequila and, after taking a couple of swallows, threw the bottle up in the air, pulled out his six-shooter, and neatly shot the bottle. The Californian noted that there was still some tequila left in the bottle, but the Texan said, "That's okay, we have plenty of tequila where I come from."

The Californian promptly brought out his bottle of white zinfandel, took two swallows, threw it up in the air, and shot it with a 9mm pistol, saying, "We have plenty of this where I come from."

The Oregonian took all this in and finally opened a bottle of Henry Weinhard's ale. He downed the entire bottle, threw it up in the air, shot the Californian with a 12-gauge shotgun he kept around for duck hunting, and deftly caught the bottle in the other hand. The Texan's jaw dropped nearly to his silver buckle and his eyes opened nearly as wide as the buckle. The Oregonian, momentarily puzzled at the Texan's reaction, finally piped up: "It's okay, we have plenty of Californians where I come from, but I can get a nickel for this bottle!"[97]

Though still substantially inchoate, the mythology of stewardship that helped unite a critical mass of Oregonians to support progressive environmental legislation in the 1960s remains part of the state's cultural milieu.

Within its familiar litany of stories the prominent features of the Oregon landscape—the Cascade Mountains, the Willamette River, the Pacific Ocean—are linked with tales of those who appreciated them enough in the past to convey the importance of their preservation. The nineteenth-century perception of the region as a "Garden of Eden" underlies the common moral of the tales, that the land is somehow special and worthy of care and that in caring for it Oregonians mark themselves as special as well. Combined with tales of political heroism from the early decades of the twentieth century, and in particular examples of citizen action meant to suggest that Oregon's system of government was as superior to other states' as its landscapes, the stewardship narrative provided a compelling context for critiques of post-World War II challenges to livability that suggested the state was under threat and perhaps even in decline. Population growth, rapid urbanization, industrial expansion, and increased competition for access to the outdoors all threatened a way of life to which residents had grown accustomed over the first half of the twentieth century and thereafter felt was part of their birthright.

Historical arguments for stewardship allowed residents to share a common understanding of what Oregon meant and to join in support of conservation measures despite the differences of class, geography, and party. The call to preserve livability was egalitarian from the outset, focusing on access to natural resources and quality of life for all regardless of wealth or political orientation, and it spoke to issues literally close to home. As such it diverged from the traditional conservation issues of the mid-twentieth century—parks and wilderness—to establish a broader political base upon concerns that people faced on a daily basis, including declining air and water quality and the impacts of growth. This did not make the Oregon movement unique; such issues had first appeared on politicians' agendas almost a century before, as eastern industrial cities struggled with the tension between economic growth and the concomitant pollution it produced.[98] What was different, however, was the encompassing use of stewardship as a conceptual umbrella, under which a variety of local concerns could be presented to the public as part of a moral crusade to save the places they inhabited from the forces of change and decay in service to future livability. The introduction to a promotional book published by the Portland-based Benjamin Franklin Savings and Loan Association in 1977 captured the sentiment well: "In recent times, Oregon has achieved a degree of standing in the nation, and elsewhere, as a place occupied by people who care about staying on the best terms with the plant and animal life of which they are a part. So Oregon is more than a state; it is, indeed, a state of mind."[99]

Tom McCall's role in this process was described by a contemporary as growing organically from his experiences as a youth in Oregon and his love for the land, culminating in a political voice that Oregonians were ready to hear: "He was able to fashion a political vision, at once conservative and progressive, uniquely suited to them. . . . McCall's support was not confined to one segment of the Oregon political spectrum, but ranged all the way from the conservative Republican establishment . . . to the committed environmentalists who, by the end of his career, came to revere him."[100] The rhetoric and political priorities of Oregon's environmental era can be viewed as both liberal and conservative, despite the state's modern reputation as a bastion of liberalism. Those who promoted conservation by calling for the preservation of livability as embodied in a previous generation's way of life were seeking to *prevent* change, not achieve it. Indeed, change in general was portrayed as a negative factor in the rhetoric of stewardship; it was presumed that the state needed a sort of static preservation that would lock resources into historical patterns of use, not a program that would dramatically alter the landscape or culture by overturning tradition. Its target was the preservation of an idealized status quo, a world in which corporations could continue to log the forests and use the rivers to dispose of industrial waste—both of which produced jobs—but would do so in responsible ways that would leave undisturbed as much territory as citizens needed for scenic and recreational purposes. Oregonians uncomfortable with the pace of change had only to look to other states for object lessons on the consequences of waste and irresponsible resource management decisions. By linking their fears with the belief that previous generations had done a better job of honoring the state's natural endowments, political leaders were able to turn fear of change into a powerful weapon *for* change, as in the case of land use planning reforms that challenged the very foundations of private property by questioning the long-assumed right of landowners to develop their land as they saw fit.

The practical legacy of Oregon's environmental era is mixed. As the *Statesman-Journal* indicated in its 1998 retrospective, many of its central accomplishments addressed pressing issues of the times but failed to anticipate the environmental challenges the state would face in the twenty-first

Fig. 29. Governor Tom McCall at press event with children to mark Cleaner Air Week, 1969 (Oregon Historical Society Photo Collection, OrHi 105877)

century. The Willamette River, for example, is today threatened by pollution from sources unforeseen at midcentury. The state's population soared from 2.09 million in 1970 to 3.8 million in 2010, an increase of over 81 percent in four decades.[101] This exceeded most of the projections available to planners in the 1960s, due largely to higher than anticipated rates of in-migration. Indeed, Oregon's birth rate is eleventh from the bottom nationally and is the lowest among the western states; population growth derived from migration suggests that tongue-in-cheek efforts to portray Oregon as undesirable indeed backfired, as some feared they would in the 1970s.[102] As a consequence of this growth, policies that were expected to preserve livability in keeping with Oregonians' sense of place in the 1960s—including open space and the rural character of all but the most densely settled areas—at best corralled growth by managing its immediate impacts. Sprawl may have been restrained, but the secondary impacts of population growth, including overtaxed infrastructure and natural systems, are evident today despite the best-intended planning efforts. Critics have quite reasonably charged that the successes of the 1960s and 1970s led to a sense of complacency that allowed Oregonians to ignore the impacts of

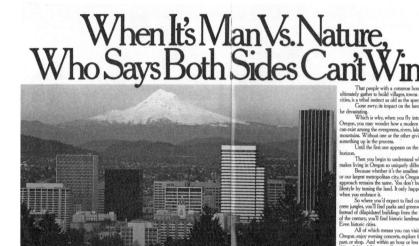

When It's Man Vs. Nature, Who Says Both Sides Can't Win?

That people with a common bond will ultimately gather to build villages, towns and cities, is a tribal instinct as old as the species.
Gone awry, its impact on the land can be devastating.
Which is why, when you fly into Oregon, you may wonder how a modern city can exist among the evergreens, rivers, lakes and mountains. Without one or the other giving something up in the process.
Until the first one appears on the horizon.
Then you begin to understand what makes living in Oregon so uniquely different.
Because whether it's the smallest town, or our largest metropolitan city, in Oregon our approach remains the same. You don't build a lifestyle by taming the land. It only happens when you embrace it.
So where you'd expect to find concrete jungles, you'll find parks and greenways. Instead of dilapidated buildings from the turn of the century, you'll find historic landmarks. Even historic cities.
All of which means you can visit Oregon, enjoy evening concerts, explore the past, or shop. And within an hour or less be skiing, fishing, hiking or sailboarding.
It may also be why so many visitors who come to Oregon for the scenery change their plans.
And end up staying.

Fig. 30. Official Oregon tourism campaign promoting harmony with nature, c. 1996 (Original in author's possession)

growth in the following decades, rather than remaining vigilant in support of the goals behind their past policies. "We have been resting on our laurels from what Tom McCall did for the past 20 years or more. In the meantime, the population is greater and more intense," proclaimed Jeff Allen of the Oregon Environmental Council in 2000.[103]

One of the more significant impacts of Oregon's environmental era is that it demonstrated the potential of bold action from government. Oswald West's celebrated 1914 directive to preserve public access to the beaches was not a particularly brave political move, nor was it that much of a departure from the commanding philosophies of the Progressive Era in which it occurred. But when Tom McCall and others called upon Oregonians to defend the environment *because they owed it to Oregon* and then offered imaginative ways to do so, new ground was broken. People's ideas about the limits of government action were challenged, and Oregon attracted substantial national attention for its efforts. "Thus evolved the Oregon Mystique," summarized travel writer Marnie McPhee, "resource-based, independence-minded, environment-conscious, outdoor oriented. It continues to characterize the state."[104] While few subsequent accomplishments provoked the sense of pride evident among the state's citizens in the 1970s, the frequent retelling of the stories and the popularity of the reflective moments offered by significant anniversaries of these acts have kept longtime residents mindful of what can be done and have helped educate more recent migrants in the mythology of stewardship as they develop their own senses of place.

From a broader perspective, these events are also testimony to the importance of cultural factors in environmental politics. Costly, controversial solutions to environmental problems cannot often be achieved simply through the force of political will; they generally require broad (or at least very vocal) support from the public to survive the opposition of lobbyists bent on preserving the status quo or even rolling back regulations to favor their patrons. Motivating voters through appeals to history, culture, and sense of place offers another route to building the requisite coalitions in support of progressive environmental legislation and, as was the case in Oregon, can help unite people of disparate interests behind a shared view of what is meaningful about a particular place. The most important concrete result of Oregon's environmental era was indeed to protect "the land," to ensure the provision of both natural amenities and critical ecosystem services through public action. As historians William Robbins and Katrine Barber conclude, "This social ownership of nature's endowment provides citizens with a collective sense of commonwealth and holds potential for developing a polity steeped in the values of a public realm, linking inhabitants to a common landscape."[105] As state planners contemplate the projected consequences of climate change in the twenty-first century—including the possibility of massive losses to the public beaches due to sea level rise—that cultural connection to the land will be critical to any efforts to mitigate the impacts.[106]

Toward the end of his second term in office, Tom McCall responded to a letter from a constituent by musing on the process of linking landscape and culture into a single community, thus making the state—and ultimately the nation—a better place to live. "There is a sense of community in Oregon that one misses elsewhere. It's obviously more than simply being familiar with one's own turf. Maybe Oregon is an anachronism, but it's a glorious anachronism—but maybe, on the other hand, it's the harbinger of something new. Whatever the case, I intend to make this sense of community part of 'the Oregon story' from now on."[107] As Brent Walth saw it, "McCall succeeded in making Oregon not just a place but a character in our lives, a protagonist in a story." McCall and the environmental issues with which he was associated became part of that story as well, a story that retains its political power and is still used to explain what makes Oregon unique. Walth concluded of McCall, "He never left us. He is still there behind that curtain of fog. His voice whispers to us, and in softness, fills the void all around. He is saying, Oregon is demure and lovely, and it is our responsibility to make it better."[108]

The currency of this unique collision of person and place and meaning may rise and fall in value over time, but evidence suggests that it is still widely accepted in Oregon and perhaps envied a bit elsewhere. In the absence of a compelling national mythology supporting environmental stewardship it is not surprising that a localized one developed in a region that was settled later than most, retained significant elements of its original natural splendor, and lagged behind its neighbors in population and industrial development throughout the twentieth century. Whether or not people in Oregon actually *were* any different from those of California, Washington, or Idaho really makes no difference; many *thought* they were, and that belief helped them achieve goals environmental advocates in other states only dreamed of reaching. The stories they continue to celebrate today—not only of Tom McCall, but of the familiar litany of environmental laws that bore Oregon to the national stage—retain power that can still be mobilized for the right cause. If their belief in the mythology of stewardship can be rekindled in the twenty-first century and used in pursuing solutions to environmental problems unanticipated by previous generations, they will be at an advantage regardless of the accuracy of the exceptionalism they celebrate.

If humans are to be accepted as part of nature, as Aldo Leopold and later ecologists have long insisted they must be, the relationship between culture and environment deserves greater attention from historians and environmental advocates alike. We cannot understand the how and why of human impacts on the environment without examining their cultural underpinnings, whether they be a taste for beef, a penchant for gold, or the belief that certain landscapes are especially worthy of preservation. The nexus of nature and culture—the intersection of history, politics, and myth—is one place where we can hope to overcome the "great divide between democracy and environmentalism" that for far too long focused attention on distant wilderness to the detriment of the places in which people lived on a daily basis, places that directly shaped the livability of their communities.[109]

The Oregon case offers just one example of the application of cultural forces in defense of the environment, but it is one widely recognized for its accomplishments and indeed forms part of the central narrative of the

Fig. 31. Governor Tom
McCall reading mail by
kerosene lamp in his office
to raise public awareness
of the energy crisis, 1973
(National Archives and
Records Administration,
Record Group 412: Records
of the Environmental
Protection Agency, LI 412-
DA-12978)

twentieth-century American environmental movement. Evidence supports the contention that increased attention to what people believe about the places they inhabit can influence their actions just as significantly as economics, political orientation, class, or other traditional driving factors.[110] In their fight to keep Oregon green its citizens spoke of debts to the past, to the land, and to the future, ideas that may not be unique but must certainly be recognized as rare in a century dominated by faith in progress, consumption, and newness as unquestioned goods. That their stories are still frequently cited as inspirational by contemporary residents suggests the mythology of stewardship might still carry the potential to serve the goal of livability, if only it could be mobilized once again as it was during Oregon's environmental era.

Notes

INTRODUCTION

The epigraph is from Walter, *Placeways*, 2.

1 Edwards and Schwantes, "Pacific Northwest as Promised Land."

2 E. W. Kenworthy, "Tough Rules Saving a Dying Oregon River: Salmon Now Swim in Waters Once Unfit for Life," *New York Times*, September 8, 1970, 50.

3 William Robbins, "Nature's Northwest: In Search of a Pacific Region," in Robbins, *Great Northwest*, 178.

4 Handley, "Idea of the Pacific Northwest," 138–39.

CHAPTER 1

The epigraph is from Joseph N. Teal, "Oregon's Heritage of Natural Resources—Shall They Be Conserved for the People?," address delivered at the University of Oregon on Commonwealth Day, February 13, 1909, Oregon State Library Reference Collection.

1 "Oregon's 20th Century Legacy: Protecting the Environment," Associated Press State & Local Wire, December 31, 1999, http://web.lexis-nexis.com, January 10, 2001.

2 Tuan, *Topophilia*, 4.

3 Eaton, "Beauty That Requires Health," 88–89.

4 D. Lewis, "Four Deaths," 414.

5 Zucker, Hummel, and Høgfoss, *Oregon Indians*, 72–73.

6 Boag. *Environment and Experience*, 146ff.

7 Jones, *Oregonian's Handbook*, 52.

8 King and Fullenwider, *Pacific Northwest*, 195.

9 Post, *Loitering in Oregon*, 19.

10 Cox. "Crusade to Save Oregon's Scenery," 179–99.

11 Dietrich, *Northwest Passage*, 298–304.

12 Schwantes, *Pacific Northwest*, 392–93.

13 Dick, "When Dams Weren't Damned," 113–49; White, *Organic Machine*, 70, 77.

14 Victor, *Atlantis Arisen*, 47; see also White, *Organic Machine*.

15 *Oregon: The Land of Opportunity*, iii–v.

16 *Coos Bay Oregon*, 61–63.

17 Whisnant, *Portland, Oregon*, 3.

18 WPA Writer's Program, *Oregon*, ix.

19 WPA Writer's Program, *Mount Hood*, 45–46.

20 Burg, "Native Son's Rambles," 231.

21 Schotzko and Granatstein, *Brief Look*; Fiege, *Irrigated Eden*, 165–67.

22 Bernat, "Convergence," 37.

23 Office of War Information, Overseas Branch, "Northwest U.S.A."

24 Booth, *Northwestern United States*, 105.

25 Frykman. "Regionalism, Nationalism, Localism," 251–61.

26 Bingham, "Pacific Northwest Writing."

27 Lyman, "Oregon Literature," 408.

28 See variously Holbrook, *Promised Land*; Neuberger, *Our Promised Land*; and Potts, "West of H. L. Davis."

29 Powell, "Somewhere Else," 54–61.

30 Neuberger, *Our Natural Resources*.

31 See W. Douglas, *Of Men and Mountains*; W. Douglas, *My Wilderness*. Douglas's autobiography, *Go East, Young Man*, is also replete with references to the environment of the Northwest and its influence on his character.

32 W. Douglas, "Hart Mountain," 175.

33 Binns, "Northwest Region," 75.

34 Harvey, *Symbol of Wilderness*.

35 "Housing: Up From the Potato Fields," *Time*, July 3, 1950.

36 Rome, *Bulldozer in the Countryside*, 127–28.

37 "Table 2: Farms and Farm Acreage According to Use, by Size of Farm: Censuses of 1920 to 1959," in Hurley, *U.S. Census of Agriculture*, 5; Robbins, *Landscapes of Conflict*, 286.

38 Eichler and Kaplan, *Community Builders*, 76–77.

39 Hatfield, "Invitation to You."

40 Rothman, "Selling the Meaning of Place," 525–57.

41 Zelinsky, "Changing Character," 113–35.

42   Stewart Holbrook in Netboy, *Pacific Northwest*, 25.
43   Glenn L. Jackson quoted in Peirce, *Pacific States of America*, 188. Typical of this period, the book's section on Oregon is entitled "For God's Sake, Don't Move Here."
44   D. McCall, *Ranch under the Rimrock*.
45   See variously Schwantes, *Pacific Northwest*, 399–403; and Walth, *Fire at Eden's Gate*, 141–53.
46   Graham, *Since "Silent Spring,"* 48–68; Carson, *Silent Spring*.
47   Schwantes, *Pacific Northwest*, 400–402.
48   Walth, *Fire at Eden's Gate*, 313–14.
49   Mark O. Hatfield, forward to Corbett-Atterbury, *Oregon Story*.
50   Sarasohn, "Regionalism, Tending Toward Sectionalism," 223–36; Walth, *Fire at Eden's Gate*, 315.
51   MacColl, "Battle to Control Land Use," 209ff.
52   Tom McCall, "Legislative Address, Governor Tom McCall, Oregon, 1973," Oregon State Archives, http://arcweb. sos.state.or.us/pages/records/governors/ guides/state/mccall/legis1973.html.
53   "People Take Warning!"
54   Douglas Yocum and Tom Stimmel, "Tom McCall of Oregon: 1913–1983," *Oregonian*, January 9, 1983, B1.
55   James, "Ecotopia in Oregon?," 20–22.
56   Wilkinson, *Pacific Northwest*.
57   "Eugene and Portland Tops on Livable City List," *Oregon Statesman*, September 20, 1977, A14.
58   "Atlantic Article Aids Legend of Great Pacific Northwest," *Oregon Statesman*, March 20, 1976, sec. 1, 4.
59   Sarasohn, "Good Life," 27–29.
60   See generally Carroll, *Community and the Northwestern Logger*; and Wilson, "Origins of the Old-Growth Forest Conflict."
61   Seideman, *Showdown at Opal Creek*, 401.
62   Raphael, *Tree Talk*, 31.
63   Ibid., 56.
64   "Communities for a Great Oregon Hosts 3rd Annual Earth Day Tour," *Mill City Enterprise*, April 23, 1992, 7.
65   Durbin, *Tree Huggers*, 195–201.
66   Lehner, "Historical Look"; "Table 3: Timber Harvest Report Data for 1942–2004," in Andrews and Kutara, *Oregon's Timber Harvests*, 5.
67   Todd, *Communicating Environmental Patriotism*, 6–7.
68   Ibid., 103.

CHAPTER 2

The epigraph is from E. T. Scoyen to Richard Neuberger, June 10, 1959, Ax 078, box 3, "Conservation, National Parks: Shoreline Bill," Neuberger Papers.

1   Cox, *Park Builders*, 6–7; see also Powell, "Land of Magic Names."
2   See Cox, *Park Builders*, 100.
3   G. Richard Leverett, "Uncle Sam's New National Park," *Oregonian*, September 14, 1938, sec. M, 7.
4   Neuberger, "Hells Canyon."
5   Richard L. Neuberger, "National Park at Mt. Hood . . . Wallowas . . . Coast?," *Oregonian*, July 23, 1939, magazine section, 8; Lary Dilsaver, telephone conversation with author, September 23, 1999.
6   Richard L. Neuberger, "Oregon Areas Eyed for National Park Status," *Oregonian*, April 28, 1940, magazine section, 6. Despite his support for the park plan, Sprague clearly did not relish the idea of extending the federal influence in his state and suggested that his choice of the coastal option was determined in part because at the time it was the smallest of the proposals in area, at just under five thousand acres, whereas the Mt. Hood option stood at just under one million and Hells Canyon slightly less than that.
7   Swain, "National Park Service and the New Deal," 316.
8   White, *Organic Machine*, 69–74.
9   Pacific Northwest Bell Telephone Company Business Research Division, *Population and Household Trends*, 12.
10   "Table 52. Oregon—Race and Hispanic Origin: 1850 to 1990" and "Table 62. Washington—Race and Hispanic Origin: 1850 to 1990," in Gibson and Jung, *Historical Census Statistics*.
11   Stanbery, *Population Growth in the Pacific Northwest*, 5.
12   Lipin, *Workers and the Wild*, 98–101.
13   Governor's Committee for a Livable Oregon, *Report of the Tourism and Recreation Committee*, 4.
14   Oregon State Highway Commission Travel Advisory Committee, *Impact of Tourism in Oregon*, 1.
15   Cox, *Park Builders*, 102–3.
16   Dilsaver, *National Parks*, 62.
17   Runte, *National Parks*, 172–73; see also Louter, *Windshield Wilderness*. Little of the Mission 66 money would end up in Oregon, though, as the state had relatively few federal parks; see "Oregon

Last in '66' Plan," *Oregonian*, March 23, 1957, 9.

18   *The National Parks: Shaping the System*, 72.

19   "Park Service Favors Deal for Caves, Dunes," *Oregonian*, March 22, 1959, 26.

20   U.S. National Park Service, *Pacific Coast Recreation Area Survey*, 89.

21   Cooper, *Coastal Sand Dunes*, 3–6.

22   Reckendorf et al., "Stabilization of Sand Dunes in Oregon."

23   Frank Herbert to Lurton Blassingame, July 11, 1957, in Herbert, Herbert, and Anderson, *Road to Dune*.

24   American Antiquities Act.

25   John B. Oakes, "Conservation: Record of Congress," *New York Times*, September 5, 1954, X14.

26   Joe Miller, "Oregon: Can the Issues Be Ignored?," *Reporter*, November 4, 1954, 33–35; "Oregon: The Neuberger Campaign," 6; John B. Oakes, "Conservation: Federal Program," *New York Times*, October 2, 1955, X29.

27   Olaus J. Murie, letter to the editor, *New York Times*, October 14, 1955, Ax 078, box 3, "Conservation, General: 1955–1956," Neuberger Papers.

28   Richard L. Neuberger, "Conservation: Prospects for 1959," *New York Times*, January 4, 1959, X43.

29   Testimony of George L. Collins, National Park Service, in U.S. Congress, House, *Hearings on H.R. 6260*, 21.

30   U.S. Congress, Senate, *S. 1526*, sec. 1.

31   Ann Sullivan, "Only Known Mainland Rookery an Oregon Tourist Attraction," *Oregonian*, March 15, 1959.

32   Richard L. Neuberger, U.S. Congress, *Congressional Record*, 86th Cong., 1st sess. (1959): 5138.

33   Ibid., 5140.

34   Ibid.

35   Ibid., 5139.

36   John F. Gribble to Senator Richard Neuberger, December 30, 1954, Ax 078, box 2, "Conservation, General: 1954–1955," Neuberger Papers.

37   Fred H. McNeil to Senator Richard Neuberger, May 2, 1955; Richard B. Knotts to Senator Richard Neuberger, July 20, 1955, Ax 078, box 2, "Conservation, General: 1954–1955," Neuberger Papers.

38   Oregon Conservationist to Senator Richard Neuberger, March 31, 1955, Ax 078, box 2, "Conservation, General: 1954–1955," Neuberger Papers.

39   "State or Federal Park?," *Oregonian*, March 22, 1959, 40.

40   "Proposed Park Legislation Draws Fire," *Siuslaw Oar*, March 27, 1959, 1, col. 4.

41   See Righter, *Crucible for Conservation*.

42   "Senator Amazed at Opposition," *Siuslaw Oar*, May 1, 1959, 3, col. 2; "Senator for Dunes Park Despite Opposition," *Oregonian*, March 28, 1959, 8, cols. 3–4.

43   "Proposed Park Legislation Draws Fire," *Siuslaw Oar*, March 27, 1959, 1, col. 4.

44   Ralph F. Middleton to Senator Richard Neuberger, telegram, [1959?], Ax 078, box 3, "Conservation, National Parks: Seashore and Dunes: 3/59–4/59," Neuberger Papers.

45   "Public Opinion Divided on Coast Park Plan," *Oregonian*, April 13, 1959, 14, cols. 1–2.

46   "Senator for Dunes Park Despite Area Opposition," *Oregonian*, March 28, 1959, 8, cols. 3–4.

47   A. Robert Smith, "Oregon's Park Plan Faces 'Cool' Attitude by Ike Administration," *Oregonian*, April 9, 1959, 4, col. 1; Engel, *Sacred Sands*, 262–82.

48   Malcolm Bauer, "Public Opinion Divided on Coast Plan," *Oregonian*, April 13, 1959, 14.

49   "Park Officials Speak on Proposed Park Area," *Siuslaw Oar*, April 17, 1959, 1; "F.B. Nat'l Park Gets Support," *Siuslaw Oar*, April 17, 1959.

50   Karl W. Onthank to Senator Richard Neuberger, April 15, 1959, Ax 078, box 3, "Conservation, National Parks: Seashore and Dunes: 3/59–4/59," Neuberger Papers.

51   Mrs. Charles W. Fisher, letter to the editor, *Oregonian*, May 10, 1959, 38, cols. 5–6.

52   John M. Hayes, "Park Plan Disliked," *Oregonian*, April 1, 1959, 20, cols. 6–7.

53   George Y. Elandson to Senator Richard Neuberger, April 15, 1959, Ax 078, box 3, "Conservation, National Parks: Seashore and Dunes: 4/59–5/59," Neuberger Papers.

54   "Lane C-C Nixes Recreation Area," *Siuslaw Oar*, April 24, 1959, 1; "More Money for Anti-Park Initiative," *Siuslaw Oar*, May 8, 1959, 1, col. 2.

55   "Hearing Set on Park Issue," *Siuslaw Oar*, May 22, 1959, 1, col. 2.

56   "Rep. Porter Opposes Senate National Seashore Bills, Declares Dunes Boundaries Not Sufficiently Clear," *Oregonian*, May 28, 1959, 4, cols. 6–8.

57   "Indians Claim Coastal Area," *Oregonian*, June 30, 1959, 14, col. 6; "Coastal Tribes Oppose Park," *Siuslaw Oar*, July 31, 1959, 1, col. 1.

58 "Recreation Area Subject of Meet,"
    Siuslaw Oar, July 17, 1959, 1, cols. 2–3.
59 "Park Need Unproved," *Oregonian*,
    August 26, 1959, 14, cols. 1–2.
60 "Senator Neuberger Raps Dune Critics,"
    Oregonian, August 28, 1959, 26, col. 4.
61 "Senator Neuberger Agrees to Modify
    Measure on Oregon Dunes," *Oregonian*,
    September 8, 1959, 8, cols. 2–8.
62 Richard L. Neuberger, "Neuberger Asks
    for Seashore Park," *Oregonian*,
    September 10, 1959, 22, cols. 4–6.
63 "Dunes Plan Wins Favor," *Oregonian*,
    September 13, 1959, 16, col. 7.
64 "Natural Resources Board Opposes
    Dunes Park Plan," *Oregonian*, September
    24, 1959, 17, cols. 1–4.
65 "Blow to Dunes Park," *Oregonian*,
    September 27, 1959, 32, col. 2; "Senator
    Raps Dunes Stand: Neuberger Sends
    Letter to Hatfield," *Oregonian*, September
    28, 1959, 13, col. 4; "Solon Demands
    Hatfield Stand on Dunes Park,"
    Oregonian, October 6, 1959, 1, cols. 7–8.
66 "Porter, Hatfield in Long-Range Debate
    over Dunes Park Policy," *Oregon
    Statesman*, October 7, 1959, sec.1, 1,
    cols. 2–4.
67 "Ex-Gov. West Urges Dune Park Okeh,"
    Oregon Statesman, October 3, 1959,
    sec.1, 2, col. 3.
68 J. Wesley Sullivan, "Coast Dunes Area
    Barely Gets Mentioned in National
    Publicity," *Oregon Statesman*, October 5,
    1959, sec.1, 4, cols. 7–9.
69 William Tugman to Senator Richard
    Neuberger, July 30, 1959, Ax 078, box 3,
    "Conservation, National Parks: Seashore
    and Dunes, 6/59–7/59," Neuberger
    Papers.
70 Lyle G. Swetland to Senator Richard
    Neuberger, September 24, 1959, Ax 078,
    box 3, "Conservation, National Parks:
    Seashore and Dunes, 9/59," Neuberger
    Papers.
71 "Sand Dunes on Oregon's Coast," 52–56.
72 U.S. Congress, Senate, *Oregon Dunes
    National Seashore*, 17–18.
73 Ibid., 21–36.
74 Ibid., 37.
75 Ibid., 59–65. See also U.S. Congress,
    House, *Hearings on H.R. 6260*, 227.
76 Crafts, oral history interview, 8.
77 U.S. Congress, House, *Hearings on H.R.
    6260*, 181; see also "Park Hearings Held
    This Week," *Siuslaw Oar*, October 9,
    1959, 1, col. 6.
78 U.S. Congress, House, *Hearings on H.R.
    6260*, 131–37.

79 Eric Allen, "Who to Believe?," *Medford
    Mail Tribune*, October 4, 1959, in U.S.
    Congress, Senate, *Oregon Dunes
    National Seashore*, 400–401.
80 U.S. Congress, Senate, *Oregon Dunes
    National Seashore*, 158.
81 Ibid., 218.
82 Ibid., 219–20.
83 Ibid., 250–51.
84 Ibid., 261–62.
85 Ibid., 267–68.
86 Ibid., 404, 546–53; see also "Governor
    Offers Aid in Dunes," *Oregonian*,
    October 9, 1959, 1, col. 4; and "Solon
    Demands Hatfield Stand on Dunes Park,"
    Oregonian, October 6, 1959, 1, cols. 7–8.
87 Oswald West to Senator Richard
    Neuberger, telegram, October 1, 1959, Ax
    078, box 3, "Conservation, National
    Parks: Seashore and Dunes, 10/59,"
    Neuberger Papers.
88 Richard Neuberger to Oswald West,
    telegram, October 3, 1959, Ax 078, box 3,
    "Conservation, National Parks: Seashore
    and Dunes, 10/59," Neuberger Papers.
89 U.S. Congress, Senate, *Oregon Dunes
    National Seashore*, 67.
90 Ibid., 355.
91 Ibid., 364–65.
92 Ibid., 361.
93 Ibid., 366.
94 Ibid., 414.
95 "Dunes Park Plan Expanded, Altered to
    Placate Criticism," *Oregon Statesman*,
    October 26, 1959, sec.1, 1, cols. 5–7.
96 "Neuberger Asks Resource Committee
    for Objections to Dunes," *Oregonian*,
    October 16, 1959, 24, cols. 3–8; "Bulk of
    Land in Park Proposal Declared Already
    Publically Owned," *Oregonian*, October
    29, 1959, 10, cols. 2–4.
97 Harold Zellerbach to Senator Richard
    Neuberger, October 29, 1959, Ax 078,
    box 3, "Conservation, National Parks:
    Seashore and Dunes, 10/59," Neuberger
    Papers.
98 "New Hope for Dunes Park," *Capital
    Journal*, October 19, 1959, sec. 1, 4, cols.
    1–2.
99 U.S. Congress, House, *Hearings on H.R.
    6260*, 16.
100 "Timber Bloc Protests Tract Swap in Sen.
    Neuberger's Dunes Park Measure,"
    Oregonian, November 1, 1959, 26, cols.
    3–8.
101 "House Sub-committee Conducts Fair
    and Dignified Hearing in Florence,"
    Siuslaw Oar, November 6, 1959, 1, col. 2.
102 U.S. Congress, House, *Hearings on H.R.
    6260*, 66.

103 A. Robert Smith, "Dunes Park Opponents Have Ally in Ike's Administration," *Oregon Statesman*, November 2, 1959, sec.1, 4, cols. 7–9.

104 Untitled U.S. Forest Service memorandum (described as "brief, informal, and personal rundown of some of the major legislation that we really want; some that we are against; and perhaps mention a few other items"), January 5, 1960, folder "Recreation : Other—Forest Service versus Park Service," U.S. Forest Service Headquarters Records.

105 Daniel Davies, "Resources Chief Reiterates Opposition to Dunes Park," *Oregon Statesman*, November 18, 1959, sec. 1, 3, cols. 1–3; "State Agency Delays Dunes Park Stand," *Oregon Statesman*, November 25, 1959, sec. 1, 3, cols. 5–9; "Revised Dunes Proposal Getting Calm Appraisal, Governor Hatfield Says," *Oregon Statesman*, November 29, 1959, sec. 1, 2, cols. 4–5.

106 "Open to Suspicion," *Capital Journal*, November 27, 1959, sec. 1, 4, cols. 2.

107 A. Robert Smith, "Rep. Porter Waits for Hatfield before Drafting Seashore Bill," *Oregon Statesman*, December 11, 1959, sec. 1, 4, cols. 7–9. See also "Seaton Says Dunes Park Has Merit," *Capital Journal*, December 3, 1959, sec. 2, 3, col. 1; and "Dunes Park Aid Offered by Johnson," *Capital Journal*, December 10, 1959, sec. 1, 1, col. 6.

108 "The Slow-Moving Dunes," *Oregon Statesman*, December 12, 1959, sec. 1, 4, col. 1.

109 Richard L. Neuberger, "Belligerent Minority," *Oregonian*, December 27, 1959, 54, cols. 5–6.

110 A. Robert Smith "Morse-Neuberger 'Honeymoon' Ends in Tiff via Mails," *Oregon Statesman*, August 15, 1957, 1; Helen Fuller, "The 'Morseberger' Breaks in Two," *New Republic*, June 22, 1959, 8–9.

111 Richard Neuberger, "Wayne L. Morse: 1956 and Beyond," *Fortnight*, May 1955, 17–20.

112 On the Morse-Neuberger relationship, see generally chapter 9, "Dick and Wayne," in Drukman, *Wayne Morse*, 240–300; and Drukman, "Oregon's Most Famous Feud," 300–367.

113 Wayne Morse, "Statement of Senator Wayne Morse on Oregon Dunes and National Shoreline Area Bills," September 1959, Conservation Papers, 1950–1967, Ax356, box1, "Oregon Dunes. Proposals,

resolutions, associated documents," Onthank Papers.

114 A. Robert Smith, "Morse's Lack of Enthusiasm May Doom Dunes Park Bill," *Oregon Statesman*, January 12, 1960, sec. 1, 4, cols. 1–3.

115 "Dunes Park Ideas Given," *Oregonian*, January 14, 1960, 5, col. 2.

116 "If, as Governor Hatfield Says . . . ," *Oregon Statesman*, January 14, 1960, sec. 1, 4, col. 2.

117 "Neuberger Will Fight Morse on Dunes Issue," *Oregonian*, January 20, 1960, 6, cols. 1–2.

118 A. Robert Smith, "Neuberger Introduces Dunes Bill," *Oregonian*, January 26, 1960, 1, col. 8; "Neuberger Asks Hatfield, Ike Regime Settle Dunes Disputes," *Oregon Statesman*, January 26, 1960, sec.1, 4, cols. 7–9.

119 "Dunes Park Opposition Deplores Hatfield Stand," *Oregonian*, February 6, 1960, 20, cols. 2–3.

120 "Park's New Boundaries Outlined," *Siuslaw Oar*, February 19, 1960, 1, col. 3.

121 "In the Sands of Time," *Coos Bay World*, February 23, 1960.

122 "Hatfield Says Neuberger Cooperates on Park Bill," *Oregonian*, February 11, 1960, 6; "Gov. Hatfield Expects Accord with Neuberger on Dunes Bill," *Eugene Register-Guard*, February 11, 1960.

123 "Poll Shows Support for New Coast Park," *Oregonian*, March 11, 1960, 17, col. 1; A. Robert Smith, "Poll Results Favor National Seashore," *Oregon Statesman*, March 14, 1960, sec. 1, 4, cols. 8–9.

124 A. Robert Smith, "Opinion Poll Results Favor Coastal Park," *Eugene Register-Guard*, March 11, 1960.

125 Undated UPI wire copy, Ax 078, box 52, [untitled scrapbook], Neuberger Papers.

126 P. Douglas, "Richard L. Neuberger," 8.

127 "Editorial Writers Pay Tribute to Neuberger," *Medford Mail Tribune*, March 10, 1960.

128 William Tugman, "Neuberger's Death Called Grievous Loss to Oregon," *Eugene Register-Guard*, March 12, 1960.

129 Richard L. Neuberger, "When I First Learned I Had Cancer," in Neal, *They Never Go Back to Pocatello*, 327; "Physicians Not Certain Cancer Causes Breakage," *Oregonian*, March 3, 1960, 6.

130 "Death Comes During Rest," *Oregonian*, March 10, 1960, 26.

131 "Senator Neuberger Ponders Campaign," *Eugene Register-Guard*, February 1, 1960.

132 "Richard Neuberger's Active, Dedicated Life," *Oregonian*, March 15, 1960, 6.

133 A. Robert Smith, "Solons Voice Praise; Flags Signal Grief," *Oregonian*, March 10, 1960, 1.

134 "Sen. Neuberger's Death Tragic Loss," *Oregonian*, March 11, 1960, 30.

135 "Park Honor Bill Readied," *Oregonian*, March 15, 1960, 6; "Interior Department Supports Dunes Park Plan," *Oregon Statesman*, April 17, 1960, sec. 1, 6, cols. 4–9; A. Robert Smith, "Seaton Reveals Ike Wants to Create Dunes Park in Oregon," *Oregon Statesman*, April 22, 1960, sec. 1, 4, cols. 5–7; "Despite Faint Hope of Passage, Backers of Seashore Bills Continue . . . ," *Oregonian*, June 12, 1960, 7, cols. 1–8.

136 Neal, *They Never Go Back to Pocatello*, xxxiv.

137 Neuberger, *Adventures in Politics*, 152–63.

138 Neuberger, "My Hometown Is Good Enough for Me."

139 Neuberger, "Oregon at 100."

140 Neuberger, "Guarding Our Outdoor Heritage."

141 A. Robert Smith, "Morse Insistence on Eliminating Condemnation Provision Holding up Dunes Legislation," *Oregonian*, October 17, 1963, 11, col. 1.

142 "Proposal for Park at Seashore Is Gaining Support in Oregon," *New York Times*, November 25, 1962, 143.

143 "Yes on Oregon Dunes," *New York Times*, July 4, 1963, 16.

144 "Morse Blocks Dunes Project," *Oregon Journal*, December 12, 1963, 8, col. 1.

145 Quaintance, "A National Seashore for Oregon?," 39.

146 U.S. National Park Service, *Parks for America*, 439.

147 McCall and Neal, *Tom McCall: Maverick*, 70.

148 "This Session Critical for Sand Dunes Issue," *Siuslaw News*, June 30, 1966, 1, col. 2.

149 A. Robert Smith, "FS Begins Plan for Dunes Park," *Oregon Statesman*, February 19, 1967, sec. 1, 4, cols. 1–4.

150 "Dunes, Either Way," *Capital Journal*, February 15, 1967, sec. 1, 4, cols. 1–2.

151 A. Robert Smith, "Newest Dunes Plan Depends on Morse," *Oregon Statesman*, May 6, 1967, sec. 1, 4, cols. 7–8.

152 A. Robert Smith, "New Dunes Park Bill Offers Middle Course," *Oregonian*, June 30, 1968, 27, cols. 1–2; A. Robert Smith, "Oregon Dunes Park Chances Improved," *Oregon Statesman*, December 1, 1968, sec. 1, 4, cols. 4–5.

153 "New Motive for Dunes," *Oregon Statesman*, April 20, 1970, sec. 1, 4, col. 1.

154 "Dunes Recreation Area Officially Dedicated," *Oregonian*, July 16, 1972; Act to Establish the Oregon Dunes National Recreation Area.

155 Nixon, "Statement."

156 Oregon Dunes NRA Dedication Ceremony Program, July 15, 1972, folder 6: Agendas, Minutes, 1972, Mss. 2537, Governor's Committee for a Livable Oregon Papers.

157 "Neuberger Visitor Center for Dunes Recreation Area," *Capital Journal*, March 8, 1972, sec. 1, 4, cols. 1–2.

158 McCall and Neal, *Tom McCall: Maverick*, 70.

CHAPTER 3

The epigraph is from Tom McCall, untitled address to Willamette Basin Task Force, May 31, 1967, MSS 625, box 4, folder "Meetings, speeches, April 1968," McCall Papers, Oregon Historical Society.

1 McCall and Neal, *Tom McCall: Maverick*, 61.

2 Tarr, "Search for the Ultimate Sink," 516–52.

3 Gleeson, *Return of a River*, 4–12.

4 *Oregon Sportsman*, 1914, as cited in Robbins, *Oregon Environment*, 22.

5 Gleeson, *Return of a River*, 12–15.

6 Robbins, *Oregon Environment*, 27.

7 Honey, *Willamette River Greenway*, 24.

8 "Not Avon Calling," *Oregon Statesman*, April 4, 1961, sec. 1, 4.

9 Gleeson, *Return of a River*, 22.

10 Ibid., 25–26.

11 Robbins, *Oregon Environment*, 33–35.

12 Gleeson, *Return of a River*, 59.

13 "A Matter of Values," *Capital Journal*, November 4, 1959, sec. 1, 4.

14 "Willamette River Filth Still High," *Oregon Statesman*, January 28, 1960, 1.

15 Jim Hollon, "Hatfield Warning on Affluence Woe," *Capital Journal*, May 6, 1959, sec. 2, 11.

16 "Pollution Control Support Received," *Capital Journal*, July 18, 1960, sec. 1, 6.

17 See generally Corbett-Atterbury, *Oregon Story*; and Lucia, *Don't Call It Or-E-Gawn*, 39–45.

18 Kerr, "What Is the Purpose," 1.

19 "End Air, Water Pollution," *Oregon Statesman*, February 29, 1961, sec. 1, 4.

20 "As Oregon Fights Dirty Air, Water," *Oregon Journal*, November 21, 1962, sec. 2, 8.

21 McCall and Neal, *Tom McCall: Maverick*, 59–60.

22 Walth, *Fire at Eden's Gate*, 142.

23 McCall and Neal, *Tom McCall: Maverick*, 60.

24 *Pollution in Paradise*, 1963, KGW TV Collection, Oregon Historical Society Moving Image Archive.

25 Ibid.

26 McCall and Neal, *Tom McCall: Maverick*, 60.

27 Walth, *Fire at Eden's Gate*, 147.

28 Ibid.

29 Lear, *Rachel Carson*, 412.

30 Rome, *Genius of Earth Day*, 23–25.

31 Carson, *Silent Spring*, 244.

32 Opie, *Nature's Nation*, 413–14.

33 Lear, *Rachel Carson*, 419.

34 "President's Science Advisory Committee (PSAC): Pesticides Report," May 15, 1963, 45, Presidential Papers, President's Office Files, Papers of John F. Kennedy, Kennedy Library, http://www.jfklibrary.org/Asset-Viewer/Archives/JFKPOF-087-003.aspx.

35 Douglas Seymour, "Solons Vote Teeth for Pollution Law," *Capital Journal*, March 26, 1963, 1.

36 Jerry Tippens, "Sanitary Authority Denies Iron Hand," *Oregon Journal*, January 3, 1963, sec. 2, 5.

37 Average total precipitation in "Period of Record Monthly Climate Summary, Salem WSO"; Gleeson, *Return of a River*, 75.

38 Floyd McKay, "Pioneer Poet's Lovely Willamette River Turned into Sewer by People," *Oregon Statesman*, September 25, 1965, 3; "Fight to Cut Wastes in Willamette River Costing Millions," *Oregon Statesman*, September 26, 1965, 9.

39 Floyd McKay, "Population and Industrial Expansion Both Will Affect Willamette Cleanup," *Oregon Statesman*, September 30, 1965, 5.

40 Udall, *Quiet Crisis*, 188.

41 "Straub Flays Mark for River Pollution," *Capital Journal*, August 13, 1965, sec. 1, 1.

42 "3 Mills Blamed for Most of Willamette Pollution," *Capital Journal*, August 17, 1965, sec. 1, 1.

43 McCall and Neal, *Tom McCall: Maverick*, 65–66.

44 Chuck Grell, "Proper Planning, Conservation Seen Oregon Need," *Capital Journal*, June 30, 1966, sec. 2, 11.

45 "An Elbow-to-Elbow Oregon?," *Capital Journal*, December 20, 1965, sec. 1, 4.

46 Dennis Buchanan, "Authority Lacks Power to Fight Ever-Growing Oregon Pollution," *Oregon Journal*, February 28, 1966, 1.

47 Eells and Nyberg, *Lonely Walk*, 45–46.

48 Dennis Buchanan, "Lawmakers, Public Hold Key to Pollution Controls," *Oregon Journal*, March 3, 1966, 7.

49 "Remarks by Secretary of State Tom McCall before United Republicans of Oregon," April 2, 1966, MSS 625, box 3, McCall Papers, Oregon Historical Society.

50 "Straub Gives River Plan," *Capital Journal*, July 20, 1966, 7.

51 Robert Straub, "Dear Fellow Oregonians," July 1, 1966, box 32, folder 19, Straub Archives, Western Oregon University.

52 "A Dream Too Thrilling for Politics," *Eugene Register-Guard*, July 22, 1966, 14A.

53 C. Johnson, *Standing at the Water's Edge*, 105.

54 McCall and Neal, *Tom McCall: Maverick*, 67–70.

55 Walth, *Fire at Eden's Gate*, 169.

56 "Sing Along with Bob," n.d., box 31, folder 19, Straub Archive, Western Oregon University.

57 "Statement by Gov. McCall on Beach Route," July 7, 1967, MSS 625, box 3, McCall Papers, Oregon Historical Society.

58 Walth, *Fire at Eden's Gate*, 171.

59 "Straub Better for Governor," *Oregon Journal*, October 6, 1966, 10J.

60 "McCall Taunts Straub on Pollution," *Oregon Statesman*, October 14, 1966, 19.

61 Floyd McKay, "Willamette Plan on Straub Slate," *Oregon Statesman*, October 7, 1966, 4.

62 Marge Davenport, "Pollution Perils Oregon's Health, Way of Life," *Oregon Journal*, October 17, 1966, 2.

63 "Air, Water Pollution Plague Oregon Areas," *Oregon Journal*, November 21, 1966, 1.

64 "Governor Tom McCall's Administration: Inaugural Message, 1967," Oregon Secretary of State, http://arcweb.sos.state.or.us/pages/records/governors/guides/state/mccall/inaugural1967.html.

65 Marge Davenport, "Get Tough Policy Adopted by State in Pollution Fight," *Oregon Journal*, February 22, 1967, 6.

66 "$105 Million Willamette Anti-pollution Plan Devised," *Oregon Statesman*, February 27, 1967, 1; A. Robert Smith, "Pulp Mill Crackdown Seen Key to Willamette Cleanup," *Oregon Statesman*,

February 27, 1967; "U.S. Agency Calls for Willamette River Cleanup," *Capital Journal*, February 27, 1967, 1; "B-C Mill Meeting Pollution Order," *Capital Journal*, February 27, 1967, 3.

67   A. Robert Smith, "State Agency Hits at U.S. Pollution Report," *Oregon Statesman*, March 31, 1967, 4.

68   A. Robert Smith, "Willamette River Report Unfair, Sen. Hatfield Says," *Oregon Statesman*, March 5, 1967, 6.

69   "Governor Unveils River 'Greenway,'" *Oregon Journal*, March 1, 1967, 2; Tom Wright, "Leaders Seek 120 Miles of Willamette River Parkway," *Oregon Statesman*, March 2, 1967, 1.

70   "Self-Solving River Problem," *Capital Journal*, March 8, 1967, 4.

71   Fujii, "Who Will Pay for Willamette Greenway?," 7.

72   "Willamette's Pollution Hides the Real Stream," *Capital Journal*, March 24, 1967, 7.

73   McCall and Neal, *Tom McCall: Maverick*, 78–79.

74   "McCall Names Self to State Sanitary Board," *Oregon Statesman*, April 26, 1967, 1; "Chairman Too: McCall Names Self to State Sanitary Board," *Capital Journal*, April 25, 1967, sec. 2, 15.

75   McCall and Neal, *Tom McCall: Maverick*, 78.

76   "McCall Self-Appointment Called Political Blunder," *Medford Mail-Tribune*, April 26, 1967.

77   "Statement by Governor Tom McCall on State Sanitary Authority Appointment," April 25, 1967, MSS 625, box 3, McCall Papers, Oregon Historical Society.

78   "McCall's Sanitary Authority Move," *Oregon Voter* 53:18 (May 6, 1967): 5.

79   "Beautiful Oregon?," *Oregon Voter* 53:18 (May 6, 1967): 3.

80   "A 200-Mile Oregon Green Way Along River Urged," *New York Times*, March 28, 1967, 25.

81   Floyd McKay, "Bill to Preserve Beauty Spots Goes to McCall," *Oregon Statesman*, May 12, 1967; "Beauty Program Backed," *Capital Journal*, May 25, 1967, 9; "Greenway Poses Questions" *Oregon Agriculture*, May 25, 1967, 7–8.

82   "Greenway Gripes," *Oregon Voter* 130:35 (September 2, 1967): 12.

83   "Statement by Gov. McCall on Pollution Abatement Bill Signing," June 19, 1967, MSS 625, box 3, McCall Papers, Oregon Historical Society.

84   Marge Davenport, "Crackdown Starts in Pollution Fight," *Oregon Journal*, July 11, 1967, 4; Walth, *Fire at Eden's Gate*, 198;

McCall and Neal, *Tom McCall: Maverick*, 83.

85   "Statement by Governor Tom McCall on Resignation from State Sanitary Authority," July 10, 1967, MSS 625, box 3, McCall Papers, Oregon Historical Society.

86   Stewart Udall, "Comeback for the Willamette River," *National Parks Magazine*, March 1968, 4–8.

87   "Who Protects the Outdoors?," *Capital Journal*, August 14, 1967, 4.

88   Tom McCall, "Willamette Basin Task Force, Marion Hotel," May 31, 1967, MSS 625, box 3, McCall Papers, Oregon Historical Society.

89   Pacific Northwest Bell, "What's It Going to Be Like by 1976?," PNB Ad No. 367-AD, [n.d.], MSS 625, box 3, McCall Papers, Oregon Historical Society.

90   E. W. Kenworthy, "Tough Rules Saving a Dying Oregon River," *New York Times*, September 8, 1970, 50.

91   Orr and Orr, *Oregon Water*, 174–77.

92   McCall and Neal, *Tom McCall: Maverick*, 82–83.

CHAPTER 4

The epigraph is from Ancil Payne, editorial, May 10, 1967, folder "Beach Bill Misc.," box 6, Administrative Correspondence 1964–1969, accession #70A-95, McCall Administration Records, Oregon State Archives.

1   McCall and Neal, *Tom McCall: Maverick*, 77.

2   *Oregon's Beaches*, 22.

3   Floyd McKay, "Beach Issue Explodes in Legislature," *Oregon Statesman*, May 8, 1967, 1.

4   Dodds, *American Northwest*, 6–12.

5   Moulton, *Journals*, 79ff.

6   Dicken, *Pioneer Trails*.

7   *Oregon's Beaches*, 10.

8   Hildreth, "Public Access," 8; Kehow, "Next Wave," 1917–19.

9   Sobel and Raimo, *Biographical Directory of American Governors*, 1273.

10   Cox, *Park Builders*, 10.

11   "Crafty Os West Hoodwinked Legislature to Get Beaches for State," *Oregonian*, May 14, 1967, 24; *Oregon's Beaches*, 11; Merriam, *Oregon's Highway Park System*, 24.

12   Merriam, *Oregon's Highway Park System*, 25.

13   "Devers Lauds Present Beach Law as Best," *Oregon Journal*, December 30, 1947, 1; "Os West Asserts Lincoln County Strip in Question; Railroad to

Investigate Claim," *Oregon Statesman*, January 4, 1948, 1.

14 Thomas P. Guerin, "A Properly Planned and Executed State Policy for Preservation of Beaches Is Needed," guest editorial, *Oregon Journal*, August 2, 1949, 16.

15 Charles A. Sprague, "It Seems to Me," *Oregon Statesman*, February 11, 1953, 1.

16 "Oregon's Coastline," *Oregon Statesman*, August 7, 1953, 4.

17 "Oregon's Threatened Beaches," *Oregon Journal*, January 31, 1957, sec. 4, 1.

18 "Preservation of Beach by Oz West Honored," *Oregon Journal*, May 21, 1958, 3.

19 Fred Martin, "Public Beaches of Oregon 'Threatened' by Two Bills," *Oregon Statesman*, February 18, 1961, 1.

20 "Senate Okehs Paper Mill Pipeline at Coast, Sends Bill to Governor," *Oregon Statesman*, February 21, 1961, 7.

21 Beulah Hand, "Fears Trespass on Beaches," *Oregon Statesman*, May 3, 1961, 4.

22 *Oregon's Beaches*, 19.

23 "State to Spend $6 Million for Access to Beach," *Oregon Statesman*, January 22, 1966, 1.

24 "Revolution on the Beach," *Oregon Statesman*, September 14, 1964, 4.

25 *Oregon's Beaches*, 19.

26 Ibid.

27 J. Richard Byrne to Glenn L. Jackson, July 14, 1966, House Highway Minutes and Exhibits, box 85, folder 2, Legislative Assembly, 1967 Regular Session, Oregon State Archives.

28 William G. Nokes to G. E. Rohde, August 15, 1966, ibid.

29 Lawrence F. Bitte to Tom McCall, August 25, 1966, ibid.

30 Sullivan, "Laying Out an 'Unwelcome Mat,'" 336–39.

31 Bender, "Castles in the Sand," 914.

32 *Oregon's Beaches*, 23.

33 Ibid., 24–25.

34 A second bill, HB 1600, was introduced simultaneously but received much less attention than HB 1601 as it simply stated that any future "seaward accretions" on the beach would belong to the state but would not affect existing beach property boundaries.

35 Dave Talbot, "State Highway Department Statement in Support of H.B. 1601," March 7, 1967, House Highway Minutes and Exhibits, box 85, folder 2, Legislative Assembly, 1967 Regular Session, Oregon State Archives.

36 Minutes, House Committee on Highways, March 7, 1967, ibid.

37 "Beach Land Bills Draw Fire from Coast," *Capital Journal*, March 8, 1967, 3.

38 "Needed Protection for Beaches," *Oregon Journal*, March 14, 1967, 10.

39 L. L. Stewart, "Testimony of L. L. Stewart on House Bill 1601," March 7, 1967, House Highway Minutes and Exhibits, box 85, folder 2, Legislative Assembly, 1967 Regular Session, Oregon State Archives.

40 Minutes, House Committee on Highways, March 23, 1967, ibid.

41 Lawrence Fred Bitte to Sid Bazett, "Re: House Bill # 1601," April 27, 1967, ibid.

42 Donn DeBernardi to House Highway Committee, March 23, 1967, ibid.

43 "Public's Access Said 'In Danger,'" *Capital Journal*, March 24, 1967, 3.

44 "How to Divide Our Wild, Moving Beaches," *Capital Journal*, March 27, 1967, 4.

45 Douglas Seymour, "Controversial Beach Measure Altered," *Capital Journal*, April 7, 1967, 7; Minutes, House Committee on Highways, April 1967, House Highway Minutes and Exhibits, box 85, folder 2–3, Legislative Assembly, 1967 Regular Session, Oregon State Archives.

46 Minutes, House Committee on Highways, May 2, 1967, House Highway Minutes and Exhibits, box 85, folder 3, Legislative Assembly, 1967 Regular Session, Oregon State Archives.

47 "Battle Lines Drawn over Beach Issue," *Capital Journal*, May 3, 1967, 7.

48 Blaine Schultz, "Owners Defend Rights to Dry Sand Seafronts," *Oregonian*, May 3, 1967; Love, *Grasping Wastrels vs. Beaches Forever Inc.*, 26–31.

49 "Gov. McCall Asks Beach Bill Action," *Capital Journal*, May 4, 1967, 1.

50 Tom McCall to Sidney Bazett, May 4, 1967, folder "Beach Bill Misc.," box 6, Administrative Correspondence 1964–1969, accession #70A-95, McCall Administration Records, Oregon State Archives.

51 "Beach Access Issue Mustn't Die," *Oregon Journal*, May 5, 1967, 14; Harold Hughes, "McCall Slaps GOP's Tabling of Beach Bill," *Oregonian*, May 5, 1967, 1.

52 Matt Kramer, "Beach Bill Revival Sought," *Capital Journal*, May 5, 1967, 5; "McCall Backs Continued Public Use for Beaches," *Oregon Statesman*, May 5, 1967, 1.

53 Matt Kramer, "Speaker Seeks to Unclog Beach Bill," *Oregon Statesman*, May 6, 1967, 1; "Battle Forecast over Beach Use," *Capital Journal*, May 6, 1967, 1.

54 McCall and Neal, *Tom McCall: Maverick*, 82; Stan Federman, "Fight Rages over Access to Beach," *Oregonian*, May 7, 1967, 1.

55 Douglas Seymour, "House Balks Beach Bill Call Up," *Capital Journal*, May 8, 1967, 1.

56 Floyd McKay, "Beach Issue Explodes in Legislature," *Oregon Statesman*, May 8, 1967, 1; "Public Claim to Dry Sand above High Tide Stirs Ruckus in House," *Oregon Statesman*, May 8, 1967, 5; Harold Hughes "'Dry Sand' Bill Survives Raid by Opposition," *Oregonian*, May 9, 1967, 1.

57 *Oregon's Beaches*, 29; "Citizen Committee Threatens Action if Legislature Bottlenecks Beach Bill," *Oregonian*, May 10, 1967, 20.

58 Ancil Payne, "KGW TV-8 Editorial," Exhibits, House Committee on Highways, May 11, 1967, House Highway Minutes and Exhibits, box 85, folder 3, Legislative Assembly, 1967 Regular Session, Oregon State Archives.

59 "House Beach Issue Vote Fails but Battle Will Continue," *Oregon Statesman*, May 9, 1967, 11; Floyd McKay, "Oregon's Beach Bill Fight Continues Hot," *Oregon Statesman*, May 9, 1967, 1; Douglas Seymour, "Monte Drafts Beach Use Zoning Plan," *Capital Journal*, May 9, 1967, 1.

60 Floyd McKay, "Beach Backers Prepare Push on Legislature," *Oregon Statesman*, May 10, 1967, 1; C. Johnson, *Standing at the Water's Edge*, 126–30.

61 Floyd McKay, "New Beach Measure Unveiled," *Oregon Statesman*, May 11, 1967, 11; "Latest Beach Bill Unveiled, Stirs up Fire," *Oregon Statesman*, May 11, 1967, 1; Douglas Seymour, "Beach Bill Amendments Revealed," *Capital Journal*, May 10, 1967, sec. 2, 9.

62 "Beach Overpopulation," *Oregon Statesman*, May 11, 1967, 4.

63 Minutes, House Committee on Highways, May 11, 1967, House Highway Minutes and Exhibits, box 85, folder 3, Legislative Assembly, 1967 Regular Session, Oregon State Archives.

64 Robert Straub, "Statement of State Treasurer Robert W. Straub to Highway Interim Committee—5/11/67," ibid.

65 Tom McCall, "Recommendation by Governor McCall for Preservation of Oregon's Beaches," ibid.

66 "New Beach Bill Stirs More Dispute," *Oregon Statesman*, May 12, 1967, 8; Floyd McKay, "McCall Slates Beach Trip to End Dispute," *Oregon Statesman*, May 12, 1967, 1; Floyd McKay, "McCall Will

Walk on Beaches Today," *Oregon Statesman*, May 13, 1967, 1.

67 Walth, *Fire at Eden's Gate*, 190.

68 "This Sand Is Your Sand, This Sand Is My Sand," *Capital Journal*, May 13, 1967, 1.

69 Walth, *Fire at Eden's Gate*, 190.

70 Matt Kramer, "McCall Okehs Beach Formula," *Oregon Statesman*, May 14, 1967, 1.

71 Walth, *Fire at Eden's Gate*, 190.

72 Early Deane, "McCall Group Finds Formula in Beach Spat," *Oregonian*, May 14, 1967, 1; Stan Federman, "Cannon Beach Motel Owner Fights for Right to Fence Off Private Beach for Guests," *Oregonian*, May 14, 1967, 23.

73 Albert M. Jennings, "Beach Bill Accord Reached," *Capital Journal*, May 13, 1967, 1.

74 "Leaders Agree on Beach Bill," *Capital Journal*, May 15, 1967, 1; Tom McCall, "Statement by Governor Tom McCall," May 15, 1967, folder "Beach Bill Misc.," box 6, Administrative Correspondence 1964–1969, accession #70A-95, McCall Administration Records, Oregon State Archives.

75 "Leaders Agree on Beach Bill," *Oregon Statesman*, May 16, 1967, 1; Floyd McKay, "Opposing Camps Reach New Agreement on Beach Measure," *Oregon Statesman*, May 16, 1967, sec. 2, 16.

76 Doug McKean, "McCall's Beach Line Pushed Seaward," *Oregon Journal*, May 17, 1967, 1; Minutes, House Committee on Highways, May 16, 1967, House Highway Minutes and Exhibits, box 85, folder 3, Legislative Assembly, 1967 Regular Session, Oregon State Archives.

77 "Beach Proposal Would Place Driftwood Area off Limits," *Oregon Statesman*, May 17, 1967, 15; Floyd McKay, "Solons Exclude Driftwood Area from Beach Zoning," *Oregon Statesman*, May 17, 1967, 1.

78 "Beach Initiative Drive Organized," *Capital Journal*, May 17, 1967, 1.

79 Harold Hughes, "Smooth Sailing Seen for Beach Measure," *Oregonian*, May 20, 1967, 7.

80 House Committee on Highways, "Statement of House Committee on Highways Concerning HB 1601," Minutes, House Committee on Highways, May 18, 1967, House Highway Minutes and Exhibits, box 85, folder 3, Legislative Assembly, 1967 Regular Session, Oregon State Archives.

81 Minutes, House Committee on Highways, May 18, 1967, ibid.

82 "Beach Bill Vote Expected Next Week," *Capital Journal*, May 19, 1967, 3; Floyd McKay, "Driftwood Is Retained in Beach Bill," *Oregon Statesman*, May 19, 1967, 1; Floyd McKay, "Broader Beach Bill Due in House," *Oregon Statesman*, May 19, 1967, 19.

83 Floyd McKay, "House Votes Beach Bill; Price Tag Is $400,000," *Oregon Statesman*, May 22, 1967, 1; Douglas Seymour, "House Passes Beach Bill, 57–3," *Capital Journal*, May 22, 1967, 1.

84 "Sixteen Feet and Sandy Crow," *Capital Journal*, May 23, 1967, 4.

85 "Motel Man to Challenge New Beach Access Bill," *Oregon Statesman*, May 19, 1967, 1.

86 Dan P. Allen, "Beach Controversy Over for Now," *Oregon Voter*, May 27, 1967, 1–6.

87 Senate Judiciary Committee Minutes, May 26, 1967, folder 5, box 98, Senate Judiciary Minutes and Exhibits, Legislative Assembly, 1967 Regular Session, Oregon State Archives. For general discussion of the property rights argument in legal context, see Meier, "*Stevens v. City of Cannon Beach*," 413–48.

88 Harold Hughes, "Foes Fail to Divert Beach Bill," *Oregonian*, June 8, 1967, 1.

89 Kenneth W. Fitzgerald, "State Capitol Spotlight," *Oregon-Washington Farmers Union* 36:11 (June 1967): 5.

90 "McCall Hails Beach Bill," *Oregonian*, July 7, 1967, 13.

91 McCall and Neal, *Tom McCall: Maverick*, 82.

92 Tom McCall to Ancil Payne, July 14, 1967, folder "Beach Bill Letters," box 6, Administrative Correspondence 1964–1969, accession #70A-95, McCall Administration Records, Oregon State Archives.

93 Tom McCall to James Chancey, May 29, 1967, ibid.

94 Tom McCall to Hugh Jennings, May 23, 1967, ibid.

95 P. C. Leineweber to Tom McCall, May 17, 1967, ibid.

96 Bricklemyer et al., "Preservation of Coastal Spaces," 279.

97 "Beaches Are for Kids" bumper sticker, n.d., mss. 11, box 2, folder 7, McLenan Papers; "Re-Elect Bob Straub: Democrat for State Treasurer," [1968], box 26, folder 14, Straub Archives, Western Oregon University.

98 *Oregon's Beaches*, 67.

99 Tom McCall, "Pacific Northwest International Section Air Pollution Control Association Conference," 8, 1967, MSS 625, box 4, folder "Meetings, Speeches, 1967," McCall Papers, Oregon Historical Society.

100 "Accomplishments in Conservation First Two Years of Governor Tom McCall's Administration," 1968, MSS 625, box 5, folder "Accomplishments in Conservation," ibid.

CHAPTER 5

The epigraph is from Paul Harvey, "Oregon Did It," *Naples (FL) Daily News*, December 19, 1972.

1 Thomas F. Brady, "Publishers Rate Environment as the 'Big Story' in U.S.," *New York Times*, April 23, 1970, 32.

2 Udall, *Quiet Crisis*, 177.

3 Nash, "Song of the Open Road."

4 "Scenery and Billboards," *Oregon Voter*, February 4, 1924, 4–6. See also Fraser, *American Billboard*.

5 "Hot Dog Signs," *Oregon Voter*, February 2, 1929, 252.

6 "Billboard Regulation," *Oregon Voter*, September 7, 1929, 327; R. W. Sawyer, "Highway Billboards," *Oregon Motorist*, January 1931, 1–5, 18.

7 "Billboards: Voluntary Zoning," *Oregon Voter*, January 31, 1931, 14; "Bill-Board Ban," *Oregon Voter*, February 15, 1941, 11.

8 "Billboard Bill Had Right Approach," *Oregon Voter*, March 7, 1953, 10; Thornton Munger, "The Invasion of Roadside Farms," *Oregon Agriculture*, April 1953, 6.

9 "Billboards or Scenery," *Oregon Grange Bulletin*, March 5, 1957, 6.

10 Arthur Krock, "Billboard Advertising on the New Highway System," *New York Times*, May 3, 1957.

11 Floyd and Shedd, *Highway Beautification*, 65–67, 74.

12 National Committee on Highway Law of the Highway Research Board, *Special Report 41*, 33–50.

13 "Oregon Solons Will Get Billboard Regulation Act," *Oregon Motorist*, September 1958, 1; "Billboard Act Would Exceed Minimum Standards," *Oregon Motorist*, November 1958, 1.

14 "Measure to Control Highway Billboards Being Initiated," *Oregon Grange Bulletin*, January 5, 1960, 1; "Petitions Ask Billboard Ban on Freeways," *Oregon Statesman*, January 12, 1960, 1; Douglas Seymour, "Issues Facing Voters: No. 15," *Capital Journal*, November 1, 1960, 2.

15   "Scenery Still There?," *Capital Journal*, January 13, 1960, 4.

16   "We'll Take Monotony," *Capital Journal*, March 7, 1960, 4.

17   Thornton T. Munger, "Roadside Protection for Farmers," *Oregon Grange Bulletin*, March 20, 1960, 4.

18   "Anti-billboard Drive Names 2 Salem Men," *Oregon Statesman*, March 26, 1960, 5.

19   "Billboard Curb Petitions Reach Half-Way Mark," *Oregon Grange Bulletin*, May 5, 1960, 1.

20   "40,000 Signers Put Billboard Bill on Ballot," *Oregon Grange Bulletin*, July 5, 1960, 1.

21   Olga M. Wilson, "Billboard Control," *Oregon Grange Bulletin*, October 20, 1960, 4.

22   "Billboard Facts and Fancies," *Capital Journal*, October 31, 1960, 4.

23   "Governor Hatfield for Billboard Control," *Oregon Motorist*, October 1960, 1.

24   "Billboard Postscript," *Oregon Statesman*, November 5, 1960, 4.

25   "New Law Despite Election," *Capital Journal*, November 11, 1960, 4; "Kill State's Golden Goose?," *Capital Journal*, November 21, 1960, 4.

26   "Billboard Ban Plans Develop Two Big Points of Conflict," *Capital Journal*, March 14, 1961, 1; "Board Could Ban Roadside Signs," *Oregon Statesman*, March 19, 1961, 5; "Billboard Restriction Bills Given Governor," *Oregon Statesman*, April 27, 1961, 14; "Two Billboard Regulation Bills Enacted," *Oregon Motorist*, May 1961, 1; "Billboard Restriction," *Oregon Statesman*, May 5, 1961, 4.

27   Floyd and Shedd, *Highway Beautification*, 66–67.

28   "Maurine in Billboards Battle," *Oregon Statesman*, June 19, 1961, 4; "Green Curtain for a Loophole," *Capital Journal*, July 15, 1963, 4.

29   Floyd and Shedd, *Highway Beautification*, 72–73.

30   Rome, *Bulldozer in the Countryside*, 122–24.

31   Cross, *All-Consuming Century*, 150–52, 169–73.

32   Kirk, *Counterculture Green*, 13–30.

33   L. Johnson, "Remarks at the University of Michigan."

34   Blake, *God's Own Junkyard*, 12–15.

35   Ibid., 109.

36   Gould, *Lady Bird Johnson: Our Environmental First Lady*, 46–47.

37   L. Johnson, "Annual Message."

38   Lady Bird Johnson quoted in Gould, *Lady Bird Johnson: Our Environmental First Lady*, 51.

39   Stewart L. Udall, oral history interview 2, by Joe B. Franze, May 15, 1969, 7–8, Johnson Oral History Collection.

40   *Beauty for America*, 253, 255, 279.

41   *Report to the President and the President's Response*, 20–21.

42   Ibid., 43, 45–46.

43   Gould, *Lady Bird Johnson: Our Environmental First Lady*, 59–66, 94–97.

44   Gould, *Lady Bird Johnson and the Environment*, 148.

45   Cloonan, Gabis, and Goode, *Estimates of the Impact*, 20.

46   Ibid., 96–99.

47   Highway Beautification Act; Floyd and Shedd, *Highway Beautification*, 82.

48   Rome, *Genius of Earth Day*, 47–54.

49   Ad Council, "Keep America Beautiful."

50   Krech, *Ecological Indian*, 15–16.

51   Douglas Gripp, "Stiffened Oregon Laws Make It Tough for Litterbugs," *Capital Journal*, June 29, 1961, 9.

52   "For a Cool, Cleaner Oregon," *Capital Journal*, March 16, 1964, 4.

53   "Land of Litter," *Capital Journal*, March 11, 1967, 4.

54   Savage and Richmond, *Oregon's Bottle Bill*, 3–8.

55   Savage and Richmond, *Oregon's Bottle Bill*, 3–8.

56   Vermont Legislative Research Service, *Bottle Bills*, 2.

57   Walth, *Fire at Eden's Gate*, 254–57.

58   Savage and Richmond, *Oregon's Bottle Bill*, 8.

59   "Ban on Non-Returnable," *Oregon Statesman*, February 3, 1969, 4.

60   Don Hall, "Bottle Bill Backers Believe in Rebates," *Capital Journal*, March 29, 1969, 3.

61   Walth, *Fire at Eden's Gate*, 261–63.

62   "Litter Growth Assured," *Oregon Statesman*, April 17, 1969, 4.

63   "Crusade against Littering," *Oregon Journal*, April 22, 1969, n.p.

64   "New Flood of Potential Litter Due," *Oregon Statesman*, December 29, 1969, 4.

65   McCall and Neal, *Tom McCall: Maverick*, 204.

66   Harold Hughes, "McCall Urges Statewide Attack on Litter," *Oregonian*, July 17, 1969, 13.

67   Walth, *Fire at Eden's Gate*, 262.

68 Matt Kramer, "Big Oregon Fight Looms over No-Return Bottles," *Capital Journal*, January 9, 1970, 1.

69 Douglas Seymour, "McCall: All-Out War on the Beer Can," *Capital Journal*, January 10, 1970, 5.

70 Floyd McKay, "'No Quarter' for Bottlers in McCall Drive on Litter," *Oregon Statesman*, January 10, 1970, 1.

71 Clarence Zaitz, "Staggering Volume of Bottles, Cans Adds to Litter Problems," *Capital Journal*, January 17, 1970, 1.

72 Stern, *Impacts of Beverage Container Legislation*, 101–6.

73 Rodney M. Pitts, "Litter Problem," *Oregon Statesman*, January 21, 1970, 4.

74 Shireman, *CalPIRG-ELS Study Group Report*, 26.

75 Clarence Zaitz, "First 'Bottle Battle' Here," *Capital Journal*, February 9, 1970, 10.

76 "Industry Has Say on 'Litter Bit,'" *Capital Journal*, February 14, 1970, 8.

77 Walth, *Fire at Eden's Gate*, 316–17; Minutes, September 12, 1969, folder 3, "Agendas, Minutes, 1969," Mss. 2537, Governor's Committee for a Livable Oregon Papers.

78 Jerry Easterling, "Non-returnables: King of the Road," *Capital Journal*, February 20, 1970, 14.

79 "Litter Foes Ask Boycott," *Oregonian*, February 3, 1970, 11.

80 Clarence Zaitz, "Ban Non-returnables, or Educate about Litter?," *Capital Journal*, June 6, 1970, 19.

81 Don Hall, "New 'Bottle Bill,' Antilitter Revenue Plan Shaping," *Capital Journal*, August 20, 1970, 6.

82 Clarence Zaitz, "'Intense' Pressure Wielded on Bottles," *Capital Journal*, October 22, 1970, 1.

83 "6 to 1?," *Oregonian*, November 1, 1970, 2.

84 Savage and Richmond, *Oregon's Bottle Bill*, 11–13.

85 "'People's Lobby' to Battle Litter," *Capital Journal*, March 1, 1971, 1.

86 Minutes, House Subcommittee on State and Federal Affairs, March 3, 1971, box 129, folder 5, Legislative Assembly, 1971 Regular Session, Oregon State Archives.

87 "Fact Sheet: The Effect on Jobs of the Trend toward Non-Returnable Containers in the Beer and Soft Drink Industries," n.d., n.p.; and Richard Chambers, "Statement of Beer Sales in Oregon by Breweries," both in HB 1036 exhibits, House State and Federal Affairs,

box 130, Legislative Assembly, 1971 Regular Session, Oregon State Archives.

88 John Buckley, "Notes with Respect to State of Oregon Legislative Hearing of Wednesday, March 3, 1971," ibid.

89 John Piacentini, "Dear Concerned Oregonians" (advertisement), *Oregonian*, March 9, 1971.

90 Minutes, May 1, 1970, folder 4, "Agendas, Minutes, 1970," Mss. 2537, Governor's Committee for a Livable Oregon Papers.

91 Minutes, House Subcommittee on State and Federal Affairs, March 11, 1971, box 129, folder 5; and Larry Williams, "Testimony Presented to the House State and Federal Affairs Committee, Concerning H.B. 1036, March 11, 1971," HB 1036 Exhibits, House State and Federal Affairs, box 130, both in Legislative Assembly, 1971 Regular Session, Oregon State Archives; Gene Maudlin, "Don't Tamper with Non-returnable Bottles," *Capital Journal*, March 11, 1971, 7.

92 "Survey Conducted; Litter Load Gleaned," *Oregon Statesman*, March 23, 1971, 5; "Survey Cites Litter Toll," *Oregon Statesman*, March 23, 1971, 5; Minutes, House Subcommittee on State and Federal Affairs, March 23, 1971, box 129, folder 5, Legislative Assembly, 1971 Regular Session, Oregon State Archives.

93 "Bottlers Offer Counter-Proposal," *Capital Journal*, March 23, 1971, 9; Minutes, House Subcommittee on State and Federal Affairs, March 23, 1971, box 129, folder 5, Legislative Assembly, 1971 Regular Session, Oregon State Archives.

94 Minutes, House Subcommittee on State and Federal Affairs, April 1, 1971, box 129, folder 5, Legislative Assembly, 1971 Regular Session, Oregon State Archives.

95 "Anti-Litter Bill Wins," *Oregon Statesman*, April 11, 1971, 4.

96 Minutes, Senate Consumer Affairs Committee, April 28, 1971, box 140, Legislative Assembly, 1971 Regular Session, Oregon State Archives.

97 Gene Maudlin, "Can Industry Admits Ecology Errors, but Protests Bottle Bill 'Destruction,'" *Oregon Statesman*, April 29, 1971, 8.

98 Walth, *Fire at Eden's Gate*, 320–22.

99 "'Bottle Bill' Might Flop in Legislature," *Capital Journal*, May 21, 1971, 1.

100 "Bottle Bill Dead?," *Capital Journal*, May 24, 1971, 4.

101 "Don't Bottle 'Bottle Bill,'" *Oregon Statesman*, May 25, 1971, n.p.

102 "Ecology's Big Win," *Capital Journal*, June 3, 1971, 4.

103 "'Bottle Bill' Significant Act," *Capital Journal*, July 3, 1971, 7.

104 Tom McCall, "Remarks by Governor Tom McCall," February 2, 1970, 5–6, photocopy in author's possession.

105 "Far beyond Our Borders," *Oregon Statesman*, July 26, 1971, 4.

106 "Federal Bottle Policy," *Oregon Statesman*, November 8, 1971, 4; "The Watchdog Is Dreaming," *Oregon Statesman*, February 17, 1972, 4.

107 Ronald Sullivan, "Jersey Plan May Limit Containers," *New York Times*, September 9, 1971.

108 "Deposit on Litter," *Nation*, July 5, 1971, 6.

109 Lesow, "Litter and the Nonreturnable Beverage Container," 210–11.

110 "Litter Bag Use Urged," *Oregonian*, February 17, 1971.

111 McCall and Neal, *Tom McCall: Maverick*, 206.

112 Walth, *Fire at Eden's Gate*, 322.

CHAPTER 6

The epigraph is from Ted Hallock, oral history interview, May 21, 1997, in Teramura, "Oral History," 49.

1   "Livability," *Oxford English Dictionary* online, September 2015, http://www.oed.com/view/Entry/109302?redirectedFrom=livability&.

2   Pinchot, *Breaking New Ground*, 326.

3   Hays, "Three Decades of Environmental Politics," 336–41.

4   "Governors Study Expanding Cities," *New York Times*, July 11, 1961, R14.

5   Cahn, "Oregon Dilemma."

6   Ehrlich and Ehrlich, *Population, Resources, Environment*, 18–23.

7   Commoner, *Closing Circle*, 12, 214–15.

8   Nease, *Man's Control of the Environment*, 2–3.

9   "Earth Day Speech," box 9, folder "Earth Day (speech material) 4/22/70," Mss. 625, McCall Papers, Oregon Historical Society.

10   McHarg, "The Plight," 19.

11   Bureau of Governmental Research and Service, *1940–1970 Population and Housing Trends*, 5.

12   U.S. Census Bureau, "1990 Census of Population and Housing."

13   Bureau of Governmental Research and Service, *1940–1970 Population and Housing Trends*, 6.

14   U.S. Census Bureau, "Table 145: Residence in 1965 of the Population 5 Years Old and Over by Race, Sex, and Age: 1970," in *1970 Census of Population*, 315.

15   Holden and Sheppard, *Migration and Oregon*, 2, 6.

16   Pacific Northwest Bell Telephone Company Business Research Division, *Population and Household Trends*, 12.

17   "Selling Off Oregon's Beauty," *Oregon Journal*, September 9, 1968, 12.

18   Fred I. Weber Jr., "Portland! One Million Persons with Stability—A 1969 Reality," *Oregon Voter*, July 5, 1969, 20.

19   "Mark Says Natural Resources Pushed," *Oregon Statesman*, July 23, 1966, 10.

20   Hatfield, *Not Quite So Simple*, 62.

21   Pacific Northwest Bell, "This Is the Willamette Valley Today. What Will It Be Like by 1976?," *Oregon Statesman*, May 9, 1967, 10.

22   Holbrook, "Yankee Go Home," 71–72.

23   Donald Sterling Jr., "Hands Off the JGB Assn.," *Oregon Journal*, April 13, 1969, 14.

24   Martin Clark, "Town Topics: 'Stay Away,' NW Fans Advised," *Oregon Journal*, January 6, 1967, 7.

25   "Polk 'Holds 'Em Off,'" *Oregon Statesman*, December 17, 1969, 4.

26   "Population Control," *Oregon Statesman*, January 2, 1970, 4.

27   Oregon State Highway Department, Traffic Engineering Division, Planning Survey Section, *Survey of Out-of-State Passenger Cars*.

28   "Our Prime Resource," *Oregonian*, July 3, 1967, 18.

29   Governor's Committee for a Livable Oregon, *Report of the Tourism and Recreation Committee*, 3–11, 16–17.

30   Minutes, September 6, 1968, folder 2, "Agendas, Minutes, 1968," Mss. 2537, Government's Committee for a Livable Oregon Papers.

31   *Sunset Travel Guide to Oregon*, 6.

32   Governor's Committee for a Livable Oregon, *Report of the Tourism and Recreation Committee*, 20, 25, 32, 45–46.

33   John McWilliams, "Out-of-Staters Jam State Parks," *Oregon Journal*, January 24, 1968, 1.

34   M. J. Smith, "Who Needs 'Em?," *Oregon Journal*, September 15, 1969, 14.

35   Stan Federman, "Threat Seen from Oregon's Tourist Advertising," *Oregonian*, July 19, 1969, 1.

36   Louis Harris and Associates, *Public's View of Environmental Problems*, 18.

37 "Valley Livability Battle Drive Due,"
    Oregon Statesman, December 31, 1969, 4.
38 Paul W. Harvey Jr., "Oregon Becomes
    Choosy in Hunt for Pollution-Free
    Industry," *Oregonian*, April 6, 1970, 12.
39 Rome, *Bulldozer in the Countryside*, 120–
    24.
40 Tom McCall, "Special Message to the
    55th Legislative Assembly On Land-Use
    Planning and Zoning," 1969 Senate
    Agriculture Minutes and Exhibits, box
    112, folder SB10, Legislative Assembly,
    Oregon State Archives.
41 Maradel Gale, interview by Derek
    Larson, October 19, 1999, recording in
    author's possession; Adler, *Oregon Plans*,
    32–33.
42 MacColl, "Battle to Control Land Use,"
    205; Macpherson, "Agricultural Roots of
    Oregon's Land Use Planning System."
43 Walter Hickel to Tom McCall, June 3,
    1970, box 9, folder "Meetings, Speeches,
    20–30 June, 1970," Mss. 625, McCall
    Papers, Oregon Historical Society.
44 Walker and Hurley, *Planning Paradise*,
    45; MacColl, "Battle to Control Land
    Use," 205; McCall and Neal, *Tom McCall:
    Maverick*, 196–97.
45 Paul W. Harvey Jr., "Tom McCall: An
    Active Kind of Governor," *Capital
    Journal*, January 14, 1970, 14.
46 "Keep McCall's Proven Leadership,"
    Oregon Statesman, October 20, 1970, 4.
47 C. Johnson, *Standing at the Water's Edge*,
    146.
48 Thomas R. Mahoney to Robert L. Straub,
    January 28, 1970, box 28, folder 12,
    Straub Archives, Western Oregon
    University.
49 "Bob Straub: The Man for Governor,"
    [n.d.], box 29, folder 9, ibid.
50 Gordon, "Oregon: Unspoiled Splendor,"
    134–36.
51 Federman, "'Plumed Knight' Rides
    Again," 4.
52 Paul W. Harvey Jr., "Blaine Society Starts
    Backlash," *Oregonian*, December 30,
    1970, 13.
53 "State Attracting More Tourists, but
    They're Spending Much Less," *Oregonian*,
    July 7, 1970, 18.
54 Oregon State Highway Commission
    Travel Advisory Committee, *Tourism in
    the Seventies.*
55 Paul W. Harvey Jr., "Tom Reviews First
    Term, Views Second," *Capital Journal*,
    January 11, 1971, 28.
56 "Oregon Borders Still Open," *Oregon
    Journal*, January 15, 1971, 12.

57 Floyd McKay, "Poor Blaine Missed
    Oregon's 'Delights,'" *Oregon Statesman*,
    February 1, 1970, 4.
58 Dan Wyant, "Please Feed the Bears," *San
    Francisco Chronicle*, October 31, 1971.
59 A. Robert Smith, "Non-Existent Society
    Still Is Alive," *Oregon Statesman*, October
    10, 1970, 4.
60 "Down with the Blaine Society," *Oregon
    Journal*, October 26, 1970, 10.
61 Kane, "Scorecard," 8–9.
62 Paul W. Harvey Jr., "James G. Blaine Is
    Still Standing Guard," *Oregon Statesman*,
    December 30, 1970, 4.
63 Gene Maudlin, "Oregon's Priorities Are
    'Straight,'" *Capital Journal*, February 10,
    1971, 14.
64 Tom Ferschweiler, "Permanent 'Visitors'
    Welcomed," *Oregon Journal*, March 9,
    1971, 8.
65 Gene Maudlin, "Quality of Life
    Diminishing in State, Advisors Report,"
    Oregon Statesman, February 20, 1971, 5.
66 Steven V. Roberts, "Oregon Not Alone in
    Shunning Growth," *Oregon Statesman*,
    March 14, 1971, 1.
67 Tom McCall, "Sixth Urban Rural
    Conference: Speech By Governor Tom
    McCall," February 12, 1971, box 15,
    folder "Meetings, Speeches, February
    1971," Mss. 625, McCall Papers, Oregon
    Historical Society.
68 Steven V. Roberts, "Some Areas Seek to
    Halt Growth," *New York Times*, March 14,
    1971, 1.
69 Barnes, "Oregon for Oregonians," 10–11.
70 "McCall Endorses Oregon Trail while
    Discouraging Squatters," *Capital Journal*,
    April 14, 1971, 7.
71 Tom Ferschweiler, "Governor Reaffirms
    Insistence on Responsible Tourist Policy,"
    Oregon Journal, April 14, 1971, 14.
72 "Oregon Gets Bad Image," *Oregonian*,
    April 14, 1971.
73 "Tourist Ad Funds Given OK," *Oregon
    Journal*, May 26, 1971, 4; "Tourists Ad
    Money On Again, Off Again," *Oregon
    Journal*, May 27, 1971, 10.
74 David Lamb, "Oregon—A Paradise Lost
    for California Immigrants?," *Los Angeles
    Times*, September 4, 1971, 1.
75 "Oregon Hostile, Papers Tells
    Californians," *Oregon Journal*, September
    7, 1971, 1.
76 Tom McCall, "League of Women Voters:
    Remarks By Governor Tom McCall,"
    September 8, 1971, box 16, folder
    "Meetings, Speeches, Sept. 1971," Mss.
    625, McCall Papers, Oregon Historical
    Society.

77 Citizens' Advisory Committee on Environmental Quality, "Report to the President and to The Council on Environmental Quality," April 1971, box 16, folder "Citizens Advisory Comm. On Environmental Quality, 6/17–18, 1971," Mss. 625, McCall Papers, Oregon Historical Society.

78 Mitchell Hider, "Is It Too Late to Save Our Valley?," *Capital Journal*, December 4, 1971, 12.

79 *Project "Foresight*," 2-1.

80 "Salem Expands by 3,001 since April, Now 72,445," *Oregon Statesman*, December 3, 1971, 1; "Northwest Is Getting Too Many People," *Oregon Statesman*, December 3, 1971, 1.

81 A. Robert Smith, "No More People, Plants in Oregon Paradise, Urges Packwood," *Oregon Statesman*, December 26, 1971, 1.

82 Forstall, *Population of Counties by Decennial Census*.

83 Oregon State Highway Division, Traffic Section, Planning Unit, *1970 Out-of-State Tourist Revenue Survey*, 4, 10.

84 Holden and Shepard, *Migration and Oregon*, 25.

85 Dan Sellard, "Ugly Californian: Why Oregon Is Getting Cooler," *Sacramento Union*, [c. 1972].

86 Bronson, *How to Kill a Golden State*, 10.

87 Palmer, "Abundance and the Remains," 3–18.

88 The term was regionally popular by the late 1960s and appeared in a *Time* magazine headline, "The Great Wild Californicated West," in August 1972.

89 "Great Wild Californicated West," 15.

90 Unsigned letter to Governor Tom McCall, August 9, 1972, Record Group 64, box 28, folder "Livable Oregon," McCall administration records, Oregon State Archives.

91 Robert Brooks Wilhite and George Michael Jones to Tom McCall, August 17, 1972, ibid.

92 Dan Carver to Governor Tom McCall, July 19, 1972, ibid.

93 Jack Pement, "Unwelcome to Oregon or Adventures of Malice in Thunderland," *Oregon Journal*, August 17, 1973, 3; Marge Davenport, "Oregon Taking a New Look at Tourism," *Oregon Journal*, October 3, 1972, 1.

94 Dan Bernstein, "How Will It Look in Year 2002?," *Capital Journal*, January 11, 1973, 13.

95 Dan Bernstein, "Land Use: No Easy Answers," *Capital Journal*, October 14, 1972, 13.

96 Weber, "Population and Quality of Life."

97 Rose, "1901 Plan for Washington, DC."

98 Mumford, *Sticks and Stones*, 147.

99 Platt, *Land Use and Society*, 215–18, 228, 233.

100 Popper, *Politics of Land-Use Reform*, 55.

101 Cullingworth, *Planning in the USA*, 50.

102 Rome, *Bulldozer in the Countryside*, 128–33.

103 Bosselman and Callies, *Quiet Revolution in Land Use Control*, as cited in Platt, *Land Use and Society*, 348.

104 1000 Friends of Oregon, *Birth of Senate Bill 100*, 4.

105 Hector Macpherson, interview by Derek Larson, October 12, 1999, recording in author's possession.

106 Macpherson, "Agricultural Roots of Oregon's Land Use Planning System."

107 Little, *New Oregon Trail*, 11.

108 Macpherson interview.

109 Jerry Easterling, "Builders Will Have to Wait on Environment," *Capital Journal*, November 11, 1972, 16.

110 Jim Close, "Proper Land Use Planning Urged at McCall Conference," *Capital Journal*, November 20, 1972, 1; Jim Close, "Land Ethic, Not Land Use, Urged on Conservation Confab," *Capital Journal*, November 21, 1972, 9.

111 "State Agency for Land Use Is Requested by Governor," *Capital Journal*, December 12, 1972, 24.

112 Macpherson interview.

113 T. McCall, untitled address, J-312–13.

114 Tom McCall, "Governor Describes Land Use Planning as Most Significant Environmental Action," press release, January 18, 1973, 5–12, Oregon State Library.

115 Little, *New Oregon Trail*, 14–16.

116 Roger Epperson, "Land Use Bill 'Hasn't Much Chance,'" *Capital Journal*, January 24, 1973, 14.

117 Minutes, January 5, 1973, folder 7, "Agendas, Minutes, 1973," Mss. 2537, Governor's Committee for a Livable Oregon Papers.

118 1000 Friends of Oregon, *Birth of Senate Bill 100*, 4; Little, *New Oregon Trail*, 19; MacColl, "Battle to Control Land Use," 214–15.

119 Leonard, *Managing Oregon's Growth*, 10–11.

120 Little, *New Oregon Trail*, 19.

121 Tom McCall, "Testimony by Governor Tom McCall to Oregon Senate Committee on Environment and Land Use: Senate Bill 100," March 6, 1973, Senate Environment and Land Use

Committee, Exhibits, SB 100–SB 104, box 60, folder 1, Legislative Assembly, 1973 Regular Session, Oregon State Archives.

122 Dan Bernstein, "Land Use Bill Gets McCall Support," *Capital Journal*, March 3, 1973.

123 Macpherson interview.

124 Dan Bernstein, "Land Use Bill Wins in Senate," *Capital Journal*, April 19, 1973, 30.

125 Little, *New Oregon Trail*, 19.

126 Ted Hallock, oral history interview, in Teramura, "Oral History"; Dan Bernstein, "Land Use Planning Bill OK'd," *Capital Journal*, May 23, 1973, 1.

127 "Oregonians Can Now Plan for Higher Quality of Life," *Capital Journal*, October 8, 1973, 4.

128 MacColl, "Battle to Control Land Use," 217; "Who's Who at LCDC," 5.

129 T. McCall, *Oregon Land Use Story*, 18.

130 "Population Planning Held Vital," *Oregon Journal*, July 22, 1974, 2.

131 "Land Use Bill OK but Not Good, Says McCall," *Capital Journal*, April 24, 1974, 19.

132 "McCall Lashes Out at Land Use Defeat," *Capital Journal*, June 12, 1974, 14.

133 Frank Allen, "McCall Urges: Get Involved in Land-Use Goals," *Capital Journal*, September 19, 1974, 1; "McCall Pleads for Land Use Planning," *Oregon Journal*, September 18, 1974, 4.

134 *Fasano v. Board of County Commissioners of Washington County*; Deits, "Fasano v. Board of Commissioners," 95–105.

135 A. Richard Immel, "Try as They Might, Folks in Oregon Can't Deter New Residents," *Wall Street Journal*, May 22, 1974.

CHAPTER 7

The epigraph is from P. Lewis, *Our Oregon*.

1 Kirsch, "Oregonians of the Century."

2 Richard Neuberger to Robert Frazier et al., March 18, 1959, MSS Ax78, box 3, folder "Oregon Dunes," Neuberger Papers.

3 Virlis L. Fischer, "Statement of Virlis L. Fischer on Proposed Oregon Dunes National Seashore," April 12, 1959, ibid.

4 Oswald West to Richard Neuberger, telegram, October 1, 1959, ibid.; McCloskey, *Conserving Oregon's Environment*.

5 Clark, "Evolution of Watershed Councils," 210.

6 On the economic impacts of the Dunes National Recreation Area, see Anderson, "Search for Solutions"; *Oregon Dunes NRA: Final Environmental Impact Statement*, chap. 3, 10; Ed Becker, Oregon Dunes Area ranger, Siuslaw National Forest, conversation with author, September 12, 1999; Lisa Romano, public affairs staff officer, Siuslaw National Forest, correspondence with author, May 21, 2015.

7 See variously "Cape Cod National Seashore 50th Anniversary Press Releases," http://www.nps.gov/caco/cape-cod-national-seashore-50th-anniversary-press-releases.htm; *The Gulf Breeze: Padre Island National Seashore News and Information* (National Park Service, U.S. Department of the Interior, Padre Island National Seashore), 2013 issue; and Susan Emery, "National Lakeshore Unveils 50th Anniversary Plans," *Northwest Indiana Times*, November 6, 2014, http://www.nwitimes.com/news/local/porter/duneland/national-lakeshore-unveils-th-anniversary-plans/article_a05c3035512d-51028d03-21b857a88f79.html.

8 "Oregon Dunes National Recreation Area," Siuslaw National Forest, http://www.fs.usda.gov/recarea/siuslaw/recarea/?recid=42465.

9 See Harvey, "Echo Park," 43–67.

10 Richard Neuberger, "Belligerent Minority," *Oregonian*, December 27, 1959, 54.

11 Jonathan H. Adler, "The Fable of the Burning River, 45 Years Later," *Washington Post*, June 22, 2014.

12 *Water Quality Control in Oregon*; Gleeson, *Return of a River*, 87.

13 Joan Laatz Jewett, "Oregon's Willamette River Needs Help, Report Says," *Oregonian*, December 17, 1997; Lisa Balick, "Willamette River Tops List of Toxic Waterways," *KOIN6.com*, April 16, 2015, http://koin.com/2015/04/16/willamette-river-tops-list-of-toxic-waterways/; Neil Mullane, "The Willamette River of Oregon: A River Restored?," in Leanen and Dunnette, *River Quality*, 67–70.

14 Oregon Department of Environmental Quality, *A River Restored: Oregon's Willamette*, n.d. [1980s], http://www.deq.state.or.us/about/video.htm.

15 "Willamette River Has a Long and Winding History," news report, KGW-TV8, Portland, OR, originally broadcast July 28, 2000; "Portland Harbor Superfund Site," U.S. Environmental Protection Agency, Region 10: The

Pacific Northwest, http://yosemite.epa. gov/R10/CLEANUP.NSF/ph/ Portland+Harbor+Superfund+Site.

16 "Willamette River Cleaner, Officials Say," *Vancouver (WA) Columbian*, June 26, 1994; "Combined Sewer Overflows," City of Portland, Environmental Services, https://www.portlandoregon.gov/bes/ article/316721.

17 "Portland Harbor Superfund Site"; Steve Law, "More River Pollution in Willamette, Cap Plan Proposed," *KOIN6. com*, June 12, 2014, http://koin. com/2014/06/12/river-pollution-found-near-omsi/.

18 "Despite Major Cleanup, Willamette River Still Has a Long Way to Go," *Los Angeles Times*, August 6, 2000.

19 "Court Backs Beach Control," *Capital Journal*, December 22, 1971, 1.

20 "California's Beach Battle Should Make Us Thankful," *Capital Journal*, May 6, 1972, 4.

21 KATU-TV, *Channel 2 News*, Portland, OR, July 5, 1997.

22 "The Beach Bill," *The Oregon Experience*, OPB television, broadcast November 12, 2007, http://www.opb.org/television/ programs/oregonexperience/segment/ the-beach-bill-/; *Oregon Shores Fall Newsletter* (Oregon Shores Conservation Coalition) 22:2 (October 2007): 1.

23 U.S. Congress, House, *Hearings before the Committee on Fisheries and Wildlife Conservation*, 55–63.

24 "Far beyond Our Borders," *Oregon Statesman*, July 26, 1971, 4.

25 Phillip Hager, "Oregon Fights Battle of Bottle with New Law," *Los Angeles Times*, October 21, 1972, 1.

26 Larry Roby, "Bottle Bill a Success—McCall," *Capital Journal*, February 12, 1973, 1.

27 Gudger and Bailes, *Economic Impact of Oregon's "Bottle Bill"*; Savage and Richmond, *Oregon's Bottle Bill*.

28 Tom McCall, "Comments of Governor Tom McCall, National Symposium on State Environmental Legislation," March 17, 1972, Mss. 625, box 18, folder "National Symposium on State Environmental Legislation, Wash. DC, 3/17/72," McCall Papers, Oregon Historical Society.

29 "Nationwide Bottle Bill Introduced," *Capital Journal*, February 7, 1975, 1; "Bottle Bill Upheld as Act of Wisdom," *Capital Journal*, September 24, 1975, 3; "Enact Federal Bottle Law," *Capital Journal*, December 10, 1975, 4; "Nation Needs Bottle Bill," *Capital Journal*,

January 26, 1977, 4; Charles E. Beggs, "National Bottle Bill Promoted by Report," *Oregon Statesman*, October 19, 1975, 5; Ginny Burdick, "A Bottle Bill for All," *Capital Journal*, October 6, 1975, 21; Comptroller General of the United States, *Report to Congress: Potential Effect of a National Mandatory Deposit on Beverage Containers*, December 7, 1977, Mss. 625, box 30, folder "Bottle Bill Issues, 1970s, I," McCall Papers, Oregon Historical Society.

30 "Bottle Bill: Follow Oregon's Lead, U.S. Told," *Oregon Statesman*, December 10, 1977, 1; "Connecticut Joins Oregon Crusade," *Oregon Statesman*, April 10, 1978; "Maine Endorsement Gives Bottle Bill Backers Hope," *Capital Journal*, November 8, 1979; "California Bans Bottle Bill," *Capital Journal*, January 29, 1980, 4; Tom Billitteri, "Michigan Getting Ready for Bottle Bill," *Capital Journal*, November 29, 1978, 5; Martin Rosenberg, "Washington's Bottle Battle Up for Vote," *Capital Journal*, May 11, 1979, sec. C, 1.

31 Russell Sadler, "Record of McCall Era Belies No-Growth Image," *Oregonian*, c. 1982.

32 Bottle Bill Resource Guide, "Bottle Bills in the USA," http://www.bottlebill.org/ legislation/usa.htm.

33 "McCall: Big Business Opposes Bottle Bill," *Statesman-Journal*, August 24, 1981, sec. C, 4.

34 Ron Blankenbaker, "Bottle Law's Real Father Nearly Forgotten by Now," *Oregon Statesman*, April 7, 1985, sec. C, 3.

35 Tom McCall, "Remarks by Oregon Governor Tom McCall, National Audubon Society Awards Dinner," November 6, 1974, Mss. 625, box 25, folder "Meetings, Speeches, Nov. 1974," McCall Papers, Oregon Historical Society.

36 Henry Richmond to Tom McCall, August 1, 1974, Mss. 625, box 31, folder "1,000 Friends of Oregon, correspondence, 1974–1982," McCall Papers, Oregon Historical Society.

37 "1000 Friends of Oregon—39 Years of Accomplishments," 1000 Friends of Oregon, http://www.friends.org/about/ history.

38 Gifford, "Planning for a Productive Paradise," 495–98.

39 *Vote No on #10*.

40 Tom McCall, "Statement of Tom McCall on Ballot Measure 10," October 24, 1978, Mss. 625, box 27, folder "Ballot Measure

10, 1978," McCall Papers, Oregon Historical Society.

41 "The Back 40: Ballot Measure 10 Defeated in 31 Counties," c. 1978, Oregon State Department of Land Conservation and Development, historical files.

42 Hector Macpherson and John Gray, open letter to "Oregonians interested in statewide land use planning," September 21, 1982, Oregon State Department of Land Conservation and Development, historical files.

43 "Tom McCall Quotes," Oregon Historical Society, http://www.ohs.org/education/tom-mccall-better-oregon/quotes.cfm.

44 Hector Macpherson, interview with author, October 12, 1999, recording in author's possession.

45 Victor Atiyeh, "Legislative Message, 1985," Oregon State Archives, http://arcweb.sos.state.or.us/pages/records/governors/guides/state/atiyeh/legis1985.html.

46 Tom McCall, untitled speech transcript, c. 1971, Oregon State Department of Land Conservation and Development, historical files.

47 Kim Stafford, *Old 100: A Celebration of Oregon's Senate Bill 100*, May 1, 1998, Oregon State Department of Land Conservation and Development, historical files.

48 Macpherson, interview.

49 DeGrove, "Following in Oregon's Footsteps," 227.

50 DLCD Planning Day Orientation, October 1999.

51 *Oregon Statewide Planning Program*.

52 "1973: Governor Tom McCall Makes Famous Speech to the Legislature," Oregon Department of Land Conservation and Development, "History of Oregon's Land Use Planning," http://www.oregon.gov/lcd/pages/history.aspx; links to \\AD\LCD\docs\history\mccall_speech_1973.wav.

53 Bricklemyer et al., "Preservation of Coastal Spaces," 268.

54 Jeff Barnard, "Oregon's Land Use Laws Threatened," Associated Press wire story, January 29, 2001; Adler, *Oregon Plans*, 223.

55 Oregon Department of Land Conservation and Development, "History of Oregon's Land Use Planning," http://www.oregon.gov/lcd/pages/history.aspx#2000_2007.

56 Oregon State Legislature, "Background Briefing on Land Use," September 2012, https://www.oregonlegislature.gov/citizen_engagement/.../LandUse.pdf.

57 Robbins, *This Storied Land*, 155.

58 Ryan, *This Ecstatic Nation*, 82.

59 Tom McCall, "Remarks of Former Governor Tom McCall Accepting First Annual Governor Oswald O. West Memorial Award," September 27, 1982, Oregon State Library.

60 Bates, "Real McCall."

61 Tom McCall "Tom McCall's Remarks on 'View of the State' Panel, Environmental Industry Conference, Washington, DC, Feb. 25, 1977," Mss. 625, box 34, folder "Speeches, 1977," McCall Papers, Oregon Historical Society.

62 George Hutton, "Mr. McCall Did Well for the State around Him," *New York Times*, January 5, 1975, E3.

63 McCall quoted in Bates, "Decision at Road's End," 30.

64 Walth, *Fire at Eden's Gate*, 429.

65 Tom McCall to Robert Sutro, January 6, 1975, Mss. 625, box 25, folder "Linfield College Offer," McCall Papers, Oregon Historical Society.

66 "In Memoriam: Tom McCall," January 12, 1983, Oregon State Library.

67 Robert Straub, "Remarks by Bob Straub, Memorial Service for Tom McCall," January 12, 1983, Oregon State Library.

68 McCormack, "Eulogy," 141.

69 "Tom McCall by Henk Pander," *Portland Public Art* (blog), June 5, 2007, https://portlandpublicart.wordpress.com/2007/06/05/tom-mccall-by-henk-pander/.

70 Thomas Vaughan, "For McCall: 'Do not Stand at My Grave and Weep,'" *Statesman-Journal*, February 20, 1983, 3D.

71 Lansing, *Portland*, 407; City of Portland Parks and Recreation, "Waterfront Park," http://www.portlandoregon.gov/parks/finder/index.cfm?action=ViewPark&ShowResults=yes&PropertyID=156.

72 Brent Walth, "Pollution in Paradise: The Moment Oregon Began to Go Green," *Willamette Week*, November 14, 2012, http://www.wweek.com/portland/article-19906-pollution_in_paradise.html.

73 Gressley, "James G. Blaine," 369.

74 Schoenfeld, Meier, and Griffin, "Constructing a Social Problem," 46.

75 Buel, "Negotiating down the Oregon Trail," 21.

76 "Oregon: People's Power," *Economist*, May 17, 1980, 19.

77 Wallace Turner, "Lumber Industry Woes Dim Good Life in Oregon," *New York Times*, March 3, 1982, A16; Svart, "Living the Ecotopian Ethic," 12.

78 Brent Walth, "An Oregon Century: Blazing Trails in the 1970s," *Oregonian*, August 27, 2007.

79 Ross, "Losing Ground in Oregon," 40–44.

80 Benner, "Life in the Silicon Rain Forest," 112.

81 Don Hamilton, "Oregon's Go Home Society Lies Dormant," *Oregonian*, August 20, 1986, C1.

82 Pike, *Destination Marketing*, 192.

83 Oregon Department of Tourism, *We've Been Saving a Place for You.*

84 Roberts, "1991 Public Interest Law Conference Opening Address," 105–6.

85 Bob Baum, "Oregonians Still Enjoy Rewards of McCall Legacy," *Oregonian*, January 10, 1993, C6.

86 Stafford, "Two Stories Becoming One," 21.

87 Smith and Gilden, "Cultural and Natural Assets."

88 "More Than Ever, Oregon Needs McCall's Doctrine," *Statesman-Journal*, Special Report Reprint: Paradise Lost: A Cloud Over Eden, August 1998, 3.

89 "Proud of Their Progress," *Statesman-Journal*, Special Report Reprint: Paradise Lost: A Cloud Over Eden, August 1998, 2.

90 Marsh, *To the Promised Land*, 443.

91 "Oregon School Woes Featured in 'Doonesbury' Comic Strip," *Eugene Register-Guard*, February 22, 2003.

92 Bill Graves and Jeff Mapes, "The Oregon Dream Vanishes," *Oregonian*, January 12, 2003.

93 Bill Graves and Jeff Mapes, "What Went Wrong," *Oregonian*, January 14, 2003.

94 Jeff Mapes, Alex Pulaski, and Gail Kinsey Hill, "The Nine States of Oregon," *Oregonian*, November 3, 2003; Peterson del Mar, *Oregon's Promise*, 248.

95 Jeff Mapes, "Lim's 'Visit Oregon, but please don't stay' Legislation Dies Quickly," *Oregonian*, April 21, 1999.

96 Lauren Dodge, "Oregon Residents Renew the Cry: You Californians, Please Get Out!," Associated Press wire story, April 5, 1999.

97 Author unknown. A search of the Internet found that the story appeared on at least forty-six web pages around the country in December 2000, suggesting that people outside Oregon found it amusing as well. It remained widespread in 2015.

98 Tarr, *Devastation and Renewal.*

99 P. Lewis, *Our Oregon.*

100 McCormack, "Eulogy," 141.

101 U.S. Census Bureau, "Oregon Population, 2010 (April 1) estimates base," http://quickfacts.census.gov/qfd/states/41000.html.

102 Kaiser Family Foundation, "State Health Facts: Number of Births per 1,000 (2010)," http://kff.org/other/state-indicator/birth-rate-per-1000/.

103 "Despite Major Cleanup, Willamette River Still Has a Long Way to Go," *Los Angeles Times*, August 6, 2000.

104 McPhee, *Western Oregon*, 28.

105 Robbins and Barber, *Nature's Northwest*, 232.

106 Johnson and Schell, "Adapting to Climate Change," 449.

107 Tom McCall to Peter Borden, March 22, 1974, record group G4, acc. #75A-12, box 39, folder "Livable Oregon," McCall administration records, Oregon State Archives.

108 Walth, "Tom McCall," 570.

109 Shutkin, *Land That Could Be*, 120.

110 Judd and Beach, *Natural States*, 251.

Bibliography

Periodical and archival listings include only the major sources consulted.

PERIODICALS

Associated Press (state and local wire service)
Capital Journal (Salem, OR)
Columbian (Vancouver, WA)
Coos Bay (OR) World
Eugene (OR) Register-Guard
Los Angeles Times
Medford (OR) Mail-Tribune
Mill City (OR) Enterprise
Nation
New York Times
Oregon Agriculture (Salem, OR)
Oregon Grange Bulletin (Salem, OR)
Oregon Journal (Portland, OR)
Oregon Motorist (Salem, OR)
Oregonian (Portland, OR)
Oregon Statesman (Salem, OR)
Oregon Voter (Salem, OR)
Oregon-Washington Farmers Union
Sacramento Union
San Francisco Chronicle
Siuslaw Oar (Florence, OR)
Statesman-Journal (formed by merger of the *Oregon Statesman* and the
    Capital Journal)
Wall Street Journal
Washington Post

ARCHIVAL COLLECTIONS

Abell, Ron, and James G. Blaine Association, Papers. Oregon Historical Society.
Atiyeh, Gov. Victor G., Administration Records. Oregon State Archives.

Charleton, David H., Papers. Oregon Historical Society.

Clark, Donald E., Papers. Oregon Historical Society.

Governor's Committee for a Livable Oregon Papers. Oregon Historical Society.

Hatfield, Gov. Mark O., Administration Records. Oregon State Archives.

Ivey Collection. Moving Image Archive. Oregon Historical Society.

Johnson, Lyndon Baines, Oral History Collection. Lyndon Baines Johnson Presidential Library.

KGW TV Collection. Moving Image Archive. Oregon Historical Society.

KOIN TV Collection. Moving Image Archive. Oregon Historical Society.

McCall, Gov. Tom L., Administration Records. Oregon State Archives.

McCall, Tom Lawson, Papers. Oregon Historical Society.

McLennan, Janet, Papers. Western Oregon University.

Neuberger, Richard L., Papers. Knight Library, University of Oregon.

Onthank, Karl, Papers. Knight Library, University of Oregon.

Oregon Environmental Council Papers. Oregon Historical Society.

Oregon State Department of Land Conservation and Development. Internal historical files.

Oregon State Economic and Community Development Department. Internal historical files.

Oregon State Legislature. House and Senate Committee records. Oregon State Archives.

Oregon State Library Reference Collection.

Straub, Gov. Robert W., Administration Records. Oregon State Archives.

Straub, Robert, Archives. Western Oregon University.

U.S. Environmental Protection Agency. *Documerica* image project. National Archives and Records Administration.

U.S. Forest Service Headquarters Records. Forest History Society, Durham, NC.

OTHER MATERIALS

Abbott, Carl, Deborah Howe, and Sy Adler, eds. *Planning the Oregon Way: A Twenty-Year Evaluation.* Corvallis: Oregon State University Press, 1994.

An Act to Establish the Oregon Dunes National Recreation Area. Pub. L. No. 92-260, 86 Stat. 99 (1972).

Ad Council. "Keep America Beautiful—Iron Eyes Cody." http://www.adcouncil.org/Our-Campaigns/The-Classics/Pollution-Keep-America-Beautiful-Iron-Eyes-Cody.

Adler, Sy. *Oregon Plans: The Making of an Unquiet Land-Use Revolution.* Corvallis: Oregon State University Press, 2012.

American Antiquities Act. 16 USC 431–33 (1906). http://www.cr.nps.gov/local-law/anti1906.htm.

Anderson, David Laurence. "A Search for Solutions to Conflicting Demands of Outdoor Recreation in the Oregon Dunes Coastal Environment." PhD diss., Oregon State University, 1974.

Andrews, Alicia, and Kristin Kutara, comps. *Oregon's Timber Harvests: 1849–2004.* Salem: Oregon Department of Forestry, 2005.

Barnes, Peter. "Oregon for Oregonians." *New Republic,* March 20, 1971.

Bates, Tom. "Decision at Road's End." *Oregon Times,* March 1978.

———. "The Real McCall." In *Profiles of Oregon: An Anthology of Articles from "Oregon Magazine," 1977 to 1987,* edited by Win McCormack, 52. Portland: New Oregon Publishers, 1986. Originally published in *Oregon Magazine,* 1978.

"The Beach Bill." *The Oregon Experience.* Broadcast November 12, 2007. http://www.opb.org/television/programs/oregonexperience/segment/the-beach-bill-/.

Beauty for America: Proceedings of the White House Conference on Natural Beauty. Washington, DC: USGPO, 1965.

Bender, Stephen W. "Castles in the Sand: Balancing Public Custom and Private Ownership Interests on Oregon's Beaches." *Oregon Law Review* 778 (1998): 913–67.

Benner, Susan. "Life in the Silicon Rain Forest." *Inc.,* June 1984.

Bernat, G. Andrew, Jr. "Convergence in State Per Capita Personal Income, 1950–99." *Survey of Current Business,* June 2001.

Bingham, Edwin R. "Pacific Northwest Writing: Searching for Regional Identity." In *Regionalism and the Pacific Northwest,* edited by William G. Robbins, Robert J. Frank, and Richard E. Ross, 151–74. Corvallis: Oregon State University Press, 1983.

Binns, John H. "Northwest Region—Fact or Fiction?" *Pacific Northwest Quarterly* 48:3 (July 1957): 65–75.

Blake, Peter. *God's Own Junkyard: The Planned Deterioration of America's Landscape.* New York: Holt, Rinehart and Winston, 1964.

Boag, Peter G. *Environment and Experience: Settlement Culture in Nineteenth-Century Oregon.* Berkeley: University of California Press, 1992.

Booth, Charles W. *The Northwestern United States.* New York: Van Nostrand Reinhold, 1971.

Bosselman, F., and D. Callies. *The Quiet Revolution in Land Use Control.* Washington, DC: USGPO, 1971.

Bricklemyer, Eugene C., Jr., et al. "Preservation of Coastal Spaces: A Dialog on Oregon's Experience with Integrated Land Use Management." *Ocean and Coastal Law Journal* 9 (2004): 239–80.

Brinckman, Jonathan. "Salmon's Quiet Comeback?" *American Forests* 105:2 (Summer 1999): 24–27.

Bronson, William. *How to Kill a Golden State.* Garden City, NY: Doubleday, 1968.

Buel, Merrie. "Negotiating down the Oregon Trail." *Earthwatch Oregon* 12:1 (January 1980).

Bunting, Robert. *The Pacific Raincoast: Environment and Culture in an American Eden, 1778–1900.* Lawrence: University Press of Kansas, 1997.

Bureau of Governmental Research and Service. *1940–1970 Population and Housing Trends: Cities and Counties of Oregon.* Eugene: University of Oregon School of Community Service and Public Affairs, 1971.

Burg, Amos. "A Native Son's Rambles in Oregon." *National Geographic* 65:2 (February 1934).

Cahn, Robert. "Oregon Dilemma." *Saturday Evening Post*, October 14, 1961, 21–27.

Carroll, Matthew S. *Community and the Northwestern Logger: Continuities and Changes in the Era of the Spotted Owl.* Boulder, CO: Westview Press, 1995.

Carson, Rachel. *Silent Spring.* Boston: Houghton Mifflin, 1962.

Clark, Lance R. "The Evolution of Watershed Councils and the Oregon Plan." *Journal of Sustainable Forestry* 13:1/2 (2001): 205–21.

Clausen, Jan. "One Fish, Two Fish." *Nation* 270:3 (January 24, 2000): 22–24.

Cloonan, James B., Stanley T. Gabis, and Rudyard B. Goode. *Estimates of the Impact of Sign and Billboard Removal under the Highway Beautification Act of 1965.* Columbia: Missouri State Highway Department, 1966.

Commoner, Barry. *The Closing Circle: Nature, Man, and Technology.* New York: Alfred A. Knopf, 1972.

Cooper, William S. *Coastal Sand Dunes of Oregon and Washington.* Memoirs, 72. New York: Geological Society of America, 1958.

Coos Bay Oregon. Portland[?]: Marshfield, Oregon, Chamber of Commerce and the Southern Pacific Line in Oregon, n.d.

Corbett-Atterbury, Vivian. *The Oregon Story.* Portland: Binford & Mort, 1959.

Cox, Thomas R. "The Crusade to Save Oregon's Scenery." *Pacific Historical Review* 37 (May 1968): 179–99.

———. *The Park Builders: A History of State Parks in the Pacific Northwest.* Seattle: University of Washington Press, 1988.

Crafts, Edward C. Oral history interview. November 7, 1969. John F. Kennedy Library, Boston.

Cross, Gary. *An All-Consuming Century: Why Commercialism Won in Modern America.* New York: Columbia University Press, 2000.

Cullingworth, Barry. *Planning in the USA: Policies, Issues, and Processes.* New York: Routledge, 1997.

DeGrove, John M. "Following in Oregon's Footsteps: The Impact of Oregon's Growth Management Strategy." In *Planning the Oregon Way: A Twenty-Year Evaluation*, edited by Carl Abbott, Deborah Howe, and Sy Adler, 227–44. Corvallis: Oregon State University Press, 1994.

Deits, Mary J. "Fasano v. Board of Commissioners." *Willamette Law Journal*, Winter 1973.

Dick, Wesley Arden. "When Dams Weren't Damned: The Public Power Crusade and Visions of the Good Life in the Pacific Northwest in the 1930s." *Environmental Review* 13:1 (Fall/Winter 1989): 113–53.

Dicken, Samuel Newton. *Pioneer Trails of the Oregon Coast.* Portland: Oregon Historical Society, 1971.

Dietrich, William. *Northwest Passage: The Great Columbia River.* Seattle: University of Washington Press, 1995.

Dilsaver, Lary. *The National Parks: Shaping the System.* Washington, DC: U.S. Department of the Interior, 1991.

Dodds, Gordon B. *The American Northwest: A History of Oregon and Washington.* Arlington Heights, IL: Forum Press, 1986.

Douglas, Paul. "Richard L. Neuberger, 1913–1960." *New Republic,* March 21, 1960.

Douglas, William O. *Go East, Young Man.* New York: Dell, 1974.

———. "Hart Mountain." In *Varieties of Hope: An Anthology of Oregon Prose,* edited by Gordon B. Dodds, 168–75. Corvallis: Oregon State University Press, 1993.

———. *My Wilderness: The Pacific West.* New York: Doubleday, 1960.

———. *Of Men and Mountains.* New York: Harper & Row, 1950.

Drukman, Mason. "Oregon's Most Famous Feud: Wayne Morse versus Richard Neuberger." *Oregon Historical Quarterly* 95:3 (Fall 1994): 301–62.

———. *Wayne Morse: A Political Biography.* Portland: Oregon Historical Society Press, 1997.

Duncan, David James. "Salmon's Second Coming." *Sierra* 85:2 (March 2000). https://vault.sierraclub.org/sierra/200003/salmon1.asp.

Durbin, Kathie. *Tree Huggers: Victory, Defeat, & Renewal in the Northwest Ancient Forest Campaign.* Seattle: Mountaineers, 1996.

Eaton, Marcia Muelder. "The Beauty That Requires Health." In *Placing Nature: Culture and Landscape Ecology,* edited by Joan Iverson Nassauer, 85–108. Washington, DC: Island Press, 1997.

Edwards, G. Thomas, and Carlos A. Schwantes. "The Pacific Northwest as Promised Land: An Introduction." In *Experiences in a Promised Land: Essays in Pacific Northwest History,* edited by G. Thomas Edwards and Carlos A. Schwantes, xiii–xvi. Seattle: University of Washington Press, 1986.

Eells, Robert, and Bartell Nyberg. *Lonely Walk: The Life of Senator Mark Hatfield.* Portland: Multnomah Press, 1979.

Ehrlich, Paul, and Anne Erlich. *Population, Resources, Environment: Issues in Human Ecology.* San Francisco: W. H. Freeman, 1970.

Eichler, Edward P., and Marshal Kaplan. *The Community Builders.* Berkeley: University of California Press, 1967.

Engel, J. Ronald. *Sacred Sands: The Struggle for Community in the Indiana Dunes.* Middletown, CT: Wesleyan University Press, 1983.

Fasano v. Board of County Commissioners of Washington County. 96 Or. Adv. Sh. 1059, 507 P.2d 23 (1973).

Federman, Stan. "The 'Plumed Knight' Rides Again in Oregon." *Smithsonian,* September 1970, 36–38.

Fiege, Mark. *Irrigated Eden: The Making of an Agricultural Landscape in the American West.* Seattle: University of Washington Press, 1999.

Floyd, Charles F., and Peter J. Shedd. *Highway Beautification: The Environmental Movement's Greatest Failure.* Boulder, CO: Westview Press, 1979.

Forstall, Richard L., ed. *Population of Counties by Decennial Census: 1900 to 1990, California.* Washington, DC: Population Division, US Bureau of the Census, 1995. http://www.census.gov/population/cencounts/ca190090.txt.

Fraser, James. *The American Billboard: 100 Years.* New York: Harry N. Abrams, 1991.

Frykman, George A. "Regionalism, Nationalism, Localism: The Pacific Northwest in American History." *Pacific Northwest Quarterly* 43 (October 1952): 251–61.

Fujii, Howard. "Who Will Pay for Willamette Greenway?" *Oregon Agriculture,* March 25, 1967.

Gibson, Campbell, and Kay Jung. *Historical Census Statistics on Population Totals by Race, 1790 to 1990, and by Hispanic Origin, 1970 to 1990, for the United States, Regions, Divisions, and States.* September 13, 2002. http://www.census.gov/population/www/documentation/twps0056/twps0056.html.

Gifford, Laura Jane. "Planning for a Productive Paradise: Tom McCall and the Conservationist Tale of Oregon Land-Use Policy." *Oregon Historical Quarterly* 115:4 (Winter 2014): 470–501.

Gleeson, George W. *The Return of a River: The Willamette River, Oregon.* Corvallis: Advisory Committee on Environmental Science and Technology/Water Resources Research Institute, Oregon State University, 1972.

Gordon, Arthur. "Oregon: Unspoiled Splendor." *Reader's Digest,* May 1969.

Gould, Lewis. *Lady Bird Johnson: Our Environmental First Lady.* Lawrence: University Press of Kansas, 1999.

———. *Lady Bird Johnson and the Environment.* Lawrence: University Press of Kansas, 1988.

Governor's Committee for a Livable Oregon. *Report of the Tourism and Recreation Committee of the Governor's Committee for a Livable Oregon.* Salem, OR[?], 1968.

Graham, Frank, Jr. *Since "Silent Spring."* Boston: Houghton Mifflin, 1970.

"The Great Wild Californicated West." *Time,* August 21, 1972.

Gressley, Gene M. "James G. Blaine, 'Alferd' E. Packer, and Western Particularism." *Historian* 44:3 (1982): 364–81.

Gudger, Charles M., and Jack C. Bailes. *The Economic Impact of Oregon's "Bottle Bill."* Corvallis: Oregon State University Press, 1974.

Handley, Michael. "The Idea of the Pacific Northwest." PhD diss., University of Kansas, 1996.

Harvey, Mark W. T. "Echo Park, Glen Canyon, and the Postwar Wilderness Movement." *Pacific Historical Review* 60:1 (February 1991): 43–67.

———. *A Symbol of Wilderness: Echo Park and the American Conservation Movement.* Albuquerque: University of New Mexico Press, 1994.

Hatfield, Mark O. "An Invitation to You from the Governor of Oregon." *Oregon Centennial Official Souvenir Program.* Portland: Oregon Centennial Commission, 1959.

———. *Not Quite So Simple.* New York: Harper and Row, 1968.

Hays, Samuel. *Conservation and the Gospel of Efficiency: The Progressive Conservation Movement, 1890–1920.* Cambridge, MA: Harvard University Press, 1959.

———. "Three Decades of Environmental Politics: The Historical Context." In *Explorations in Environmental History: Essays by Samuel P. Hays,* 334–78. Pittsburgh: University of Pittsburgh Press, 1998.

Herbert, Frank, Brian Herbert, and Kevin J. Anderson. *The Road to Dune.* New York: Tor Science Fiction, 2005.

Highway Beautification Act. Pub. L. 89–285 (1965).

Hildreth, Richard. "Public Access to Shorelines and Beaches: Alternative Approaches and the Taking Issue." In *Water as a Public Resource: Emerging Rights and Obligations (Summer Conference, June 1–3).* Boulder: Natural Resources Law Center, University of Colorado Law School, 1987. http://scholar.law.colorado.edu/water-as-public-resource-emerging-rights-and-obligations.

Holbrook, Stewart. *The Far Corner: A Personal View of the Pacific Northwest.* Sausalito, CA: Comstock Editions, 1986.

———. ed. *Promised Land: A Collection of Northwest Writing.* New York: McGraw-Hill, 1945.

———. "Yankee Go Home." *Look,* March 27, 1962.

Holden, Arnold, and W. Bruce Sheppard. *Migration and Oregon—1970: Patterns and Implications.* Corvallis: Oregon State University/Rockefeller Foundation Project "Man's Activities as Related to Environmental Quality," 1974.

Honey, William D., Jr. *The Willamette River Greenway: Cultural and Environmental Interplay.* Corvallis: Water Resources Research Institute, Oregon State University, 1975.

Hurley, Ray. *U.S. Census of Agriculture: 1959 Final Report.* Vol. 1, pt. 47, *Counties.* Washington, DC: Bureau of the Census, 1961.

James, Peter. "Ecotopia in Oregon?" *Portland Magazine* 6:3 (March 1979).

Johnson, Charles K. *Standing at the Water's Edge: Bob Straub's Battle for the Soul of Oregon.* Corvallis: Oregon State University Press, 2012.

Johnson, Courtney B., and Steven R. Schell. "Adapting to Climate Change on the Oregon Coast: Lines in the Sand and Rolling Easements." *Journal of Environmental Law and Litigation* 28 (2013): 447–514.

Johnson, Lyndon B. "Annual Message to the Congress on the State of the Union." January 4, 1965. In Gerhard Peters and John T. Woolley, *The American Presidency Project*, http://www.presidency.ucsb.edu/ws/?pid=26907.

——. "Remarks at the University of Michigan." May 22, 1964. In Gerhard Peters and John T. Woolley, *The American Presidency Project*, http://www.presidency.ucsb.edu/ws/?pid=26262.

Jones, Edward Gardner, ed. *The Oregonian's Handbook of the Pacific Northwest*. Portland: Oregonian Publishing, 1894.

Judd, Richard W., and Christopher S. Beach. *Natural States: The Environmental Imagination in Maine, Oregon, and the Nation.* Washington, DC: Resources for the Future, 2003.

Kane, Martin. "Scorecard." *Sports Illustrated*, January 18, 1971.

Kehow, James M. "The Next Wave in Public Beach Access: Removal of States as Trustees of Public Trust Properties." *Fordham Law Review* 63:5 (1995): 1913–51.

Kerr, R. E. "What Is the Purpose of an Interim Committee on Natural Resources?" *Oregon Agriculture* 17:8 (August 25, 1959).

King, William A., and Elmer D. Fullenwider. *The Pacific Northwest: Its Resources and Industries*. San Francisco: South-Western Publishing, 1938.

Kirk, Andrew J. *Counterculture Green: The Whole Earth Catalog and American Environmentalism*. Lawrence: University Press of Kansas, 2007.

Kirsch, Walden. "Oregonians of the Century." *KGW Evening News*. KGW TV, Portland, OR. Originally broadcast November 26, 1999.

Knapp, Gerrit. "Land Use Politics in Oregon." In *Planning the Oregon Way: A Twenty-Year Evaluation*, edited by Carl Abbot, Deborah Howe, and Sy Adler, 3–24. Corvallis: Oregon State University Press, 1994.

Krech, Shepard, III. *The Ecological Indian: Myth and History*. New York: W. W. Norton, 1999.

Lansing, Jewel. *Portland: People, Politics, and Power, 1851–2001*. Corvallis: Oregon State University Press, 2003.

Leanen, Antonius, and David Dunnette, eds. *River Quality: Dynamics and Restoration*. Boca Raton, FL: Lewis Publishing, 1997.

Lear, Linda. *Rachel Carson: Witness for Nature*. New York: Henry Holt, 1997.

Lehner, John. *Historical Look at Oregon's Wood Product Industry*. Salem: Oregon Office of Economic Analysis, January 23, 2012.

Leonard, H. Jeffrey. *Managing Oregon's Growth: The Politics of Development Planning*. Washington, DC: Conservation Foundation, 1983.

Lesow, John W. "Litter and the Nonreturnable Beverage Container: A Comparative Analysis." *Environmental Law* 2 (Winter 1971): 197–217.

Lewis, David. "Four Deaths: The Near Destruction of Western Oregon Tribes and Native Lifeways, Removal to the Reservation, and Erasure from History." *Oregon Historical Quarterly* 115:3 (Fall 2014): 414–37.

Lewis, Paul M. *Our Oregon.* Portland: Beautiful Oregon Publications, 1977.

Lipin, Lawrence M. *Workers and the Wild: Conservation, Consumerism, and Labor in Oregon, 1910–1930.* Urbana: University of Illinois Press, 2007.

Little, Charles E. *The New Oregon Trail: An Account of the Development and Passage of State Land-Use Legislation in Oregon.* Washington, DC: Conservation Foundation, 1974.

Louis Harries and Associates. *The Public's View of Environmental Problems in the State of Oregon.* Portland[?]: Louis Harris and Associates, 1970.

Louter, David. *Windshield Wilderness: Cars, Roads, and Nature in Washington's National Parks.* Seattle: University of Washington Press, 2010.

Love, Matt. *Grasping Wastrels vs. Beaches Forever Inc.: Covering the Fights for the Soul of the Oregon Coast.* Pacific City, OR: Nestucca Spit Press, 2003.

Lucia, Ellis. *Don't Call It Or-E-Gawn.* Portland: Overland West Press, 1964.

Lyman, H. S. "An Oregon Literature." *Oregon Historical Quarterly* 2:4 (December 1901): 401–9.

MacColl, E. Kimbark. "The Battle to Control Land Use: Oregon's Unique Law of 1973." In *Politics in the Postwar American West,* edited by Richard Lowitt, 203–20. Norman: University of Oklahoma Press, 1995.

Macpherson, Hector. "The Agricultural Roots of Oregon's Land Use Planning System, or How in the World Did Oregon Become a National Leader in Growth Management?" Unpublished remarks before the Oregon Planning Institute, September 5, 1996. Oregon Department of Land Conservation and Development historical files.

Marsh, Tom. *To the Promised Land: A History of Government and Politics in Oregon.* Corvallis: Oregon State University Press, 2012.

McCall, Dorothy Lawson. *Ranch under the Rimrock.* Portland: Binfords & Mort, 1968.

McCall, Tom. *The Oregon Land Use Story.* Salem: Executive Department, Government Relations Division, January 7, 1974.

———. Untitled address before the Legislative Assembly. *Journals and Calendars of the Senate and House of the Fifty-Seventh Legislative Assembly. Regular Session. House Journal.* January 8, 1973.

McCall, Tom Lawson, and Steve Neal. *Tom McCall: Maverick.* Portland: Binford & Mort, 1977.

McCloskey, Michael. *Conserving Oregon's Environment: Breakthroughs That Made History.* Inkwater Press, 2013. Ebook location 2377.

McCormack, Win. "Eulogy: Tom McCall's Challenge to Oregon." In *Profiles of Oregon: An Anthology of Articles from "Oregon Magazine," 1977 to 1987,* edited by Win McCormack. Portland: New Oregon Publishers, 1986. Originally published in *Oregon Magazine,* 1983. http://www.winmccormack.com/poli_mccall_eulogy.htm.

McHarg, Ian L. "The Plight." In *The Environmental Crisis: Man's Struggle to Live with Himself,* edited by Harold W. Helfrich Jr., 15–31. New Haven, CT: Yale University Press, 1970.

McPhee, Marnie. *Western Oregon: Portrait of the Land and Its People.* Helena, MT: American Geographic, 1987.

Meier, Peter C. *"Stevens v. City of Cannon Beach:* Taking Takings into the Post-*Lucas* Era." *Ecology Law Quarterly* 22 (1995): 413–48.

Merriam, Lawrence C., Jr. *Oregon's Highway Park System, 1921–1989: An Administrative History.* Salem: Oregon Parks and Recreation Department, 1992.

Miller, Joe. "Oregon: Can the Issues Be Ignored?" *Reporter,* November 4, 1954.

Moore, Harry Estill, and Howard W. Odum. *American Regionalism: A Cultural-Historical Approach to National Integration.* New York: Henry Holt, 1938.

Moulton, Gary E. *The Journals of the Lewis and Clark Expedition.* Vol. 6, *November 2, 1805–March 22, 1806.* Lincoln: University of Nebraska Press, 1990.

Mumford, Lewis. *Sticks and Stones: A Study of American Architecture and Civilization.* New York: Boni and Liveright, 1924.

Nash, Ogden. "Song of the Open Road." In *Many Long Years Ago.* New York: Little Brown, 1945.

National Committee on Highway Law of the Highway Research Board. *Special Report 41: Outdoor Advertising along Highways: A Legal Analysis.* Washington, DC: National Research Council, 1958.

The National Parks: Shaping the System. Washington, DC: U.S. Department of the Interior, 1991.

Neal, Steve, ed. *They Never Go Back to Pocatello: The Selected Essays of Richard Neuberger.* Portland: Oregon Historical Society Press, 1988.

Nease, Jack, ed. *Man's Control of the Environment: To Determine His Survival . . . or to Lay Waste His Planet.* Washington, DC: Congressional Quarterly, 1970.

Netboy, Anthony, ed. *The Pacific Northwest: An Impressionistic Picture Illustrated with Photographs.* Garden City, NY: Doubleday, 1963.

Neuberger, Richard L. *Adventures in Politics: We Go to the Legislature.* New York: Oxford University Press, 1954.

———. "Conserving Our Great Outdoors." *New Leader,* February 20 1956, 1–23.

———. "Guarding Our Outdoor Heritage." *Progressive,* January 1959.

———. "Hells Canyon, the Biggest of All." In *They Never Go Back to Pocatello: The Selected Essays of Richard Neuberger,* edited by Steve Neal, 15–23. Portland: Oregon Historical Society Press, 1988.

———. "My Hometown Is Good Enough for Me." *Saturday Evening Post,* December 16, 1950.

———. "Oregon at 100." *Sports Afield,* June 1959.

———. *Our Natural Resources—and Their Conservation*. Public Affairs Pamphlet no.230. Washington, DC[?]: Public Affairs Committee, 1956.

———. *Our Promised Land*. New York: Macmillan, 1938.

———. "Our Vanishing Resources." *Common Sense* 14:11 (December 1945): 17–19.

Nixon, Richard M. "Statement about Signing a Bill Creating the Oregon Dunes National Recreation Area." March 24, 1972. *Public Papers of the Presidents, 1972*. Vol. 498. Washington, D.C.: USGPO, 1972.

Office of War Information, Overseas Branch. "Northwest U.S.A." *The American Scene*, no. 10. 1945. Video. YouTube. https://youtu.be/nVAnqix86M0.

1000 Friends of Oregon. *The Birth of Senate Bill 100*. Salem: 1000 Friends of Oregon, [1998?].

Opie, John. *Nature's Nation: An Environmental History of the United States*. New York: Harcourt Brace, 1998.

Oregon: The Land of Opportunity. Portland: Portland Chamber of Commerce, 1939.

"Oregon: The Neuberger Campaign." *New Republic*, October 25, 1954, 6.

Oregon Department of Tourism. *We've Been Saving a Place for You*. Salem: Oregon Department of Tourism, c. 1989.

Oregon Dunes NRA: Final Environmental Impact Statement. Portland: US Forest Service, 1994.

Oregon's Beaches: A Birthright Preserved. Salem: Oregon State Parks and Recreation Branch, 1977.

Oregon Shores Conservation Coalition. *Oregon Shores Fall Newsletter* 22:2 (October 2007).

Oregon State Highway Commission. Travel Advisory Committee. *The Impact of Tourism in Oregon*. Salem: Oregon State Highway Commission[?], 1973.

———. *Tourism in the Seventies . . . Is Oregon Ready for It?* Salem: Oregon State Highway Commission, 1970.

Oregon State Highway Department. Traffic Engineering Division. Planning Survey Section. *Survey of Out-of-State Passenger Cars*. Salem[?]: n.p., 1960–70.

Oregon State Highway Division. Traffic Section. Planning Unit. *1970 Out-of-State Tourist Revenue Survey*. Salem[?]: Oregon State Highway Division, 1970.

Oregon Statewide Planning Program. Salem: Oregon Department of Land Conservation and Development, 1997.

Orr, Elizabeth, and William Orr. *Oregon Water: An Environmental History*. Portland: Inkwater Press, 2005.

Pacific Northwest Bell Telephone Company Business Research Division. *Population and Household Trends in Washington, Oregon, and Northern Idaho, 1970–1985*. Seattle: Pacific Northwest Bell Telephone Company, 1972.

Palmer, Tim. "The Abundance and the Remains." In *California's Threatened Environment: Restoring the Dream*, edited by Tim Palmer. Washington, DC: Island Press, 1993.

Peirce, Neal R. *The Pacific States of America: People, Politics, and Power in the Five Pacific Basin States*. New York: W. W. Norton, 1972.

"People Take Warning!" 1973. The Next American System. *Blueprint America: PBS Reports on Infrastructure*. May 20, 2009. http://www.pbs.org/wnet/blueprintamerica/reports/the-next-american-system/video-people-take-warning-1973/?p=658.

"Period of Record Monthly Climate Summary, Salem WSO, 1/1/1928 to 12/31/2005." Western Regional Climate Center. http://www.wrcc.dri.edu/cgi-bin/cliMAIN.pl?orsale.

Peterson del Mar, David. *Oregon's Promise: An Interpretive History*. Corvallis: Oregon State University Press, 2003.

Pike, Stephen. *Destination Marketing*. New York: Routledge, 2011.

Pinchot, Gifford. *Breaking New Ground*. New York: Harcourt, Brace, 1947.

Platt, Rutherford H. *Land Use and Society: Geography, Law, and Public Policy*. Washington, DC: Island Press, 1996.

Popper, Frank J. *The Politics of Land-Use Reform*. Madison: University of Wisconsin Press, 1981.

Post, Mae Celeste. *Loitering in Oregon*. n.p.: 1914.

Potts, James Thompson. "The West of H. L. Davis." PhD diss., University of Arizona, 1977.

Powell, E. Alexander. "The Land of Magic Names: How a Globe-Trotter . . . Stumbled upon Treasure Trove in the Northwest Corner of His Own Continent." *Sunset* 31 (July 1913): 66–75.

Powell, Michael. "Somewhere Else: Ambivalent Images of Oregon in American Postwar Narrative." *Pacific Northwest Forum*, 2nd ser. 2:3 (Fall 1990): 54–61.

Project "Foresight": First Phase. Salem [?]: Project Foresight, December 1971.

Quaintance, Charles, Jr. "A National Seashore for Oregon? A Study in Legislative Problem Solving." *Oregon Law Review* 44:1 (December 1964) 1–41.

Raphael, Ray. *Tree Talk: The People and Politics of Timber*. Covelo, CA: Island Press, 1981.

Reckendorf, Frank, Don Leach, Robert Baum, and Jack Carlson. "Stabilization of Sand Dunes in Oregon." *Agricultural History* 59 (1985): 260–68.

Report to the President and the President's Response: White House Conference on Natural Beauty. Washington, DC: USGPO, 1965.

Righter, Robert W. *Crucible for Conservation: The Creation of Grand Teton National Park*. Boulder: Colorado Associated University Press, 1982.

Robbins, William, ed. *The Great Northwest: The Search for a Regional Identity*. Corvallis: Oregon State University Press, 2001.

——. *Landscapes of Conflict: The Oregon Story, 1940–2000*. Seattle: University of Washington Press, 2004.

——. *The Oregon Environment: Development vs. Preservation, 1905–1950*. Corvallis: Oregon State University, 1975.

——. *This Storied Land*. Portland: Oregon Historical Society Press, 2005.

Robbins, William G., and Katrine Barber. *Nature's Northwest: The North Pacific Slope in the Twentieth Century*. Tucson: University of Arizona Press, 2011.

Roberts, Barbara. "1991 Public Interest Law Conference Opening Address." *Journal of Environmental Law and Litigation* 6:105 (1991).

Rome, Adam. *The Bulldozer in the Countryside: Suburban Sprawl and the Rise of American Environmentalism*. New York: Cambridge University Press, 2001.

——. *The Genius of Earth Day: How a 1970s Teach-In Unexpectedly Made the First Green Generation*. New York: Hill and Wang, 2013.

Rose, Julie K. "The 1901 Plan for Washington, DC." *City Beautiful: The 1901 Plan for Washington D.C.* American Studies Department, University of Virginia, Spring 1996. http://xroads.virginia.edu/~cap/citybeautiful/plan. html.

Ross, Kelly. "Losing Ground in Oregon." *Reason*, April 1983, 40–44.

Rothman, Hal. *The Greening of a Nation? Environmentalism in the United States since 1945*. New York: Harcourt Brace, 1998.

——. "Selling the Meaning of Place: Entrepreneurship, Tourism, and Community Transformation in the Twentieth-Century American West." *Pacific Historical Review* 64:4 (November 1996): 525–57.

Runte, Alfred. *National Parks: The American Experience*. 3rd ed. Lincoln: University of Nebraska Press, 1997.

Ryan, Terre. *This Ecstatic Nation: The American Landscape and the Aesthetics of Patriotism*. Amherst: University of Massachusetts Press, 2011.

"Sand Dunes on Oregon's Coast." *Sunset: The Magazine of Western Living*, October 1959.

Sarasohn, David. "The Good Life: A Forum on Oregon's 'Livability.'" *Oregon Magazine* 10:4 (November 1980).

——. "Regionalism, Tending Toward Sectionalism." In *Regionalism and the Pacific Northwest*, edited by William G. Robbins, Robert J. Frank, and Richard E. Ross, 223–36. Corvallis: Oregon State University Press, 1983.

Savage, John F., and Henry R. Richmond. *Oregon's Bottle Bill: "A Riproaring Success."* Portland: Oregon Student Public Interest Research Group, 1974.

Schoenfeld, A. Clay, Robert F. Meier, and Robert J. Griffin. "Constructing a Social Problem: The Press and the Environment." *Social Problems* 27:1 (October 1979): 38–61.

Schotzko, R. Thomas, and David Granatstein. *A Brief Look at the Washington Apple Industry: Past and Present*. SES 04-05. Pullman: Washington State University, c. 2003.

Schwantes, Carlos Arnoldo. *The Pacific Northwest: An Interpretive History.* Rev. and enl. ed. Lincoln: University of Nebraska Press, 1996.

Seideman, David. *Showdown at Opal Creek: The Battle for America's Last Wilderness.* New York: Carroll and Graf, 1993.

Shireman, William, et. al. *The CalPIRG-ELS Study Group Report on Can and Bottle Bills.* Berkeley: California Public Interest Research Group, 1981.

Shutkin, William A. *The Land That Could Be: Environmentalism and Democracy in the Twenty-First Century.* Cambridge, MA: MIT Press, 2000.

Smith, Courtland J., and Jennifer Gilden, "Cultural and Natural Assets for Willamette Basin, Oregon Sustainability." Paper presented at the Tenth Biennial Conference of the International Institute of Fisheries, Economics, and Trade, Corvallis, OR, July 11, 2000. http://ir.library.oregonstate.edu/xmlui/handle/1957/30559.

Sobel, Robert, and John Raimo, eds. *Biographical Directory of American Governors.* Vol. 3. Westport, CT: Meckler Books, 1978.

Stafford, Kim. "Two Stories Becoming One." *Oregon Quarterly* 76:2 (Winter 1996).

Stanbery, V. B. *Population Growth in the Pacific Northwest, 1940–1950.* Portland: Columbia Basin Inter-Agency Committee/United States Department of Commerce, 1950.

Stern, Carlos, et. al. *Impacts of Beverage Container Legislation on Connecticut and a Review of the Experience in Oregon, Vermont, and Washington State.* Storrs: Department of Agricultural Economics, College of Agriculture and Natural Resources, University of Connecticut, 1975.

Sullivan, Jennifer A. "Laying Out an 'Unwelcome Mat' to Public Beach Access." *Journal of Land Use and Environmental Law* 18:2 (Spring 2003): 331–54.

Sunset Travel Guide to Oregon. Menlo Park, CA: Lane Books, 1968.

Svart, Larry. "Living the Ecotopian Ethic." *Earthwatch Oregon,* April–May 1982.

Swain, Donald C. "The National Park Service and the New Deal, 1933–1940." *Pacific Historical Review* 41 (August 1972): 312–32

Tarr, Joel. *Devastation and Renewal: An Environmental History of Pittsburgh and Its Region.* Pittsburgh: University of Pittsburgh Press, 2004.

———. "The Search for the Ultimate Sink: Urban Air, Land and Water Pollution in Historical Perspective." In *Environmental History: Critical Issues in Comparative Perspective,* edited by Kendall E. Bailes, 516–52. New York: University Press of America, 1985.

Teramura, Kami A. "An Oral History of the Visions and Intentions behind Oregon's Land Conservation and Development Act: Senate Bill 100." Master's Project, Community and Regional Planning Program, University of Oregon, 1997.

Todd, Anne Marie. *Communicating Environmental Patriotism: A Rhetorical History of the American Environmental Movement.* New York: Routledge, 2013.

Tuan, Yi-Fu. *Topophilia: A Study of Environmental Perceptions and Values.* New York: Columbia University Press, 1974.

U.S. Census Bureau. *1970 Census of Population.* Vol. 1, pt. 39, *Characteristics of the Population: Oregon.* Washington, DC: USGPO, 1973.

———. "1990 Census of Population and Housing: Population and Housing Unit Counts." https://www.census.gov/population/www/censusdata/90pubs/cph-2.html

———. "Resident Population and Apportionment of the U.S. House of Representatives: Oregon." January 30, 2000. http://www.census.gov/dmd/www/resapport/states/oregon.pdf.

———. *Statistical Abstract of the United States: 1996.* 116th ed. Washington, DC: Census Bureau, 1996.

U.S. Congress. House. *Hearings before the Committee on Fisheries and Wildlife Conservation and the Environment on Public Access to Beaches, H.R. 10394 and H.R. 10395.* 93rd Cong., 1st sess., October 25–26, 1973. Serial No. 93-25.

U.S. Congress. House. Subcommittee on Public Lands of the Committee on Interior and Insular Affairs. *Hearings on H.R. 6260 to Establish the Oregon Dunes National Seashore.* 86th Cong., 1st sess., October 30–31, 1959.

U.S. Congress. Senate. *S. 1526: A Bill to Establish the Oregon Dunes National Seashore in the State of Oregon.* 86th Cong., 1st sess.,1959.

U.S. Congress. Senate. Subcommittee on Public Lands of the Committee on Interior and Insular Affairs. *Oregon Dunes National Seashore: Hearings before the Subcommittee on Public Lands.* 86th Cong., 1st sess., October 5, 1959.

U.S. National Park Service. *Pacific Coast Recreation Area Survey.* Washington, DC: U.S. Department of the Interior, 1959.

———. *Parks for America: A Survey of Park and Related Resources in the Fifty States, and a Preliminary Plan.* Washington, DC: U.S. Department of the Interior, 1964.

Udall, Stewart. "Comeback for the Willamette River." *National Parks Magazine*, March 1968, 4–8.

———. *The Quiet Crisis.* New York: Holt, Rinehart, & Winston, 1963.

Vermont Legislative Research Service. *Bottle Bills.* 2012. http://www.uvm.edu/~vlrs/?Page=Environment/environment.html.

Victor, Francis Fuller. *Atlantis Arisen; or, Talks of a Tourist about Oregon and Washington.* Philadelphia: J.B. Lippincott, 1891.

Vote No on #10. Portland: Citizens to Save Oregon's Land, 1978. Oregon State Department of Land Conservation and Development historical files.

Walker, Peter A., and Patrick T. Hurley. *Planning Paradise: Politics and Visioning of Land Use in Oregon.* Tucson: University of Arizona Press, 2011.

Walter, Eugene Victor. *Placeways: A Theory of the Human Environment.* Chapel Hill: University of North Carolina Press, 1988.

Walth, Brent. *Fire at Eden's Gate: Tom McCall and the Oregon Story*. Portland: Oregon Historical Society Press, 1995.

———. "Tom McCall and the Language of Memory." *Oregon Historical Quarterly* 113:4 (Winter 2012): 570–83.

Water Quality Control in Oregon. Salem: Department of Environmental Quality, State of Oregon, December 1970.

Weber, Fred I., Jr. "Population and Quality of Life." *PGE Area Development and Research Forum*, no. 31 (July–August 1972).

Whisnant, Archibald, ed. *Portland, Oregon: The World's Greatest Lumber Producing Center*. Portland, OR: n. p., c. 1940.

White, Richard. *The Organic Machine: The Remaking of the Columbia River*. New York: Hill and Wang, 1995.

"Who's Who at LCDC." *Earthwatch Oregon*, April 1974.

Wilkinson, Jon. *The Pacific Northwest*. The United States Geography Series. McGraw-Hill video. 1976. https://archive.org/details/ PacificNorthwest1976.

Wilson, Mark Shelton. "Origins of the Old-Growth Forest Conflict (1971– 1989): A New Model for Resource Allocation." PhD diss., Oregon State University, 1994.

Wood, Ruth Kedzie. *The Tourist's Northwest*. New York: Dodd, Mead, 1916.

WPA Writer's Program. *Mount Hood: A Guide*. New York: J. J. Little & Ives, 1940.

———. *Oregon: The End of the Trail*. Portland: Binfords & Mort, 1940.

Zelinsky, Wilbur. "The Changing Character of North American Culture Areas." In *Regional Studies: The Interplay of Land and People*, edited by Glen Lich, 113–35. College Station: Texas A&M University Press, 1992.

Zucker, Jeff, Kay Hummel, and Bob Høgfoss. *Oregon Indians: Culture, History and Current Affairs: An Atlas and Introduction*. Portland: Western Imprints/Oregon Historical Society, 1983.

Index